S0-ATI-143

PUBLIC OPINION

BERNARD C. HENNESSY

Director, National Center
for Education in Politics

WADSWORTH PUBLISHING COMPANY, INC.
BELMONT, CALIFORNIA

CAMROSE LUTHERAN COLLEGE
LIBRARY

TO ERNA

Without whose interference
this book would have been
written earlier but less well.

© 1965 by Wadsworth Publishing Company, Inc., Belmont,
California. All rights reserved. No part of this book may be re-
produced in any form, by mimeograph or any other means, without permission in writing from the publisher.

L.C. Cat. Card No.: 65–22881
Printed in the United States of America

HM
261
H 4 / 6526

FOREWORD

Those who are or soon will be voting citizens of the United States have every reason to be interested in the workings of public opinion. No force is more powerful in American government. Cynics believe that public opinion matters little and that policy is made by some mysterious "They"; but the cynics are wrong. The ways in which public opinion enters into the democratic decision process in this country are indeed complex and subtle. But the relationship between public opinion and public policy certainly does exist in a most significant way.

This book helps the reader to appreciate the true role of *vox populi*. In the first portion, it summarizes the available scientific methods for ascertaining objectively what public opinion on any issue really is. It presents a readable, interesting description of the working of public opinion in various institutions of the American political structure.

Like most ideological issues, the role of public opinion in our country's politics is usually debated in a greatly oversimplified fashion. There is a naive model of democracy according to which one ought to be able to poll the public on each and every issue, find out how the majority vote, and expect the government to act accordingly. If American democracy is held up against that sort of unrealistic model, it can easily be denigrated.

But, as Dr. Hennessy points out, public opinion cannot be conceived that simply. Within the public there are some people who care intensely about any given issue and others who care hardly at all. It is not even true that all people would want their judgments to be weighted equally. Often we feel that some things are not our business and should therefore be decided by those who are affected. On many issues, wide segments of the public want only a result and have no definite view about how to achieve it. The public, for example, wants peace; but few members of the public believe that their judgment on diplomatic moves to keep peace is better than that of the Secretary of State. Thus, the relationship between the public's view at any moment about what the government does is far from a mirror image.

However, if you doubt that the American government pays attention to public opinion, just ask any public officeholder how much he worries about public reactions to what he does. Few congressmen, bureaucrats, governors, or mayors have any doubt that public opinion in this country is a vital force. Nevertheless, even with his deep consciousness of the impact of public opinion, the public official may still underestimate it, for he is apt to take into account only those aspects of public opinion that he feels as pressure on himself. He is not aware of public opinion to the extent to which he himself shares in it. He has grown up within the political culture of the country, and he therefore acts in conformity to its public opinion quite voluntarily, since it is his opinion, too. The student who understands American public opinion understands a great deal about American politics.

Ithiel de Sola Pool

PREFACE

A book about public opinion should be more than a collection of poll results packaged together with some essays on democracy and some facts about the mass media. It should deal systematically with opinion formation, opinion measurement, opinion change, and the relationships between opinions and public policy.

It seems to me that the material in such a book has to come from many disciplines. Though written for political scientists, it has to incorporate a good deal of social psychology, plus a smattering of biology, anthropology, and economics, because the making and remaking of opinions is a general phenomenon of human life and not one limited to the art and science of government. Nonetheless, I think a public opinion text should also be frankly political, and it should put opinion making and opinion change in a political context. Thus, it has to include a section on the theory and practice of the opinion-policy process.

The theory of this book is non-Jeffersonian, pluralistic, relativistic—and quite tentative. The practice is that of campaigns, political parties, pressure groups, and the institutions-plus-personnel of government. The practice orientation of this book is designed to facilitate student fieldwork. It is a matter of my experience, and that of others, that students who engage in survey research while studying public opinion almost invariably develop a strong appreciation for the variety of public opinion, for the difficulty of its measurement and meaning, and for the recognition of the linkages between opinions and public policy. Because I think fieldwork to be so important, and because the student should get into the field early in the semester or quarter, I have placed the section on measurement first in the book. However, the measurement section is self-contained. Teachers who do not share my enthusiasm for fieldwork may begin, if they like, with Chapters 5 and 6 before Chapter 1, or they may take up the measurement section (Chapters 1–4) between Chapters 18 and 19.

The unity of this book depends upon three social psychological concepts. First, as an aid in explaining opinion formation, I have adapted and somewhat generalized the notion of the funnel of causality, first used in *The American Voter*, by Angus Campbell, Philip E. Converse, Warren E. Miller, and Donald E. Stokes. Second, I have revised the statement of the opinion-policy process which I published first in *The Southwestern Social Science Quarterly*, in March 1958; in this statement (Chapter 6), I relate political pluralism, opinion distributions, and policy making. Then, in the three final chapters, I consider the relation of functional and dissonance theories of opinion change to each other, and politically (by means of the opinion-policy process), to the dynamics of American government.

One more point: the "case story" that introduces the text is an only slightly disguised version of a campaign in which I was once involved. This story highlights and exemplifies the thorny problems of democratic theory and practice that crop up whenever political actors attempt to understand or influence voters' opinions. It is meant to be interesting in itself and a gentle introduction to the more straightforward text material that follows; but it also raises in realistic form questions to which the reader is repeatedly returned in various contexts to the end of the book.

More than the author of other kinds of books the writer of a text is indebted to many persons known and unknown. To all my students, from those at the University of Arizona, where as a novice I had a chance to teach the public opinion course in 1954, to those at the University of Rhode Island who heard the book dished up as lectures in the summer of 1964 go my thanks for many valuable suggestions given with more grace than their captive condition demanded. To my colleagues at those two universities, so widely separated in geography and in style, and to that band of American social scientists with whom I have had the good fortune to work through NCEP Affiliates, I owe and offer appreciation.

More especially, I am grateful to the members of the M.I.T. Center for International Studies and the Harvard Human Relations Department for the opportunity to read and listen and talk in their presence during 1956–1957. Ithiel de Sola Pool of M.I.T. and James A. Robinson of The Ohio State University read the manuscript and made many helpful suggestions. William P. Irwin, Charles O. Jones, and Robert J. Huckshorn, my political science colleagues at NCEP, were uniformly supportive. They and others of NCEP's staff, Connie Delaney, Maureen Drummy, Pat Mewhinney, Anne Million, Margaret Ryan, and Anna Schwartzberg, gave of their varied talents more than I had any right to ask—all of which I acknowledge, again, with gratitude.

Bernard C. Hennessy

CONTENTS

NORTH vs. FREDERICK:
A CASE OF OPINIONS
AND VOTES

The children's record player blasted out scratchily at full volume: "John Henry was a railroad man . . ."

John Henry North shouted from David's room to his wife: "Ruth, why couldn't we get a radio ditty out of this? It could go:

'John Henry is a candidate
Who thinks good government cannot wait.
Give him your help 'fore it is too late . . .' "

"John, for goodness sake, come on out here. Never mind the ditty! Don't you know that whole gang will be coming over in half an hour and we haven't really thought through precisely what we want to get done tonight."

"Okay."

He turned off "John Henry" and stood for a moment looking at the picture on the little twenty-five-cent record. The John Henry on the label was a powerful man, stripped to the waist, holding a great steel hammer over his head, about to drive a spike up tight against the rail flange. North wondered whether this poor, uneducated Negro had ever thought about fame. Or whether he had even local fame before some other gandy dancer, probably, had made up this song for his children, for their children, for their children, and eventually for Little Golden Records, Inc.

The two John Henrys had practically nothing in common. North was well educated. Furthermore, he was not poor. His father had left him some money, and he had a comfortable income as an associate professor of Economics at Greenville State University, plus some royalties from a rather successful introductory text he had written in 1958. He and Ruth had a large, but unpretentious split-level house in a new section of the city, with plenty of room for themselves and their two sons. And, of course, he was not Negro.

"Well," Ruth said, when he came out to the kitchen, "that ditty might help you with the Negro vote, but only a few of them vote and you've got those already."

"Yeah, I guess that's right."

John pulled a chair from the kitchen table and sat by Ruth at her disorderly little desk. She put a paper in front of him. "Here's the agenda for tonight."

"Uh, uh. We're not going to call it that, remember? Tonight we're just talking about the possibility of my running for mayor of Greenville."

"But you are, aren't you?"

"*We* think I am, and all the people who will be here tonight know that it's a possibility, but the main thing is to let them convince themselves that it's a good idea. If we had an agenda, it might look to some as though they were here to implement a decision rather than to make one."

"Yes, although I think maybe you can be too subtle and indirect at times." . . .

John had been talking in a rambling, quiet way for about ten minutes. He had opened his remarks by going over a number of things "which you all know": that he felt he would like to run for public office; that, if he could say so without sounding immodest, he thought he had some special training and experience that could be used in city government; that the present mayor was barred by city charter from seeking a third term; and that he had explored the situation with a number of people ("including most of you here tonight") and had received a lot of encouragement, plus one or two comments *dis*couraging him ("for which I'm equally thankful").

"The decision ought to be made tonight, one way or the other," he said, "because we would need over six hundred signatures on the nominating petition, and would have only about five weeks to get them, and then only about six weeks from filing date to the primary." He looked quickly from one side to the other with a friendly, "your turn" expression.

Dick Cassidy sat in an armless easy chair next to the fire. He took the silence as a moment to move slightly away from the heat. Several others watched him slide his chair, and taking this as an invitation to kick off the discussion, he pulled one ankle up on his other knee and leaned forward in his chair.

"I think you're right, John, and I'd like to see you go for it. But *you* have to make the decision, because in the end you have to do the bulk of the work. I've got some time and a little money to give you, and I think you can probably pick up a lot of support. But it's going to be amateur support, and a lot of it wasted. I know from Steve's campaigns that enthusiastic amateurs can't elect a guy alone. The candidate has to get around and show the flag at every little church group and card party."

Cassidy was the owner of a small public relations firm. He had gotten into the business two years ago, when Steve Eliot had decided to run for Congress and had asked Dick to handle his campaign publicity. At the time, Dick had been assistant city editor on the evening paper; before that, he had been, as one of his newspaper colleagues described him, "a hot-shot, liberal, college newspaper editor." Eliot had made it, and, as congressman from the fourth district, he had put Cassidy on his payroll, part time, to handle his constituency business. He had three small rooms in the old Fenner Building downtown, and the delicate marriage of the Congressman's public business and the publicity man's private business was written on the three doors: on the door to room 106 was "Congressman Steven Eliot, Walk In"; room 108 had on it "Congressman Steven Eliot, Enter Room 106"—and the door was kept locked; room 110 had, simply, "Richard Cassidy, Public Relations." The other offices connected in series with 106, where Dick's secretary sat behind a desk with two phones.

"You're right, Dick," John returned. "I'd thought of it this way: This is May 30th and the nominating signatures have to be in the city clerk's office on July 7th. That's about five and a half weeks. We can get the petitions out within a week. My classes are over June 9th, and that gives me four solid weeks for collecting signatures myself, bird-dogging my friends into getting signatures, and planning the campaign in detail."

Beth Flanders jumped into the conversation. "You're not really very well known, John, outside of university circles and your work in NAACP and on the Advisory Committee for the City Planning and Zoning Commission." Beth was fortyish, had two children in high school and one in junior high, and was married to a quiet (some said hen-pecked) lawyer. She was active in the League of Women Voters and past president of the Planned Parenthood Federation—all in all, not badly described by Dick Cassidy, who, for some reason or other, didn't especially like her, as "a busy do-gooder." She was, however, a great friend of Ruth's.

"You know, Beth is right," observed Wally Sewell—and then, between puffs of a big, curved pipe—"and there isn't any reason to think that the Planning and Zoning bit is going to help you. Half the builders hate your guts, especially the big operators who build the cardboard tract homes like the one Prudence and I live in; those boys will open up their checkbooks for 'Gumshoe,' and all the good little simple-minded homeowners you've been trying to protect against faulty wiring and leaky roofs won't know or care what happens to you."

Sewell was an assistant professor of philosophy and, as such, thought himself both worldly-wise and hard-boiled. In this case, he had a point, and everyone knew it.

Arthur P. "Gumshoe" Frederick would be a hard man to beat in the Democratic primary. In his early sixties, he had, as he described it, "kicked around in politics since I was old enough to run errands for old Boss Milligan down in the second ward; you remember Milligan's fight to get Janoski off the City Council, and how Milligan and I parted company when I made the speech for Janoski at the caucus on my twenty-first birthday; and then how we set up those four straw candidates in 1926, and how I got the nomination with only 39 per cent of the vote, and . . ." Oh, Gumshoe Frederick did talk, and mostly about himself; but he was friendly, and popular in the sense of being known to the voters; and, so far as anyone knew, he was personally money-honest, even though that might not be said about all his friends. A thorough pragmatist, he had never been accused of having any particular philosophy or convictions about government and elected officers. He blew where the wind blew him, but always with a laugh and a warm, look-in-the-eye handshake. You couldn't, as the fellows used to say in the Lawyers Club, help but like Gumshoe.

Nobody except his bitterest political enemies—and he had made a few—ever called him Gumshoe to his face. Arthur P. Frederick was not proud of his nickname. He had earned it, or at any rate had acquired it, during one of the several periods when he was out of office—to be exact, after his two terms as chairman of the County Board and before his two terms as U.S. Congressman, an office from which Steve Eliot had removed him two years before in a close and heated primary fight. Frederick had put some money during this off-period into a private detective agency, which after about three years of intermittent shady dealings had collapsed in the glare of a perjury trial and the district attorney's investigation of a large, intercity vice ring. It was never clear just what Frederick's relations with the outfit had been; from his newly won office in Washington he denounced the owner of the agency; and it was not until his race with Eliot, some three years after the scandal, that his involvement became known. All the facts were still not out, and probably never would be; but he ran so well against Eliot despite this handicap, especially in the city, where he had a slight edge over the younger man, that he felt confident about the mayoralty race coming up.

There was a lot of talk that evening. Bill Mason, one of John's graduate students, was eager: "We can get a hundred students to work for Dr. North! We'll go door to door, we'll pass out literature, I know we can do it!"

Others were less optimistic. But at nine-forty-five, when the first few made homeward motions, John offered to sum it up.

"Then it's agreed, is it, that I'll get the nomination forms, and we'll go ahead with the petition gathering? If that goes well, we'll plunge in with an announcement of candidacy on the day we file the petitions, which ought to be about the end of June. Okay?"

When the others had left, Ruth and John sat down with Dick to a second cup of coffee. Dick was still talking business.

"Let's summarize this thing, John. I can give you as much free time as I can take from Steve's campaign and the three others which I've taken on a paying basis, as you know. I'll work with you and Ruth, Wally, and Bill Peterson as a kind of strategy committee. I'll do the layouts for literature and posters, get the billboards, and arrange for the newspaper space and the radio and TV spots. Let's the five of us get together Friday night at my house—or over here if you like—and lay out the total publicity thing. Meanwhile, you get on the petitions. Don't forget to keep a file card on every petition and on every man, woman, and child who offers you even a good wish."

At the door, Dick's last charge was: "Remember, John, you're apt to lose, so make the running for it fun in itself."

On Friday, the five met again in a working session. Bill Peterson had not been at the earlier meeting, but he was a close friend of the Norths, and was valuable especially as a grass-roots politician of long standing. He had been a precinct committeeman for ten years and a member of the city and county central committees; for the past three years, he had been on the county executive committee. Because he was an architect, his name sometimes appeared on the plans for new city and county buildings, but no one ever thought he was interested in politics only because of the few jobs that his political friends might throw him. Besides having a deep interest in city planning that went back to his undergraduate days at Yale, he was "hooked" on politics the way some people get hooked on marijuana or bingo. Being a bachelor, he had time and money enough to enjoy his weakness.

When they were all seated at Ruth's kitchen table, Dick passed around copies of a typewritten sheet:

NOTES ON OVER-ALL PRIMARY CAMPAIGN PLANS

1. Problem: To get one more vote than Gumshoe

2. Assets: Clean record
              Appeal to independents
              No special enemies
              Particular appeals to certain groups:
                  University community and its satellite groups
                  Negroes
                  Jewish organizations
                  Some groups interested in city planning (?)
                  Some church groups

3. Liabilities: Not well known to mass of voters
                Weak where Gumshoe is strong:
                     With veterans and service-club types
                     With the regular party workers
                Money:
                     Not enough
                     No source of large amounts
4. Over-all Strategy: A. Play to own strength and away from Gumshoe's
                         1. Use "young man with vision" theme
                         2. Project competence + confidence
                         3. Make virtue of poverty; pitch for many small contribu-
                            tions instead of "large money with strings"
                         4. Draw volunteers and enthusiasm from groups where
                            strong to:
                              a) keep the faithful aroused
                              b) spill over into overlapping and complementary
                                 groups
                      B. Go after the marginal, uncommitted persons and groups
                         1. Sprightly, punchy publicity (see attached)
                         2. Plenty of good old door-to-door perseverance, by *candi-
                            date* and friends

"There," John said, after reading it through. "Clean young egghead reforms dirty politics!" He looked at Dick and smiled.

"Okay, okay. These are just some notes off the top of my head, but I think there's nothing unusual here. It's just straightforward strategy stuff. How does it look to you, Bill?"

"I think you've got to be careful about playing up university connections and university groups. We've got to make John into a regular guy. One who hasn't been spoiled by being bright and well educated. The average voter is full of contradictions here: on the one hand he shares what might be called, I suppose, a cultural and social bias in favor of higher education, but, on the other hand, the Ph.D. is a foolish sort of guy who forgets his umbrella in the art gallery. Use the university connection all we can for getting workers and the pro-university vote out quietly. But I'd say that in the publicity stuff John should no more than be identified as 'Professor of Economics, Greenville State University.'

"To some extent," Bill added, "the same thing goes for the Negro and Jewish vote. These people are committed to many of the same things John has been working for, and the word will spread among them to those who don't already know him. We don't need any pitches to those whole groups except, probably, a plank about John's being for an equal-accommodations ordinance if he wants to put that in."

"What we want to do, as I see it," said Ruth, "is to create a public opinion that's favorable to John."

Dick smiled. "I hope you won't think me unchivalrous if I qualify, and maybe even change here and there, a lady's statement: What we want to do is to make favorable the opinions of publics *that count*. And the publics that count for us are those in which we have some reason to believe a majority will be favorable to John—and will vote for him. And, further, these publics, like all publics, are made up of individual men and women who can vote or influence others to vote.

"For our purposes, the big, shapeless public (if it exists), which is supposed to be the sum total of all the people, is of no interest or consequence. For that matter, I think that the public, in the sense of everybody, or that public opinion, in the sense of everybody's opinions on everything, is the most useless, misleading, and perhaps dangerous idea going.

"If we think of many publics, each consisting of those who have an interest in some common tradition, social institution, or idea, and if we think of each of these publics as being made up of individuals, with each individual being in many publics both simultaneously and consecutively, then we can begin to get hold of what our problem is. We want to motivate the individuals in these many publics in such a way that, from all these publics, John will get at least one more vote than Gumshoe.

"We've just talked about the Negro vote. We could have said 'those who have a sense of public relating to their Negro-ness.' 'The Negro vote' is the politicians' shorthand for the existence and importance of something known to them long before there were professional sociologists. In the same way, politicians talk about the housewives' vote, the business vote, the Italian vote, and the votes of all of the major blocs—'publics,' you see—which they can identify, and to which they will try to direct specific appeals.

"We're dealing with a patchwork of publics, and our job is to put them together in such a way that, when the votes are counted, the publics in which John is strong have been more activated than those publics in which Gumshoe is strong.

"I didn't mean to make this long speech, Ruth. But I'm kind of a buff on the delicate art of 'creating public opinion'—I think it's your phrase—and I never pass up a chance to expound."

Bill could see that Ruth was not wholly pleased at being "lectured" by Dick.

"Okay," he said, "let's get on with it. Dick, let's go over this other sheet. I think there'll be more questions on this." He picked up the other paper that Dick had passed around.

SUGGESTED USE OF NEWSPAPER, RADIO, AND TV

Newspaper:
1. Thirteen-week series, Sundays, 1 column wide, 5 inches deep.
   a) Each with different message; but
   b) Each with small picture; slogan, if good one can be hit on.
2. Election-eve pitch ? ? ?

Radio:
1. 480 five-second spots. Eight per day for the ten days just before (and in-cluding) election day.
2. 108 thirty-second spots. To be moved around during daytime and early evening hours, three per day for the six days before and including election day. Themes: schools, parks and recreation, public health, juvenile de-linquency, police and fire protection, etc.
3. Sponsor some brief (fifteen minutes maximum) musical programs on the two specialized stations. ? ? Discuss.

Television:
1. 100 five-second spots, divided among the three channels, with many during prime time, early in campaign.
2. 21 sixty-second spots, seven each for the three channels. One on each channel early, other six divided two each for the last three days before primary day. All prime time.
3. No long programs. Rely on unpaid time, commercial and university station.

"Okay," said Dick, "let's talk about these things."

"In the first place, with mass media, you're probably going after the 'don't knows' and the 'don't cares,' the two biggest classes of voters that the pollsters find at this stage in every local election. Most of the people who are registered Democrats—to limit this to the primaries for the moment—either don't know you, or Gumshoe, or both, or they do know you and don't give a damn.

"But a lot of the 'don't knows' and 'don't cares' will vote in the end; so we have to make a pitch for them. *Name familiarity,* to give it a term often used in my profession, is what we're shooting for among the 'don't knows.' We want them to get to know who John is. Of course, there are some dangers here. They may find out who he is and vote against him because of it. But the odds are that if they know who one guy is, and don't know who the other guy is, they will vote for the guy whose name they know. Here, obviously, Gumshoe has the advantage on us now, and probably will throughout the campaign, because he is already known to more people than John is, and he will do a certain amount of name-familiarity campaigning, just as we will, which will refresh those who have forgotten who he is and will tell others for the first time.

"I would say in our case, however, that we want to push John's name rather than rely on any anti-Gumshoe vote. But maybe you want to con-sider taking the other strategy."

"Well," Ruth put in, "I would say we want to tell them about John, not about Gumshoe."

John looked at her with a mixture of sweetness and toleration. "There may be some people who don't want to know that I'm the best husband in the world."

"Please," said Bill, "no domestic hearts and flowers. We old bachelors can't stand it. Let's have Dick get on with this publicity razzle-dazzle; then, when he's through, I'll tell you what wins elections."

Dick smiled. "I know what you're going to say, Bill, and you're right about personal contact. But, in this city of 170,000, personal contact won't do it alone. You've got to have personal contact *plus* mass contact. Right?"

"Right."

"Okay, then, to get on. This paid stuff, in all three media, is almost wholly for name familiarity. We'll have little messages sprinkled in, and even an idea or two, but what we want to get across is simply that John North exists and that he's a good guy.

"Two years ago, during Steve's campaign, I got the newspapers to give me a regular commercial contract for a thirteen-week series. Before that, they had charged the straight one-time cost for each ad, no matter how many times you ran it or one like it. And you know that all political stuff in newspapers, radio, and TV is cash on the barrelhead *before* the show goes on. This hasn't changed; they still demand payment in advance; but I did get the papers to allow the series rate. That helps a little, but it's still expensive. And you know, too, that you can't take an ad in the morning *Herald* without having the same ad in the evening *Press-News*. They're both owned by Greenville Newspapers, Incorporated, and sell only packaged ads."

"Isn't that illegal?" Ruth asked. "Why should we have to buy more than one ad?"

"I don't know," Dick answered. "It's sometimes annoying, often useless, and always expensive—but illegal? I don't know. In our case, it's okay. We want to hit both the morning and afternoon readers. I suggest Sundays—actually appears in the evening paper on Saturday night—because it seems that people often spend more time with the weekend paper. And I'll try to have the boys in make-up put it on the entertainment page, where the movie ads and TV programs are listed—there's some evidence that more people look at this page than at any other. If we can't get it there, I'll shoot for the funny section, then for the front of the paper somewhere."

John broke in. "I think we get the picture here. You want these items to get my name in print, and to say a little something each week. Thus, I might say something about planning and zoning this week, then, next week, a little squib about extending the civil-service coverage to more of the Parks and Sanitation Department employees."

"Yes, that's the idea, although I'm not sure about your example of civil-service coverage, unless you could get some of the present patronage appointees to work for you in the hope that you'd blanket them in after the election. Otherwise, I don't see the political mileage in it."

Ruth frowned. "Dick, you've got a little leverage to use on everyone, haven't you?"

Bill turned to Ruth with an exaggeratedly machiavellian smile, and said, "That, my dear, is politics." And then he said to Dick, "I see you've got a question mark after this 'election-eve pitch.' I'd go farther than a mere question mark. I'd chuck it out. Every candidate puts an election-eve ad in the paper. Who the hell reads them? And who the hell phones those jillions of numbers for 'a ride to the polls'? My experience is that you spend your money, you tie up a phone or two that you could use to better advantage otherwise, and the three old ladies who do call for a ride vote for the other guy anyway, either out of ignorance or out of a desire to prove to themselves that you can't buy their vote. You might catch a few votes this way, although I'm not certain of it, but in any case not nearly as many as you'd get by hiring a couple of fellows with that fifty dollars and having them work some neighborhood where you know you're strong but where the turnout is apt to be weak without personal attention. Right?"

Dick agreed, and the election-eve ad was abandoned.

"Okay," Dick continued, "let's go down to radio. First, let's think for a moment about who listens to radio, and when they listen. Since the onslaught of TV, the character of radio listening has changed. The big radio-listening times now are the commuting times, and during these periods—say, seven to nine in the morning and four-thirty to six-thirty in the evening—the normal housewife and teenage audience is swelled by a good share of people listening to the 35,000,000 car radios we now have in this affluent society. But this is not an audience that will concentrate on a program, or listen attentively, or listen for very long. That's why spot announcements and short musical selections are the main bill of fare, and the disc jockey is everywhere the kingpin of the —"

"Of course! That's what's happened," John interrupted. "I'd never realized it."

Dick continued. "So we have to tailor the political stuff to the audience and the best times. Fortunately, spots are pretty cheap. The 480 five-second spots we ought to divide among the six radio stations according to their audience ratings, so we have an average of about eight per day per station for the ten days just before and including election day. The air is filled with political spots at this time, and we lose much of the effectiveness of this, and so does every other candidate, but it's also characteristic of the radio audience that there are many relatively indifferent persons, who may or may not vote even though registered, and who are late deciders. If they don't really care, and if they somehow manage to get to the polls, they're apt to pull the lever by the name they last heard.

It's simple; it may not be good; it certainly isn't Jeffersonian philosophy; but that's the way it is.

"In the same way, the 108 thirty-second spots should average out to three a day per station for the six days before and including election day. These, being longer, can carry a simple message. John ought to record these himself in his most sincere voice, and say a little something on each one about how he's better than anybody. The five-second spots are going to cost us about a buck apiece and the thirty-second about a dollar-fifty or a dollar-seventy-five.

"The last item here, under radio, is about the possibility of sponsoring some brief musical programs on WWOG, the daytime station that plays mainly religious stuff, and on WCAA-FM, our 'good music' station. I'd like to try it, as a little experiment, and I think for a hundred bucks we could get a fair amount of time and maybe more than a hundred bucks of good will. Shall I check it out?"

Nods around the table.

Ruth broke the momentary silence. "Dick, this is going to be awfully expensive, isn't it?"

"Yep. Campaigning is expensive. Even mayor's campaigns. There's no help for it, my dear."

John said, "When we've finished with the television section here, let's go over the campaign costs and think about what this will total and what else we'll need to spend."

"Yes, we can do that," Dick returned. "The TV thing isn't tricky, except that I'd like to try out a different timing arrangement. One of the big problems for the campaigner is that TV becomes saturated with political ads during the two or three weeks before the election. Many of the viewers tend to resent this avalanche of spot announcements, and some get downright mad when their favorite shows are taken off the air for some of the long political programs and coverage. It may be that excessive TV advertising actually loses some votes for some candidates. We don't really know enough about what might be called the *social psychology* of television campaigning.

"But I think maybe we can avoid, to some extent, being harmed by this saturation effect, and still get the value of TV for name identification, if we have a bunch of five-second spots very early in the campaign, and then have fewer and somewhat longer spots immediately before election day. So I'm suggesting 100 five-second spots for early August perhaps, and 21 sixty-second spots for the last three days. These are expensive, but if we sew up the time right now, we can be pretty sure of getting prime time for the last 21 and a share of prime time for the earlier, shorter ones.

"The best time for political stuff on TV is, in my experience, just before news programs or commentary between five-thirty and nine-thirty in the evening. In between programs that have high audience ratings is also good—actually, said by many of the so-called experts to be the best time—but I'm a so-called expert who thinks it's best to have the political spot nestled right up next to the opening of a newscast. Attention at that moment is high, and there's a psychological readiness for something of *public* importance. At other times, the viewer is unreceptive to a political advertisement, especially if it has to share a minute break with a detergent ad and a cigarette ad, even if it comes between his favorite westerns. Anyway, the TV spot, like the radio spot, is largely for name familiarity. If John seems instinctively like the 'good guy,' we'll pick up some marginal votes here.

"Finally, I'd caution against long, paid programs. I'm sure we can get John on Marty Brogan's show on Channel 4; we can probably get on a couple of the morning housewife's shows—what are they, 'Coffee Break,' and what's the one on Channel 11? And there'll be some film coverage of John's speeches. Also, I suppose we can get a couple of appearances on the university's station, although here again we want to be careful not to overplay the university connection."

Bill asked, "Would you have John make a little issues-pitch on the sixty-second TV spots just before election day?"

"Yes, that's what I had in mind. But I don't think we ought to make those up much in advance; we may want to use them for charges or countercharges that might be necessary at the end of the campaign. I expect anything from Gumshoe, and, though I think our best strategy is to stress what a good, able, guy John is and let them make their own comparisons, still, Gumshoe may give us a few blasts—especially if he gets worried—and that we can't ignore."

Before the strategy meeting broke up that night, the major outlines of the whole plan of operation were in shape. The total budget of $4,500 was divided $3,000 for the primary and $1,500 for the general. Ruth complained that it would break them, but Bill and Dick were optimistic about raising half or more from people and groups not yet brought into the campaign. Money was Bill's job, and Dick was to handle publicity, leaving Ruth to arrange meetings and to coordinate John's activities. John, as is always planned for a candidate, was to be free for attending meetings, coffees, speaking, and getting out to the shopping centers and to door-to-door work in selected areas.

Four and a half weeks later, on July 1, John Heny North announced his candidacy for mayor of Greenville. Dick wrote the press release, which was used almost verbatim by the evening paper. He had arranged beforehand to give it to the evening paper's political writer because, during the campaign, the evening paper would get fewer of the stories first. Most of the newsworthy political events occur in the evening and are therefore covered first by the next morning's paper. The morning paper used most of the information from the release, but rewrote it, and used a column-wide picture of John, which had also been supplied by Dick.

The campaign theme, "The Candidate with a Program," was introduced in the announcement. It was, as all agreed, an old phrase, and not very catchy; but the use of it centered on the hope of distinguishing John's background and his emphasis on ideas from Gumshoe's style of campaigning, which Bill described as "issueless conviviality." The North strategy committee, tied together by daily and often lengthy telephone conversations, had kicked the theme around a great deal. Puns on John's name were considered—"Go North for Mayor," and "Vote True, North for Mayor"—but they had agreed that a smart-aleck slogan might be worse than none at all. In the end, they decided to put on each printed advertisement and close each radio and TV spot with the simple appeal: "North for Mayor: The Candidate with a Program." Each of the newspaper ads, each of the billboards to be rented for six weeks before the primary, and each of the longer TV spots were then to spell out in as much detail as possible the points in this "program." One dealt with civil-service reform, one with land-use planning and zoning, one with the extension of the municipal water system, and one with the bond issue to build a new sewage treatment plant.

When the campaign got fully underway, the days and nights were filled for each of the core North workers. John was out, all the time, it seemed, meeting people door to door, at supermarkets, at factory gates, or at small house parties. He sat down and talked with groups of women in the afternoon and with men and women in the evening. Ruth, it seemed, was home on the telephone from eight-thirty in the morning until nine-thirty at night—arranging, planning, scheduling, and rethinking tactical matters at every turn. Dick and Bill were less wholly involved, but each gave four or five nights a week to the campaign. And in the midst of it all, they got together one evening—at eleven, after the last function of the day—*and they agreed that they didn't have the slightest knowledge of how it was going.*

Dick called it the "political horse latitudes."

"Every politician," he said, "asks every other politician, 'How's it going?'—by which he means 'What is your over-all assessment, at the moment, of my (or your) chances?' And they never *know* how it's going, although they will give an answer in the hope—always a vain hope—that the subsequent conversation will provide a bit of information to rationalize their optimism or calm their fears."

This was the situation: Each of the people close to John's campaign dared not trust himself or his friends because he knew that their whole orientation was inbred; they talked only or almost only to their own supporters. The world seemed, in such circumstances, to be a rosy place, and Gumshoe's chances seemed next to nil. But the older politicians, Bill and Dick, fought the Norths' optimism—and their own. They knew that in the opposition camp the subjective sun also shone. A true picture would be hard to get, if it could be got at all.

Dick decided to take a careful poll of voter knowledge and interest three weeks before primary-election day. He made up a questionnaire, asking about voter background, intention, and knowledge of the candidates. He threw in a number of irrelevant questions, and asked about candidates in several other races (one of whom was a paid client of his). He told the North workers who were recruited for the interviewing not to reveal whose poll they were taking until their interviews were over.

Dick chose six sampling areas, consisting in each case of one precinct alone or of two adjoining precincts, to represent a socioeconomic and political cross section (according to registration figures and previous voting patterns) of the city. In each of these sampling areas, he chose from fifty to seventy Democrats at random from the official voters' list. This gave him a sample of 365 persons; and the 13 volunteer workers to whom these were assigned, 35 persons to each worker, were told to interview all of those persons, and only those persons, whose names they had.

At the end of the interviewing, after the many delays and frustrations and misunderstandings that untrained people always experience in polling, Dick had 277 useful interviews. The breakdown indicated that this sample seriously overrepresented the women (61 to 39 per cent) and quite seriously overrepresented the higher socioeconomic groups in the city. Some adjustments were possible, however; and after these were made, the survey indicated that of those who knew John, about half intended to vote for him. But the critical finding was that only a little over 60 per cent of those who said they intended to vote in the Democratic primary knew John, whereas nearly 90 per cent knew Gumshoe. It was bad news, and hard to believe, so contrary was it to the impressions built up by constant association with supporters and well-wishers. It confirmed the sense of the name-familiarity strategy. But was there time enough remaining to get John known?

This question was answered ten days before the election, when the campaign took a dramatic turn. At a meeting of the downtown American Legion post, Gumshoe attacked John for being a conscientious objector in World War II. He declared that John lacked the proper patriotism to hold public office—*any* public office—and suggested that he was a coward. Further, Gumshoe hinted that John was a subversive, noting that John was a member of the American Civil Liberties Union, which had been criticized by the House Un-American Activities Committee, had co-sponsored a number of activities with organizations on the Attorney General's list, and five of whose board members had previously been members of now defunct organizations on the Attorney General's list.

The newspapers carried page-one stories: "Frederick Says North Unfit for Office; Mayorality Candidate's Patriotism Challenged." All the TV and radio newscasts carried the story as the top local item.

The problem of getting John known had been solved.

The morning after Gumshoe's speech, the North strategists gathered for breakfast and talk. The first reaction of each was to fight back, quickly and sharply. It was suggested that John go on TV, in a Greenville version of Vice-President Nixon's "Checkers" speech of 1952, and talk about his World War II decision, as a Quaker; to explain in humble detail why he had made that decision, and to question the relevance of his personal belief in pacifism to the issues and problems upon which his fitness for the office of mayor should be decided.

But, as they talked over the possibility of this course, each revealed that he had been contacted, in the few hours between Gumshoe's speech and their morning meeting, by two or three of John's supporters who felt that this charge would help John more than it would hurt him. These persons were themselves outraged by Gumshoe's charges, and they were confident that the inherent injustice and unfairness of the attack would result in others' rallying to John's cause. Freedom of religion was involved, these people declared, and in so slanderously attacking a man, Gumshoe would lose the respect and support of many voters.

The more the North strategists thought about this argument, the more realistic it became. The wish, in this way, became the father of the course that they decided to follow.

John would write a letter to the papers, to be printed in the letters to the editor. He would explain that during World War II he had decided to serve in an unpaid work camp rather than violate his religious views; he would deplore this irrelevant mudslinging by his opponent and hint that it was merely a desperate gamble resulting from his opponent's sure knowledge that John could not be beaten on the issues; and he would say that he could not elevate such a low attack on his religion (and, mind you, on *all* religions) by making it a central matter in the remaining few days of the campaign; he would end the letter by asking the editors and the voters to keep their eyes on the city's problems, and to vote according to their judgment of who was better able to meet these problems.

The reaction to the letter, as far as the North campaign workers could tell, was overwhelmingly favorable to John.

But, at the gossip level, it was deliberately spread by Gumshoe's friends in the city-hall circles that John was un-American, and—even worse from the point of view of the patronage employees—that he would

throw them all out and put in "a bunch of civil-service do-gooders."
Other rumors were spread—some maliciously, but most, no doubt, simply
by way of innocent storytelling as the petty politicians responded to
the ubiquitous question "What do you hear?" It was said that John was
not really a Quaker, because he didn't go to the meeting house regularly
(which was true), and that his conscientious objection was therefore the
fakery of either a Communist or a coward; facts, as usual, were wholly or
partially ignored. That the Communist line, when John was a conscientious objector, had declared all-out support for the war, and that
John had rejected an opportunity for noncombatant service in the army,
which would have combined safety with glory and pay—these facts were
not allowed to interfere with the enjoyment of the gossip.

The North strategy of ignoring the rumors and backstairs gossip
persisted to the end. On the night before the election, John was on TV
(in a change from the original plan), answering questions that were phoned
in. Of the fourteen questions asked during the program, five had been
previously arranged for by John's friends. ("Just insurance against the
unlikely event that we don't get any good spontaneous questions," Dick
had explained.) Of the other nine, two were on John's stand as a conscientious objector and one was a new absurdity—that a textbook in one of
John's classes had been written by a "Communist sympathizer." None
of these charges was answered, and the final note of the campaign was a
quiet and sincere appeal by John for rational voting on the issues and
on the man who could best do the job.

Twenty-four hours later, the political career of John Henry North
was over. Gumshoe Frederick scored a three-to-two victory. Out of
16,182 votes cast, John got 6,211; Gumshoe, 9,971.
Why?

In the week following the election, the North strategists puzzled
over the outcome. Dick Cassidy concluded that the underground campaign of rumor and gossip had turned the trick for Gumshoe. "We
should have met the charges openly and forcefully," he declared; "we
should have hit them back." His evaluation was reinforced when he
heard that in another state a congressional candidate had been attacked
for his pacifism, and that this candidate had skillfully fought back—he
even had a former commander of that state's Disabled American Veterans
appear on TV in his behalf—and he had won.

On the first evening of this postmortem (political postmortems, unlike those of the coroner, go on forever), Wally Sewell was, as usual,
quietly smoking his big, curved pipe. "That *may* be true, Dick, but
I've got another view of John's defeat. Let's look at it this way: we have

about 170,000 people in this town, of whom 90,000 may be of voting age. Maybe 80,000 of those can meet the requirements to be voters, and maybe 70,000 of these are registered —"

"Actually," Bill broke in, "it's a little less than 70,000."

"Okay. And of these 70,000, about 40,000 Democrats were eligible to vote in the primary last Tuesday—right?"

"Right."

"How many voted? About 16,000. Or about 40 per cent. Gumshoe got out the vote; we didn't. You know, he had the city patronage boys, probably a hundred of them, bringing in their families and friends; he told them he'd keep them; John didn't say anything to them, but instead talked to the League of Women Voters types—saving your grace, Beth (with a nod and smile to her)—who probably voted for you all right, but wouldn't for the world try to induce another person to vote for you. Likewise, you had the liberal, the university, and the Negro vote. But did they work for you? Of course not. Your issues-oriented university friends went down and voted for you—all two hundred of them! And how many of the Negroes voted? If 40 per cent of the whole electorate got out, what percentage of the Negroes got out? Maybe 15 per cent, and some of those voted for Gumshoe because they hold city jobs; they may believe in your 'equal-accommodations ordinance,' but poor men vote their stomachs, if they vote at all—and our Negroes, as I'm sure you don't need to be told, are poor.

"So, where does that leave the smear campaign? Yes, it was helpful to Gumshoe, because it gave his boys something to talk about, and maybe some of his professional and veteran friends got in a few more votes because of it. But, on the whole, I doubt that you were smeared to death. You lost because of the hole in the democratic theory. The voting public doesn't really take to rational campaigns, to thinking out the issues, to weighing the qualifications of particular candidates for particular offices. We muddle through because the level of the elected officials is about even with, maybe slightly higher than, the level of the median man in the street. But you're an extraordinary man—no flattery, John, I mean it—and extraordinary men don't easily get elected in a democracy. And that's why democracy is, as Winston Churchill is supposed to have said, 'the worst of all forms of government, except any other.' "

The argument between those who supported Dick's smear theory of John's defeat and those who accepted Wally's belief in the inherent-apathy-of-democracy theory went on into the late hours. Does either explanation make sense? Are there still other theories, or other factors, that ought to be considered?

PART ONE

MEASUREMENT

The primary election in the mythical town of Greenville constituted one measurement of public opinion. The opinion that was measured was the choice expressed by the 16,182 adults who voted in the contest between John Henry North and Arthur P. Frederick. The opinion that was effective was that of the 9,971 persons who chose Frederick over North.

Was that public opinion—the decision of about one tenth of the Greenville adults, or about 6 per cent of all the people of that town? One could hardly say that it was not, in some sense, an expression, and another measurement of public opinion.

Yet something seems wrong with the notion that the opinion of 10 per cent of the adults (the *effective* opinion in this election) constitutes *public* opinion. What about the 8 per cent of the Greenville adults who voted for North? Is their opinion, because it was minority opinion, not to be counted as part of public opinion? And what of the 80 per cent of the Greenville adults who expressed no choice at all in the election? Some of these may have had an opinion on the question of which of these two candidates ought to be accepted as the Democratic nominee for mayor of their city; should their views be ignored because they were not expressed? What about those who were less than twenty-one years old? Or those whose voting rights had been temporarily or permanently taken away? Are these people not part of the public and may they not have an opinion?

The answers to these questions depend—as do most of the interesting questions in the social sciences—upon how you define the terms. As we shall see, there is less than complete agreement on the meanings of the terms that are used in the study of public opinion.

But in order to avoid the perfectly reasonable objection that might be raised at this point—namely, how can we measure public opinion if we don't yet know what it is we are trying to measure—a tentative definition may be given here. Let's say that *for any given issue, public opinion is the collection of views, measurable or inferable, held by persons who have an interest in that issue.*

In Chapter 5, this first definition will be given some qualification and elaboration. Meanwhile, taking this tentative definition of public opinion, let us consider in the next few pages the business of how public opinion is *measured.* Measurement is taken up here because *fieldwork,* if at all possible, ought to accompany the study of public opinion. It is not enough just to read a textbook or articles about how someone else measured public opinion or what someone else found about the opinions that publics hold on the vital or trivial issues of the day. Although such reading is essential, it should be supplemented by serious fieldwork.

No chemist would believe for a moment that lectures and reading alone constitute a satisfactory undergraduate course. Laboratory work is essential to the understanding of chemical theories. The case can be made nearly as strongly for laboratory work in what have come to be called the *behavioral sciences*—a fancy term for the study of man's individual and social behavior. Much of political science can be grouped under this academic roof, as can all of sociology and much of psychology, anthropology, economics, and history. Anthropologists and sociologists have recognized the importance of fieldwork for many years. Political scientists, for whom this book is primarily written, are placing an increasingly greater emphasis on fieldwork in their courses. This emphasis is all to the good, and a movement to which it is hoped this book can contribute.

We therefore take up the measurement of public opinion, in the hope that the following discussion may help you plan a field project that you will engage in while reading the rest of the book.

OPINIONS DIRECT
AND REPRESENTATIVE

1

1.1 The Social Importance of
Opinion Measurement

The measurement of public opinion is, in its simplest sense, finding out what people think. So defined, it is as old as society; and it developed, without being named, along with the other characteristics—language, the division of labor, and habits of cooperative work—that marked the latter stages of the "descent of man."

Gradually, during the long development of humanity, the mature individuals began to realize that certain desires could be more easily met by cooperation than by antagonism. It became apparent that seven men from neighboring caves could combine their strength to kill an animal that no one or two or three could kill, and that the meat and hide and bones thus obtained would supply their families with more than they would get if each hunted smaller animals alone. Perhaps it was mutual defense against a neighboring clan that drove primitive man into cooperative action.

But cooperation brings division of work. Two men chase the animal in; two more stand behind rocks in the narrow pass and plunge their fire-hardened spears into the beast as it thunders past; two others entangle it in stout vines as it thrashes in its death agony. Six men, and three very distinct jobs.

It may happen that, by common consent, the strongest of the young men are detailed to be the spear thrusters, a job that demands the utmost strength and agility. These men find that they can begin to give more and more of the directions and orders because the others are more dependent on them than they are on the others. *Social status* and *power* thus arise; and unless there are counter situations and factors which lead to others' getting status and power, the spear throwers may become a favored class in this rudimentary community.

It may, of course, be quite otherwise. The old men, resigned to be the beaters-in during the hunt, may have developed some simple religious doctrines and rituals which give them authority as the teachers of the myths and legends. The anthropologists tell us that veneration of the aged appears to have been more common than the social exaltation of the strongest, but that both of these groups rank, usually, in power and authority above the diggers, or the weavers, or those who shape the simple tools.

The differentiation of social status in even the smallest and simplest societies occurred long before there were any reliable records of precisely how such differentiations developed. For our purposes, it is enough to note that social differentiation was always accompanied by the development of some kind of communication, by *gestures* and *verbalization,* and that it created situations in which it was frequently important for some people to know what certain numbers of the others thought about matters of common interest. One cannot imagine such a simple community without also imagining a collection of the more influential men sitting around a fire or flat rock—"council rocks" are still common landmarks wherever there were tribes of American Indians—discussing things that were important to them all.

Although the societies and the meetings were vastly different, the council of Mesopotamian warriors in 10,000 b.c. and the yearly New England town meeting served the same purposes for running society. *Functionally,* these meetings were similar. Each constituted, among other things, a *measurement of opinion.* By the time of the development of New England democracy in the seventeenth and eighteenth centuries, there were other ways of measuring opinion; there were church meetings, plenty of them; there were handbills and simple newspapers; there were officials whose job it was to communicate regularly with the people with regard to public matters. But the *meeting* and the *vote,* or the "sense of the meeting," have been fundamental ingredients in the measuring of opinion for thousands of years.

1.2   The Political Importance of Opinion Measurement

In every community since the beginnings of social man, there has been some concern for the opinions of the people. Among the power holders of every society there has been attention to the thinking and desires of the masses. Even before political leadership was distinguishable from religious or tribal-blood leadership this must have been, to some degree, the case.

Later, when the division of statuses produced kings, it can be said that no king was ever absolutely absolute. Even in the time when absolutism was a fairly respectable indoor theory, no king could afford completely to ignore the wishes of the population.

It may be helpful to differentiate between what might be called *positive public opinion,* on the one hand, and mere *acquiescence,* on the other. It can be argued that all rulers of all time have needed the acquiescence of the masses, but not necessarily the support of positive public opinion. To the extent that the masses were uninterested, unable, or unwilling to think or act with regard to public affairs, positive public opinion, as we know it, was of no consequence. Until fairly recently, as anthropological history goes, the masses had no education, no information from outside their own little villages, and no human energy left over after obtaining scant physical needs. They had few or no opinions regarding public matters.

Daniel Lerner has found that, even today, many Middle Eastern peasants are unable to conceive of public events outside their own villages. They cannot imagine what the nonpersonal world is like. They are unable to place themselves in the role of another person. When the interviewers asked the Turkish villagers questions which required them to imagine themselves as head of a government, editor of a paper, or manager of a radio station, they often simply could not respond. Lerner says:

> The strenuousness of such demands upon persons untutored in empathic skills was underlined by the many respondents, in every country, who thought of suicide rather than imagine themselves in these exalted ranks. "My God! How can you say such a thing?" gasped the shepherd, when Tosun put such questions to him.[1]

This lack of opinion among the masses, and the inability even to conceive of the holding of opinions on matters relating to large publics, was the almost universal condition until well into the modern period of Western history.

Concurrent with these social and economic factors, which prevented any real sense of publicness in the opinions of the masses (and complemented fact with theory), was the prevailing doctrine of premodern time that the masses had no business entertaining notions about public matters even if they were capable of doing so. Doctrines of divine right for priests and kings persuaded rulers and ruled alike that it was not the business

---

[1] Lerner's discussion of this lack of "empathy" ("the capacity to see oneself in the other fellow's situation"), and the consequences of this lack for the modernization of traditional societies, is a vital contribution, and part of a pioneering book, which no student of human behavior should fail to read. Daniel Lerner, *The Passing of Traditional Society* (New York: The Free Press of Glencoe, 1958), p. 70.

of the people to think or say anything except those simple thoughts and words which were appropriate to "that station in life to which they had been called by an omniscient Providence."

Thus, both theoretical and practical elements combined until fairly recently to impede the development of positive public opinion. The dumb acquiescence of the masses was mandate enough to legitimate, in this sense, whatever government existed.

Gradually, however, with the advent of technological changes that created some leisure and freed a few persons from the margins of survival, and with both the discovery of new land and the rediscovery of old learning, there came into existence in the Western world a new set of beliefs about the relationship between the rulers and the ruled.

Machiavelli, whom political scientists both claim and deny as patron saint, stands more or less at the bridge between old and new. He recognized that it is useful and preferable to gain the positive support of the people, but that the passive toleration of the masses is a most necessary minimum for stability. The ruler, he says, "who has but a few enemies can easily make sure of them without great scandal, but he who has the masses hostile to him can never make sure of them, and the more cruelty he employs the feebler will his authority become; so that his best remedy is to try and secure the good will of the people."[2]

1.3   Political Representation and Opinion Measurement

When the number of persons whose opinions count is very small, as in primitive societies and in tiny self-governing communities, whether public or private, the opinions of all can be measured. Nonpublic organizations, such as church congregations, social clubs, and economic groups, may also conduct their business by meetings of the whole membership, by mail balloting, or by questionnaires sent to each person. As we shall see, these private *primary groups* constitute an important element in the larger network of public opinion. But restricting our consideration to governmental units, we may say that only the unlimited town meeting (and perhaps some special districts of very small power and geography) is based on the idea that the opinions of *all* the voters will be measured; in theory, there is no element of representation. This idea is the basic tenet of *direct democracy,* of course, and to put it in terms of the measurement of opinion is simply another way of illuminating it.

---

2 N. Machiavelli, *The Discourses* (New York: Random House, Inc., Modern Library Edition, 1940), p. 162.

Today, however, many New England towns have adopted what is called the "limited town meeting," in which a number of persons are chosen to gather annually to vote on the questions placed before them by the town officials. In these meetings, the opinions of some are assumed to be *representative* of the opinions of all. With the choosing of such persons to decide on the main issues in the name of all the townsmen, direct democracy, and its simple, one-step measurement of opinion, has been abandoned. In the election of these representatives, the opinion of the whole voting population is still asked. But the measurement of whole opinion is only on the question of which persons are to be chosen to decide thereafter for a limited time on the issues that come before the meeting. Thereafter, on all matters except new elections, public opinion cannot be measured by a simple vote of the whole population, but only by a two-step process, in which the vote of the representative meeting is assumed to *reflect* the opinions of all the people. That this process introduces distortion is certain. But it is equally certain that the public business in all except the smallest communities could not be carried out otherwise.

Size, then, is the limiting factor to the direct measurement of opinion. For making governmental policy, the town meeting is simply not effective when there are more than three or four hundred voters in attendance. The congressman or congressional candidate cannot obtain the opinions of all voters (or all who are eligible to vote, or all adults, or all people) in his district. The maker of some new detergent called *Slosh* cannot measure the reactions of all housewives to his product. In these cases, some kind of representation device must be introduced. The opinions of *some* of the people are measured, and, from these measured opinions, deductions are made about the opinions of all.

This two-step process, oversimplified here, is a form of *sampling*. Whether it is good sampling or bad sampling depends, most importantly, on whether accurate deductions can be made from the measurement of the representative group. Thus, it may be said, in a sense, that there is bad representation and good representation.

The measurement of public opinion is as important in a society as is the extent to which the support of the masses is necessary, or is thought to be necessary, for the legitimating or the operation of government. Briefly, the importance of public opinion (and, therefore, of the measurement of public opinion) depends on the degree of democracy in the society. Insofar as there are theories that say that the people have a right to influence their governments, so far is public opinion important.

As a practical matter, political leaders are selective in their assessments of public opinion. They try, first of all, to measure the opinions of those people who have the greatest influence on their own future and the future of those policies they most support or oppose. John Henry North had the potential Democratic voters polled. The legislator looks first to the opinions of the most influential men of his district.

Which persons and groups are important to officials depends not alone on the officeholders' individual beliefs and preferences, but also on those notions of political representation that find acceptance in the political theory of the time. Since the sixteenth century, according to Samuel Beer, four rather distinct views of representation have marked British politics. The "old Whig" theory had it that Parliament represented the whole people. Edmund Burke believed in this theory; he said in his famous "Speech to the People of Bristol" that although he represented the people of that town, he also represented all other, similar towns (a maritime "interest") and, beyond that, all the people of England. Such a belief disposed him to think relatively little of the judgment of his constituents on the issues of the day. He had small interest in measuring opinions in the streets of Bristol.

The old Whig view of representation gave way gradually, but never entirely, to what Beer calls the "liberal" theory of representation. In this theory, the predominant view was that each member of Parliament represented not particular groups of people or historical "interests," but the great middle class. A member's independent opinion on the issues of the day was as good as any other member's, and, collectively, the opinions of the whole Parliament were, almost by definition, those of the dominant, Victorian middle class. Members of Parliament, holding such a theory of representation, needed to spend little or no time in calculating the opinions of the public upon whose favor they depended, since, in practice, they thought as did the voters in the "shopkeeper democracy" of the time and, in theory, they were under no obligation to discover what differences might have existed between their opinions and those of their constituents. Beer, quoting Richard Pares, calls the period from 1832 to 1867 the "golden age of the private M.P."[3]

Following the Representation of the People Act of 1867, however, a new pattern of voting called forth a new theory of representation. Beer calls this the "radical" theory, and says that popular majoritarianism lay at the bottom of it. The tendency was for the member of Parliament to be reduced to the status of a mere delegate, registering the interests of those groups (agriculture, business association, labor unions) that supported his election. Thus, the emphasis shifted to devices for expressing and measuring public opinion; and the views of various elements or publics were

[3] This discussion of British theories of representation is from Samuel Beer, "The Representation of Interests in British Government: Historical Background," *American Political Science Review*, LI, No. 3 (1957), 613–650. Quotation from p. 632.

most readily expressed by means of political-action organizations (pressure groups) and political parties. All three of the great British parties of the present century were formed in the period 1867 to 1910. The development of the radical theory of representation, thus, depended heavily on organizations that reflected, or claimed to reflect, public opinion.

The last theory of representation that Beer identifies in modern British thought is what he calls the "collectivist" theory of representation. This might better be called the "theory of party government," since the main theme of this theory is that the political party in power, as a coalition of social groups, represents the whole nation. Party opinion, as formed in the party organization and its constituent groups, is the opinion that counts. The individual is not wholly lost in this process, however, because he participates in forming both group and party opinion. He also participates basically, at each general election, by choosing between the parties; but his opinion is not *directly* of much consequence to his representative.

Each of these theories of representation looked to a different segment of the population for the opinions that count. The old Whig theory held that the people could decisively give an opinion only when they cast a vote; at other times, their opinions on specific issues might be given, but they would not be sought; they would be largely superfluous in any case, because the personal view of the representative was the determining opinion. There was, in short, little need to measure public opinion.

Under the liberal theory of representation, the legislator had even greater independence; as long as he personally took care of the interests of the powerful bourgeoisie, the class from which he himself probably came, he had no need to be sensitive to other opinion.

After 1867, radical theory of representation required the representative to seek out the opinions of a vastly expanded electorate. This was best accomplished by attention to the many pressure groups that were created, in large part, expressly for the purpose of bringing opinion to bear on legislators, and by association with one or other of the increasingly powerful mass parties.

Finally, the party-government theory of representation depends, for the organization of opinion, on the internally democratic, but disciplined, machinery of the party itself. This theory is perhaps of less interest than the other, to Americans, although the debate over "more responsible parties" is a long, serious, and still healthy one among American political scientists and politicians.

The importance, to us, of Beer's excellent summary of British theories of representation is that the public opinion that is measured is, politically, the opinion that is influential; and the importance of popular influence is apt to be assessed differently at different times and in different places. Although George Gallup may sometimes measure opinion that is merely interesting or curious, the politician in every time and place attempts to measure the opinion that makes a difference to the theory and practice of government.

INFORMAL DEVICES
AND STRAW POLLS

2

2.1 The Simple Ingredients of
Everyday Opinion Measurement

Whether opinion sampling is good or bad, it always involves *asking, listening,* and *reading.* The politicians in John Henry North's case asked each other, "What do you hear?" The candidate, the market researcher, the commercial pollster, and just about every active person listens constantly and interprets what he hears, consciously or unconsciously, into a measurement of opinion.

Asking is not necessarily associated with listening. The lounger on the street corner, without asking, picks up information, which he may use to measure opinion. The wartime spy may measure public morale without ever asking the home-front worker how he feels.

Usually, asking and listening are vitally interrelated parts of all opinion measurement. The politician asks his friends and acquaintances and, on the basis of their responses, attempts to create in his mind a picture of public opinion. The pollster asks his respondent broad or narrow questions in as much detail as he or his employer thinks is necessary.

Much measurement of opinion is done by reading. The candidate reads the newspapers in his district. The editor of one paper reads other papers. The entrepreneur, looking for a new location for a store, reads the business news, specialized suburban papers, and the public records of new subdivisions and home construction. All these people are, in some degree or other, sampling public opinion by reading. It is perhaps unnecessary to point out that their information, and the conclusions drawn from this information, may be seriously distorted; for they are probably reading an unrepresentative sample of an unrepresentative sample. Since newspapers are themselves not representative of all the opinions held by all of the people, they are, to that extent, inevitably distorted. Since the sample of newspapers read by the candidate, the editor, or the businessman is in turn unrepresentative of all newspapers, another necessary distortion occurs. Of the more than 1,700 daily newspapers and 8,000 weekly newspapers in the United States, few individuals can read more than four or five. By using a well-organized staff, and a cadre of home correspondents, a congressman can perhaps get reports or clippings from all the papers in his district. But the editor and businessman probably cannot so adequately organize their reading samples of other papers, and they may seriously mismeasure the public opinion, or public opinions, of concern to them.

Nonetheless, the distortion in most reading samples is readily compensated for in everyday situations. Each of us evaluates almost automatically the representativeness and validity, for our purposes, of the reading samples we employ in measuring the segment of public opinion that is important to us. The businessman distrusts the optimism of the *Paradise Valley Shoppers News* for the market potential of the new Paradise Valley subdivision. He will react more enthusiastically to the County Registrar of Deeds' report that 80 per cent more residence lots were sold in Paradise Valley than in any other subdivision in the county. In the measurement of opinion, we evaluate everything about our reading samples, and weigh them with all the other factors that go into making up our judgments.

The endless measuring of opinion is a process in which we all share in various degrees, for opinion measuring is inevitable in every social situation. Most of this "horseback" opinion measuring is of little general consequence. It is of no political importance whether a person accurately measures the opinions of others in private situations that involve only his relationships with them. Nor do we especially care whether an individual accurately measures the opinions of his neighbors toward his plan to paint his house a bright purple, although there may be circumstances in which such a plan becomes a genuine public issue.

But we do care whether the mayor gets a good picture of the citizens' opinions of his proposal for a fundamental change in the structure of city government.

2.2 "Ear to the Ground": Politicians Measure Opinion

We have said that all opinion measurement involves some combination of reading, asking, listening, and thinking. The person who is interested in public questions, whether he is a government official, party activist, pressure-group leader, or League of Women Voters independent, will use all of these methods in assessing the views of publics. From the viewpoint of the holders of political power, keeping one's "ear to the ground" meant, before the advent of scientific polls, collecting printed and spoken opinions and discounting them according to the influence of those who enunciated them.

The politician avidly reads newspaper stories and other expressions of opinion. He reads specialized publications, such as the newsletters of organizations that operate in his area or are interested in matters that interest him. He reads his mail carefully and always answers it, with greater or lesser attention, depending on who the letter is from and how it is written. Beyond this, he sees people and talks with people. He asks and he listens. In short, in his measurement of opinion, he conducts informal interviews.

It seems to be true, as it was in the case of John Henry North, that politicians talk mainly to other politicians. They probably spend half or more of their talking time, except when they are on a planned sidewalk hunt for opinions (or more likely for votes), in conversation with other politicians. But this leaves considerable talking time for nonpoliticians—for family, for friends whose friendship is based on nonpolitical considerations, and for casual contacts. Although families and nonpolitical friends tend to get little time from politicians—the *virus politicus* is a consuming malady that allows little private life—politicians often talk to casual contacts and constituents.

In his contact with ordinary people and voters, an important consideration is the kind of job the politician holds and the place in which he holds it. A local executive or legislator (a mayor or city councilman, a county clerk or supervisor, or a state legislator who represents a district that is in the state capital) will have a clear advantage over a nonlocal in gauging, through casual interviews and observations, opinion that is significant to him. The congressman who represents the 10th Congressional District of Virginia, and lives in Arlington, just across the Potomac from Washington, can go home every night. But only two or three congressmen share this advantage. The rest necessarily live separated for many months from constituents whose opinions they would like to judge personally day in and day out; some congressmen who live in the East and Northeast may go home on most or every weekend; Western congressmen may get home only once or twice during the session, if at all.

Geography, then, is quite important. But the type of job is also important. It probably can be said that, by and large, local officeholders whose jobs take them constantly into the public are better able to maintain themselves in office through re-election than are nonlocals. Generally speaking, a county superintendent of highways will be less vulnerable at the polls than a coroner or county clerk. Other things being equal (they rarely are), a mayor is less likely to misjudge opinion than is a city clerk; a councilman who is also a vice-mayor, and who therefore attends more citywide functions than his fellow councilmen, is less likely to misjudge opinion or to fail of re-election than are the other members of the council. In summary, a variety and number of contacts of what we call the *informal-interviewing type* are helpful to the politician with his "ear to the ground."

But the politician doesn't have to initiate all the contacts—even all the verbal and interviewing-type contacts. Aside from letters, officeholders and candidates are constantly seen or telephoned in person by constituents who seek favors, redress of wrong, and advice. Some of these people represent organized groups—pressure groups—but many of them are just plain people with just plain gripes.

"There's a hole in the street out in front of my house. Can't you do something about it?" City and county officials hear this kind of complaint all the time. It is a contact. It is an interview. It is also a measurement of opinion.

If people from all over the district are calling their councilman about holes in the street, then he knows that the streets are in pretty bad shape (a thing that he might be expected to know without such calls), and he also knows that there's a certain amount of feeling among the public that something should be done about it.

Reading, listening, asking, and talking—these are ways the politician has always kept his "ear to the ground." Door-to-door canvassing is not new in politics. The good precinct captain has done it for years. He has not done it scientifically, using the mathematical laws of probability, but his practical judgment and knowledge of his area may be so keen that his assessments are accurate enough for his purposes. There are many stories of ward and precinct politicians who can predict the vote in their areas within one or two percentage points.[1] This is not surprising in areas that are small, and intensively "worked."

An early attempt to assess the ability of party politicians to predict elections was made by Claude E. Robinson in 1932. He collected two types of data from the presidential election campaign of 1928. First, he gathered Republican estimates by county from three states. He compared these forecasts with the actual election returns, and calculated the "plurality error" (the difference between the *estimated* plurality and the *actual* plurality) for each county. He found that the plurality errors

---

[1] Preston E. Peden, of the Chicago Association of Commerce and Industry, says that he knows "one Republican precinct captain in Chicago (an attorney for a large packing company) who can predict within one or two votes the outcome of any election in his precinct." In James A. Gathings, ed., *Politics and the American Businessman* (Lewisburg, Pa.: Bucknell University, 1960), p. 62.

ranged from 0.1 per cent to 52 per cent, and that the average plurality error by county was 13 per cent for two of the states and 14 per cent for the other.[2] Second, from a number of political leaders and newspaperman, Robinson compiled a list of estimates by state and political party. He listed "trustworthy" estimates of Democrats in eight states, and found that their median plurality error in 1928 was 18 per cent; Republican estimates in sixteen states showed much better predictive validity, having a median plurality error of only 7 per cent.[3]

The differences between their predictions and the actual vote is striking testimony to the proposition that politicians tell themselves what they want to hear. Robinson says that politicians, in estimating their future, suffer from the "elation complex." He says that this is a necessary self-delusion, for "men who believe they are whipped are almost sure to be beaten"; but it "constitutes the chief weakness in the predictive technique of the politician," for it "opens the door to delusions of grandeur and power, and causes otherwise normal men to see great and sweeping victories where fate holds crushing defeat in store."[4]

The "elation complex" seems to have been at work on October 12, 1960, when the leaders of New York State's Democratic Party, Michael Prendergast and Carmine de Sapio, predicted an "overwhelming victory" for the Kennedy-Johnson ticket. So great was their enthusiasm that they saw the Democrats sweeping upstate counties not carried since the mid-1930s and "on the verge of winning control of the state legislature."[5] The Kennedy ticket won in New York, to be sure, but not so sweepingly as to affect the solid Republican victories at all other levels in the state.

Another informal technique of opinion measurement is *crowd analysis*. It has only recently been elevated to the level of a "science" and been sanctified by disinterested research. One may suppose that since the beginning of political speechmaking (which means since the beginning of politics, and the beginning of civilization as well) the speechifiers and their friends have tried to interpret the behavior, size, and attentiveness of crowds, and to gauge crowd responses to particular words, phrases, and styles of oratory.

Adolf Hitler, who had great oratorical talents of the demagogic variety, was clearly aware of the possibilities of measuring both opinion and the effectiveness of speech techniques from the reactions of crowds.

---

2 *Straw Votes: A Study of Political Predicting* (New York: Columbia University Press, 1932), pp. 6–8.

3 *Ibid.*, p. 9.

4 *Ibid.*, p. 10.

5 New York *Herald Tribune,* October 13, 1960.

It was his belief that all great political movements were fired by the "magic power of the spoken word, and that . . . particularly the broad masses of the people can be moved only by the power of speech"—by, as he put it, "the firebrand of the word hurled among the masses . . . [and] not the lemonade-like outpourings of literary aesthetes and drawing-room heroes."[6] Hitler stressed the importance of the emotional "feedback" that speakers get from crowds, a phenomenon that, if speakers are sensitive to it, can be turned to advantage:

> . . . the speaker gets a continuous correction of his speech from the crowd he is addressing, since he can always see in the faces of his listeners to what extent they can follow his arguments with understanding and whether the impression and the effect of his words lead to the desired goal. . . .
>
> He will always let himself be borne by the great masses in such a way that instinctively the very words come to his lips that he needs to speak to the hearts of his audience. And if he errs, even in the slightest, he has the living correction before him. As I have said, he can read from the facial expression of his audience whether, firstly, they *understand* what he is saying, whether, secondly, they can *follow the speech as a whole,* and to what extent, thirdly, he has *convinced* them of the *soundness* of what he has said. If—firstly—he sees that they do not understand him, he will become so primitive and clear in his explanations that even the last member of his audience has to understand him; if he feels—secondly—that they cannot follow him, he will construct his ideas so cautiously and slowly that even the weakest member of the audience is not left behind, and he will—thirdly—if he suspects that they do not seem convinced of the soundness of his argument, repeat it over and over in constantly new examples. He himself will utter their objections, which he senses though unspoken, and go on confuting them and exploding them, until at length even the last group of an opposition, by its very bearing and facial expression, enables him to recognize its capitulation to his arguments.[7]

In democracies, too, political actors are compelled to be attentive to the size, composition, and behavior of crowds. The possibilities of manipulating crowds are much reduced in democratic environments, mainly because in democracies other messages and stimuli compete with those given to crowds by the government. Nonetheless, the democratic politician desires large, enthusiastic crowds for three reasons. First, he needs the support and votes of the individuals in the crowd. Second, he hopes for a bandwagon effect; he wants to rouse the individuals in the crowd to persuade other voters as well as give their own votes, and he wants to make his cause seem popular to those who are not in the crowd. Third, he needs the crowd for what we have called feedback; he can sense, in the

---

[6] Adolf Hitler, *Mein Kampf,* trans. Ralph Manheim (Boston: Houghton Mifflin Co., 1943), p. 107.

[7] *Ibid.,* pp. 469–471. Italics in original. Reprinted by permission of Houghton Mifflin Company.

way Hitler did, how he is doing. Even if he cannot always amend his lapses or improve his delivery of a speech under way, he can learn from such feedback to revise or ignore his less successful appeals (or phrases, or figures of speech), and to emphasize in later speeches the more successful elements.

The most famous of all American campaign blunders seems now, in the light of recent scholarship, to have resulted largely from a failure to assess crowd reaction. In 1884, James G. Blaine was the Republican presidential nominee opposing Democrat Grover Cleveland. On the evening of October 29—only one week before election day—Blaine spoke in New York City to a large group of Protestant ministers and divinity students. He was introduced that evening by the Rev. Dr. Samuel D. Burchard, who said, among other things, that the assembled ministers supported Blaine and would not identify themselves with the Democratic Party, "whose antecedents have been rum, Romanism and rebellion."

It had been assumed for many years that Blaine did not hear Burchard's remark. In any case, he did not repudiate the remark on the spot—nor, indeed, until three days later.

In 1955, a memorandum of U.S. Supreme Court Justice John Marshall Harlan came to light. A few months after the 1884 election, Justice Harlan had had dinner with Blaine and had written:

> The Burchard incident was referred to by Mr. Blaine, and he said that the utterance of the words "Rum, Romanism and Rebellion" stunned and amazed him for the moment and *went through him like a knife;* that in responding to Burchard's address of welcome he made no allusion to those words, for the reason that, at the time, he did not think they were heard except by a few of those present who stood very near to Dr. Burchard, but who did not seem to recognize their mischievous effect; that, at the instant, he determined not to appear to have heard what Burchard said, as he supposed that more harm would be done by noticing his remarks than by passing them by without observation.[8]

Commenting on Blaine's critical moment of decision, David G. Farrelly says:

> What emerges from the Harlan version is an understanding of the momentary predicament that faced Blaine. With a quick decision demanded of him, Blaine reacted promptly to the situation as he discerned it. Of course if there had been a public address system in those days, everyone in the room would have heard Burchard's remark. Then Blaine would still have had a decision to make, but under those circumstances he might very well have repudiated Burchard on the spot. Indeed, speculating editorially two days before the election, the *New York*

---

8 " 'Rum, Romanism and Rebellion' Resurrected," *Western Political Quarterly*, VIII, No. 2 (1955), 269. Italics in original. Reprinted by permission of the University of Utah, copyright holder.

Times pointed out that Blaine was usually quick enough and that an immediate disclaimer would have been to his benefit.[9]

Here, clearly, is an example of misjudging crowd feedback. Blaine had been unable to tell that the persons in attendance that night—especially the newspaper reporters—had heard the anti-Catholic remark of his introducer. He misjudged the crowd, mishandled the situation, and lost the election. New York's electoral votes would have put him in the White House, and he lost them by a scant 1,149 popular votes. Indications are, had Blaine's minister supporter not uttered this famous epithet, or had Blaine repudiated him on the spot, that Blaine would not have lost the less than six hundred voters who could have made him President of the United States. Blaine himself said, shortly after his defeat, "As the Lord sent upon us an ass in the shape of a preacher, and a rainstorm, to lessen our vote in New York, I am disposed to feel resigned to the dispensation of defeat, which flowed directly from these agencies."[10]

One of the several innovations of the presidential campaign of 1960 was the employment by the Kennedy strategists of a "crowd analyst." George Belknap, a political scientist on leave from the University of California, joined the Kennedy entourage for one week in early October to make some "scientific" assessments of the Kennedy crowds. According to the *New York Times,* Belknap was to "appraise the meaning of the Kennedy crowds in terms of their influence, if any, on the outcome of the Presidential election . . . [and] to gauge crowd reactions to politically significant words, phrases, and themes with a view to advising the candidate on their use."[11] Belknap's analyses of the reactions to Kennedy's speeches seemed to show that Kennedy's linking the name of former Republican presidential candidate Thomas E. Dewey with that of Vice-President Nixon recalled a Republican defeat and enlivened the Kennedy audience. On the other hand, it was reported that Belknap's calculations had dampened the optimism of some of Kennedy's aides by indicating that Kennedy's crowds were smaller than untrained local officials and newsmen had been estimating.

William S. White has defined "crowdmanship" as "the science of inflating the size of the audience and thus trying to outpropaganda the crowd estimates of the opposition candidate."[12] White uses the word "science" loosely for, despite Belknap's best efforts, the reporting of

9 *Ibid.*

10 *Ibid.,* p. 270.

11 *New York Times,* October 7, 1960.

12 *Arizona Daily Star,* October 22, 1960.

crowd size remained in 1960, as in campaigns before, essentially a matter of propaganda artistry. On October 26, 1960, Vice-President Nixon spoke from the state capitol steps in Columbus, Ohio. The New York *Herald Tribune,* supporting Mr. Nixon, said (October 27, p. 12) the crowd was "variously estimated at from 75,000 to more than 100,000"; the *New York Times,* supporting Kennedy, said (October 27, p. 30) the Columbus police chief had first estimated the crowd at 30,000 and had later said 150,000 had gathered. The *Times* also gave some indication of how seriously the political parties take their crowdmanship; fifty-nine busses were chartered by Ohio Republicans to take demonstrators to the capitol steps—one hundred, it was said, had been used the night before to pack supporters into the Cincinnati Gardens.[13]

2.3   Straw Polls

Claude E. Robinson says that a straw poll is "an unofficial canvass of an electorate to determine the division of popular sentiment on public issues or on candidates for public office."[14] The first known attempts to measure electoral opinion on a mass scale were the so-called "straw polls" developed by newspapers in the nineteenth century.

In the summer of 1824, the *Harrisburg Pennsylvanian* sent out reporters to check on popular support for the four presidential contenders of that year. On July 24, the paper reported that a "straw vote taken without discrimination of parties" showed Jackson to be the popular choice over John Quincy Adams, Henry Clay, and William H. Crawford.[15]

Polling and political prediction has been, as the *Encyclopaedia Britannica* declares, "an intermittent practice of U.S. journalism"[16] during the last 150 years. Toward the end of the nineteenth century, the *New York Herald* became more regular in its forecasts for local and state as well as national elections. During presidential campaigns, the *Herald* collected estimates from newsmen and political leaders in many parts of the country and predicted the Electoral College votes by state. In 1908,

---

[13] The honors for 1960 crowdmanship seem to have gone to the Democrats, despite Republican efforts in Ohio. At a New York City rally held for Kennedy by the International Ladies Garment Workers Union, David Dubinsky, union president, claimed there were 250,000 persons present, and that it was the greatest rally ever held in America, "or even the world." The *Herald Tribune* reporter, Peter D. Franklin, estimated 75,000 at Dubinsky's rally.

[14] "Straw Votes," *Encyclopedia of the Social Sciences* (1937), XIV, 417.

[15] John M. Fenton, *In Your Opinion* (Boston: Little, Brown and Co., 1960), p. 3.

[16] "Public Opinion Surveys," *Encyclopaedia Britannica* (1955), XVIII, 744.

this paper began a collaborative effort with Cincinnati, Chicago, and St. Louis papers. Later, this group was joined by three other papers (in Boston, Denver, and Los Angeles), conducting polls in thirty-seven states in 1912 and thirty-six in 1916. Other papers, and some magazines, including the *Farm Journal*, began in the same period to make election predictions based upon opinion surveys of one kind or another. By 1920, it was clear that straw polling was more than an "intermittent practice."

The chief problem in straw polling, as commonly conducted, is that it is almost impossible to ensure that the persons giving their opinions are representative of all the persons whose opinions are presumably being measured. There is no certainty that the microcosm (the *sample*) is like the macrocosm (the *universe*). For instance, straw polls are often conducted through the distribution of ballots in commercial or recreational places; the ballots are marked by those who care to mark them, and the results are tabulated by the conductor of the poll. Thus, the Rheingold Brewing Company each year "elects" a "Miss Rheingold" by straw vote. Ballots, including pictures of six young ladies who are candidates for the office, are placed in bars and liquor stores in the Rheingold distribution area. Patrons who are moved to vote in this election may do so. The fathers and brothers of the nominees may vote as often as they please— either to assure the election or the defeat of their own, depending on their views of the desirability of the office. As a pleasant tavern pastime, in which American girlhood is honored through the device of popular election, this practice is surely unobjectionable. Like most advertising, it has no pretensions to social or political importance, and, hence, deserves no more consideration here.

The quadrennial "National Popcorn Poll," using essentially the same techniques as the Miss Rheingold contest, deserves, perhaps, a closer look. Jim Blevins, an enterprising popcorn processor of Nashville, Tennessee, has conducted his poll in every presidential election since 1948. He has predicted the winner each time. He prints the names of the presidential candidates on his containers, and the buyer "votes" by picking either the Democratic or the Republican carton. In movies, the popped corn is given out in the partisan containers, and in stores and supermarkets the unpopped corn is labeled.

Meanwhile, back at the Blevins headquarters in Nashville, a staff of tabulators records the candidates' sales by state. In 1960, the Associated Press reported that Blevins had 20,000,000 Nixon and Kennedy corn-container "ballots" in the moviehouses and supermarkets. On the basis of returns up to the week before election, the popcorn pollsters forecast Kennedy's election. Despite the closeness of the 1960 race, and an error of 3.3 per cent, Blevins retained his perfect record of predicting the winner.

Besides the distribution of ballots in the Rheingold or the Blevins-popcorn manner, straw votes are frequently obtained by mail. Newspapers and commercial polling organizations use the United States mails for *one-way* or for *two-way* balloting. In the first case, coupons printed in the paper can be clipped and returned by readers who care to do so. In this way, popular opinion can be solicited for all manners of things from the most valuable baseball player of the season to plans for the international control of atomic energy. The two-way ballot is a ballot or questionnaire mailed out to all, or some percentage of, the persons whose opinions are to be polled. Newspapers, magazines, or membership organizations may attempt in this way to measure support for policies or candidates.

Each presidential election brings a rash of such polls. The Associated Press reported on October 6, 1960, that Nixon "won a 69 per cent majority in a presidential-preference poll published by the *Omaha World Herald* Thursday."[17] So far, the story looked good for the Nixon candidacy. The *unrepresentativeness* of the poll, however, is clear from the rest of the story. The *World Herald* had published the ballots in its Sunday edition (circulation: 260,511) and 1,262 had been returned from readers in seven states. The paper had earlier supported Nixon editorially.

On October 19, 1960, the *New York Times* correspondent reported from Rome, New York, that the *Rome Daily Sentinel* had polled its own small sample of voters in that city. Ten persons in each of its twenty-two precincts were asked for whom they intended to vote. The result: 47.3 per cent for Kennedy, 35.9 per cent for Nixon, and 16.8 per cent undecided.[18] In this case, if the undecideds had been distributed on the same basis as the decideds—a technique that is not always wise—the *Sentinel* would have predicted the Kennedy vote at 56.8 per cent. Since the actual Kennedy vote in the city of Rome was 57.5 per cent, the *Sentinel* poll had a surprisingly small margin of error. The *Greensboro Daily News* conducted a straw poll in Guilford County, North Carolina. Ballots were sent to every sixth voter in each precinct of that county, which was chosen because it had voted for the winner in every presidential election since 1928. The Greensboro straw poll produced an error of 3.9 percentage points, about the average error of all newspaper election polls in 1960.[19]

The best-known straw poll of this century was that conducted by the *Literary Digest* magazine from 1916 to 1936. In the Hughes-Wilson presi-

[17] *Arizona Daily Star,* October 7, 1960.

[18] *New York Times,* October 19, 1960.

[19] *Greensboro Daily News,* November 6, 1960. An unsystematic sample of fourteen newspaper polls in 1960 yielded an average error of 3.5 percentage points. Bernard C. Hennessy and Erna R. Hennessy, "The Prediction of Close Elections: Comments on Some 1960 Polls," *Public Opinion Quarterly,* XXV (1961), 405–411.

dential contest in 1916, the *Digest* asked its readers simply to send information about popular sentiment; it also took a postcard poll among its subscribers in the five key states of Illinois, Indiana, New Jersey, New York, and Ohio. In 1920, the *Digest* mailed 11,000,000 ballot cards to test public reaction to possible presidential candidates; this was, in a sense, an unofficial presidential primary. In the fall of 1924, the magazine mailed 16,500,000 ballots to owners of telephones and automobiles in the United States, asking their choice between the presidential candidates of that year. In the presidential poll of 1928, over 18,000,000 ballots were mailed. Furthermore, the *Literary Digest* conducted three nationwide polls on prohibition, in 1922, 1930, and 1932.

Although the *Digest* polls were widely quoted and commented upon by other magazines and newspapers, the chief reason for their establishment and growth seems to have been their advertising and subscription-getting value. With each ballot card, a subscription blank was mailed to the prospective straw voter. Robinson reports that "as a result of the 1930 postcard poll on prohibition, which was mailed to 20,000,000 people throughout the nation, the *Literary Digest* . . . was able to say, 'Almost overnight we have advanced circulation tremendously.'"[20]

The *Literary Digest* flourished during the 1920s and early 1930s. The elections of 1924, 1928, and 1932 were accurately predicted, and there seems to be some evidence (when measured against official referenda in ten states) that the polls on the prohibition amendment caught the trend in favor of repeal between 1926 and 1932.

But in 1936, after its gigantic blunder of predicting an Electoral College majority for the Republican presidential nominee, Alfred M. Landon, the *Literary Digest* went out of the polling business forever. Shortly thereafter, in 1938, it went out of *all* business forever.

What had happened?

The short answer is that the errors that had been inherent from the first in the *Literary Digest's* polling procedure were compounded and exaggerated in 1936. Their poll cards, as we have noted, were mailed to persons whose names were obtained from telephone books and automobile-registration lists. Two factors were operating in 1936 to produce from this sample a Republican response that was wholly unrepresentative of Republican strength among voters at large. The first factor has been much discussed: in the serious economic depression of the early and middle 1930s, there was more telephone and automobile ownership in middle-income and high-income homes than in low-income homes. Thus, the relatively more well-to-do were polled by the *Literary Digest*; but the support of these people for the Republican Landon was overwhelmed in

[20] Robinson, *Straw Votes* (see footnote 2), p. 51.

the election by the larger numbers of the less-well-off, not included in the *Digest* poll, who voted heavily for Democrat Franklin Roosevelt.

Another factor operated in 1936 to swell the Landon column in the *Digest* poll, and thus mislead its editors. As in all mail polls, those who felt most strongly on the matter returned the cards in greater numbers. Thus, the *Digest's* heavy return from enthusiastic Landon supporters— which probably, in the context of the 1936 campaign, meant rabid Roosevelt opponents—was balanced hardly at all by enthusiastic Roosevelt supporters, who were probably not polled. This imbalance, caused by the distribution system, was aggravated by the more apparent error of sampling mainly the middle and upper classes. In sum, the *Literary Digest* came a cropper because of a serious *sampling error,* plus the failure to assess, and discount, the heavy return from voters with unrepresentative political motivations.

Had the *Literary Digest* editors cared, and had they read Robinson's book *Straw Votes,* they might have made adjustments to prevent, or at least minimize, the 1936 debacle. Robinson pointed out in 1932 that the *Digest* had consistently overpredicted the Republican votes in 1924 and 1928:

From this consistent overestimation of the Republican vote arises the hypothesis that the "tel-auto" population (owners of telephones and automobiles) which forms the *Literary Digest* "electorate" is more Republican than the voting population at large; hence, under the *Digest* sampling methodology, overprediction for this party can be expected from year to year, and the predictive error shown by one poll can be used to correct the bias of the succeeding poll.[21]

Using this predictive-error method of adjusting the *Literary Digest* poll results to compensate for the Republican overprediction, Robinson established a "corrected" *Digest* prediction for 1928 of 6 per cent average plurality error by states. He found this adjusted prediction to be better than any nationwide poll in that year except that of the Hearst newspapers, which had a 5 per cent average plurality error.[22] Robinson also pointed out that the *Literary Digest* could hardly have been expected to change its polling methods—since, as a business, its success depended on subscriptions from the auto and telephone owners who were polled— but that it might have adopted techniques of adjustment in analyzing its returns.

21 *Ibid.,* p. 72. Parentheses in original.

22 *Ibid.,* p. 67.

SURVEY RESEARCH 3

On October 31, 1960, Republican Vice-Presidential candidate Henry Cabot Lodge told a campaign audience in Paterson, New Jersey, that public opinion polls were "passing fads." "In the future," Mr. Lodge is reported to have said, "people are going to look back on these polls as one of the hallucinations which the American people have been subjected to. . . . I don't think the polls are here to stay."[1]

This observation can hardly represent the considered judgment of Mr. Lodge. It is part of the campaign strategy, related to the "elation complex," for a candidate to discount poll results, and polls, when they show him to be running behind. A possible exception to this rule was President Truman, who, in 1948, said that the pollsters were wrong when they forecast his defeat. As it happened Truman *was* elected. But Truman's election was close, and it was not hallucination but a number of relatively small errors by overconfident—and to some extent careless—pollsters that accounted for the failure to predict Truman's victory.

If the polls had not been here to stay, they would have disappeared after the 1948 surprise, just as the *Literary Digest* and its poll went out of existence after its 1936 surprise. The truth seems to be that public opinion polling, as conducted by trained and careful personnel, has established its usefulness, its accuracy, and its permanence.

3.1   The Emergence of Scientific Polling

Modern public opinion polling has origins in the journalistic straw votes, as we have seen; in the field of *market research;* in the development of *psychological*

---

[1] *Washington Post and Times Herald*, November 1, 1960.

testing; and in the application of the *mathematical laws of probability and sampling* to human behavior.

Market research is the study of factors affecting the sales and potential sales of goods or services. The "Committee on Definitions" of the American Marketing Association said in 1948 that market research is "the gathering, recording, and analysis of all facts about problems relating to the transfer and sale of goods and services from producer to consumer."[2]

The earliest market research reported by private enterprise was that of N. W. Ayer and Son in 1879. For a manufacturer of threshing machines, the Ayer company assembled crop statistics throughout the country and gathered information about the circulation and advertising rates of newspapers in appropriate areas. Generally, however, the market research business seems not to have grown quickly in the forty years after 1879. Albert B. Blankenship says that some manufacturers and advertising agencies had research staffs before World War I, but that

no real impetus in this movement occurred until after the war. The excess of production capacity and a shrinkage of markets at that time forced a shift of executive attention from production to marketing. New markets and new appeals had to be found, and the marketing research specialist began to come into his own.[3]

In the transition from the prewar *production orientation* to the postwar *consumer consciousness* of American business, the market researcher's objective was to find out who wanted what packaged how. Prior to this change in approach—indeed, since the beginning of exchange economies —the maker made items as he saw fit (or was able), and offered them for barter or sale where he could and as they were. However, in the 1920s, in the transition to a consumer economy, the makers found that new technology and new transportation opened the possibility of creating, so to speak, mass products fashioned to mass desires. For instance, in the early years of this century, a unit of the Quaker Oats Company, which had milled oats for porridge since 1856, found that cereal grains could be "shot from guns," renamed, repackaged, and sold at a higher rate of trade, if the market could be puffed up like the product. From such a simple and unterrifying beginning has come the present multimillion-dollar business in breakfast cereals, jingles, contests, coupons, and juvenile antics on morning TV shows.

Thus, new technology in manufacturing was important for the growth of market research. But even more important was the develop-

2 Quoted in Lyndon O. Brown, *Marketing and Distribution Research* (New York: Ronald Press Co., 1949), p. 5, n. 3.

3 Albert B. Blankenship, *Consumer and Opinion Research* (New York: Harper & Row, Publishers, 1943), p. 5.

ment of new packaging and merchandising methods. Market research discovered that a more attractive package may lead to bigger sales (although attractiveness is not a quality that all agree on—a designer may be convinced that his label or container is irresistibly striking, but if the consumers *do* resist it, sales remain low). Cigarette companies have engaged in a great deal of market research, and it is said that the American Tobacco Company changed from a green package in the early years of World War II not so much because "Lucky Strike green has gone to war," as it patriotically proclaimed, but because it found that a white package was more attractive to women smokers.

Much of the market-research activity of the 1920s and 1930s depended on a minimum level of psychological and sociological knowledge. Meaningful market research—beyond the mere collection of economic and demographic facts—could not have emerged before there was at least some understanding of human attitudes, motivation, conditioning through repeated stimuli, and the creation and reinforcement of habit.

Finally, in addition to substantive psychological knowledge, some understanding of testing devices and techniques was necessary before attitude and opinion measurement could claim to be scientific. Most important of the procedural factors, and underlying the usefulness of survey questions, interviewing techniques, and data analysis, is the application of the mathematical laws of probability. The Swiss mathematician Jean Bernoulli first described the science of probability in 1713, but only fairly recently has this knowledge been used for measurement in business and in the social sciences.

The basic proposition of probability is that, given chance conditions and a finite number of elements, single elements or combinations thereof recur in an infinite series with predictable regularity and frequency. For example, a single die has six sides and, on any given throw, is as apt to come up on one side as on any other (assuming that it is perfectly balanced); thus, there is an equal probability (designated $1/6$) for each number on the sides to appear. The number on two dice total from 2 to 12, but the possibility that some combinations will consist of identical numbers means, for instance, that 7 is more apt to appear than is 2. The reason is that only one combination gives a sum of 2 (a 1 on each die), 3 (a 1 on one die and a 2 on the other), 11 (a 5 on one and a 6 on the other), or 12 (a 6 on each), whereas there are two combinations each for 4, 5, 9, and 10 (you work them out), and three combinations for 6, 7, and 8. Thus, in twenty-one throws of a pair of dice, you might expect to get 2, 3, 11, and 12 once each; 4, 5, 9, and 10 twice each; and 6, 7, and 8 three times each. You will not get such a distribution, of course, because *upon each of the twenty-one throws, the same number of combinations is separately possible no matter what combination comes up any other time.* This is the meaning of the statement that individual cases can never be predicted by the laws of probabilities—only the distribution of aggregate (collected) cases can be predicted. (But, in opinion sampling, this is precisely what we want to do—predict the range and distribution of aggregate cases.) So, if we throw the dice one thousand, ten thousand, or a hundred thousand times, we can be sure that, within some predictable range of error, 2, 3, 11, and 12 will each come up $\frac{1}{21}$ of the time; 4, 5, 9, and 10 will each come up $\frac{2}{21}$ of the time; and 6, 7, and 8 will each come up $\frac{3}{21}$ (or $\frac{1}{7}$) of the time.

Some sophistication in understanding probability and sampling was necessary before pollsters could hope to measure public opinion reliably by gathering opinions only of selected persons in the public. Primarily, this sophistication was achieved in American industry, through its experience with production control and product standardization.

Random, spot inspection and regular, "nth"[4] inspection have been used for many years in mass-production lines when continuous inspection of each item is competitively unnecessary or economically prohibitive. For instance, a manufacturer of hairpins may find it necessary to check the size, strength, coating, and bends of only one out of one hundred thousand of his products; a maker of vitamin tablets may have to run standardization tests on only one tablet out of every ten thousand produced. In both cases, the laws of probability are being used; from the inspection of the few, valid inferences, within known margins of error, can be made about the many.

Once there was understanding of the way in which sampling could be used to predict the uniformity of things that shared characteristics, it was only a step to sampling the characteristic attitudes and opinions that people are assumed to share.

3.2   Scientific Polling Comes of Age

In the years just before 1935, a number of academicians became concerned about the methodology of opinion polls. Claude Robinson, whose book *Straw Votes* was mentioned earlier, W. L. Crum, of Harvard University, and Henry C. Link, of the Psychological Corporation, engaged in

---

[4] N is the mathematician's way of saying "the given number." It probably meant, originally, just "number"; but now it means the number selected, or the number (often hypothetical) referred to, and frequently the number designating the interval size used. If one wants a sample of six cards from a bridge deck, one way is to choose every eighth card; eight in this case is the "nth" number.

experimental work of great importance to the emerging field. In 1935, *Fortune* magazine introduced its Fortune Survey, under the direction of two market-research experts, Elmo Roper and Paul Cherrington. The Roper poll, as the Fortune Survey became known, has been a continuing feature of that magazine. Archibald M. Crossley, who had been in market research since 1926 (Crossley, Inc.), began in 1936 to do incidental political polls, which have been carried in Hearst and other subscribing newspapers.[5]

The American Institute of Public Opinion (AIPO)—the Gallup poll —issued its first release in October 1935, only three months after *Fortune* got into the field. George Gallup, the founder of AIPO, had earlier taught Journalism at Drake, Northwestern, and Columbia Universities. In 1932, he had become research director of Young and Rubicam, a New York advertising agency. Gallup described the formation and objective of the AIPO in these words:

> After a preliminary period of experiment, beginning in 1933, the American Institute of Public Opinion, with the cooperation and support of a number of American newspapers, began a series of week-by-week national polls which have continued to the present day. The Institute's purpose was to perform the function of fact finding in the realm of opinion in the same general way as the Associated Press, the United Press, and the International News Service functioned in the realm of event. This attempt to improve and objectify the reporting of what people think met with warm response and active encouragement from editors throughout the country.[6]

For reasons which are not entirely clear—except, perhaps, for the presence at Princeton University of Hadley Cantril and Harwood Childs,[7] both early public opinion experts—scientific public opinion polling was initially centered in Princeton, New Jersey. The American Institute of Public Opinion, the Claude Robinson Polls, Inc., and the Opinion Research Corporation still have headquarters in Princeton. *Public Opinion Quarterly,* the professional journal of the field, has been published at Princeton University since 1937. This quarterly is also the organ of the American Association for Public Opinion Research, a fraternal and con-

---

[5] For a delightfully informal account of the Roper and Crossley polls, and other early opinion research endeavors, see David Wallace, "A Tribute to the Second Sigma," *Public Opinion Quarterly,* XXIII (1959), 311–315.

[6] George Gallup and Saul Forbes Rae, *The Pulse of Democracy* (New York: Simon and Schuster, Inc., 1940), p. 46. Reprinted by permission of Simon and Schuster, Inc.

[7] Cantril has been Director of the Office of Public Opinion Research, an endowed agency of Princeton University, since 1940. Childs' textbook *An Introduction to Public Opinion* (New York: John Wiley & Sons, Inc., 1940) was the first, and for many years the best, in the field.

ference organization for scholars in the field. The Princeton public opinion experts neatly complement and reinforce one another, both academically and commercially.

In the years since Roper and Gallup pioneered the systematic and scientific sampling of American public opinion, many other individuals, institutions, and centers of study have emerged both here and abroad. Before the outbreak of World War II, Gallup organized or cooperated with British and French institutes of public opinion. The British Institute has maintained a continuous existence since 1938. The French Institute was reconstituted after V-E Day, and these two Gallup affiliates have been joined since 1945 by others in more than a dozen countries. Gallup coordinates these agencies through his International Association of Public Opinion Institutes. Other public opinion polling organizations exist abroad outside the Gallup empire; but only one, Mass Observation, has had notable influence on the development of public opinion study in the United States.

Since the early days of scientific opinion measurement, a few nonprofit or governmentally sponsored polling agencies have been established in the United States. The most important of these are the Bureau of Applied Social Research, the National Opinion Research Center, and the Survey Research Center. (In government, the fears of a suspicious Congress have prevented systematic and open opinion research by federal agencies. A number of departments—Agriculture, Commerce, and Interior —have conducted opinion research under the guise of gathering statistics or economic data, and some—State Department and the United States Information Agency—have contracted with commercial pollsters for special studies.) The Bureau of Applied Social Research was the first of these academically connected organizations to engage in the scientific study of opinions and attitudes. In 1936, the Rockefeller Foundation decided to support a study of the social effects of radio; the directors of this project were Paul Lazarsfeld, Hadley Cantril, and Frank M. Stanton—then a research officer and more recently president of the Columbia Broadcasting System. This study was institutionalized at Columbia University in 1937, when Lazarsfeld joined the faculty there. The Bureau of Applied Social Research was established at Columbia University the same year; its objectives, support, and procedures are described as follows:

The Bureau carries out a program of basic and applied research under grants and commissions from philanthropic foundations, government agencies, social welfare and other nonprofit organizations, and business and industrial firms. In addition, it provides facilities for research initiated by faculty members; encourages the development of new methods of social research; provides opportunities and materials for training both graduate students and visiting scholars;

and, through its publications, makes available to lay and scientific audiences the results of its investigations.[8]

The National Opinion Research Center (NORC) was established at the University of Denver in 1941 by Harry H. Field, who was its director until his death in 1946. The Field Foundation made the initial grant to NORC to develop public opinion measuring techniques, to conduct surveys at cost for governmental agencies and other nonprofit organizations, and to provide graduate training at the University for public opinion research. In 1947, NORC was moved to the University of Chicago, where it continues to do contract work for governmental agencies and private groups concerned with public policy.

The development of the University of Michigan's Survey Research Center neatly illustrates the interdependence of governmental and academic activities in the field of attitude and opinion measurement and in behavioral-science research generally. The Michigan Center grew out of the Division of Program Surveys that the U.S. Department of Agriculture had established in 1939 to do field studies of existing and potential federal agricultural policies. During World War II, this unit broadened its operations to include studies of public finance and citizen reactions to public-finance policy.

At the conclusion of the war, the key members of this research organization set for themselves new objectives with an emphasis on the conduct of research oriented toward the solution of more basic scientific problems than could be studied effectively within the framework of governmental administrative service. They determined to seek, as a group, an association with an academic institution that could offer greater freedom in the conduct of research, greater effectiveness through association with a teaching faculty in the social sciences, and greater opportunities for contributions to the social sciences through teaching and publication of research results.[9]

In August 1946, some members of the Division of Program Surveys, led by Rensis Likert, head of the Division, and Angus Campbell, moved to Ann Arbor. Likert became the first director of the Survey Research Center. In 1948, another war-spawned research group, the Research Center for Group Dynamics, was added to the Survey Research Center to create the combined Institute for Social Research. When Likert became director of the Institute, Campbell succeeded him as director of the Survey Research Center. The two research centers, and the Institute as a whole, are supported by government and private contracts, foundation grants, and Uni-

8 Bureau of Applied Social Research, *A Report on the Year 1958–59* (New York: Columbia University, February 1960), p. 1.

9 *Institute for Social Research 1946–1956* (Ann Arbor: University of Michigan, n.d.), p.33.

versity of Michigan contributions. Since 1946, the Survey Research Center has conducted a number of important studies in American political behavior. In each of the four presidential elections from 1948 to 1960, it undertook elaborate investigations of the voting and nonvoting publics. The general character of the continuing study was described in 1956 (see footnote 9) as follows:

Through this series of interrelated studies, the Political Behavior Program has focused on two general objectives: (1) the detailed documentation of the behavior of the electorate in the national elections, and (2) the analyses of the motivational factors which underlie the political participation and partisanship of the individual citizen.

The results of this research program have been published in a series of important books, monographs, and journal articles since 1949.

In 1957, a library of polling data, the Roper Public Opinion Research Center, was established at Williams College, Massachusetts. The Center has collected sample survey data from many American and foreign opinion researchers, and has made these data available to educational and nonprofit agencies. As of July 1, 1964, raw data from 3,200 surveys had been placed in the Roper Center by more than seventy cooperating research groups. According to the director of the Roper Center, the following services are available: (1) direct access to original card decks by scholars working at the Center; (2) the distribution of duplicate decks on a loan-contract basis for six to twelve months; (3) tabulations by the Center's own staff on a contractual basis; and (4) a recently established Associate Library, to make data available through regional subcenters at educational and other nonprofit institutions.[10]

3.3 Survey Techniques

The objective of public opinion surveys is to obtain responses to uniform questions from a select number of persons (the *sample*) who, according to criteria thought to be relevant, are representative of the whole group of people (the *universe*) about whom one wants information. The sample, then, either ought to be an exact miniature of the universe,

---

[10] Philip K. Hastings, "International Survey Library Association of the Roper Public Opinion Research Center," *Public Opinion Quarterly*, XXVIII (1964), 331–333. See also, on data repository and retrieval questions, Philip E. Converse, "A Network of Data Archives for the Behavioral Sciences," *Public Opinion Quarterly* (1964), 273–286.

or it ought to be constructed so that the ways in which it differs from the universe will lead to valid information about the universe.

In the first instance, suppose that the pollster wants to study class feeling about price controls in a country in which 30 per cent of the population are in the lower socioeconomic class, 55 per cent are in the middle, and 15 per cent are in the upper. If the pollster is limited to two thousand interviews, he will seek out six hundred persons in the lower class, eleven hundred in the middle, and three hundred in the upper class. Assuming that he takes other measures to prevent bias, he will have a sample which, on class lines, is as near a small universe as he can obtain. He may then project the results from his two thousand interviews directly onto the whole universe with some reasonable certainty of being accurate.

Suppose, however, that the purpose of the pollster's study is to learn about the popular acceptance or rejection of government price controls. The pollster may then reason that the views of the upper class are more significant for policy making—first, because of the direct impact of these views on governmental decisions, and, second, because of their influence on the views of the middle and lower classes—and he may decide, therefore, to oversample the upper-class segment. In this way, he will deliberately construct a sample that is not representative of the socioeconomic universe, in order to obtain a sample that is more representative of the universe of influence—which, in this case, is more important to him than mere socioeconomic correspondence between the sample and the universe.[11]

In the construction of a scientific public opinion survey, several distinct steps may be seen:

1) Statement of information desired.
2) Identification of the universe.
3) Determination of sample size and type.
4) Construction of the questionnaire.
5) Recruitment and training of interviewers.
6) Fieldwork.
7) Processing and analysis of data.

---

[11] For example, in 1947 the Survey Research Center deliberately oversampled high-income areas to bring more library users into a study of information sources. See Angus Campbell and Charles A. Metzner, *Public Use of the Library and Other Sources of Information* (Ann Arbor: Institute for Social Research, University of Michigan, 1950), p. 62.

In the same way, the directors of a survey of American college teachers decided to oversample the large *schools* and at the same time keep their sample of large-college *teachers* in strict proportion to their numbers in the universe. For their procedures in doing this, and for an informative discussion of other sampling techniques used, see Paul F. Lazarsfeld and Wagner Thielens, Jr., *The Academic Mind: Social Scientists in a Time of Crisis* (New York: The Free Press of Glencoe, 1958), Appendix I, pp. 371–377.

These steps are not all of equal magnitude, nor are they equally demanding of the time and energy of the pollster. However, it can be argued that they are of equal importance, since, like the links of a chain, each is vital to all. No matter how precise and sophisticated the theoretical formulation of sample and questionnaire, if there is any breakdown in the steps involving the collection, processing, or analysis of data, the survey fails. In turn, if the right questions are not asked of the right people, perfection in these steps is fruitless.

3.4   Statement of Information Desired

All too frequently, students begin fieldwork in public opinion without any but the foggiest notion of what they want to find out. Given the somewhat artificial situation in which such "laboratory practice" occurs, this is perhaps not too surprising. But it is surprising to find, as one often does in political polling—and as is said to be the case in commercial market research—that persons who have a real need for survey work are often unable, at first, to say what they want to discover.

If the candidate is to spend his money wisely, he has to be able to tell the pollster what kinds of information he wants from what kinds of people in his constituency. For instance, if he wants to know what issues and themes to stress in his campaign, it is of little worth to him to gather responses about the public image of his opponent—he cannot hope that the question "What is there about Mr. X which you especially like or don't like?" will evoke responses that he can use as guidelines for his whole campaign. The responses that he gets may give him valuable hints on how to exploit his opponent's weaknesses, but they will tell him nothing about what issues may interest the electorate.

Suppose the mayor or the city manager asks the pollster to find out whether the residents of his city are in favor of slum clearance and urban renewal, and the pollster reports a good response to such questions as "Would you favor the redevelopment of the Old Town section?" Nevertheless, the mayor's proposal may be defeated in the referendum to authorize the project because the pollster did not ask the citizens "Would you support a $200,000,000 bond for the redevelopment project?" and because he did not ask the residents of the Old Town area whether they would be willing to live elsewhere if necessary. This kind of error can hardly be blamed on the pollster or his techniques—although, in these exaggerated examples, it is apparent that some of the fault would lie with him for failing to help his client define his goals.

3.5   Identification of the Universe

Whose opinions are to be sampled?

To gather information about possible ways of increasing its circulation by changing contents, should a magazine sample its readers or its nonreaders? To learn the tastes in styling of potential buyers of its Cadillacs, should General Motors choose a sample from below the $5,000-income class or from above $10,000-income class? Should it interview only men in the selected income group, as many women as men, or 70 per cent women? Should the candidate take as his universe the potential voters in his constituency, or only the habitual voters, or (for primary elections) only those who are registered in his party?

The question of whose opinions to measure, like the question of what information is desired, depends on the factors of the individual case. Public opinion surveys are not, and never will be, substitutes for thinking about social cause and effect, nor for decisions based on facts and opinions that are not derived from opinion surveys. The opinion survey is a tool, with clear limits of usefulness and no magic whatever.

3.6   Sample Size

The number of people to be interviewed in any poll depends in large part on the importance that the sponsors place on being able to make an accurate prediction, and on the money available for the conduct of the poll.

Public opinion surveys are expensive. (You will discover why when you undertake fieldwork in your class project; even the best interviewer cannot gather many interviews in a day, if he uses the techniques that keep distortion at a minimum.)

Ignoring for the moment that cost is an important limiting factor, how large should the sample be? The answer is that *the sample should be large enough to ensure that the results are within those limits of chance error that satisfy the sponsor.*

To explain this answer, we must refer to the mathematics of probability. If we assume (a) that there is a real but unknown distribution of all possible answers to a question, (b) that our sample is random (every person is just as likely to be chosen as every other person), and (c) that our techniques are capable of obtaining the true opinion from each person—if we assume all these things, we will be able to tell how accurate the responses are. For example, if opinion divides 70 per cent *yes* and 30 per cent *no* on any question in a nationwide sample of only 756 interviews, the chances are 997 to 1,000 that this 70–30 response is not more than 5 per cent inaccurate. If the sample is as large as 17,000, the probable error is reduced to less than 1 per cent, given the same 70–30 division of *yes* and *no* answers. If the indicated division of opinion is 50–50, the sample must consist of 900 interviews to obtain a 997-to-1,000 chance of less than 5 per cent error, or over 22,500 interviews to reduce the error to less than 1 per cent. These examples refer only to *the error attributable to size of sample,* the so-called *chance sampling error.* This sort of error is wholly a matter of statistical probability and should not be confused with any errors that may arise from faulty sample selection or imperfect interviewing.

The size of the sample is not the major source of error in most opinion surveys. When errors occur, in almost every case it is not because too few persons were interviewed, but because the wrong persons were wrongly interviewed. As early as 1940, George Gallup declared that "both experience and statistical theory point to the conclusion that *no major poll in the history of this country ever went wrong because too few persons were reached.*"[12]

In the first year of the American Institute of Public Opinion, Gallup conducted a number of experiments on the effects of sample size alone. He describes one of these experiments in the following excerpt:[13]

In 1936, a survey of 30,000 ballots asked the question: "Would you like to see the N.R.A. revived?" The first 500 cases showed a "no" vote of 54.9 per cent. The complete sample of 30,000 cases returned a "no" vote of 55.5 per cent. In other words, the addition of 29,500 cases to the first 500 cases in this instance made a difference of 0.6 per cent in the national findings. Here are the figures:

	NUMBER OF CASES	PERCENT VOTING AGAINST REVIVING THE N.R.A.
First	500 ballots	54.9
First	1,000 ballots	53.9
First	5,000 ballots	55.4
First	10,000 ballots	55.4
All	30,000 ballots	55.5

The effective use of relatively small samples is illustrated in the polling before the 1960 presidential election. The major nationwide poll

---

[12] Gallup and Rae, *Pulse of Democracy* (see footnote 6), p. 68. Italics in original.

[13] *Ibid.,* p. 72.

forecasts all came within two percentage points of the actual vote results
(see Table 3–1).

Table 3–1. *Percentage Error of Forecasts by
Major Polls in 1960 Presidential Election*

		PREDICTION*		RESULTS†		
POLL	SAMPLE SIZE	NIXON	KENNEDY	NIXON	KENNEDY	PERCENTAGE ERROR
A.I.O.P. (Gallup)	8,000	49.0	51.0	49.9	50.1	.90
Roper Poll	3,000	51.06	48.94**	49.9	50.1	1.16
John F. Kraft, Inc.	2,000	48.42	51.58††	49.9	50.1	1.48
Princeton Research Service	Unknown	48.00	52.00	49.9	50.1	1.90

* All data in these two columns taken or interpolated from *The New York Times,*
November 8, 1960, p. 16, and November 10, 1960, p. 48.
** Four per cent undecided distributed according to the decided vote.
† Percentage of the two-party vote.
†† Five per cent undecided distributed according to the decided vote.

A sample of a few thousand—or maybe even one thousand—is capable,
statistically, of producing an accurate reflection of the opinions of a
hundred million or more people. Contrary to what may appear to be
common sense, very large samples (say ten thousand to fifty thousand) are
not much more accurate than medium-sized samples (fifteen hundred to
five thousand), and the improved results of such large samples are almost
never worth their costs.[14]

For the purposes of any class projects in which you might be engaged,
carefully constructed samples of one hundred to five hundred cases will
usually result in a low enough chance error. When your project involves a
fairly small universe (a ward, a legislative district, a small city, a county,
or even several counties), the size of your sample need not be very large
to obtain reasonably reliable results—provided, always, that you have
selected the persons to be interviewed according to relevant criteria.[15]
The best student handbook for undergraduate research design is undoubtedly *Survey Research* (1963), by Charles H. Backstrom and Gerald D.
Hursh, available in paperback from its publishers, Northwestern University Press, Evanston, Illinois.

14 If you have your doubts or would like more information, see any good book on
statistics; or, if you prefer a less mathematical discussion, see Albert B. Blankenship,
Consumer and Opinion Research (New York: Harper & Row, Publishers, 1943), Chap.
9; or Leonard Doob, *Public Opinion and Propaganda* (New York: Holt, Rinehart and
Winston, Inc., 1948), pp. 112–124.

15 For an illuminating discussion, with many examples, of the use of small samples, see
Hadley Cantril, *Gauging Public Opinion* (Princeton, N.J.: Princeton University Press,
1944), pp. 150–171.

3.7 Sample Selection

More important than the size of the sample, beyond some minimum, is the *type* of sample chosen. We have seen that the early straw pollsters interviewed anyone they happened to meet. The so-called "inquiring reporters" of many newspapers still talk to people that they haphazardly encounter. But serious attempts to measure opinion always involve interviewing people who are in some sense *representative*.

Representativeness in a sample is ensured only by some combination of two devices: *stratification* and *randomness*. Stratification is the selection of criteria upon which to divide the universe. The decision to stratify in some ways rather than other ways is always a human judgment, based on the relatedness of the stratification factors to the information desired. Thus, the pollster has to decide whether he wants a sample that is representative of all ages, all economic groups, both sexes, both urban and rural dwellers, or of any other grouping he deems relevant.

The market researcher for Slenderella, Inc., studying potential locations for new "health salons," wants to know whether women who can afford to patronize his client's establishments actually want to do so—and, if they do, where and how far they would be willing to drive to a salon. Earlier experience of the company indicates, let us suppose, that farm women and women from lower-income neighborhoods patronize these shops only in negligible numbers. The researcher may decide, then, to sample urban and suburban women, and those in certain income classes.

Likewise, the candidate, assessing his strength and the issues in his constituency, wants to know how he is faring among men and women voters and among voters in different age groups, economic brackets, and ethnic or religious groups, and maybe those in different education or professional groups. If he is running for mayor of a mining town where there are sixty men for every forty women, it will not do for him to sample homes on weekday afternoons or to be satisfied with a stratification that results in a sample consisting of 60 per cent of women.[16]

The national surveys conducted by large opinion measuring organizations commonly use, as stratification factors, economic class, social class, age, sex, and geography. These pollsters, like all others, consider their research design and what they want to find out, and say to themselves something like this: "For the ideas we are trying to test or the kinds of

---

[16] An example may help make clear the principles of stratification; see the study reported in Bernard Hennessy, "Politicals and Apoliticals: Some Measurements of Personality Characteristics," *Midwest Journal of Political Science,* III (1959), 336–355.

information we hope to get, what kinds of people do we want to interview?" This, in a homely, over-all way, is what we mean by selecting relevant attributes in choosing the sample.

3.71   "Quota Control" Samples

From 1936 to 1948 the national polling organizations almost exclusively used a system of sample selection called *quota control*. Gallup describes this method as follows:

> In building their miniature electorates for the election of 1936, the three modern polls selected geographic district, urban-rural balance, economic status, age, and sex as the basic factors controlling the divisions of political opinion. The Crossley and Institute polls took the state as the geographic unit, while the *Fortune* survey modeled its sampling on the nine major census areas of the United States. To control the proportion of votes from cities and farms, from the various economic classes and age groups, and from men and women, quotas were established for each of these major groups to mirror the actual divisions in the population as a whole. . . . The Crossley and Institute polls . . . established their quotas on the basis of estimates of probable voting participation, and ballots were actually selected from each group in accordance with estimates of actual voting. The Institute used the additional check of controlling the political composition of its sample by obtaining Democratic voters, Republican voters, and third-party voters in the same proportion as the citizens of each state declared themselves in the previous presidential election in 1932.[17]

When the system of quota control is used, the quotas are assigned by the central office to the various stratification groups thought to be important in the sample. In a national sample of 2,000 the pollster may decide to interview 1,000 men and 1,000 women, 250 farm dwellers, 900 town and small-city dwellers, 850 big-city and suburban dwellers, 450 from the lowest-income class, 1,200 from the middle-income class, 350 from the highest-income class, 900 Democrats, 700 Republicans, and 400 independents or third-party supporters. Interviewers then select in their areas a certain number of persons who fall within these categories—e.g., 16 farm women and 17 farmers, 12 persons from low-income areas, 20 Democrats. (The categories overlap, of course, and one interview may produce a low-income Democratic farmer.) During the fieldwork phase, the interviewing plans are constantly being adjusted by the interviewers and the central office, to ensure the proper stratification of the whole sample.

Quota sampling has inherent and obvious potentials for error. Inter-

17 Gallup and Rae, *Pulse of Democracy* (see footnote 6), pp. 73–74.

viewers cannot be expected to choose the "right" respondents, even when given explicit instructions about the numbers of persons to interview from each of the categorical groups, or *strata*. The interviewer may consciously or unconsciously bias the results by his selections. He may not like the looks of a particular house or he may gather all his interviews in one section of a city, one precinct of a ward, or one apartment house in the block. He may go out only in the afternoon, or only in the evening, or he may avoid Negroes, Jews, or people who speak a foreign language.

The experience of all polling organizations is that interviewers who are allowed to choose their respondents tend to undersample the poor, the less well educated, and the racial and ethnic minorities. To minimize this bias, some of the polling organizations attempt to reduce the interviewer's discretion in choosing respondents within the quota. They may require a certain percentage of evening interviews (especially from their women interviewers), or they may require that all interviewing be done in the respondent's home or that no more than two interviews be obtained in any one block. The National Opinion Research Center, for instance, has warned its interviewers that

interviewing farmers in town, as a regular practice, would seriously weaken our rural cross-section in that some selective process may be operative in their presence . . . probably a higher proportion of farmers with good cars than of those with poor cars will be in town—or more of those with money to spend than of those living on marginal income.[18]

3.72 "Area Random" Samples

Despite such efforts to reduce bias in the selection of respondents, quota sampling is generally held to be more error prone than sampling systems that designate all the individuals to be interviewed.[19] Such systems are sometimes called *pinpoint*[20] or *specific-assignment* sampling,

[18] *Interviewing for NORC*, rev. ed. (Denver: National Opinion Research Center, 1947), p. 125.

[19] See Joseph R. Hochstein and Dilman M. K. Smith, "Area Sampling or Quota Control? —Three Sampling Experiments," *Public Opinion Quarterly*, XII (1948), 73–80; and Charles F. Haner and Norman C. Meier, "The Adaptability of Area Probability Sampling to Public Opinion Measurement," *Public Opinion Quarterly*, XV (1951) 335–352.

[20] G. Gallup, "The Future Direction of Election Polling," *Public Opinion Quarterly*, XVII (1953), 203; or E. Benson, C. Young, and C. Syze, "Polling Lessons from the 1944 Election," *Public Opinion Quarterly*, IX (1945), 467–484.

but the most common term seems to be *area random*. This term is not very helpful, however, since all sampling systems use geographical areas in some way or other, and *randomness,* in the strict sense, may not be employed in these types of samples. We will adopt the term *area sample,* remembering for this discussion that the important feature, the one that distinguishes this method from quota control, is that all individual respondents are predetermined by the survey designers either through purposive and systematic selection or by a series of random choices.

The first step in creating an area sample is the division of the universe into smaller units called *primary sampling areas.* The selection of these primary sampling areas may be the result of judgments relating to the hypotheses or information to be studied. Of the six hundred precincts in a city, twenty may be chosen for political, economic, ethnic, or other reasons related to the study. Or the primary sampling units may be chosen by *chance* methods—e.g., by taking every thirtieth precinct (*selection by constant intervals*) or by drawing the thirty numbers out of a hat (*random selection*). If chance methods are used, all parts of the universe must be covered by the smaller areas (with no overlap), and each of the smaller areas must have as good a chance of being selected as any other.

For samples drawn from a large geographical universe, such as the whole United States, it is often desirable to choose secondary or subsampling areas. Thus, the primary sampling areas might be six hundred of the more than three thousand counties in the nation. From these six hundred units, thirty secondary sampling areas (cities, parts of cities, and townships) might be drawn. When intermediate areas of this kind are used, they should be selected, like the primary areas, purposively or by chance.

The next step in obtaining an area sample is the determination of all the dwelling units within the chosen geographical areas from which the individual respondents are to be selected. Sometimes these can be determined from public or quasi-public sources—from city or county maps, directories or lists, or from the records of utilities or construction companies. Often, however, it may be necessary for the field staff (perhaps the interviewers themselves) to locate every dwelling unit in the sampling areas.

Next, a number of dwelling units are chosen, almost always by constant-interval or random selection, from the complete list of such units. Finally, a particular person is designated in each of the chosen dwelling units. All such persons together constitute the sample. Figure 3–1 illustrates the process through which, in area sampling, the respondents are chosen by successive steps from the universe.

CAMROSE LUTHERAN COLLEGE
LIBRARY

151
HEN / 6526

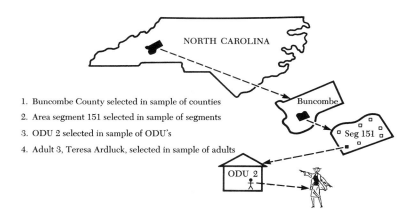

Figure 3–1. Example of Sampling in Four Stages

Wherever random selection is used throughout, every eligible person in the universe has the same chance of being selected for the sample as every other eligible person. This process is the ultimate form of what Stephan and McCarthy call *selection in accordance with a probability model*. They point out that such a procedure attains the following desired results:

a) it makes it possible to state in advance the probability that any given individual will be included in the sample and the relation of this probability to the probabilities for other individuals, without requiring a complete list of all population elements . . . and

b) it clusters the selected respondents from a geographic point of view and thus effects economies in the amount of travel required to contact the selected respondents.[21]

However, most public opinion polling necessitates a judicious mixture of the elements of both quota-control and area-random sampling, with (a) stratification of the universe for deliberate and nonrandom reasons, (b) selection of sampling areas either for deliberate reasons or by chance, and (c) chance selection of individual respondents. Table 3–2, taken from Stephan and McCarthy, illustrates the possibilities for such mixtures of techniques.

It may be helpful, finally, to have a description of an actual survey design. Burns Roper, a partner of Elmo Roper, summarizes in the follow-

21 Frederick F. Stephan and Philip J. McCarthy, *Sampling Opinions: An Analysis of Survey Procedure* (New York: John Wiley & Sons, Inc., 1958), p. 41.

Table 3–2. Possible Combinations of Sampling Procedures in a Three-State Selection of Adults from a City

SAMPLING STAGE	UNIT OF SAMPLING	PROCEDURES THAT MIGHT BE USED IN SELECTION
1	Blocks	a. Random b. Systematic c. Purposive
2	Dwelling units within blocks	a. Random b. Systematic c. Selection left to interviewer
3	Adults from within dwelling units	a. All adults interviewed b. Random selection of a single adult c. Selection left to interviewer, subject to quota restrictions

Source: Frederick F. Stephan and Philip J. McCarthy, *Sampling Opinions: An Analysis of Survey Procedure* (New York: John Wiley & Sons, Inc., 1958), p. 42. Slightly revised.

ing passage the way in which the Roper sample was drawn for their pre-election poll of 1960.

We started with a sample of counties throughout the United States. These counties were drawn at random proportionate to population and were subsequently validated for all of the ascertainable data we could find to ensure that they were representative of the nation's population. For the purposes of our election studies, 125 of these preselected counties were drawn at random. Within each of these 125 counties, specific cities, towns or rural areas were drawn—again at random proportionate to population. Two towns and/or rural areas were selected in each county. Blocks or portions of rural routes were selected within each of the towns or rural areas that were drawn. These, again, were selected at random proportionate to population. I believe the number of blocks and/or rural route segments was either three or four per county (distributed over the two towns and/or rural areas that were picked within the county). Each of the selected blocks or rural segments was designated as a "female block," meaning that only women were to be interviewed in those blocks or route segments. For each block or route segment so selected, an adjoining block or rural segment was also selected. These constituted the male blocks. Interviewing on the female blocks was done during the daytime hours; interviewing on the male blocks was done in the evening or on weekends. A starting point for each block or route segment was designated by us, and the interviewers then proceeded from these starting points around the block or rural route segment in a manner prescribed by us. They called on each household until they had completed the specified number of interviews per block. (The number of interviews varied from one study to another, but it was approximately five interviews per block.) The only additional requirement was that upon completion of all the female blocks, certain age quotas had to be filled—so many women 21–34, so many 35–49 and so many 50 and over. Aside from being sure they met these quotas by the time they completed all their female blocks, the interviewers interviewed women on the female blocks in sequence from one house to the next. Interviewing on the male blocks was parallel, except for the hours of interviewing.[22]

3.8   Construction of the Questionnaire

In this section, we will think of the questionnaire as meaning, in general, the total of all the questions asked—or, even more broadly, as the total material used for the elicitation of responses from each person interviewed. Normally, the questionnaire will consist of one or more printed, mimeographed, or typewritten sheets on which questions are written. But, in some surveys, cards, posters, or other display materials may be used to clarify or enlarge upon the written or spoken questions or to increase interviewing uniformity and reliability. When such supplementary items are used, they should properly be thought of as part of the questionnaire.

Questionnaires are so much a part of our everyday life that it may seem, at first, that the construction of such a list of questions is a task that any reasonably well-educated and honest person could do as effectively as any other. One is tempted to believe that straightforward answers can be evoked by simple, straightforward questions. Unfortunately, this is not always so. Aside from the etymological vagaries of English (and all other languages), each questionnaire constructor and each respondent brings to each question his own particular and often highly unusual meanings and nuances. One does not have to be a semanticist to appreciate, after the shortest attempt at question construction, the significance of what Stuart Chase has termed "the tyranny of words."

3.81   Specification, Division, and Tacit Assumption

A helpful general treatment of questionnaire construction may be found in an article called "The Art of Asking Why," by Paul R. Lazarsfeld.[23] In his article, Lazarsfeld says that three principles govern the crea-

---

[22] Personal communication, December 1, 1960.

[23] "The Art of Asking Why: Three Principles Underlying the Formulation of Questionnaires," in Daniel Katz et al., eds., *Public Opinion and Propaganda* (New York: Dryden Press, 1954), pp. 675–686, reprinted from *National Marketing Review*, I (1935), 32–43.

tion of clear, concise questions. The first principle is *specification*. This principle has to do with what the question means: What kind of information do you want to get? What kind of goals do you have? Do you want to influence someone to do something? Do you want to describe what you're selling, or what you're offering? Do you want to change opinions as well as measure them? These queries are related to the kinds of things the interviewer, or the person making the *schedule* (as questionnaires are often called), asks himself; they are not questions he asks the respondent, unless he asks them in translated form.

The second of Larzarsfeld's principles is the principle of *division*. The intention of the question constructor here is to make it possible for the respondent to answer meaningfully. The main ingredient in this principle is the attempt to differentiate the wording of the questions according to the past experience of the respondent, or to put each question into a framework that is significant for the respondent.

The principle of division does not mean that questions cannot, under some circumstances, be technical or complex; it means only that they should be understandable to the persons asked to respond to them. One field survey done by the University of Wisconsin was primarily a study of farmers' attitudes toward new farming methods. The farmers were asked about such modern farm practices as *side-dressing corn,* for example, *with nitrogenous fertilizers.* If you ask the man on the Brooklyn street about these things, he will stare blankly. If you asked an urban dweller such a question, you would be seriously violating what Lazarsfeld calls the principle of division. You must try to enable the respondent to answer in terms which he understands and within the context of his past experience.

This principle, in a way, may be more important for market research than it is for political surveys, because political surveys rely on certain assumptions about political opinion holding. We assume that the man on the street, who is probably eligible to be a voter, knows something about politics. This is perhaps an unrealistic assumption; all we know about the social psychology of opinion holding indicates that most men on most streets don't know very much about the kinds of things that the political opinion pollster asks them. Nonetheless, for opinion bearing on public policy, no questions at all are possible unless they are put into some kind of political context. For instance, you may ask a person what he thinks about the situation in Berlin: "Should we agree on the status of a free city for Berlin, involving some military pullback on both sides?" You may ask him this question, but he says he doesn't know a thing about it. He doesn't know, and he doesn't care. But you cannot say to yourself, "Obviously, we're going to have to rephrase this question, to put it in the context of this man's experience," because there is nothing on the question in the man's experience. However, if you're doing market research about toothpaste, you may ask a person: "What kind of toothpaste have you used within the past six months?" He may recall that he's had some Ipana, his wife bought some Gleem on sale, and he thinks they had a tube of Colgate around the house. If you ask him then: "Well, which kind do you think has the best flavor?" he can answer you; and you've asked a better question and made a better approach to market research on toothpaste than had you asked him simply: "Which toothpaste has the best flavor?"

Lazarsfeld's third principle is that of *tacit assumption*. A most insightful and important observation lies at the base of this principle. "People don't answer," Lazarsfeld says, "what you say but what they think you mean." This point is very simple, in a way, but one that needs to be remembered and constantly brought to our attention when we make questions. As an example of the phenomenon of tacit assumption, Lazarsfeld relates the case of the British lady of rank who answered her friend's question "Is anyone staying with you?" with "No," even though the house was full of servants. The lady took the question to mean, "Is anyone of our class, anyone we would think to be *anyone,* staying with you?" This tacit assumption ruled servants out of the answer, because *people respond, not to what you literally say, but to what they think you mean when you say it.*

3.82 Forms of Questions

Structurally, there are three kinds of questions asked in public opinion studies: *dichotomous, multiple choice,* and *open end.*

The dichotomous question is, like the pawn, both lowly in rank and vital to the game. Dichotomous means, simply, two sided: *yes-no, true-false, plus-minus.* Though the limitations of the dichotomous question are clear, it has great importance for all kinds of simple fact and opinion gathering. It is used especially in obtaining biographical or census-type data: "Are you married? Do you own your home? Are you a registered voter? Do you belong to a labor union?"

The multiple-choice question is a type with many subtypes, such as checklists, rank orderings, and matching-answer questions. Sometimes referred to as the "cafeteria" question, it gives the respondent some alternatives beyond the very confining yes-no choice of the dichotomous question. On the other side, however, it avoids the utter subjectivity and nearly insolvable problems of coding and analysis that open-end questions give rise to. It is widely used in public opinion research precisely because it is a compromise, structurally, between the other two types.[24]

Open-end questions are answered in the respondent's words and style. Because the answers are wholly idiosyncratic, they cannot be analyzed with complete precision. However, what is lost in analytical precision is gained in richness and subtlety of response. In the hands of skilled interpreters, enough responses can be categorized to make for analyses that are frequently more penetrating, and possibly more valid, than the rigid results of dichotomous or multiple-choice questions. Nevertheless, generalizations are hazardous, and outside advice may be a disservice to the investigator who wants to know when to employ open-end questions; his own thoughtful judgment is the best guide.

3.83 Kinds of Information Desired

Consistent with Lazarsfeld's principle of specification, we may explore the kinds of information that any question may attempt to elicit. There seem to be four such kinds of information.

First, there are questions that elicit *direct facts*. These are sometimes called *census-type* questions. "How old are you? Where do you live? Did you vote in the last election?" Normally these questions can be specific, and there is no reason to make them open ended; most census-type questions can be dichotomous or cafeteria in form.

Second, there are questions that elicit *direct information*—usually opinions, but sometimes facts—on one or more points. Example: "Will you vote in the coming election?" These questions can normally be dichotomous or checklisted, but open-end questions may also appear. The example "Will you vote in the coming election?" deals with intentions and is therefore more subjective than pure census-type questions.

Third, there are questions that elicit *indirect* or *inferential material*. They can be dichotomous, or multiple choice, but open-end questions have been increasingly used.

The kind of question used depends upon the kind of information desired. If one wants to elicit more general opinions rather than specific, factual information, dichotomous questions are used less and open-end questions are used more. At the subjective end of the order, the two-

---

[24] For a helpful discussion of the uses of multiple-choice techniques, see Paul F. Lazarsfeld, "The Controversy over Detailed Interviews—An Offer for Negotiation," *Public Opinion Quarterly*, VIII (1944), 38–60; also reprinted in Katz et al., *Public Opinion* (see footnote 23), pp. 687–701.

choice dichotomies, and the multiple-choice checklists, become less useful. A third-order example, then, might be: "Do you feel strongly about the candidates running in this election?"

The fourth kind of question has to do with eliciting *attitudes and material for background and richness in analysis.* You might ask: "How important is politics to you?" or "Please describe your family history of interest and activity in politics." Even some of these questions can be answered yes or no; but at this level of complexity, detail, or psychological depth, where opinions run into attitudes, yes-no questions are not very helpful. Dichotomous questions can be good jumping-off points when you follow them with probing. "Were your parents active in politics?" If *yes,* "What offices or activities did your father or mother engage in?" Thereafter, you have to spell it out in the respondent's own language—or in yours, if you aren't a very good interviewer.

3.84   Wording and Phrasing the Questions

It is most important that you use words, insofar as possible, in the way your respondent uses them. Once, in talking with a neighbor about the British Queen, I said I had no strong feelings about royalty although I was basically a republican. Though my remark must have appeared to be a curious *non sequitur,* she replied: "I'm a Republican too, although I can't support the most conservative leaders in our party." The mistake was mine; I could hardly have expected her to know that a small-*R* republican was a person opposed to monarchical government.

Avoid technical and rarely used words. Here is an example from the study, mentioned earlier, of Wisconsin farmers and their acceptance of new farm practices: "Farmers learn about new things in farming in different ways. From which of the following have you got most information about new things in farming?" (Followed by sources of information to be ranked.) All of these words are common. This question was written by sociologists who don't always express themselves so simply. They may have wanted to ask about "innovations," which would have been more accurate than "new things," but they wisely resisted that temptation.[25]

---

[25] One researcher applied the Flesch "readability" formula to three national poll questionnaires and found that 91.6 per cent of the questions were too hard for 12.4 per cent of the population, that 73.4 per cent were too hard for 23.2 per cent, and that 9.8 per cent of the questions were too hard for 72.6 per cent of the population. Fay Terris, "Are Poll Questions Too Difficult," *Public Opinion Quarterly,* XIII (1949), 314–319.

There are times when technical words can be used. In the Wisconsin study, we were interviewing farmers who knew about nitrogenous side-dressing for corn. Most adult Americans would not know about this technique; but all the interviewed farmers, even those who were not using it, knew what it was. They had heard about it from the county agent or read about it in farm magazines. They could be asked about such technical terms—about barn driers, strip-cropping, alfalfa-brome mixtures, and 2–4–D weed control—because they could reasonably be expected to be familiar with them. Common sense and judgment about the people you are going to interview will tell you how much technical material you can introduce in the questions.

A third suggestion about words and phrases: the form should be conversational. Don't ask: "For whom do you intend to vote?" Most people don't talk that way. Say: "Who do you intend to vote for?" or "Who do you think you'll vote for?" or "If the elections were held today, which of these candidates do you think you'd vote for?"

It is equally important not to talk down to your respondents. There is a stage when the developing interviewer may try to get too folksy. This may not be quite as bad as being stuffy and academic, but it is bad. You have to hit some median: on the farm, you can't lapse into dialect; when interviewing teenagers you can't adopt their adolescent slang. You will encounter the temptation, especially when you are talking with people of limited education, and you may try to rephrase the questions closer to their language. But if they get the notion that you're talking down to them, it is quite destructive of rapport. They expect people who have considerably more formal education than they to speak differently, to use different words—not words they don't understand but words they don't ordinarily use. If you try to turn yourself into "one of the boys," you may not get as good results as when you use your own words. Don't turn yourself into something you are not; you have to be perfectly honest and relaxed about being yourself.

The fourth suggestion is that you try not to ask leading questions, which tend to predetermine the answers. Such questions sometimes reflect cultural values. For instance, we asked the Wisconsin farmers, "Do your children between twelve and nineteen have regular chores?" This question was a matter of fact, to be answered yes or no. But the follow-up question was: (If *yes*) "Do you regard these chores more as a duty or for teaching them responsibility?" This follow-up question was worthless. Only one or two out every one hundred farmers replied that chores were a duty. The idea of teaching children responsibility in a democracy had been driven home to these respondents through all the channels by which attitudes are shaped in our society; those who might have thought that it was a duty for children to work for parents could hardly have been expected to say so.

When opinions are being sought about matters of little importance to the respondents, care must be taken not in insert irrelevant factors about which the respondents have strong feelings. In the late 1930s and early 1940s, the polling brotherhood conducted a series of experiments on the choice of wording, the ordering of questions, and other matters of technique. Cantril reports one study in which two matched samples of 1,555 persons each were given questions that were supposed to measure opinion on the same issue, but which were worded somewhat differently. One national sample was asked: "Do you approve of Sumner Welles' visit to European capitals?"; the other was asked: "Do you approve of President Roosevelt's sending Sumner Welles to visit European capitals?" In each sample, 43 per cent approved of the visit; but of those who were asked the second version, 31 per cent disapproved (as compared with 25 per cent of those who were asked the first version), while 26 per cent had no opinion (as compared with 32 per cent among those who were asked the first version). The clear inference is that the inclusion of the name of President Roosevelt, about whom many people had strong feelings, moved 6 per cent (9 per cent of the women and 3 per cent of the men) from "no opinion" to "disapprove."[26] To this extent, at least, the second version of the question was measuring opinions about the President rather than opinions about the visit by the Undersecretary of State.

In addition to the tendency to give irrelevant answers suggested by the wording of the question, people like to give answers that they think the interviewer is eager to hear—especially when the questions are about issues that the respondent doesn't care very much about. Since they don't care very much about most matters of public affairs and public policy, they tend to give the respectable answer, or the answer they think is most acceptable to the great middle class. If you ask them: "Do you think it's a responsibility for everyone to take part in politics in a democracy?" 99 per cent will say yes. But if you ask them: "Have you ever given any money to a political party?" perhaps 5 per cent will say yes.[27]

Sometimes indirection is necessary to cut through socially acceptable answers to the truth. A celebrated example of indirect techniques was used some years ago in a study of bowery bums in New York City.

[26] Hadley Cantril, "Problems and Techniques: Experiments in the Wording of Questions," *Public Opinion Quarterly*, IV (1940), 330–332.

[27] For a rather technical discussion of the polling difficulties caused by respondent rationalization and socially acceptable distortion, see Richard F. Carter, "Bandwagon and Sandbagging Effects: Some Measures of Dissonance Reduction," *Public Opinion Quarterly*, XXIII (1959), 279–287.

A group of sociologists were interviewing a number of these men, and they asked: "Are you married?" They found that an unbelievably large number were not married and never had been. They began to doubt the answers, and wondered whether they were asking the question properly. When they changed the question to read: "Where is your wife?" they got results. The men who had no wives said: "I'm not married," but all the others indirectly admitted that they were. When a man said: "She's in Kalamazoo," the interviewer would check "married."

One way to get bad questions out of your schedule is to do some *prepolling*. Go out and use your tentative questionnaire in fifteen or twenty—or as many as you need—interviews. Prepolling should be as much like the real thing as possible, and conducted under circumstances similar to those you anticipate meeting. Prepolling is a very important and necessary step, if you are to do a serious and accurate job of interviewing. Some of the polling organizations, especially the academic groups, do a great deal of prepolling. They may go through three or four drafts of the questionnaire, prepolling between each draft. It is expensive and time consuming, but there isn't any alternative to it, because the people who are involved in the planning of the research or the survey cannot always anticipate the problems that come up. You may think the question is clear, but if you ask five people and you get five different interpretations of what the question means, you've got a bad question—even though it may look like a good question to you. One of the occupational hazards of field research is that you get immersed in it and begin to take many things for granted. You think because you know what a question means, that everyone else will know. Such an assumption is a serious mistake, and can be avoided only by careful prepolling.

3.9   Recruitment and Training of Interviewers

The measurement of public opinion necessitates, at every stage, a judicious mixture of art and science. The determination of the sample size and composition is increasingly scientific. Interviewing, despite some success with applied psychology, remains largely a matter of artistry.

The ideal interviewer is like the ideal statesman, the ideal administrator, the ideal teacher, the ideal business executive, the ideal father or mother, and the ideal friend. He is understanding, intelligent, kind, insightful, patient, modest, well appearing, and soft spoken. He is also a good listener.

In the less than ideal world, a good interviewer ought to possess three essential qualities: (a) he should be at ease with himself and with others in social situations; (b) he should be sensitive to the many subtle cues given by the respondent; and (c) he should know when and in what ways to adapt his own behavior to the situation of the moment. If, in addition to these qualities, he has a keen intellect, and a warm sense of humor, he cannot fail in the interviewing business.

Commercial polling organizations attempt to retain many part-time and a few full-time interviewers in every section of the United States. The work is attractive to middle-aged, college-educated women who may have a few hours each day and a car at their disposal. The managing editor of the Gallup Poll had this to say, in the summer of 1960, about his interviewers:

There are about a thousand members on the Gallup Poll's national field staff. About seven out of ten are women. Most are engaged in some other full-time employment—there are schoolteachers, social workers, housewives, bank clerks, automobile salesmen, a photographer's model, a chiropractor and a professional hypnotist. A majority of the Gallup Poll interviewers have college educations; a recent count revealed nine with Ph.D. degrees.[28]

There is a popular notion that people who like to talk make good interviewers. Generally speaking, this notion is a misconception. The interviewer's job is neither to talk at length nor to engage in amiable or spirited discussion, but, with the fewest words and in the shortest time, to stimulate *the respondent to talk about the right things*. It is probably more important for the interviewer to be a good listener than a good talker.

Finally, in this partial list of desirable qualities, interviewers ought to have an inordinate capacity to tolerate nonsense—not tomfoolery, of course, but intellectual non-sense. Academicians and others who believe that logic does or should determine human opinion and behavior can only rarely make good interviewers. Such persons are apt to talk back or to despair (or both) when respondents display great amounts of illogic, superstition, prejudice, and ignorance. The interviewer simply must tolerate nonsense; he cannot argue with the respondent.

Tolerating nonsense, in a larger setting, is only one way in which the interviewer maintains a straightforward and matter-of-fact air during the interview. He should try to disguise any except the mildest emotion, while maintaining an appearance of interest and attention to the responses. Facial expression and nods of the head are often more important than words. Relaxed pauses may frequently be broken by the respondent's

[28] John M. Fenton, *In Your Opinion* (Boston: Little, Brown and Co., 1960), p. 12.

recollection or statement of something that would not have been obtained had the interviewer hurried on to the next question. All the other devices of the good listener—especially the meaningless little oral encouragements like "Yes, I see," "That's interesting," "Then what?" and "Why?"— should be called upon by the interviewer to help maintain a sympathetic but matter-of-fact atmosphere. In the selection of interviewers it is important to find persons who naturally and easily adopt these techniques in all their conversations.[29]

It seems certain that pre-job or on-the-job training cannot help the interviewer who is deficient in the personality and behavioral qualities described above. Many things about interviewing can be wholly or partly learned, however. The interviewer should understand enough about the way in which the sample was chosen and about the objectives of the study so that he can satisfy the understandable interest of the average respondent in these matters. Certain more or less standard phrases—to introduce oneself, to develop rapport, to get on with the questioning, to prevent irrelevance—can and should be learned by the interviewer. He should be trained in techniques that contribute to successful interviewing: to minimize distraction for the respondent, to write quickly and use abbreviations, to be consistent in interpreting questions and in probing. Although the more subtle aspects of interviewing cannot be learned in a training program, it is important for the understanding of operating procedures alone, if for no other reason, that attention be given to group and individual instruction for interviewers.

3.10 Fieldwork

Selecting the sample may involve some fieldwork. In area sampling, members of the central staff or of the interviewing staff may have to make a map or list of all the dwelling units in the smallest sampling area. The fieldwork with which we are concerned consists of those activities in which the respondents are directly involved—from the time of the first interviewer-respondent contact, through the interviews themselves, and through all efforts to complete the planned number of interviews.

---

[29] Despite a good deal of attention to these problems, it seems likely that class and other subcultural biases of interviewers influence survey reports. Katz found that the results of a set of economic, social, and political questions asked by middle-class interviewers differed significantly and systematically from results when the same questions were asked by working-class interviewers. Daniel Katz, "Do Interviewers Bias Poll Results?" *Public Opinion Quarterly*, VI (1942), 248–268.

3.101 Initial Contact

In some studies it is necessary or desirable to make appointments with each respondent. The interviewing of prominent persons—the so-called "elite study"—usually requires this. Such appointments can be made either by the central directors of the project or by the interviewer himself. Interviewing in quota-control sampling, and in all surveys of the indiscriminant, straw-vote type, need no prior contact with the respondent; indeed, such contact is impossible, because the respondent is unknown and unknowable in advance.

Between "elite studies" and the wholly anonymous selection of respondents exists a range of sample types in which the individual respondent may be known. He may be known by name or perhaps by a categorical designation, such as the *oldest person* (or women, or man) at the given address, the *chief wage or salary earner* at the address, or all *adults*. When the respondent is identifiable by name or by group, it may be helpful to give him notice that he is to be approached for an interview. Pollsters are by no means agreed on the effects of prior notice, however, and the decision in every instance has to be made on the basis of the facts and the expectations of that particular study.[30]

Sometimes letters are sent to all intended respondents a few days before the interviewer is to arrive. These letters inform the person to be interviewed about the study in very general terms; but more importantly, according to those who practice prior contact, they establish the authenticity of the person or organization making the study and psychologically prepare the respondent to be interviewed. These advantages are more apt to result in cases where high-prestige polling agencies, such as governmental or academic units, are interviewing relatively unsophisticated persons.

It is doubtful whether the commercial market research organization can increase rapport for its interviewers by giving prior notice to those to be interviewed. The advantage here may lie with the nonprofit polling group of unquestioned educational or research reputation, and especially if this group is studying opinion about public issues. If you can honestly say that the study you undertake is part of your college work, you may find that increased effectiveness results from prior notice to intended respondents.

If you send letters or call respondents—the first is preferable—you

---

[30] For some testimony on the question of prior notice, see R. C. Nuckols, "Study of Respondent Forewarning in Public Opinion Polls," *Journal of Applied Psychology,* XXXVII (1953), 121–125.

should be very careful to give them enough information about your study to make them aware of its general nature, but not enough to allow them to prepare for particular questions. You should err, if at all, in the direction of generalization and even vagueness rather than give them an opportunity to gain information or obtain or change their opinions about matters which are included in the questionnaire. There is a serious possibility of introducing bias and distortion into your study, and if a letter cannot be sent without the creation of such distortion, you should not send it at all.

If you do send a letter, it should (a) note the scientific and representative character of the sample in which the respondent's name appeared, (b) stress the importance to the study of completing each planned interview, (c) state (if true) that there are no personal or potentially embarrassing questions to be asked, (d) frankly admit the amount of time being asked of the person, and (e) predict as nearly as possible when the interviewer will call. You probably should not give any except a general return address and no encouragement for those who receive the letter to call you. If someone calls you and says he cannot or does not want to be interviewed, your chances of persuading him otherwise are quite small; your odds of getting the interview are much greater if such resistance arises on his doorstep, face to face. You should not, in any case, worry about refusals at this stage—or ever. Refusals are rare in public opinion polling conducted by respectable organizations and reasonably accomplished interviewers. The technique of prior notice, where it can be applied, is one of the ways in which refusals can be reduced.

3.102   Mood and Environment for Good Interviewing

Social psychologists like to talk about the importance of *rapport* in successful interviewing. *Rapport* is merely a fashionable French word, meaning to be in harmony with or to work well with. There appears to be no close English synonym, and the French word may be necessary as well as fashionable. Understanding, sympathy, empathy, cooperation—these are all implied in rapport, but it is more than any of them. We can hardly do without the word, though it sometimes seems pretentious.

The interviewer's best device in aiding rapport is no device at all; rather, it is a simple, easy, and friendly naturalness. The volatile, glib, and entertaining interviewer may appear to do very well, even if he is tense and, to some degree, "acting"; he may receive high praise and turn in workmanlike and richly annotated schedules. But the schedule should reflect the likeness of the respondent, or at least bear his imprint, and not be transmuted through the personality of the interviewer.[31]

This plea for the "soft sell," for an attitude on the part of the interviewer of sympathetic neutrality, is all the more important in view of the secret weapon that the interviewer has working for him: the desire of almost every respondent, once he is satisfied that there is no personal threat involved in the interview experience, to be cooperative. This almost universal attitude, however, is both a boon and a danger. The sensitive interviewer will take advantage of it, to help the subject search for what he thinks. The insensitive, tense, or inexperienced interviewer may find that—consciously or otherwise—he allows the respondent to say what the respondent thinks the interviewer wants to hear. This danger is doubly strong when, in addition to an underlying desire to cooperate (which reaches almost desperate proportions in some respondents, and possibly ought to be investigated psychologically), the respondent has few if any opinions at all about the subject of the interview. In such circumstances, one objective of the interviewer ought to be to prevent the emotional circuitry by which his own opinions work their way into the schedule through the person and the words of the respondent. In extreme cases, it may be necessary for the interviewer quietly, almost off-handedly, to test the reality of some of the responses by repudiating his own opinions. In any case, a consistent what-do-*you*-think approach, in manner as well as in speech, is recommended for the interview.

Your interviews should always take place in surroundings familiar to the respondent.[32] Other persons should not be present. If responses are recorded on the spot (the usual and recommended practice), the interviewer, not the respondent, should do the writing. In trying to prevent irrelevance, the interviewer should steer toward some middle ground— to be felt at the time, not predicted in advance—between a resignation to any amount of wandering and a courtroom adherence to admissible evidence. Long interviews may be completed at a later time, if necessary, but the presumption of good practice is to make it to the end in one sitting; no moment in time is like any other, and the joining of an

[31] These comments refer only to interviewers who are part of a term project and who will not have responsibilities for analysis. In a one-man field study, the interviewer may very well intrude his artistry at every stage—design and interviewing included—since this is inevitable in the analysis and in the reporting. I am only saying here that, insofar as possible, the stochastic artistry of many interviewers ought to be minimized when there are many interviewers.

[32] Here again it is dangerous to use the word *always*. Familiar surroundings may not be necessary, or even desirable, for depth interviewing. Lane sought the quasi-clinical surroundings of his own office for extended interviews with the fifteen persons whose opinions and attitudes were obtained for one study. Robert E. Lane, *Political Ideology* (New York: The Free Press of Glencoe, 1962).

interview obtained in two halves is more than the mere addition of later to earlier responses. Hurried interviews are almost always unsatisfactory; come back later rather than try for a thirty-minute interview in fifteen. Likewise, common sense warns against distractions during the interview.[33]

3.103   Rephrasing and Probing

In some studies, the experienced interviewer may be allowed considerable latitude in interpreting a schedule to some of the respondents. If many persons have difficulty with the ideas or words, the questionnaire is faulty and the pretesting was manifestly inadequate. But even with the best possible schedule *some* questions will need interpretation to *some* persons. A few rules may be suggested.

First, resist rephrasing any question as long as possible. Try repeating the question once, or even twice, word for word as asked the first time. If the respondent still looks blank, or says, "What do you mean?" you will have to say what you mean as simply and as matter-of-factly as possible.

Second, do not feel compelled to get a quick answer, or perhaps, in the end, any answer at all. This is sound advice for all questions, not only for those the respondent does not understand. Pauses are to be expected, and you can make them work for you; let the respondent come forward to break them. Even if his answer is to some extent made up for the occasion, it is probably better than any that you might make up for him by impatiently rephrasing or reorienting the question. A "don't know" answer, in these circumstances, may be much better than a "well, if you mean this, then I think that" answer.

Third, if you do rephrase a question, try to be consistent in your subsequent rephrasing of the same question. Likewise, if you give background information or examples to one puzzled respondent, give the same information to all other puzzled respondents. You should also report such rephrasing to the director of the fieldwork and to the other interviewers. If the situation seems to warrant it, you may get the agreement of all interviewers on standardized rephrasing for troublesome questions.

---

[33] I was once maneuvered into interviewing a farmer while he sheared a sheep; and another time, a housewife while she prepared lunch for her children momentarily due from school. Neither was worth doing, and I probably should have thrown both schedules away. I did not; but I excuse myself by remembering that I was being paid by the interview, and knew less (and needed the money more) than I do now. I hope my former boss knows more now, too, and pays his interviewers by the hour.

When answers are unclear, or when the subtlety or the variety of meanings (or causes) of the respondent's answers can be elaborated, the interviewer should seek additional or alternative responses. The easiest technique for eliciting such responses is almost always the best. Simple expressions of interest will usually suffice: "Why?" "How do you explain that?" "Oh? What makes you say so?" Sometimes just a murmur or a thoughtful "Hmmm" will invite more extended answers. This matter of probing is important and difficult. Probing refers to the elaboration of responses rather than to misunderstanding or lack of understanding of questions. But, like the need to interpret questions, the need for probing is usually highly personal and idiosyncratic. As the interpretation of questions calls for rephrasing by the interviewer, the interpretation of answers sometimes calls for probing by the interviewer.

At other times, specific questions, supplementary to the main one, may be required, or the interviewer may ask for examples. Antecedents, results, or relationships to other questions on the schedule, may also be explored.[34] When this sort of probing is necessary, the rule of *maximum uniformity* should be kept in mind: treat all responses and all respondents as nearly alike as possible and consistent with the other judgments that go into the search for meaning and accuracy.

3.104 "Not at Home": Call-Backs and Substitutions

The results of a public opinion survey can be severely biased or even rendered useless by the failure to interview all or nearly all of a sample that is based on the specific assignment of respondents. Those who are not at home the first time the interviewer calls tend to differ in their occupations, work habits, age groupings, and sex from those who are at home. Accordingly, the not-at-homes tend also to differ from the at-homes in their opinions.

---

[34] The experts are by no means agreed on the value of probing, or of anything resembling what is sometimes called a "depth interview." See Henry C. Link, "An Experiment in Depth Interviewing on the Issue of Internationalism vs. Isolationism," *Public Opinion Quarterly*, VII (1943), 267–279, on the claim that the *real* reasons for opinion or behavior can be discovered by intensive interviewing. He says:

> Our experience has been just the contrary. If people cannot give the reason for their behavior at once and almost without thinking, the pressure to make them produce reasons often results in a process of rationalization. The more they try to explain their motives, the more elaborate their rationalizations, and the less valid their reasons. (Pp. 268–269.)

One study, the first reported work on not-at-homes, was conducted in 1943 by the Special Surveys Division of the Census Bureau. Each respondent was assigned to an interviewer who kept a careful record of all calls necessary to complete each interview. It was found that for certain kinds of analyses, errors of over 5 per cent would have been committed if only those responses from persons interviewed on the first call had been considered. The conclusion of the authors of this report is unambiguous:

> People easily found at home on the first call differ significantly from those found at home only after repeated calls. The latter occur in large enough proportions to make it important for repeated calls to be made in order to represent them on sample surveys. Unless such a course is followed, samples will be distorted in the direction of too large a proportion of response from households with characteristics of the stay-at-homes.[35]

Varying your hours of interviewing according to your experience in the area (or your pre-interviewing knowledge of the area), asking neighbors when the hoped-for respondent is usually home, or, in the most difficult cases, telephoning for an appointment—all these tactics should be used in the attempt to reach each person assigned. Considerations of time and money and the urgency with which you need the particular not-at-homes for stratification purposes will determine how much energy should be spent to reach the 100-per-cent-interviewed mark or near it. Make a number of call-backs, marking on your schedule or field notes the time and circumstances of each, before dropping the name.[36] Consistency is important, both among the cases handled by the same interviewer and among all the cases handled by all the interviewers; if you make four call-backs for some not-at-homes, make the same number for the others. Where inexperienced interviewers are used—or where many interviewers are used, experienced or not—agree at the outset on the minimum number of call-backs to be made.

When the required number of call-backs have been made, or when the value of obtaining the particular interview is not worth additional effort, the question of substitution may arise. (In practice, the question of substitution should be raised and settled in the early planning of the study.) Whether substitution is required, encouraged, permitted, or forbidden will depend on the judgment of the study designers. It would be folly to generalize about the wisdom of any substitution policy. Whatever policy is adopted ought to be uniformly followed, especially if substitu-

[35] Ernest R. Hilgard and Stanley L. Payne, "Those Not at Home: Riddle for Pollsters," *Public Opinion Quarterly*, VIII (1944), 261.

[36] One study indicates that three calls (two call-backs) are usually enough to insure sample representativeness. Robert Williams, "Probability Sampling in the Field: A Case History," *Public Opinion Quarterly*, XIV (1950), 316–330.

tion is required according to some procedural formula (for example, interviewing a person of the same sex in the dwelling unit with the next higher street or building number). In small samples especially, call-back and substitution policies are important, since the introduction of systematic bias by only a few cases can have serious effects on the results.

3.11 Processing and Analysis of Data

At the completion of the fieldwork in any public opinion study, *all* material ought to be kept for the use of those who do the analysis and write the reports. Field notes and the scribbled remarks of interviewers may sometimes contain facts or hints that are vital to the analysis. Even the maps and procedural materials used by the interviewer may be useful later and should be collected at the end of the fieldwork. The rule of the pack rat is a good one to follow: *save everything.*

The processing of survey data cannot be so easily discussed. In recent years, the technological possibilities of machine processing have been so enormously increased that a small library—most of it understandable only to experts—could be assembled. Fortunately, in a general textbook, no extended treatment of electronic data processing is possible or desirable. It is enough to suggest that if your study and materials are relatively complex and important, in your judgment and in the judgment of those who are familiar with them, you should investigate the use of punch cards (e.g., Hollerith, or "IBM," cards) for the storing, sorting, and, on some machines, the comparative examination of data. Processing data in this way always involves some intermediate tasks—principally, the coding of responses and the punching of cards—into which error may be injected; but these efforts and risks are almost always worth taking for the increase in speed and variety of analysis that is possible with card-punched data.

No matter how much quantitative analysis one is able to do with public opinion poll data, the evidence is hardly ever clean-cut and neatly stacked for or against his hypotheses. At this stage in the history of social science, conclusive findings are very rare, and analyses that purport to be conclusive ought to be looked at long and suspiciously.

There is no reason, therefore, to apply only statistical tests to your data, nor to present only quantitative analyses. Although it is generally supposed that quantitative and other objective forms of interpretation are to be preferred in dealing with survey data, it is quite proper to engage in the subjective art of speculation and to apply, under certain conditions, tests of taste, aesthetics, and value preferences. Scientific method and the rules of fair play require only that all analyses be described in enough detail to avoid misleading others, and that all conclusions, however arrived at, are presented as modestly and as simply as possible.

3.12   A Concluding Note

Despite the remarkable growth in both the use and accuracy of public opinion surveys since the middle 1930s, some problems remain. For instance, it is not always certain that the desire for accuracy is foremost in the minds of those who engage pollsters or determine the conditions under which they work. Both the commercial and political results of opinion polling are frequently determined to some extent by the wishes rather than the findings of investigation. The half-truth is more common than either the whole truth or the whole lie.

But, to suggest that ethics and motives are unavoidably impure in the use of opinion polling is merely to restate a truism of man's behavior. A profound truism—and one that is compulsively ignored by utopians of every persuasion—but a truism nevertheless. Polling as a career and as an aid to careers cannot rise above the standards of the other human thoughts and acts to which it is related. Some of the implications of this truism are considered in the section on Public Opinion and Democracy.

For the purposes of this chapter, however, we have assumed the desire for complete accuracy in opinion measurement. On the purely technical side, we have seen that there are many opportunities for error in the opinion survey and that the means for eliminating these errors do not exist as yet. We have also seen that the size of the sample is not, generally speaking, a problem in scientific polling. Beyond some fairly small minimum—fifteen hundred or two thousand for a national sample and comparatively fewer, perhaps as few as five hundred, in a smaller universe—the size of the sample does not determine accuracy beyond some usually insignificant degree.

The way in which the sample is chosen, however, is critical to the accuracy of the survey. So are the way in which the questions are constructed and ordered in the total questionnaire, the way in which the interview is carried out in all of its aspects, and the way in which the responses are subjected to quantitative and qualitative analysis. In all of these steps, the artistry of the designer, the interviewer, and the analyst blend with the more mechanical, routine, and uniform elements.

The judicious use of polling science and political artistry is described by O. N. Malmquist, political editor of the *Salt Lake Tribune,* in reviewing his procedures for the *Tribune's* 1960 presidential poll in Utah:

Our 1960 poll was conducted as follows: we selected two sets of sixty voting districts in Salt Lake City. We took approximately 2 per cent of the total voting strength of the city in each of two rounds, sending interviewers house to house and taking only one vote from each house. The voting districts were selected on the basis of income, housing and past voting patterns.

In Salt Lake County outside the city we took a similar sample twice by telephone, using telephone exchanges to distribute the sample among the various economic areas.

To cover the remainder of the state I took crews of interviewers into the most populous counties and followed the same procedures except as to the selection of sampling areas. I have been traveling over the state for thirty years making political soundings and polling, so I selected the areas to be polled on the basis of past voting records and my judgment of the varying political characteristics.

For the smaller counties I selected six, which over the years have voted substantially the same pattern as all the counties not polled individually, and used them to collect a sample representing the voting strength of the entire group.

While we make direct and personal contact with the voters polled, we do not use question and answer interviews. I prefer a printed ballot, with candidates and questions, so preferences can be marked in squares, like a regular ballot. Our pollers carry small locked metal ballot boxes so that the voters can respond to our questions and then place the ballot in the box without being personally identified. Many voters, of course, do not desire secrecy and merely instruct the poller to mark the ballot as they designate. But a substantial number who would not respond to spoken questions will respond on a secret ballot.

I suppose this system could be called a combination of scientific and judgment polling.[37]

The objective of scientific polling is to bring more and more survey factors into the class of elements that can be handled mechanically, routinely, and uniformly. In the twenty years between 1933 and 1953,[38] the practitioners of opinion research established their claim, on the basis of this fundamental criterion, to have developed the "scientific measurement of opinion." That the science is by no means complete, and will probably never be complete, makes their achievement not less but more exciting.

[37] Personal communication, February 11, 1961.

[38] Neither 1933 nor 1953 stand out in the history of opinion polling with any commanding claim as era markers—as the dates of great discoveries or publications are (with some dubious simplicity) said to be. The first may fairly represent the time in which the marriage of mathematics and social psychology produced one of its most valuable offspring, the scientific sampling of human populations. The second marks the time in which the figurative child of this marriage reached his majority after an adolescence filled with many "crises of identity," of which the 1948 election was the most traumatic.

METHODOLOGY: THE ATTACKS ON THE POLLSTERS

4

Public opinion polling has been attacked by a variety of critics with a variety of arguments. Some critics believe that the polls would be a boon to democracy if the polls did what they claim to do—measure the opinions of the significant publics about important issues and political persons. Others declare that not only do the pollsters fail to do what they claim, but that evil and injury to democracy would follow *if* they did what they purport to do; accurate and reliable polling, these critics assert, would be a disservice to democracy. Since in this part of our text we are concerned with the techniques of measurement, we shall consider here only the criticisms of polling *methodology* and the way in which data are analyzed and reported.

4.1   Criticisms of Sampling

Probably the most common complaint against the pollsters is that they do not achieve representative cross sections of the universe whose opinions they aspire to measure. Beyond the questions about the representativeness of samples dealt with above, only two points need to be made.

The first is less general and refers to the measurement of opinions and the prediction of behavior from *subsamples*. For example, although a nationwide sample of two thousand voters may be adequate for predicting a presidential election, a proportionate number of respondents in any single state will not be a sufficient sample for predicting the presidential vote in that state.

Oversimplified, the primary question of sample size is: How small may a sample be, even for a small universe? Cantril indicates that two hundred is about minimum for any useful sample, and that samples of less than fifty are

not even worth experimenting with.[1] Despite this warning, the pollsters
have reported their results state by state, or have reported results for important states, during presidential campaigns. However, if we make the
unrealistic assumption that the respondents in a sample of two thousand
are distributed throughout all fifty states according to the population of
each state, the prediction for a state of seven million would have to be
based on a sample of seventy-seven interviews, for a state of three million
on thirty-three interviews, and Nevada's prediction on the basis of a sample
of two voters. This breakdown, of course, is a *reductio ad absurdum;* but
it illustrates the impossibility of predicting state votes from subcells of
national samples. The importance of the electoral-college system to the
presidential race, however, makes it imperative to consider state-by-state
forecasts, and the pollsters continue to do so. Furthermore, although
many one-state studies are done and much information is traded among
the pollsters, subsample breakdowns are still made from national samples
—despite the clear warning of a 1944 congressional report that "The size
of the samples used for many of the States was not large enough, even if
properly drawn, to ensure reliable individual State estimates based solely
on polls of the voting population."[2]

   The second point about sample size is only to suggest that techniques
are well known and available for creating samples that, within rather
small limits, closely resemble the universe from which they are drawn.
If all the pollsters do not use these techniques—and some do not—those
who have the responsibility for such surveys and those who use the results
are obliged to assess for themselves and their readers what the consequences of their technological imperfections may be. Some polling for
commercial purposes—and perhaps even for political purposes—may quite
honestly be done with less than the best techniques, when, for reasons of
cost or time, no better can be employed. But, in such cases, the procedures and probable errors should always be described whenever the results are used.

   Fairness requires not only that the pollsters describe their sample
design and actual sample but that they describe the analytical assumptions and devices on which their reports or conclusions are based. For
instance, the handling of the "don't know" responses has always been a
source of disagreement among pollsters and of confusion among laymen.

1 Hadley Cantril et al., *Gauging Public Opinion* (Princeton, N.J.: Princeton University
Press, 1944), pp. 130–131, 150–171, 298. Cantril's samples, between fifty and one hundred
in size, were all experimental, all were limited to small geographical areas, and all
produced rather large errors.

2 *Congressional Record,* August 22, 1960, p. 15778.

The "don't know" dilemma is one of the unsolved problems about which pollsters ought to be quite candid—and for which, if they are not candid, they deserve to be rebuked.

In pre-election polls of the who-do-you-intend-to-vote-for variety, a "don't know" is reported as "undecided." The terms are used interchangeably, but the problem of interpretation does not therefore disappear. Are the "undecideds" truly undecided or just indifferent? If they are indifferent, most of them probably will not vote at all; if those who vote divide between the candidates, the category can be ignored. It is likely, however, that the few voters among the indifferent will choose the candidates favored by their friends, their neighbors, or their socioeconomic class; through the use of such indices, an intelligent prediction may be made of the distribution of these votes. The ultimate choice of the true undecideds may otherwise be predicted by the use of *expected correlations* between individual behavior and socioeconomic factors; but it may be necessary, in addition, to look for idiosyncratic clues in each questionnaire. However the undecideds are handled, the pollsters have an obligation to disclose—and the readers have a right to know—the process by which the analysis was made.

An example of the inadequate reporting of procedures comes from the 1960 presidential campaign. Columnist Joseph Alsop, a sometime pollster himself, reviewed the AIPO's first poll of the campaign under the title "What Gallup Left Out."[3] Gallup's first poll had shown Nixon 50 per cent, Kennedy 44 per cent, and undecided 6 per cent. Alsop noted that "the almost incredibly low percentage of undecided voters" was arrived at after (a) another 6 per cent of Nixon or Kennedy "leaners" had been distributed according to their leanings, (b) about 20 per cent of all the ballots had been completely eliminated from the analysis, and (c) a weighting system to reduce the national effects of regional distortion had been applied. Although the distribution of the leaners seems to have increased the Kennedy percentage, the other two analytical processes substantially reduced the over-all pro-Kennedy figure.

Alsop said that his comments were not "intended to suggest that Dr. Gallup has been cooking his poll," but:

Like the throwout of suspected nonvoters, this synthetic character of Dr. Gallup's published national percentages may well be known to sociologists and other students. Statistician Perry made no bones about it, when questioned. But

---

[3] Congressman Abraham J. Multer, inserting Alsop's column into the *Congressional Record*, very aptly noted: "Mr. Speaker, there are polls and polls. Some are rigged; some are just poorly conducted. Others are just badly analyzed. Without further comment, I am pleased to call attention to a good review of a bad poll." *Congressional Record*, August 22, 1960, p. A6234.

it is certainly unknown in the political community, where the Gallup results are therefore misunderstood. . . .

It seems a fair bet that the Democrats actually had a modest over-all majority in Dr. Gallup's unprocessed ballots.

A handful of votes would produce such a majority, because of the narrow base of Dr. Gallup's famous percentages. In the last poll, the nationwide sample was about 1,600 ballots. About 20 per cent were thrown out, and the final sample was under 1,300 ballots. A single Gallup percentage point would, therefore, represent not more than 13 votes. And the mere transfer of 39 votes either way would have altered Dr. Gallup's nationwide percentages, to show Kennedy running dead-even with Nixon, or to show Nixon leading Kennedy, 53–41.[4]

The remedy, in Alsop's view, requires the AIPO to release more raw data:

. . . this poll has become a fairly major, extra-legal institution of American politics. For this reason, such things as unannounced transformations of "leaners" into "decideds" do not serve the public interest.

Dr. Gallup's industrial and commercial clients may be best served by facts carefully processed and homogenized in the undoubtedly expert Gallup manner, but the public interest demands something more when Dr. Gallup puts on his political-institutional hat. In this role, Dr. Gallup also ought to provide all the unprocessed facts.[5]

While it is difficult to quarrel with Alsop's request for *all* the facts, it might also be suggested that Gallup and other pollsters have a responsibility to give the public their analyses—for their expertness in the field would be to some large degree wasted if they merely turned large amounts of raw data loose on the public. In their analyses, they should feel the obligation to make clear (a) each step in the analytical process and (b) each assumption that influences their interpretations. In this way, the laymen may obtain the experts' analyses and the experts may be checked by other experts.

The practical difficulties of this kind of reporting, however, are apparent: discussions of assumptions and explanations of procedures are apt to be too dry, technical, and uninteresting to be included in news stories. The requirements of crisp reporting and of analytical exactness may be incompatible. Normal newspaper reporting of public opinion measurement cannot be expected to meet the ideal requisites of social-science research, although conscientious journalism might make more use of feature stories and expert critiques in reporting poll data.

Some critics of modern polling point out that the "don't know" categories, aside from being inadequately interpreted, are generally underestimated. A number of reasons are advanced to explain this under-

4 *Ibid.*, p. A6235.

5 *Ibid.*

estimation. For one, it is argued that the structure of the questionnaire and the social-psychological pressures of the interview situation account together for a serious error in measuring "real" opinion. However, it is unavoidable that brief and somewhat superficial interviews of the kind done by pollsters—"superficial" as opposed to the intensive interviews of psychology and psychiatry—must be structured to some considerable degree. Questions are often of the dichotomous or cafeteria sort, and the respondent finds it easy to give definite rather than "don't know" answers. In most cases, he does so without any danger of being exposed by later questions, even when he does not have any opinion. The use of two-step or other screening questions has been recommended to filter out the "knows" from the "don't knows." Unfortunately, in political polling, filter questions of this sort are not yet in common use—again, one suspects, for reasons of time and expense.

4.2   Do They Tell the Truth?

In addition to the possibility that the "don't knows" are generally underestimated, as a result of the structuring of questionnaire items, there is evidence that persons polled by opinion measurers tend to overstate their interest, knowledge, and conviction on public questions. The theories and expectations used to describe and delineate the behavior of what Walter Lippmann calls the "omnicompetent citizen" seem to require the public to know everything and have an opinion on everything. As a result, the average respondent feels some compulsion to have an opinion and to express it. His self-respect as a citizen rides to some degree on his ability to respond "yes" or "no"—a "don't know" is an admission that he has not attained the impossible norm impressed upon him by practically all of our society's norm makers, from first-grade teachers to League of Women Voters pamphlets. In various ways, the sensitive interviewer with a well-constructed questionnaire may minimize this social pressure; but, in all opinion measurement, actual or potential distortion from it exists in unknown amounts. The careful pollster recognizes this source of error and guards against it at every stage in his work.

This brief consideration of the problems of measuring "don't knows" leads readily into a different but related criticism of the pollsters. It has been said that respondents will not give honest answers to many of the questions asked in opinion surveys. Lindsay Rogers, whose dyspeptic book *The Pollsters* is one of the most celebrated attacks on opinion measurement, wonders whether "public opinion is ever the sum of the answers that people are willing to give to strangers," and quotes the view of the director of Mass Observation that *"public opinion is what you say out loud to anyone. It is an overt and not necessarily candid part of your private opinion."*[6]

Although it appears to be true that persons will not always tell exactly what they think when asked, it is of no value to leave the matter with such a useless generalization. Whether truth will be obtained in any instance seems to depend on (a) what the question is about, (b) who asks the question, and (c) what the respondent thinks will be done with his answer.

Indications are that a considerable number of people incorrectly answer even factual questions for which the truth can be checked from public records. One study of 920 Denver adults, conducted in early 1949, found invalidity in one-seventh to one-fourth of the answers to questions about voting in six earlier elections.[7] Thirteen per cent of the respondents who said they had voted in the November 1948 presidential election actually had not.[8] Inquiry about contributions to the 1948 Denver Community Chest drive produced an even greater amount of what the authors of the study call "invalidity"; 34 per cent of all respondents who said they had given to the drive had not. The authors surmise that "social pressures and a belief that the responses would not be checked were the major factors behind the high level of invalidity."

Nonetheless, a great deal of invalidity is caused by downright lying,[9] especially in response to questions about which there is only one socially proper or respectable answer. Hyman reports a considerable discrepancy between self-reported and actual behavior in the cashing of war bonds in 1943, the use of war posters, and industrial absenteeism. "The distortions," he says, "are significant enough to suggest that, at least with respect to behavior having a prestige character, the results of public opinion polls should be used only with the greatest caution."[10]

It is not surprising, perhaps, that respondents will lie about their behavior when the truth is ego damaging; but in the Denver study, 10 per cent of the respondents claimed to have valid drivers licenses and

---

[6] (New York: Alfred A. Knopf, Inc., 1949), pp. 37, 41–42. Italics in original.

[7] Hugh J. Parry and Helen M. Crossley, "Validity of Responses to Survey Questions," *Public Opinion Quarterly*, XIV (1950), 61–80.

[8] In Waukegan, Illinois, 22 of a sample of 204 (10.8 per cent) gave untruthful answers when asked whether they had voted in the 1950 election. Mungo Miller, "The Waukegan Study of Voter Turnout Prediction," *Public Opinion Quarterly*, XVI (1952), 397.

[9] Kindness requires us to believe that some of the invalidity is caused by failure to remember, or failure to understand the question properly.

[10] Herbert Hyman, "Do They Tell the Truth?" *Public Opinion Quarterly*, VIII (1944), 559.

had not, 9 per cent said they had public library cards and had not, 3 per cent claimed to own automobiles and did not, and 3 per cent claimed to own their homes and did not.[11] A few persons claimed *not* to have these items and actually did; but, if we take the percentage of underreporters as the measure of honest error, we are left with presumed liars, in this study, of 8 per cent on auto licenses, 7 per cent on library cards, and 2 per cent each on car and home ownership.

The accumulated evidence from these and other studies of response validity indicates that distortions and untruth are almost certain to exist in all poll data. Leo Crespi argues that conscious fraud is rare, and that distortion exists largely as a result of respondent disinterest, fatigue on long schedules, and a desire to appear informed and helpful.[12] It seems hard to believe, however, that fatigue or a desire to be helpful would prompt a respondent to misrepresent pure census-type data like car or home ownership. There appears to be a hard core of liars on even the most socially neutral questions—a group that is joined by many as the questions become increasingly ego related. This matter demands the practiced judgment of the conscientious poll taker and analyst; estimates of the importance of distortion and what can be done about it have to be made for each case on its own conditions.

It is equally impossible to generalize, at this stage in the development of opinion measurement, about the effects of strangers as interviewers. The implication in Rogers' criticism is that people are more apt to tell the truth to their friends than to strangers. The answer to this implication is yes and no. A number of psychological theories suggest (and interviewing experience attests) the notion that some kinds of people will be more candid about some things with strangers than with friends. All interviewers have heard truths from respondents who would under no conditions tell them to friends or neighbors. And it may be—although it has not been proved, nor even tested, to my knowledge—that opinions on political issues are more freely given to strangers. A case can at least be made that the impersonal stranger, once he is established in the respondent's eyes as a reputable fact gatherer, is more apt to be trusted with a confidence than is someone the respondent must see on a day-to-day basis. This suggestion is the subjective side of the argument that "strangers may be more often confided in than friends."

An even stronger argument could be made to justify the respondents' giving confidences to strangers. Although the average respondent cannot be expected to appreciate it at the time of the interview, every interviewer realizes that there are two factors in the polling process that tend

---

11 Parry and Crossley (see footnote 7), p. 72.

12 Leo P. Crespi, "The Cheater Problem in Polling," *Public Opinion Quarterly*, IX (1945), 431–445.

to separate names from data in the collection and analysis of poll results. In the first place, there is a thoroughgoing air of anonymity about every opinion study—even, to a considerable extent, about elite studies. Often names are not known at all, and even when, as in most cases, they are or can be known, poll takers maintain a pervasive indifference toward them. Although there appears to be no discussion of this presumption of anonymity in the literature (perhaps because it is so much taken for granted by the social scientist), it probably results from the fact that the opinion researcher is interested primarily in *collected opinions;* i.e., in the aggregate views of categorical and social groups. His emphasis is necessarily on the many, and though each respondent is important in the building of his sample, each alone is, generally speaking, insignificant.

The second factor is simply this: to remember names, and to associate particular opinions with particular persons, would not be humanly possible for the interviewer or the analyst even if he wanted to do so.[13] Names uselessly clutter up the minds of the persons who analyze opinion data. Thus, just as in large-scale statistical work the institutional tendency is to ignore names, so at the personal level the rule of economy tends to prevail. Since names are irrelevant and inconvenient, anonymity is practical as well as ethical.

The pollster's presumption of anonymity probably has little effect on the respondent's willingness to give candid answers to survey questions. As polling becomes increasingly common (even the most vigorous critics expect more rather than less polling), and as there is a constant improvement in the public understanding of opinion measuring, then the expectation of anonymity on the part of the polled may begin to equal the presumption of anonymity that already exists for the pollster. One need be neither naive nor prophetic to see that when such a condition is reached, it will be necessary to stand Rogers' criticism on its head. Meanwhile, there is no reason to believe that people in general are less honest in interviews with strangers than with friends.

4.3   Validity and Reliability

Validity in polling has to do with whether the respondent's real opinion is discovered. But, strange as it may seem, for some purposes and under some circumstances it may not matter whether real opinon is re-

---

13 Emotionally maladjusted persons, or chronic gossips, may seek employment in survey work; such persons could do great damage to their employer and to the reputation of opinion researchers generally. For this reason, the honest pollster takes great care in the selection and training of his field staff and his central-office analysts.

vealed. Although the psychologist may be concerned with the correspondence between private opinion (what the individual *really* thinks) and public opinion (what he *says* he thinks), the political sociologist is primarily interested in the correspondence between the individual's public opinion and his related behavior. If the individual says he believes in building new schools, and he votes on the bond referendum accordingly, the political scientist has, for his purposes, a rational set of data, even if the individual is secretly opposed to building new schools. If the individual supports candidate X in pre-election polls and votes for candidate X in the election, it is, for most political analyses, irrelevant whether or not he really likes candidate X. Although the reasons for liking or disliking a policy or a candidate are important for strategic purposes—and tests of logic and relevancy may be necessary for certain kinds of analyses— the first practical test for the political meaning of public opinion is not the ultimate truthfulness of inner conviction but the internal consistency of public opinion and public behavior.

To the political scientist, *reliability* is probably more important than *validity*. Reliability is judged by the reproducibility of a measurement result. A testing technique is said to have high reliability when it consistently measures the same dimensions with similar results. Thus, an intelligence test is reliable when it measures the *same dimensions* of the intellect of all children given the test at any single time and when successive measurements of individuals show *consistently similar results*. It is not a valid intelligence test when elements unrelated to intelligence (for example, style of language or other learned cultural factors) are measured along with native intellectual ability—it may not be valid, but it is reliable when it shows consistent measurement results.

Are public opinion polls, in this sense, reliable? Some evidence is available. In one interesting experiment, the National Opinion Research Center sampled voter intentions in Boulder, Colorado, and on election day had all voters fill out a second ballot immediately after they had cast their official ballots. The pre-election poll turned out to be very close on candidate choice (an error in each of two contests of less than 1 per cent) and quite close on two of the three policy questions on the ballot. A rather large error on the third referendum may have been explainable for reasons not pertinent to the question of polling reliability.[14]

Another test of poll reliability used gross national-survey data gathered over several years. In 1944, Cantril collected the results from comparable studies and comparable questions that had been obtained by four independent polling organizations. His most general and significant find-

14 Harry H. Field and Gordon M. Connelly, "Testing Polls in Official Election Booths," *Public Opinion Quarterly*, VI (1942), 610–616.

ing involved a set of ninety-nine pairs of comparable questions, on which he reported that the average difference between the results was 3.24 percentage points.[15]

Despite these and other attempts to check the reliability of polling, one interesting early suggestion has apparently not yet been followed. Over twenty years ago, Lucian Warner declared that the "ideal empirical check" of sample survey results would be to interview the whole universe at the same time that the sample was being interviewed. Such a check could be made in a community of five-to-ten thousand persons without great cost. Warner believed that

> The original survey should employ the methods currently accepted and should sound opinion on a variety of topics. The 100 per cent canvass of the population should be made simultaneously to avoid the possibility of a shift in opinion. A large regiment of workers should be employed that the work might be complete [sic] within a single day.[16]

Although such an experiment would be neither as easy nor as significant as Warner thought, it or some modification of it would seem worthwhile.

If prediction error in election forecasting is taken as a measurement of poll reliability the summary judgment of Louis Harris on election-prediction accuracy may be taken as a tentative conclusion for the problem of polling reliability. Harris said, "Sampling, for all the claims, is still not so precise as to warrant much less than a 3 per cent margin of error (and this is generous on the low side)."[17]

Validity, of a kind, and reliability may be measured by the correspondence of pre-election polls and election statistics. From the technical point of view, this is a major reason why opinion pollsters like the chance to forecast elections. Elections constitute one of the rare means for checking poll results—perhaps the only regular and systematic test that is not experimentally staged nor based on a number of demographic and sociological assumptions. The "givens" in an election are regularized, anticipated, and (aside from possible bandwagon effect) beyond the influence of the pollster.

The margin of error between the predicted popular vote and the actual vote for a candidate is a rough test of the validity of the prediction for that election. For a number of elections, these errors may be taken collectively as a gross estimation of poll validity. Similarly, the differences

15 Hadley Cantril, "Do Different Polls Get the Same Results?" *Public Opinion Quarterly,* IX (1945), 62.

16 "The Reliability of Public Opinion Surveys," *Public Opinion Quarterly,* III (1939), 390.

17 "Election Polling and Research," *Public Opinion Quarterly,* XXI (1957), 115.

between or among poll forecasts for the same political race constitute a
test of reliability. When aggregated, they may give us clues as to the
general reliability of polls.

The average error for all 245 national, sectional, state, and local
election predictions made by the Gallup Poll from 1936 to 1950 was four
percentage points.[18] Since 1948, however, Gallup and the other major
political pollsters have vastly improved their polling techniques and their
understanding about political behavior. In six presidential and congressional elections, 1950 through 1960, the Gallup agency has averaged an
error of *less than 1 per cent*.[19]

In the 1960s, whatever the exact margin of error of polling, polls are
useful to political actors and to students of politics. Careful opinion
polling is an item of sound strategy for candidates, and it has passed the
pragmatic test of being tried and found helpful. Shortly after the 1960
election, President-Elect Kennedy visited his defeated rival and asked:
"How do you evaluate the private polls you had taken?" Vice-President
Nixon replied: "Miraculously accurate."[20]

4.4   Measurement of the Intensity of Opinion

It is charged, finally, that the polls distort the "truth" about public
opinion because they do not measure the intensity of opinions. Rogers
says the pollsters are unable "to tell us the loudness of the yeses and noes
they say they hear":

A public opinion poll tells us nothing about the eagerness or enthusiasm of
those who wish that something be done, or about the indifference or bitterness
of those who do not want it done. Until the pollsters do both these things, they
will not "chart" opinion or "register" sentiment. They may claim to count a
pulse, but they cannot boast of reading a thermometer.[21]

Those who criticize the pollsters for their unconcern with intensity of
opinion appear to miss the mark. Since the beginning of scientific polling,

[18] George Gallup, "The Gallup Poll and the 1950 Election," *Public Opinion Quarterly*,
XV (1951), 21.

[19] Paul Perry, "Election Survey Procedures of the Gallup Poll," *Public Opinion
Quarterly*, XXIV (1960), 531–542; and, by the same author (who is president of the
Gallup Organization, Inc.), "Gallup Poll Election Survey Experience, 1950 to 1960,"
Public Opinion Quarterly, XXVI (1962), 272–279.

[20] *New York Times*, July 22, 1962. The news story indicated that $1,500,000 was the
estimated cost of confidential candidate polling in the campaigns of 1960.

[21] Rogers, *Pollsters* (see footnote 6), p. 47.

the serious practitioners have recognized the importance of measuring what Rogers calls the "loudness of the yeses and noes."[22] On the other hand, and despite the undoubtedly genuine concern with the problems of intensity and the techniques of dealing with these problems, the pollsters have not improved their practice very much since the early days. Here again the pollsters, like most men, know better than they do. Louis Harris is no doubt one of the most thoughtful experts in the field, and one of the most candid; he admitted in 1958 that, with regard to election polling, "qualitative dimensions of intensity and firmness of opinions have rarely been systematically analyzed, but may make a real difference in any kind of precise percentage-point result."[23] During a campaign, the journalistic pressures and the pressures from the clamoring players of the great game of politics seem to prevent the application of the most refined (which are usually the most costly and almost always the slowest) research tools. The headlines seem inevitably to make their own conditions when attention is focused on political opinions; qualifications of findings, scales of pluses and minuses, and rows of gray figures without black and white winners and losers do not appeal to the consuming public in periods of high political fever. But when political fever gives way to the other fevers recorded by the mass media, who will pay for the energies of Gallup's nine hundred interviewers, the analysts, and the machine time to consider carefully the intensity with which pro-Kennedy voters liked Kennedy (or disliked Nixon) or whether the "no" received in answer to the question "Do you favor federal aid to education?" was really "I guess not" or "No! And as head of the States Rights League I'm speaking against it every night"?

When seen in this light, this criticism becomes much like the other procedural charges made against pollsters. The pollsters, when they are able to resist economic and journalistic pressures, are aware that they do not have magical devices with which they can accurately map, like aerial photographers, each ridge and furrow of public opinion. Nor do they believe—even though in fanciful and unguarded moments they may seem to believe—that they can perfect democracy singlehandedly if the rest of us will just have faith in them. On the whole, it is unfair to charge them with such vanities. What they may fairly be charged with, as the most sensitive among them will agree, is a failure to explain at every opportunity and in

---

22 See, for example: F. Allport, "Polls and the Science of Polling," *Public Opinion Quarterly*, IV (1939), 249–258; Daniel Katz, "The Measurement of Intensity," in Cantril *Gauging Public Opinion* (see footnote 1), pp. 51–65; George Gallup, "The Quintamensional Plan of Question Design," *Public Opinion Quarterly*, XI (1947), 385–393; and P. R. Hofstaetter, "Actuality Measure in the Study of Public Opinion," *Journal of Applied Psychology*, XXXVII (1953), 281–287.

23 Harris, "Election Polling" (see footnote 17), p. 115.

as much detail as the given situation permits the limitations and qualifications that ought to be attached to every poll result.[24] They ought to report modestly and conservatively, and to stress much more than they do that every statement described as a "result" or "finding" is not a fact but an approximation of a fact. Possibly, ultimate candor ought to move them to say something like this at the beginning of each poll release: "We have been as careful as possible to keep errors out of our work, but we know the chances are that the following approximations are wrong by as much as 3 to 4 per cent (or perhaps even more, depending on the ways in which some people would have us calculate the error). Still, experience indicates that the methods we have used in obtaining these careful guesses about public opinion are better than any other methods that we know. Here, then, are the results of our measurements. . . ."

[24] After reviewing all schedules and other analytical materials used by three research groups in a study of social scientists teaching in U.S. colleges, David Riesman concluded "that roughly 10 per cent of the interviews misfired in some decisive fashion." "Some Observations on the Interviewing," in Paul F. Lazarsfeld and Wagner Thielens, Jr., *The Academic Mind* (New York: The Free Press of Glencoe, 1958), p. 271. Since the study that Riesman reviewed was a model of care and precision, we may assume that 10 per cent is something like a minimum for interviewing error—that at least one of ten interviews "misfires in some decisive fashion." However, this assumption does not mean that the accumulated quantitative results are 10 per cent in error, for many of the errors cancel out in the summing.

PART TWO

PUBLIC OPINION AND DEMOCRACY

The three chapters that follow deal with the meaning of public opinion. In Chapter 5, consideration is given to definitions of public opinion—some old, some new, and all imperfect. The definitional elements of the term *public opinion* are identified and briefly described. The chapter includes a definition (also imperfect) which I favor because I find it more useful than other definitions as a shorthand expression for what we mean when the term *public opinion* is used by students of government and society.

Chapter 6 also deals with the meaning of public opinion—with its meaning in the theory and practice of democracy. Although there are passing references to public opinion in nondemocratic societies in this book, our almost exclusive focus is on public opinion in democracies—especially our own democracy. Accordingly, the model developed in Chapter 6 is a representation of what I have called the *opinion-policy process* in a pluralistic society. I hope the model may have some usefulness for analysis of the relations between opinions and policy in Western democracies generally, but I mean it primarily to apply to the United States.

In the last chapter of Part Two we relate democratic theory to public opinion measurement. Do the polls serve democracy? This question might well be the title of Chapter 7 as well as the title of an important article referred to in that chapter. The answer—to give it away at once, but in a form which tells you very little—is yes and no, but mainly yes.

THE MEANING OF
PUBLIC OPINION

5

Students of human behavior find it necessary to use many terms for which there is no agreement about precise meanings. *Character, personality, urbanization, marginal utility, liberty, order,* and *justice*—these are only a few of the terms that social scientists use, often with more confidence than is warranted, day in and day out. The chemist knows that *water* is H_2O with, at worst, a percentage of measurable impurity; but the political scientist can never be sure just what constitutes an *independent voter.*

It is apparent, therefore, that we must agree on certain definitions, in order to understand one another, while recognizing that there is often some measure of arbitrariness in any definition that we may agree to accept.

5.1 Definitions of Public Opinion

There are almost as many definitions of public opinion as there are writers on public opinion. We must go back to Machiavelli—as is so often the case for political scientists—to find the term *public opinion* first used in its modern sense. In the *Discourses,* he declares "that a wise man will not ignore public opinion in regard to particular matters, such as the distribution of offices and preferment"; but, like many of the writers who followed, he apparently felt that the term was so well known and understood that it needed no defining.

Rousseau is sometimes said to have been the first modern political thinker to make an extended analysis of public opinion. Rousseau exhibits not only a concern for the relations between governmental policy and the opinions of individuals, but even, in some places, a modern understanding of public opinion as it relates to majority rule and representation in a democracy. Thus he appreciates that opinions have their origin not in man's physical nature, or in supernatural causes, but in social relationships.[1] He is also aware that all governments rest fundamentally on opinion rather than on law or coercion,[2] and that in social change no government may be very far ahead of popular opinion.[3] Some of his comments on majority rule, when divorced from his mystical and contradictory discussions of the "general will," are remarkably modern. On the use of ordinary and extraordinary majorities, for example, he says:

First, the more grave and important the questions discussed, the nearer should the opinion that is to prevail approach unanimity. Secondly, the more the matter in hand calls for speed, the smaller the prescribed difference in the numbers of votes may be allowed to become: where an instant decision has to be reached, a majority of one vote should be enough. The first of these two rules seems more in harmony with the laws, and the second with practical affairs. In any case, it is the combination of them that gives the best proportions for determining the majority necessary.[4]

Despite some significant contributions to an understanding of public opinion, it would be too much to say that Rousseau was, in any sense, the father of modern public opinion. His analysis is not systematic; and, as Hans Speier has remarked, "Even Rousseau, who put public opinion in its modern place, demanding that law should spring from the general will, still spoke of opinion also in the traditional, predemocratic way."[5]

As a social and political phenomenon, public opinion was of little

[1] Jean Jacques Rousseau, "The Social Contract," *The Social Contract and The Discourses,* trans. G. D. H. Cole (New York: E. P. Dutton & Co., 1913), p. 105.

[2] "Along with these three kinds of law [constitutional, civil, and criminal] goes a fourth, most important of all, which is not graven on tablets of marble or brass, but on the hearts of the citizens. This forms the real constitution of the State, takes on every day new powers, when other laws decay or die out, restores them or takes their place, keeps a people in the ways in which it was meant to go, and insensibly replaces authority by the force of habit. I am speaking of morality, of custom, and above all of public opinion; a power unknown to political thinkers, on which, nonetheless, success in everything else depends." *Ibid.,* pp. 44–45.

[3] Rousseau was aware, too, that governmental policy reciprocally shapes popular opinion: "It is certain that all peoples become in the long run what the government makes them: warriors, citizens, men, when it so pleases; or merely populace and rabble, when it chooses to make them so." "A Discourse on Political Economy," *ibid.,* p. 243.

[4] "The Social Contract," *ibid.,* p. 89.

[5] "Historical Development of Public Opinion," *American Journal of Sociology,* LV (1950), 378.

concern to the holders of power before the ideological revolution of the eighteenth century. It was quite clear that the effect of the equalitarian and majoritarian ideas of Locke, Rousseau, Condorcet, Jefferson, and the other thinkers of the period 1650–1800 was to widen the base of political power. Prior to this period, it did not matter much what the public thought—the public had no way to make its opinions either known or effective in determining policy. But the emphasis on political equality and individualism, coupled with the perhaps more important technological and economic changes of the eighteenth century, meant that a growing part of the hitherto voiceless public would be able to influence governmental policy; and when the public begins to influence policy, it becomes important what the public thinks. Thus, by the opening of the nineteenth century, the term *public opinion* had gained a fairly wide usage among the educated classes.

But not all of the educated classes were happy with the increasing importance of public opinion. Sir Robert Peel, writing to a friend in 1820, fulminated against "that great compound of folly, weakness, prejudice, wrong feeling, right feeling, obstinacy, and newspaper paragraphs, which is called public opinion." De Tocqueville, in the 1830s, associated public opinion and the dangers of a mediocre, unstable, but all-powerful (perhaps tyrannical) majority.

By the end of the nineteenth century, the importance of public opinion was seen by statesmen, politicians, and a few academicians. Woodrow Wilson, Lord Bryce, and A. F. Bentley were aware of many of the theoretical and practical implications of popular opinion in the democratic state. But it was not until World War I that a fairly widespread interest was created in the study of public opinion; to some extent this interest was an outgrowth of the real and alleged use of propaganda by both sides in that conflict.

The modern study of public opinion dates, probably, from A. Lawrence Lowell's *Public Opinion and Popular Government,* published in 1913, and Walter Lippmann's *Public Opinion,* published in 1922. Writers of the 1920s and the 1930s, building on the newly organized concepts and materials of the psychologists, psychiatrists, and sociologists, developed a great many theories and hypotheses, thousands of pages of data, and a good deal of conceptual advancement—attended, perhaps inevitably, by some confusion. One thing is certain: everyone got into the act. Public opinion courses are taught in American universities[6] by po-

---

[6] In general, European universities do not offer separate courses in public opinion. See W. A. Robson, ed., *The University Teaching of Social Sciences: Political Science* (New York: UNESCO, 1954), pp. 188, 190, 199.

litical scientists, sociologists, social psychologists, and journalists; and everyone expects that anthropologists, currently the most imperialistic of academicians, will take it up the day after tomorrow.

But do these people agree on what public opinion is? The short answer is they do not. Edward M. Sait was not able to convince many of his academic fellows that "there should be no question about what we mean by calling opinion 'public'; we mean, in the light of long-established usage, the opinion of the people, the opinion of the community."[7] Sait had no patience with those "sociologists and psychologists [who], without the support of any previous authority, have tried to substitute a meaning of their own." But these unsupported sociologists and psychologists were searching for greater precision of definition—they wanted to know *what* public and *what* opinion?—and they have not been entirely unsuccessful in making the term into a sharper and more usable tool for the study of human behavior.

Leonard W. Doob, in *Public Opinion and Propaganda,* says that "public opinion refers to people's attitudes on an issue when they are members of the same social group."[8] This includes most of the factors other definers think important, but there is some ambiguity about what, precisely, he means by "members of the same social group." Another writer, David Truman, declares: "Public opinion . . . consists of the opinions of the aggregate of individuals making up the public under discussion. It does not include all the opinions held by such a set of individuals, but only those relevant to the issue or situation that defines them as a public."[9] Arthur Kornhauser says that "Public opinion may best be thought of for the present purpose as the views and feelings current in a specified population at a particular time in regard to any issue of interest to the population."[10] Other definitions could be given,[11] but these will serve to illustrate the agreements and disagreements among the experts on the meaning of public opinion.

At this point, it might be useful to put forward a tentative definition, which draws upon and to some extent synthesizes these and other definitions. We may say that *public opinion is the complex of beliefs*

---

7 Howard Penniman, ed., *Sait's American Parties and Elections* (New York: Appleton-Century-Crofts, Inc., 1948), p. 95.

8 (New York: Holt, Rinehart and Winston, Inc., 1948), p. 35.

9 *The Governmental Process* (New York: Alfred A. Knopf, Inc., 1951), p. 220.

10 "Public Opinion and Social Class," *American Journal of Sociology,* LV (1950), 335–336.

11 See, for example, Daniel Katz et al., eds., *Public Opinion and Propaganda* (New York: Dryden Press, 1954), pp. 50–51.

*expressed by a significant number of persons on an issue of public im-
portance.*

5.2 Factors in the Definition of Public Opinion

It may be of some value to examine this definition by looking more
carefully at its basic elements—at what might be called the *factors* of
public opinion. There appear to be five such factors, which are considered
in this and in most of the recent attempts to define public opinion.

5.21 Presence of an Issue

There is, in the first place, a virtual consensus that public opinion
gathers around an *issue.*

In common usage, *public opinion* often appears to be a generalized
term, describing something like a collective attitude or a public mood.
People often say, for instance, that everyone should respect public opinion,
that public opinion is wise, or that public opinion is unwise. Carlyle
maintained that "public opinion is the greatest lie in the world" and
Lincoln once said that it "generally has a strong underlying sense of
justice." But a moment's thought will convince us that this common way
of speaking about public opinion—as if it were an abstract political or
social force—is at best unfruitful, because even when the term is used in
this generalized sense, the users imply the presence of an issue, or a combination of issues. Lincoln presumably meant that, over the years, the
people, if allowed to express their views on issues of wide concern, will
usually choose wisely and justly.

For our purposes, an issue may be defined as a contemporary situation with a likelihood of disagreement. There seems to be no useful
purpose in speaking of public opinion on whether men should breathe or
trees should grow; the element of controversy must be at least implied. It
is also helpful to think of the issue as involving contemporary conflict, to
distinguish opinion from law (as codified policy) and custom (as traditional behavior patterns).[12]

---

[12] Floyd H. Allport, "Toward a Science of Public Opinion," in Katz, *Public Opinion*
(see footnote 11), pp. 58–59, reprinted from *Public Opinion Quarterly,* I (1937), 7–23.

5.22   The Nature of Publics

There must be, in the second place, a recognizable group of persons concerned with the issue. This is the *public* of public opinion. The concept of a public that we subscribe to here was made famous by John Dewey, principally in his book *The Public and Its Problems*. Dewey maintained that there are many publics, each of them consisting of individuals who together are affected by a particular action or idea. Thus, each issue creates its own public, and these publics will normally not consist of the same individuals who make up any other particular publics, although every individual will, at any given time, be a member of many other publics. For example, a man may be a church member, a bridge player, a carpenter, a father, a rider of streetcars, and a member of a little-theater group. When an issue concerning bridge players arises, he will join with other bridge players to form the *bridge-playing public,* and the opinion of these people becomes, for this issue, the *public opinion*. This view of the transient, occasional, and issue-centered public is dramatically illustrated by Ogle's story of fifty men in a London blackout:

As an example [of the formation of a public], let us suppose that during a London wartime blackout fifty men were lost in the dark and fog of the night. After long wandering, one of them found that he seemed to have stumbled into a blind alley and that his further progress was barred by walls on three sides. He then decided to sit down and wait until the lights came on, or until the dawn appeared. Suppose that one by one, and silently, all fifty wanderers were drawn by an inscrutable providence to the same place and that all of them made the same decision—to await the coming of the dawn. At this point, let us assume, fifty men were all congregated in a small space and each was unaware of the presence of the others. A small crowd had gathered, but we would have been unable to speak in terms of a public, as far as any practical manifestation of behavior was concerned. Each man would behave as if he were alone. Now let us suppose that one of the men struck a match. Those nearest to him then became aware of the fact that they had company, and before long every one in the group would have recognized that fact. From that moment, we might speak in terms of group consciousness; and consequently, from that moment, we might expect manifestations of public opinion.[13]

We are primarily interested in the issues, and in the opinions of the publics that form around the issues, that are relevant to what we may broadly describe as the theory and practice of government. But the formation and re-formation of publics and public opinions is by no means limited to political life; it pervades all social behavior.

---

13 Marbury Bladen Ogle, Jr., *Public Opinion and Political Dynamics* (Boston: Houghton Mifflin Co., 1950), p. 43. Reprinted by permission of Houghton Mifflin Company.

5.23   The Complex of Beliefs in the Publics

The third major factor in public opinion has to do with the *distribution* of opinion on an issue. This factor is what we have called the "complex of beliefs."

On each issue, the interested public will divide itself into two or more different points of view. Not all these points of view will be contradictory or mutually exclusive. The number of views that can be differentiated, however, will be a function of the attitudes and previous experiences of the individuals who make up the public, as well as a function of the complexity of the issue. A relatively simple issue, of interest only to a fairly homogeneous public, will not generate the variety of views produced by more complex issues. The erection in the city park of a monument to an elder statesman, if it becomes an issue at all, may produce only two or three points of view; whereas the introduction of a comprehensive master plan and zoning ordinance for a city may produce a dozen or more recognizably different opinions. But, in each case, the total constellation of views generated on the issue is what we mean by the phrase "complex of beliefs."[14]

The proposition that public opinion is always a composite of two or more identifiable points of view is subject to at least one qualification: in a democracy, those issues upon which policy has to be made normally produce a coalescence of the various views into a majority and a minority opinion at the final point of decision. Thus, when policy is finally made, by vote, a dichotomous situation is presented to the voters, who have only two choices; one of these choices becomes the majority view and the other becomes the minority view.

5.24   The Expression of Opinion

The fourth important factor in our definition of public opinion is the *expression* of the various views that cluster around an issue. Words, spoken or printed, are the most common form of expression of opinion, but, at

---

[14] The disposition of the people who "don't know" on any issue presents a difficult problem. It seems reasonable to believe that the "don't knows" consist of two kinds, (a) those who have no opinion because they do not care about the issue, and (b) those who do care but have suspended judgment. Theoretically, the "don't cares" might be excluded from the complex of views at any given moment; politically, however, it is important to consider them as people who might become "do cares" and thereby change the balance in the complex of views. Those who care but have suspended judgment may be thought of simply as representing one view in the complex.

times, gestures—the clenched fist, a stiff-arm salute, even the gasp of the crowd—will suffice to express opinion.

Among the authorities, there is no agreement that public opinion must be defined in such a way that expression is required. Doob, for instance, speaks of both "internal" and "latent" public opinion. When the attitudes that people possess regarding a certain issue "are not expressed," he says, "reference can be made to *internal public opinion*."[15] Supposedly, three factors determine whether or not these internal opinions become external opinions: (1) the motivational strength of the attitudes involved, (2) the rules of the social group involved (in a police state, for example, attitudes hostile to the state will not become externalized), and (3) the limits of the available media of communication.

One difficulty with Doob's concept of internal public opinion is that it is not clearly enough distinguished from attitude—although he makes an effort to distinguish it by declaring that internal public opinion is made up of sharpened, specific attitudes of individuals. Another difficulty, and a more serious one, is simply that an internal opinion is not public. There can be no sense of identification among individuals (the *sine qua non* of a public) who have not made known in some way their common interest, no matter how strongly they feel these interests internally.

Doob's other variety of "unexpressed public opinion," what he calls "latent" opinion, refers to "attitudes of people regarding an issue when those attitudes have not yet been crystallized or when they are not being evoked or are not affecting behavior."[16] This is subject to the same kind of criticism as the idea of internal public opinion. Latent opinion is what might be called *potential* public opinion; but it is difficult to see the usefulness of such a classification. When individual thoughts are not expressed, they are *private* opinions; when they are expressed, they become public opinion, assuming the other conditions to be present.

It may be said that the term *latent public opinion* is important to describe a situation in which a considerable number of individuals hold attitudes or general predispositions that may eventually crystallize into opinions around a given issue. But this is nothing more than a description of the psychological or social-psychological matrix in which opinion is made, and the opinions themselves are neither identifiable nor measurable until they are actually expressed. It seems, then, unnecessary to complicate the definition of public opinion further, with the notion of unexpressed opinion; for our purposes, expression, in some form, is one of the essentials of public opinion.

---

15 Doob, *Public Opinion* (see footnote 8), p. 39. Italics in original.

16 *Ibid.*, p. 40.

5.25   Number of Persons Involved

The last factor in the definition of public opinion is the *size* of the public that is interested in the issue. In our definition, the question of numbers is conveniently and deliberately hedged by the phrase "a significant number of persons," with the intention of excluding those minor issues and minor expressions of individuals that are essentially private in nature. For example, we are not really concerned with the distribution of opinion among Mary Jones's friends about the color of Mary's hair. If riots start in the dormitory over the color of Mary's hair, the number of persons, and the issue itself, may become significant; but, normally, small groups of persons concerned with essentially personal, trivial, or private matters cannot develop what may properly be called public opinion.

We need to make two points concerning what we have called "a significant number of persons." First, although the question of the majority-minority distribution is of special importance in the making of political decisions, our conception of the size of the public demands neither that a majority of the persons affected by the issue hold opinions on that issue nor that a majority view be discernible on any particular issue. Second, we want to know whether the interested public, or any of the various views held by members of the interested public, is *effective* either in changing the views of that public's marginal members or in attracting nonmembers into the public. In short, does the complex of views on the issue have any effect or is it capable of having an effect upon the opinions or the behavior of those who are not members of that public? (Since the political scientist is primarily interested in the effect of opinion upon political decisions, this problem is usually posed in terms of the influence of public opinion upon the making of policy.)

Allport believes that the degree of the effectiveness of the opinion is the most important element for analysis, and that effectiveness is a function not only of numbers but of the intensity of feelings and of "the *strenuousness of the effort* which individuals will make toward the common objective."[17] He thus agrees (as have all the others who have considered the importance of numbers) with Lowell, who said, "individual views are always to some extent weighed as well as counted."[18]

[17] Allport, "Toward a Science of Public Opinion" (see footnote 12), p. 60. Allport would use potential effectiveness as one of the main criteria in selecting issues and publics for study. It is difficult to object to his suggestion.

[18] A. Lawrence Lowell, "Public Opinion and Majority Government," in Katz, *Public Opinion* (see footnote 11), p. 14.

We may say, then, that "a significant number of persons" means, in each case, a different and perhaps unascertainable number; the presumption is simply that this number is capable of producing some effect—an effect that is as much a result of the intensity of opinion and the organization of effort as it is of the sheer size of the public.

5.3 Summary

In this chapter, we suggested that public opinion is the complex of beliefs expressed by a significant number of persons on an issue of public importance. Each of the five main elements in this definition is important to an understanding of public opinion, and to an understanding of how public opinion is differentiated from mores, social custom or habit, and from private interests of no general concern to the larger groups in the society. An issue is a matter with a possibility of disagreement that is of some general concern to the community, not just to individuals. The public consists of those affected by, or aware of, the issue; there is no general public as such, but many publics, each created by an issue in which it is interested. The ideas, feelings, and points of view of the members of those publics must be expressed; the awareness of the public nature of the issue is itself indicated in part by expression, for unexpressed opinions are not identifiable, not measurable, and not public. The *complex of views* includes all the expressed points of view that cluster around the issue and are held by the public; the number of such views depends on the psychological factors at work among the individuals in the public and on the complexity of the issue; the resolution of the complex of views into a minority-majority division is a special problem of democratic decision making. The phrase *a significant number of persons* relates to the size of the public, and means a different number in each case—though not small numbers concerned with essentially private matters; *significance* may in part be measured by effectiveness, or potential effectiveness, which are functions of intensity and organization as well as of sheer numbers alone.

DEMOCRACY AND THE OPINION-POLICY PROCESS

6

This chapter is about the meaning and importance of public opinion for the life of the democratic society. In what sense can it be said—or should it be said—that the people really rule in a democracy? Do majoritarian principles demand that the opinions of 50 per cent plus one of the people on each particular issue be turned into policy? Who *are* the people? What methods are available to make certain that opinion is properly known? Are sheer numbers enough, or ought one to consider, as many have suggested, quality of opinion as well? These are some of the questions that arise in any consideration of public opinion in a democracy.

Although we are not concerned here with public opinion in societies in which democratic theory and practice are weak or nonexistent, it may be useful to tie together, in a few words, two statements that are basic to public opinion in any society. First, we have said that public opinion is the complex of beliefs expressed by a significant number of persons on an issue of public importance. Second, we have suggested that public toleration—if not support—is necessary for the continuation of any existing government and that, in this sense, despotic and arbitrary governments maintain their power only because nongovernment elements are unwilling or unable to change them.

Nondemocratic governments may exercise power for many years in societies where the preconditions of democracy do not exist. In such societies, popular opinion as we know it, and especially as we defined it in the last chapter, may be inchoate, unexpressed, or suppressed. In all such societies, public opinion—if it could be said to exist at all —may be quite unrelated to governmental policy; one could not expect any regular and positive correlation between what the people thought and what their governments did.[1] In contrast to such societies are those in

[1] Anthropologists tell us that, in the very simplest societies, traditional and customary ways of thinking and behaving determine not

which the opinions of the people are unfailingly reflected in public policy. In the range marked by these extremes, it is apparent that an almost infinite number of relationships is possible between the public opinion of a society as defined in the last chapter and the governmental policies of that society. The possible relationships between opinion and governmental policy are illustrated in Figure 6–1. Two points need to be made

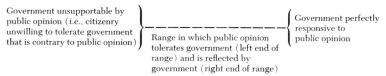

Government unsupportable by public opinion (i.e., citizenry unwilling to tolerate government that is contrary to public opinion)

Range in which public opinion tolerates government (left end of range) and is reflected by government (right end of range)

Government perfectly responsive to public opinion

Figure 6–1. Relationship between Opinion and Governmental Policy

about this simple diagram. First, we want to avoid the error, alluded to in an earlier chapter, of thinking about public opinion as a disembodied "will" unrelated to specific issues. We are in danger of falling into this error when we speak of public opinion tolerating government, supporting government, or being reflected by government. But we can avoid the difficulties of such mischievous generalizations by thinking of this relationship between opinion and government either as the practical summary of many opinions of many publics on many issues, or as the public opinion on the issue of the popular supportability of the government. If the government is intolerable, it means that so many publics have felt their opinions to be so disregarded on so many issues that the government must be replaced. This situation, in terms of the relations between opinions and governments, is the point of revolution, the point at which public opinion on the issue of the supportability of government is simply that the government is *in*supportable. At the other end of the range is the government that is perfectly responsive, and the point at which public opinion on the issue of the supportability of government is that the government is wholly supportable.

The second observation about the diagram is that it indicates nothing *directly* about the structure, organization, or processes of any government. One ordinary set of definitions about types of government divides them according to the numbers of persons who exercise political power. Thus the classical philosophers Plato and Aristotle declared that governments in which only one person ruled were monarchies, those in which a few

---

only all opinions but all governmental policy. No doubt our statement should be modified to allow for such societies; but, for better or worse, "simple" societies have almost disappeared from our world.

ruled were aristocracies, and those in which many ruled were democracies. In theory, monarchies and aristocracies may be placed at any position on the range. The all-powerful king or dictatorial committee may be as responsive to public opinion as is the purest democracy; but there is a fair presumption that the one man or the few men will be less willing to respect public opinion, or less able to measure it, than will the government of the many. In practice, nondemocratic governments that are benevolent and successful tend to evolve into democracies; a concern for public opinion has always brought with it a concern for increasing the number of persons who share the political power. Likewise, as more persons have gained the right to choose leaders, and to become leaders themselves, more attention has been paid to the opinions of interested publics.

Therefore, as a practical matter, democracies are more apt to pay attention to, and to relate themselves to, and, as a consequence, be more responsive to public opinion than are nondemocratic governments. Although monarchies or aristocracies may sometimes be deliberately responsive to public opinion, attention to public opinion (beyond the minimum level of public acquiescence) is not a necessary part of governments by one or governments by the few. However, responsiveness to public opinion is an essential ingredient of democratic government.

Our concern in this chapter will be wholly with the relevance and the relationships of democracy and public opinion. This attention is justified because of the theoretical considerations set out in the preceding paragraphs, and because the general focus of our study is on the meaning, importance, and dynamics of public opinion for the political life of our own democracy.

6.1 Opinions and Policy Oversimplified

The *opinion-policy process* is the way in which what people think is related to what government does; no more complicated idea is intended. Simple as this definition is, it contains all of the questions giving rise to all of the thought and talk and violence of all of man's political history. It is the biggest political question that could be propounded.

Yet it appears, at first glance, that it would be easily settled in democratic societies. Democracy is government by the people; what the people think ought to be exactly what the government does.

The obvious model for this simplistic view is the small, self-contained, homogeneous community where public opinion and democratic practice are seen in their simplest form: the New England town. At the town meeting, when more than half of the voters' hands go up, the policy is decided; and it might be said that public opinion has declared itself.

But even here the matter is not quite so simple. Suppose the town meeting decides on January 1 (and all voters are present—an unlikely but convenient assumption) to adopt a budget providing $20,000 for snow removal, but that it becomes apparent toward the end of the fiscal period that more money must be appropriated or the roads must remain unplowed. What then? A special meeting, or a decision by the selectmen? If the latter method is followed, the originally well-defined relationship between public opinion and policy is destroyed. The selectmen may, indeed, decide to do the very same thing the people would want, were they again to vote on it—but this is at best only a chance identification of majority opinion and public policy.

Another problem further complicates what appeared at first to be ultrasimple. What about the minority? What of the views of that less than half of the townspeople who did not want to spend the $20,000 (preferring to spend either more or less or nothing at all) for snow removal? Surely their views should be included in the public opinion that is important to the workings of democracy.

The example of the New England town meeting only serves to indicate that there is no simple relationship between public opinion and democratic practice.[2] The traditional idea of the place of public opinion in a democracy suffers from several serious faults. It tends to ignore both custom and emotion, it assumes faultless social communication, and it demands what Walter Lippmann calls the "omnicompetent citizen" (i.e., it ignores specialization of function). It is probably not applicable, in anything like its ideal form, to a modern, industrialized, urbanized, and specialized society.

6.2   The A Priori Requirements of Traditional Democratic Theory

In order to understand more fully the role played by public opinion in the democratic state, it may be helpful to examine certain of the assumptions in the traditional theory of democracy, and to compare this theory with political behavior in the democratic state. The theory of democracy developed mainly in the eighteenth and nineteenth centuries may be examined for our purposes in terms of (a) the basic premise of individualism and (b) the qualities alleged to be necessary in each individual.

[2] For some comments on "the conditions for town-meeting discussions" and their absence today, see Stanley Kelley, Jr., *Professional Public Relations and Political Power* (Baltimore, Md.: Johns Hopkins Press, 1956), pp. 225–232.

6.21   The Basic Premise of Individualism

The intellectual fathers of democracy presupposed a sociopolitical situation in which the individual was the basic unit of the body politic. The relations of rulers and ruled were those of man to man; of agent to principal, in the legal sense; and of equal to equal, in the sense of natural rights; with the rulers being first among equals and subject to displacement in the practical matter of decision making. In their dislike of aristocracies, the democratic theorists of the eighteenth and early nineteenth centuries tended to de-emphasize, if not abolish conceptually, all of the group relationships that bind society together and so strongly influence individual behavior. Man the political animal stood alone, being responsible to and influenced by nothing but his reason, his conscience, and his rights. The opinions he held as an individual were to be somehow (perhaps by majority vote alone) translated into policy—a policy that was supposed to serve the interests of the whole by serving the interests of the individual himself.

This theoretical framework, from the sociological point of view so unrealistic, appears to have resulted primarily from three ideas widely held by the principal writers on democracy. Democratic theory was, in the first place, closely associated with the idea of the social contract as the origin of government. If, as the contract theory held, government was the result of a deliberate and, for the most part, voluntary agreement among individuals, and there was no legitimate power other than (a) that which had been placed in the government by the individuals, and (b) that which the individuals retained, then there was no need for intermediate groupings. Even in the version of the contract (e.g., Hobbes's) that supported absolutism rather than democracy, the relationship was direct between the individuals and the sovereign. It is not surprising, therefore, that the democratic theorists, who believed for the most part in contract as the origin of government (a belief exampled in the American Constitution), tended to abstract all of the sociopolitical environment except the individual and the government.

Nor is it surprising that these same thinkers, who, in the second place, were devoted to the idea of natural rights, should conclude that all of these rights, or, more precisely, all of these rights that were of political consequence, resided in the individual and in no place else. They could not see that groups could be described as needing or deserving liberty, equality, and freedom of choice. On the contrary, as a practical matter, they were generally interested in reducing the liberty and freedom of choice of certain groups—primarily, the remains of the feudal aristocracy, churchmen who had political pretensions, and holders of land and commercial grants.

Finally, the framers of traditional democracy were heavily influenced by an economic individualism that interacted with and reinforced their political individualism. For those who could believe that the economic life of the community would be regulated by the "unseen hand" arising from the individualistic pursuit of self-interest, it was apparently very easy to believe that political individualism was sound—especially when *its* hand (majority decision by vote) was *seen*. Also, to the economic individualist, the function of any government was to be limited to keeping order and protecting rights (it was to be, in Lassalle's famous phrase, "a nightwatchman state"), and this kind of government, uncomplicated by broad social functions, should surely be so simple and so obvious that no elaborate mechanism need intervene between the individual and his government.

For these and other reasons, the framers of the democratic theory based much of their theory on the unrealistic notion of man's sociological nakedness. They largely ignored the rich and complex group relations that existed even in the relatively simple agricultural society of 1800 and that today determine and condition the opinions of the individual in so many ways.

6.22   Qualities Alleged to Be Necessary in Each Individual

Traditional democratic theory assumed, in addition to the sociological nakedness of the individual, that each of the members of the electorate would be interested in the issues, motivated by principle, aware of facts, and capable of choosing rationally. It may be worthwhile to look briefly at each of these allegedly necessary qualities and survey their relevance to voter behavior in our democracy.

The notion that each of the citizens who have a share of political power should be interested in public issues is one that has informed democratic ideals since very early days. Both the Athenians and Romans, at various times, chose officials by lot on the assumption—probably valid in that context—that the amount of interest and knowledge in public affairs was about equal, citizen for citizen. In contemporary democracy, as one means of justifying universal suffrage and the one-man-one-vote principle, it is still convenient to postulate some minimum level of interest in public affairs for all citizens.

But the evidence is undeniable that voters today do not all have an interest in public issues. On the contrary, the "don't care" group on many issues runs as high as the "do care" group.[3] This indicates a departure from the presumed norm of citizen interest that is all the more striking when one considers that the polled individual probably exaggerates his interest in order more nearly to approximate the democratic ideal.

Traditional democracy assumes, further, that each member of the electorate is motivated by principle and does not make political decisions either on habitual or whimsical grounds. That is to say, the individual forms his opinions because he believes in the rightness or the utility of certain principles, which he applies in each case to the issue before him. According to some theorists, the individual must be motivated by a sense of community interest; but, in the writings of others, the point is not clear and, for them, it may be that the narrowest notion of self-interest is enough. In any case, there is agreement among them that fancy, indifference, custom, or mere habit should not motivate opinions on public issues. Here again, the facts as we know them belie the theory. The habitual vote (those who vote a straight ticket irrespective of candidates or issues) is variously estimated from 60 to 80 per cent. In 1948, the "Dixiecrats" won all of those states (and only those states) in which they ran as the official Democratic party candidates;[4] it would seem a likely inference that southern voters tend to cast their ballots for the Democratic label regardless of what it stands for.[5]

There is much other evidence that many Americans are traditional voters, in the sense that they always cast their vote for the same party. In July 1942, the American Institute of Public Opinion asked a cross section

---

[3] Lazarsfeld and his associates found that in Erie County, Ohio, less than one third of the electorate professed great interest in the election of 1940. Paul F. Lazarsfeld et al., *The People's Choice* (New York: Duell, Sloan & Pearce, Inc., 1944), p. 45. The Survey Research Center of the University of Michigan, in its study of the 1952 presidential campaign, reported that 37 per cent of the sample claimed to have been "very much interested" in the campaign, that only 21 per cent thought that "it would make a good deal of difference" which party won the election, and 32 per cent said it would make no difference at all. Angus Campbell et al., *The Voter Decides* (Evanston, Ill.: Row, Peterson & Co., 1954), pp. 34, 38. If this is typical of voter attitudes on such highly publicized matters as a presidential election, what must be concluded about the public apathy on issues that receive less attention?

[4] V. O. Key, Jr., *Politics, Parties, and Pressure Groups,* 3rd ed. (New York: Thomas Y. Crowell Co., 1952), p. 288.

[5] In 1948, this traditionalism was stronger than the race issue for southerners. Otherwise, in those states where the regular Democratic candidates, committed to uphold the civil-rights sections of the national platform, and the States Rights Party candidates, opposed to the civil-rights sections, were both on the ticket, voters would have voted for the latter slate. In Georgia, for example, the States Rights candidates were forced to run under their own label and they captured only 20.9 per cent of the total vote, compared with over 60 per cent for the regular Democratic party. *Statistical Abstract of the United States 1956* (Washington, D.C.: Government Printing Office, 1956), p. 339.

of Americans whether they normally voted a straight or a split ticket, and 40 per cent admitted that they voted a straight ticket.[6] Some recent evidence indicates that ticket splitting is increasing and that the habitual vote in elections for major office is dwindling.[7] This may be the long run trend; but in the foreseeable future, half or more of American voters will vote quite blindly for their party.

Campbell and his associates cite the following comment as illustrative of the traditional voter's attitude:

> It's hard to explain, but I've always been a Republican and I just don't know why or anything about the reasons, issues, or such. I just think they're better than the Democrats in everything, nothing in particular.[8]

It might be asserted that this voter is forming his opinion on the basis of principle—the principle being adherence to his party. But this assertion is hardly more than a quibble, and it is unquestionably not the kind of principle that the makers of traditional democratic theory required of their citizen.[9]

Another assumption made by traditional democracy is that the voter, in making political decisions, is aware of the relevant facts. He is supposed to have not only a knowledge of the issue itself but also enough background and peripheral information to form an opinion that, in the light of the principles he applies, makes sense and is capable of being defended intelligently. Here again, just to state this assumption is to expose its unreality. Martin Kriesberg estimates that about one third of the electorate is unfamiliar with almost any given event in American foreign relations,[10] and there seems to be no question but that the people in any

---

[6] Hadley Cantril, ed., *Public Opinion 1935–1946* (Princeton, N.J.: Princeton University Press, 1951), p. 832. For a more recent study of relevant factors, see Angus Campbell and Warren E. Miller, "The Motivational Basis of Straight and Split Ticket Voting," *American Political Science Review*, LI (1957), 293–312.

[7] See Joseph S. Clark, *Congress: The Sapless Branch* (New York: Harper & Row, Publishers, 1964), pp. 37–38; and Richard E. Neustadt, *Presidential Power* (New York: John Wiley & Sons, Inc., 1960), p. 4.

[8] Campbell, *Voter Decides* (see footnote 3), p. 92.

[9] The idea of party regularity, however, is not a mere quibble in the context of the modern thought that interposes a responsible party between the individual and his government.

[10] "Foreign Policy and Opinion at Home: Dark Areas of Ignorance," in Lester Markel, ed., *Public Opinion and Foreign Policy* (New York: Harper & Row, Publishers, 1949), p. 51. For a study of some of the variables involved in the relationship between opinion holding and information, see Philip K. Hastings, "Level of Information and Opinion Content," *Political Science Quarterly*, LXIX (1954), 234–240.

highly developed and complex society will be substantially uninformed about most of the political issues that confront them.

The final assumption of traditional democracy is that the voter makes his decision rationally, in the light of the preceding three factors. He is supposed to form his opinion on the basis of his reason alone, excluding from the process all emotion, prejudice, and fancy. Here, more than in any of the other assumptions, the contrast between expectation and perform- ance has been most obvious and most deplored. Even if we suppose no rigorous meaning for the term "rational,"[11] it is apparent that most of the voters do not decide political matters with the care that they give to, say, the purchase of a new car or the investment of their savings. If one excludes the indifferent from what are normally called the "independent" voters, there may be a small residue of persons who make their choices essentially on a rational basis; but no one will contend that these persons are numerous in American political life.

The contradictions that emerge from this brief survey of the require- ments for opinion formation in traditional democracy and of the electoral behavior in democratic practice, indicate why democratic theory has undergone significant revision in recent years.

Gordon Allport, with a pessimism only partially concealed by his professed hopes for the future, declared that "Up to now the 'behavioral sciences,' including psychology, have not provided us with a picture of man capable of creating or living in a democracy." He argues that demo- cratic theory still requires "that a man possess a measure of rationality, a portion of freedom, a generic conscience, propriate ideals, and unique value."[12] Traditional democratic theory presupposed, in addition to these qualities, faultless communication and mastery of all relevant facts—so that Allport's "requirements" are at least more attainable than Jefferson's. Further, we might agree with Allport's criteria if we could infer that not every man needs to have these democratic virtues, but only that in the col- lective or statistical sense they must be operative in the formulation of policy. Thus, although psychology (especially a narrow individual psy- chology) does not now offer us a picture of the democratic *man,* a political sociology may nevertheless give us a picture of the democratic *society.*

We must therefore look at the kind of social and political environ- ment presupposed for democratic policy formation.

---

[11] For a number of possible meanings for the term pertinent to this discussion, see Bernard Berelson, "Democratic Theory and Public Opinion," *Public Opinion Quar- terly,* XVI (1952), 324–326.

[12] Gordon W. Allport, *Becoming: Basic Considerations for a Psychology of Personality* (New Haven, Conn.: Yale University Press, 1955), p. 100.

6.3 Sociological and Institutional Factors Prerequisite to Opinion Formation in a Democracy

One testimony to the unity of democratic thought lies in the fact that all of the writers, traditional and modern alike, agree on the necessity for certain sociological and environmental conditions in the operation of popular government. Among these conditions, invariably, is the maintenance of some basic agreement on values and goals.

6.31 Homogeneity of Values and Interests

The earlier writers phrased this precondition in terms of a uniform moral and ethical code and a shared conception of public interest. The traditional point of view is well described by Lippmann. In his classic work on public opinion, he says of Jefferson and others that "In the self-contained community, one could assume, or at least did assume, a homogeneous code of morals. The only place, therefore, for differences of opinion was in the logical application of accepted standards to accepted facts."[13]

It is quite probable that there was a high measure of value agreement (at least among the franchised) in 1800. Those who did not agree with the moral code could always move on to the frontier. The relatively small, simple, agricultural communities of that time probably demonstrated sufficient solidarity of interests and ideals to make this a reasonable precondition for democratic practice. It is also probable that the same degree of homogeneity does not exist today in any of the industrialized societies that describe themselves as democracies.

It may not be entirely necessary to expect homogeneity with respect to common moral codes or values. The modern writers tend to describe this minimal precondition in terms of procedural consensus and the relative maximization of individual values within agreed-upon institutions.[14] Berelson has described the necessary homogeneity in these terms:

[13] Walter Lippmann, *Public Opinion* (New York: Harcourt, Brace and World, Inc., 1922), p. 275.

[14] See, for example, Robin Williams, Jr., *American Society: A Sociological Interpretation* (New York: Alfred A. Knopf, Inc., 1951), pp. 204–205, 209; and Herbert McClosky, "Consensus and Ideology in American Politics," *American Political Science Review*, LVIII (1964), 376–378.

Liberal democracy is more than a political system in which individual voters and political institutions operate. For political democracy to survive, other features are required; the intensity of conflict must be limited, the rate of change must be restrained, stability in the social and economic structure must be maintained, a pluralistic social organization must exist, and a basic consensus must bind together the contending parties.[15]

The nature and extent of the basic moral and political values and procedures which must be commonly accepted are not clearly understood. James W. Prothro and Charles M. Grigg conducted a careful field study to gather evidence on the extent of consensus in two American communities. Ninety-five to 98 per cent of their respondents agreed on basic democratic statements such as "Public officials should be chosen by majority vote" and "The minority should be free to criticize majority decisions." If agreement to this kind of culturally prescribed abstraction is what is meant by substantive consensus, then the American democracy seems to have it. But when more specific statements were derived from these generalizations, Prothro and Grigg found that "consensus breaks down completely," and that "respondents in both communities are closer to perfect discord than to perfect consensus on over half the statements."[16] This study leads the authors to conclude that agreement on democratic principles is unnecessary beyond the most general, superficial, and verbal levels:

Assuming that the United States is a democracy, we cannot say without quali-fication that consensus on fundamental principles is a necessary condition for the existence of democracy. Nor does it appear valid to say that, although con-sensus need not pervade the entire voting population, it must exist at least among the highly educated, who are the carriers of the creed. Our data are not inconsistent, of course, with the qualified proposition that consensus on fundamental principles in a highly abstract form is a necessary condition for the existence of democracy. But the implication of political theory that consensus includes more specific principles is empirically invalid.[17]

Beyond this minimal agreement on values and interests, viable democracy is usually understood to rely upon the following institutional and environmental factors: (a) freedom of communication, (b) time for deliberation, and (c) continuing nonpartisan administrative procedures. These factors constitute what might today be called the elements of the democratic belief. These elements are critical to democracy. That they may be consciously understood and believed in by all the people is unnecessary;

---

[15] Bernard Berelson et al., *Voting* (Chicago: University of Chicago Press, 1954), p. 313.

[16] "Fundamental Principles of Democracy: Bases of Agreement and Disagreement," *Journal of Politics*, XXII (1960), 286.

[17] *Ibid.*, p. 293.

that they be understood by those who play influential roles in the opinion-policy process, and be acquiesced in by the rest, seems vital to the maintenance of a workable democracy.

6.32   Freedom of Communication

There has always been agreement among democrats, traditional and modern alike, that freedom of communication is one of the basic sociological factors upon which democratic discussion and decision making depends. The precise limits of this freedom, and the extent to which the individual must be able to speak or write his opinions, have been debated by many wise men over the years—and must be debated anew by each generation of democrats. But there has never been any doubt that on public matters each person must be allowed to think, and say, anything which does not deny to others a like freedom. On this principle, no further generalization is either necessary or possible. Its application, in any community that aspires to democracy, is a matter of specific historical and sociological conditions, and cannot be pursued here.

6.33   Time for Deliberation

That there must be sufficient time for the public in a democracy to consider all of the relevant facts in the detail which the occasion demands is another procedural principle that follows inescapably from the premise that the people shall in some way cooperate in making policy. In Jefferson's day, it might not have been open to doubt that there was time for deliberation in solving public problems; but this factor may no longer be taken for granted. The probability seems to be that modern technology has placed democracy at a serious disadvantage in its struggle for survival against antidemocratic ideas and powers. Technology is not all on one side. But, on balance, it appears that radio and television can only shorten to some limited extent the time that democracies require for careful discussion of public policy.

6.34   Continuing Nonpartisan Administrative Procedures

It seems quite certain that neither Thomas Paine, nor any of his friends in the formative period of democratic thought, ever used the rather stuffy phrase "continuing nonpartisan administrative procedures." But they thought about this requirement for democratic practice, and they described it as the necessity for good faith and the willingness to carry out as well as revise majority decision. The essence of this factor is that there must be known and accepted ways for changing policies and changing majorities. It is, of course, related to the ideas of freedom of communication and time for deliberation, but it is more than either of these. It is the notion that the government must have power to govern, although this power is limited and temporary, and that devices must exist for changing the government and the policy in nonrevolutionary ways. This factor was no less necessary (although it was simpler) in 1800 than it is today. Fortunately, in those democracies that have a relatively long history of nonviolent party rivalry and some agreement about bureaucratic impartiality, this requirement for democratic practice appears to be a matter of procedural consensus confirmed in usage. For new democracies, the possibility that this requirement may not be forthcoming is a real and constant threat.

6.4   Public Opinion in Modern Democratic Practice

We have seen that the a priori requirements in traditional democratic theory are unrealistic norms for individual political behavior and quite at odds with observed citizen participation in the opinion-policy process. Yet we in the United States and the people in perhaps a dozen other countries have governments that are in large manner democratic— that demonstrate responsiveness to popular desires, protection of individual liberties, and the other broad imperatives demanded by democratic thought.

This apparent paradox has in recent years been widely recognized and at least partially resolved through a reexamination and revision that makes democratic theory more consistent with the facts of modern life. In order to understand the emerging theory of the opinion-policy process, we may briefly analyze the basic factors operative in the liberal, pluralistic society.

6.41   The Fundamental Importance of Groups

An individual may believe that, in the words of Sancho Panza, "Naked came I into this world, and naked shall I go out." But during the whole of his life, he is subject to hundreds of sometimes conflicting, sometimes complementary group memberships and interrelations. The postulate of sociological nakedness laid down by the pioneer democrats is not now and never was consistent with the facts of human life. On the contrary, the basic fact with which all social analysis starts—especially analysis of those modern political societies which are our major concern here—is the mutual interaction and influence of individuals and groups.

We may categorize the groups in our society into five basic types: (a) kinship, (b) economic, (c) moralistic-ritualistic, (d) artistic-recreational, and (e) political.

Kinship groups are determined by blood or marriage ties of an immediate or extensive nature, the principal identifiable groups in primitive societies. Even in modern Western societies, these groups may be the most important, although they are relatively less stable and less permanent than in simple societies. Insofar as kinship groups remain the basic transmitters of social norms and traditions, and continue to be the chief socializer of the child, they have first place among the groups in which individuals share values and expectations.

Economic groups, in the sense in which we know them in modern society, are largely a result of the specialization of labor and the complex patterns of an exchange economy. However, *slaves, freemen, workers,* and *warriors* are group distinctions (at least partly economic in origin) known to the most ancient societies. Occupational and craft groups were important in Western Europe at least as far back as the early Middle Ages. In the modern democratic society, it cannot be said that economic factors determine political factors, or even that there is an unfailing relationship between economic and political factors. But there is no doubt that there are opinion tendencies in each income and occupation group[18] and that these are subject to reinforcement by the organization of political pressure groups.

Moralistic-ritualistic groups (churches, secret societies, lodges, for example) exist for the confirmation and encouragement of transcendental ends. The need for an ultramaterialistic sense of purpose is so strong in most individuals, and the likelihood of achieving it by private means (in the manner of Thoreau or Schweitzer) is so improbable, that moralistic-ritualistic groups appear to be a necessary part of any society. They provide a ritual certainty as an antidote to the insecurity of human life. Equally important in the Western world, they introduce an area of cooperation into a society that is at least nominally competitive; here (at least in theory) idealism does not have to be tempered with prudence, materialism is devalued, and no stigma is attached to one's having been unsuccessful in competition.

Artistic-recreational groups fill the need for creativeness, beauty,

---

[18] For one of a number of relevant studies, see Richard Centers, *The Psychology of Social Classes* (Princeton, N.J.: Princeton University Press, 1949).

physical exercise, and camaraderie but are distinguished from the moralistic-ritualistic groups by being relatively less concerned (perhaps unconcerned) with ethical, spiritual, or philosophical issues. Garden clubs, athletic associations, singing or drinking organizations are examples that come to mind at once.

The last type, those groups overtly political in whole or part, includes political parties (partisan organizations interested in obtaining government offices) and pressure groups (partisan or nonpartisan organizations interested in promoting issues).[19] Political parties will normally not be included in any of the first four categories, but a pressure group may be—in fact, probably will be—a group of another type, only specifically and perhaps periodically participating in the opinion-policy process.

Although this typology of groups in modern society may be conceptually useful here, it is not meant to be definitive. In the study of group organization and function, much more sophisticated classification has been and will be produced.[20] The important point for this discussion is that public opinion is filtered, colored, and transformed in countless ways by individual and group subjectivization of fact and other opinion.

6.42   Public Opinion, the Group Struggle, and Public Policy

Gross measurements of public opinion are interesting and important, but they are not controlling factors in the determination of particular policy issues. All the pertinent studies indicate that generalized public opinion (in the manner of Gallup's national polls) is not a factor of the highest priority in legislative decision making.[21] Whether administrators make more use than legislators of this kind of public opinion is still

[19] This follows the accepted distinction between parties and pressure groups set forth (among other places) in David Truman, *The Governmental Process* (New York: Alfred A. Knopf, Inc., 1951), pp. 33–39; and Key, *Politics* (see footnote 4), p. 24.

[20] The already vast literature on group studies is ably, but only partially, summarized in Harold H. Kelley and John W. Thibaut, "Experimental Studies of Group Problem Solving and Process," in G. Lindzey, ed., *Handbook of Social Psychology* (Reading, Mass.: Addison-Wesley Publishing Co., Inc., 1954), II, 735–785; see also George C. Homans, *The Human Group* (New York: Harcourt, Brace and World, Inc., 1950); and Truman, *Governmental Process* (see footnote 19), *passim.*

[21] See L. E. Gleeck, "96 Congressmen Make Up Their Minds," *Public Opinion Quarterly*, IV (1940), 3–24, at 8; "Congressional Uses of Polls: A Symposium," *Public Opinion Quarterly*, XVIII (1954), 121–142, especially 123–129; and Leonard A. Marascuilo and Harriett Amster, "Survey of 1961–1962 Congressional Polls," *Public Opinion Quarterly*, XXVIII (1964), 497–506.

an open question; but the indications are that administrators, too, are more heavily influenced by specialized clientele, other officials, and pressure groups.[22]

Gallup-type reports are important insofar as they help legislators and administrators recognize and delineate the gross limits and patterns of their political environment. These reports are keys to the general tenor of public interest, apathy, support, or disaffection in such matters as the over-all record of an incumbent, the suitability of candidates, or the fitness of political parties. These feelings of individuals, when measured and collected, might better be called public attitudes than opinions, for, as Berelson points out, they are principally matters of taste, habit, and a pattern of predispositions associated with family, social, and economic factors.[23]

The public opinion that counts in policy making is a complex of views, group and individual, that should perhaps be called public opinions or the opinions shared by members of publics.[24] These opinions play upon decision makers in a variety of ways and in a medley of voices to influence the declared policy, which is "the equilibrium reached in the group struggle at any given moment."[25] The decision makers—principally, legislators and administrators, but frequently the courts also—have a large measure of flexibility, as "countervailing powers" may be played off against one another.[26] In the same way, the citizens, organized into

[22] Martin Kriesberg, "What Congressmen and Administrators Think of the Polls," *Public Opinion Quarterly*, IX (1945), 333–337. See also the wealth of pertinent information scattered throughout Harold Stein, ed., *Public Administration and Policy Development: A Case Book* (New York: Harcourt, Brace and World, Inc., 1952).

[23] Berelson, *Voting* (see footnote 15), p. 311.

[24] Harwood L. Childs, *An Introduction to Public Opinion* (New York: John Wiley & Sons, Inc., 1940), pp. 41–42. For a discussion of the difference between the general (national) public opinion and the opinions of subpublics, see Harvey Glickman, "Viewing Public Opinion in Politics: A Common Sense Approach," *Public Opinion Quarterly*, XXIII (1959), 495–504, especially 500–502.

[25] Earl Latham, "The Group Basis of Politics: Notes for a Theory," *American Political Science Review*, XLVI (1952), 390.

[26] The notion of countervailing powers is comprehensively developed in J. K. Galbraith, *American Capitalism: The Concept of Countervailing Power* (Boston: Houghton Mifflin Co., 1952); and, in a more political context, in the works of David Truman (see footnote 19) and Earl Latham (see footnote 25).

For an interesting and suggestive criticism of the "group-theory of politics," see C. Wright Mills, *The Power Elite* (New York: Oxford University Press, 1956), pp. 125–126, and Chapter 11, "The Theory of Balance," pp. 242–268. Mills, for all his insight, seriously confused the sociological group balance of David Truman and David Riesman with American constitutional checks and balances and with the concept of balance of power in international relations.

pressure groups, are able to take advantage of the rivalries among competing leadership groups.[27]

6.43 A Model of the Opinion-Policy Process in Modern Democracy

With the immediately foregoing discussion in mind, it may be possible to attempt a summary formulation of the most recent thinking on the opinion-policy process. In this synthesis, we may avoid at least some of the inadequacies of traditional theory. Thus, democracy might be defined as

a governmental system in which a large electorate is fairly frequently allowed to decide upon the general tendencies of governmental action, mainly by choosing officials, from competing leadership groups, to make specific policy. In the intervals between elections, the people, individually and collectively, are encouraged to discuss and debate policy and freely to communicate their opinions to the leadership groups.

The relation of public opinion to public policy may then be discussed in terms of the two major, but in no operational sense separable, problems of democratic practice: (a) the majority-minority problem and (b) the direct-representative problem.

6.431   The Majority-Minority Problem

The group theory of politics complicates, but does not abolish, the majoritarian problem in democratic practice. The question of whose interests are to be advanced in the group struggle leads inevitably to the concern for majorities and minorities. We need not go into the philosophical or moral reasons for the majoritarian principle in democratic theory. Rather, the practical reasons for the principle, and some of the operational difficulties, ought to be examined briefly in terms of the thinking summarized in the model suggested here.[28]

Emil Lederer has pointed out that, in a democracy,

[27] For some brief but incisive comments on this leadership competition within the group-theory analysis of contemporary democracy, see Robert Dahl, "Hierarchy, Democracy, and Bargaining in Politics and Economics," in *Research Frontiers in Politics and Government* (Washington, D.C.: Brookings Institution, 1955), pp. 3–59.

[28] See Robert A. Dahl, *A Preface to Democratic Theory* (Chicago: University of Chicago Press, 1958), Chapter 2, "Populistic Democracy," pp. 34–62, for a careful analysis of some operational problems associated with the majoritarian principle; see also his helpful summary note on the literature, p. 36.

When a decision has to be taken . . . as in voting for a political party or for a special measure, this vast complexity that forms opinion must be reduced to a clear-cut issue. The technique of every political or administrative body requires the reduction of complicated matters to a "yes" or "no"; majority rule is inevitable whenever unanimity is unattainable.[29]

This collapsing of all relevant viewpoints into a dichotomized question (or a series of dichotomized questions) is unnecessary during the period of discussion and general consideration within and among the interested publics. But as soon as a decision must be reached at any level, dichotomization is strongly indicated. Mathematically, it is difficult to obtain majority consent for policy when more than two relevant alternatives are presented, and this difficulty increases as the number of alternatives increases. Thus, as a practical matter, a democracy has to make up its mind by means of a series of either-or questions and answers: Shall we adopt Plan A or Plan B? Or, more typically, shall we adopt Plan A, *yes* or *no?* This, *at the point of decision,* is the necessary dichotomy out of which majorities are made.

Although public opinion, in its most total sense, is not majority opinion but the whole complex of views on an issue of public importance, there is apparently no way to escape calling the opinion that by a vote-counting process is carried into policy in a democracy *majority opinion.*[30] In the dichotomized situation necessary for making decisions, this leaves that less-than-half opinion, which is, again inescapably, *minority opinion.* Thus, the precompromised opinions that constitute (when compromised) the majority and minority opinions in Figure 6-2 are what we have called the complex of views of which gross public opinion is made.[31] As soon as a policy decision is necessary in a democracy, those who decide the policy must produce a majority view—and they will usually produce a fairly homogeneous minority view—thus producing a majority opinion. This opinion will be produced among the electorate itself in a direct democracy (Fig. 6-2), and in the legislative body in a representative democracy (Fig. 6-3).

[29] "Public Opinion," in Max Ascoli and Fritz Lehmann, eds., *Political and Economic Democracy* (New York: W. W. Norton & Co., Inc., 1937), pp. 284–293, at p. 286. Lowell also stressed the need for limiting alternatives at the choosing stage. A. Lawrence Lowell, *Public Opinion in War and Peace* (Cambridge, Mass.: Harvard University Press, 1923), pp. 127–128, 134–137, 148–150.

[30] Precision requires us to distinguish legislative decision making from election: the choice of one candidate, when three or more are running, is frequently an expression of what might be called *plurality opinion.*

[31] The model presented in Figures 6-2 and 6-3 is not concerned with the psychology of decision making but only with the way in which expressed individual and group opinions are related to governmental policy. The model itself says nothing about why or how people or groups develop their opinions on public issues.

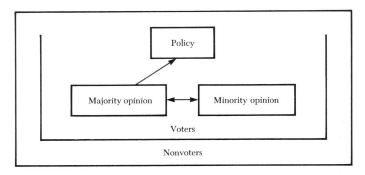

Figure 6–2. Model of Opinion-Policy Process (On Issues) in Direct Democracy

6.432   The Direct-Representative Problem

Representative democracy interposes a decision-making body between the electorate and the public policy. But this addition of what we can call the *legislative level* makes the interaction of public opinion and policy considerably more complex.[32] As in the case of direct democracy, a majority and a minority opinion will be produced on each of the either-or propositions that constitute the last stage of policy making. But in representative democracy, this simple division takes place only in the legislature. Although the complex of views that makes up general public opinion on any issue is capable of being ordered, through compromise, to produce majority and minority opinions, this is unlikely to happen; and when it does happen, the majority opinion among the public may not be the majority opinion at the legislative level. Thus, we need to introduce the idea of *effective opinion*. In direct democracy, and at the legislative level in representative democracy, majority opinion is always effective opinion. But at the level of the general electorate in representative democracy, it is possible (as in Fig. 6–3) for a minority coalition of individual and group opinions to become effective opinion. An example of this case is the long-standing public support (ranging from 60 to 70 per cent) for universal military training coupled with the persistent defeat of such bills in Congress.

[32] For a perceptive discussion of the difference between voting-opinions and issue-opinions in representative government, see Gerhart D. Wiebe, "Public Opinion between Elections," *Public Opinion Quarterly*, XXI (1957), 229–236.

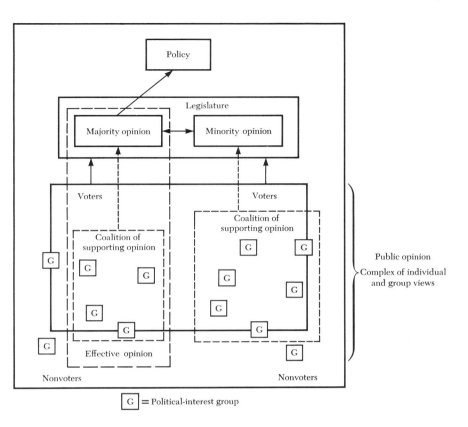

Figure 6–3. Model of Opinion-Policy Process
(On Issues) in Representative Democracy

Effective opinion appears to turn on the degree of participation, intensity of effort, and efficiency of organization among the various individuals and groups who constitute the involved public on any particular issue. But to make this generalization is only to say that who gets what depends on who supports what points of view, how strongly they feel on the matter, and what methods are available to further their ends. Any more detailed understanding must be pursued in terms of specific issues and in the context of particular time and space. When this is done we may be able satisfactorily to identify majority, minority, and effective opinion in the given case, but our knowledge of other cases will not be furthered. Still, this generalization may offer some understanding of the over-all opinion-policy process, and it may also serve as a crude matrix for the investigation of policy decisions on specific issues.

6.433   Governmental Agencies in the Opinion-Policy Process

A brief comment seems necessary to clarify a relationship that is not explicitly shown in Figure 6–3. Lines of influence (voting and communications) in this schematic representation run from groups and voters to the legislature. For illustrative purposes this oversimplification seems justified. For a clearer understanding of democracy in action, however, a further point needs to be made; namely, that self-government involves a reciprocal relationship between nongovernmental networks of groups and individuals and governmental networks of groups and individuals.

This enriched view of the opinion-policy process necessitates an understanding that (a) governmental agencies other than legislatures influence (often decisively) policy outcomes, and that (b) all such governmental agencies and their individual officials may influence the continuous dialogue through which opinion and policy are shaped.

Governmental officials and agencies—especially executive and administrative but frequently judicial too—become involved as individuals and as groups in the opinion-policy process at the prelegislative level. They may be thought of as elements in the majority and minority coalitions that support legislative voting alignments. It is probable that governmental units, when participating in the group struggle, must be regulated by extraordinary restraints both self- and law-imposed; in a democracy they cannot be allowed to use the same kinds and degrees of devices permitted to nongovernmental groups.[33] Despite these limitations, the opinion-policy process may be thought of as a two-way street. Governmental elements shape public opinion through public affairs and information programs, through the intentional effects of experimental and demonstration projects and the largely unintentional effects of countless administrative decisions in the carrying out of legislative policy, and in subtle "feedback" to nongovernmental agencies—which tailor their demands and strategies accordingly.

6.5   The Legislator's Dilemma

The obligation of governmental officials to be sensitive to public opinion and, in some measure, to reflect the views of the citizens is most dramatically posed in the legislator's dilemma: Should the elected repre-

---

[33] For some pertinent comments on the influence of governments in opinion formation, see Francis G. Wilson, "Public Opinion: Theory for Tomorrow," *Journal of Politics*, XVI (1954), 610–611, and 616–617.

sentative regard it as his duty to vote as he thinks his constituents want
him to or should he exercise his independent judgment? This dilemma is
one that appointed officials share, in slightly lessened degree, with elected
officials; but the classic case is framed as a problem in legislative responsibility. "The bald issue," as V. O. Key, Jr., put it, "appears in the contrast
between the representative bound by instructions from his constituents
and the representative bound by conscience to exercise his best judgment
in the interest of the nation."[34] In their interviews with legislators in
four states, Wahlke, Eulau, Buchanan, and Ferguson found that legislators
do in fact regard their responsibilities in one or the other of these two
quite separate ways. The "delegate" role, according to this study, is
adopted by legislators who tend to follow what they take to be the instructions of their constituents, and "they seem to imply that such con-
sultation [with constituents] has a mandatory effect on their behavior."
The legislator who adopts the "trustee" role "sees himself as a free agent
in that, as a premise of his decision-making behavior, he claims to follow
what he considers right or just, his convictions and principles, the dictates
of his conscience."[35]

Although this dilemma can never be resolved as a matter of principle
or "right," it may be helpful to distinguish between the representative's
obligations with respect to the basic *values* of his constituents and his
obligations with respect to the *opinions* of his constituents. *Values* I define
here, as elsewhere in this book, as long-term, enduring, basic preferences
toward objects; opinions are shorter-term and more specific orientations
toward objects. It is of some use in clarifying legislators' responsibilities to
say that legislators ought to try to realize the long-term value orientations
of their constituents; but on matters of opinion, on which constituents are
likely to change their views and on which specialized information may be
available, the legislators' views ought to take primacy over those of their
constituents.[36]

This difference between values and opinions seems to be, in part,
what Edmund Burke had in mind when he wrote his defense of the
legislator's freedom of conscience. He says of the legislator's relations
with his constituents: "Their wishes ought to have great weight with
him; their opinions high respect; their business unremitted attention.

---

[34] *Public Opinion and American Democracy* (New York: Alfred A. Knopf, Inc., 1961),
p. 481.

[35] John C. Wahlke, Heinz Eulau, William Buchanan, and LeRoy C. Ferguson, *The
Legislative System: Explorations in Legislative Behavior* (New York: John Wiley &
Sons, Inc., 1962), pp. 272, 276.

[36] I am indebted to James A. Robinson for insight into this distinction and, indeed,
for some of the phrasing of this paragraph.

It is his duty to sacrifice his repose, his pleasure, his satisfactions, to theirs —and above all, ever, and in all cases, to prefer their interest to his own." Without doing too much violence to Burke's philosophy, I think one can read "their values" for "their interest" here. "But," Burke goes on, "his unbiased opinion, his mature judgment, his enlightened conscience he ought not to sacrifice to you, to any man, or to any set of men living. . . . Your representative owes you, not his industry only, but his judgment; and he betrays, instead of serving you, if he sacrifices it to your opinion."[37]

6.6   The Opinion-Policy Process: Good or Bad? A Postscript

Whether it is good or bad that in a representative democracy the opinion-policy process may produce policy contrary to majority opinion (on those apparently rare occasions in which gross public opinion becomes measurably polarized) is, in the end, a matter of individual judgment. It depends upon how majoritarian one wants one's democracy. Most of those who made the United States Constitution thought that this possibility, inherent in representation, was a good thing, and the writers of the *Federalist Papers* defended their deliberate effort to block the effectiveness of majority opinion.[38]

But even without such deliberate efforts, representative government may frequently make minority opinion into effective opinion. As long as the legislator may choose to listen to any one of the numerous, conflicting, and inaccurately measured voices of the people, just so long may he and his colleagues either mistake or ignore the majority coalition of opinion. Whenever policy is made by agents (as distinguished from *plenary* policy making in a direct democracy), the one-to-one relation of opinion and policy predicated by majoritarian democrats becomes difficult if not impossible to demonstrate.

It is doubtful, however, whether it is either theoretically or practically important that minority opinion sometimes becomes effective opinion. In the first place, majority public opinion may be wrong, in that it may adopt a position incompatible with the future operation of the democratic

[37] *Burke's Politics: Selected Writings and Speeches of Edmund Burke on Reform, Revolution, and War,* ed. Ross J. S. Hoffman and Paul Levack (New York: Alfred A. Knopf, Inc., 1949), p. 115.

[38] For instance, they declared that equal representation in the Senate would discourage "the propensity of all single and numerous assemblies to yield to the impulse of sudden and violent passions, and to be seduced by factious leaders into intemperate and pernicious resolutions." *The Federalist, No. 62.*

process. The history of civil liberties in the United States contains many minority defenses of basic democratic rights in the face of widespread, possibly majority opinions that would deny these rights.

The frequent persecutions of unpopular people and groups during national crises has been too common in American life to justify any easy assumption that public policy invariably ought to be determined by gross public opinion. The witch hunts that followed both World Wars and the systematic discriminations at state and regional levels against racial, religious, and labor groups (Negroes, the Jehovah's Witnesses, and union organizers) have all, at certain times and places, threatened procedural and substantive rights indispensable to democracy itself. On the whole, in each of these types of antidemocratic activities, a minority dedicated to civil liberties has defended and acted to restore democratic practice.[39]

Stouffer's study of attitudes toward civil liberties in the United States convincingly documents the greater respect for the First Amendment among the leadership minorities than among the public at large in the United States.[40] His finding that community leaders are uniformly more tolerant of social and political nonconformity prompted Janowitz to question the "political assumptions . . . that public opinion is fundamentally healthy, has long-term perfectibility, and is a central guide for public policy."[41] Janowitz recognizes the antimajoritarian implications of his question, but he is justified in wondering whether "education which turns out to be a key correlate [of toleration] will continue to raise the level of public tolerance."[42]

In the second place, power, broadly defined to include the wielding

---

39 That minority elites may at times acquiesce in antidemocratic activity is also apparent—the ejection of duly elected Socialists from the New York State Legislature in 1921 and the forced relocation of the West Coast Japanese in 1942 are cases in point. But, generally, they have been much more zealous than nonelites in maintaining the democratic environment.

40 Samuel Stouffer, *Communism, Conformity, and Civil Liberties* (Garden City, N.Y.: Doubleday & Co., Inc., 1955), Chapter 2, "Are Civic Leaders More Tolerant Than Other People?" pp. 26–57.

41 Morris Janowitz, review of Stouffer (see footnote 40), *Public Opinion Quarterly*, XX (1956), 353.

42 *Ibid.* Henry Steele Commager, in his *Majority Rule and Minority Rights* (New York: Peter Smith Reprint, 1950), makes an excellent case against judicial review of federal legislation and demonstrates that it has not in general protected civil liberties—even though he passes too lightly over the liberal record, since 1925, of federal-court nullification of *state* restrictions. It is more pertinent to the argument here, however, to point out that Commager is concerned with the possibility of an unrepresentative minority (the courts) frustrating the will of the representative minority (the legislatures). He seems to be quite aware that the defense of minority rights also involves the important action of the tolerant leadership minority in checking (through institutional and political devices) the frequent intolerance of mass opinion (pp. 58–60).

of conscience and of moralistic factors in addition to its more traditional components, makes policy in human affairs. For the democrat, the issue is not the existence of the power struggle, but the political, economic, and social conditions within which the struggle takes place. These conditions and the way they are institutionalized determine whether or not the policy-making process can be termed democratic in the light of the elements described under Heading 6.3 in this chapter.

Thus, the democrat need not be alarmed by what may appear to be unpopular policy. As long as the open, liberal, society is preserved—as long as what David Truman calls the "democratic mold" is maintained—he himself may participate, even if only through group membership, in the opinion-policy process.

It may be argued that many individuals and many groups cannot, in fact, compete in the power struggle on an equal basis with other individuals and groups, because the resources (mainly money) necessary for competition are unevenly distributed in the society.[43] It seems undeniable that the inequality of resources will produce inequality of power at any given time in the policy process, thus giving very real advantages to certain groups.

But no equal power distribution is to be expected—or perhaps even to be desired. The power pendulum, and therefore the policy pendulum, is bound to fluctuate over time; and during periods of rapid social change it is apt to swing widely. But in the not-too-long-run perspective, something like a balance may be expected as long as the opportunity to mobilize opinions, organizations, and pressures is kept open. The state, as the principal umpire of the power-policy struggle, will probably have to invoke the rules (and actively intervene) more often on the side of the economic underdog than on the side of the topdog.[44] But this is no cause for alarm—except for those who think that the function of the state is to maintain their own power positions (a not uncommon point of view!). The group-policy-struggle concept implies no mechanistic process, and the state is quite properly moved by humanistic principles, and perhaps, to some degree, by its own interests as a group.

[43] C. Wright Mills, in *The Power Elite* (see footnote 26), makes this contention explicitly at pp. 110–115 and 125–129.

[44] Dewey himself never believed that the group analysis was a neo-laissez-faire conception: "Our doctrine of plural forms is a statement of fact; that there exist a plurality of social groupings, good, bad and indifferent. . . . It does not intimate that the function of the state is limited to settling conflicts among other groups. . . . Our hypothesis is neutral as to any general, sweeping implications as to how far state activity may extend." John Dewey, *The Public and Its Problems* (New York: Holt, Rinehart and Winston, Inc., 1927), p. 73. See also Morton Grodzins, *The Loyal and the Disloyal* (Chicago: University of Chicago Press, 1956), pp. 56–60, for a statement of the activist role of government in the pluralistic society.

That this open power policy and opinion-policy process is characteristic of liberal democracy is noted by all the latter-day analysts, whether sociologists or political scientists.[45] This openness, this constantly changing pattern of opinions, pressures, and policy within a framework of procedural consensus appears to be at once the essence and the best indication of democracy in action.

[45] William G. Carleton even affirms that "Democracy is the system of the future because democracy alone is consistent with the pluralistic and multigroup society which industrialism inevitably creates. All other types of government are essentially oligarchic, and oligarchies represent too few groups to satisfy modern pluralistic societies." "Is Democracy to Blame?" *Virginia Quarterly Review*, XXXIII (1957), 228.

OPINION MEASUREMENT IN THE DEMOCRATIC SOCIETY

7

7.1 Public Opinion and the Perfection of Democracy: A Simplistic View

Some of the early public opinion pollsters apparently believed that their work would make possible the achievement of the last stage in the evolution of self-government. They thought or at least wrote as though they thought that the ultimate step in the long march to democracy could now be taken. Democracy, they seemed to say, means that all persons participate in making governmental decisions; decisions are made on the basis of opinions about issues, and polling techniques make it possible for the first time accurately to measure the opinions of large numbers of persons. Therefore, polling makes possible the perfection of democracy.

Polling enthusiasts who talked in this way were fond of quoting the English nobleman James Bryce on the nature of public opinion in a democratic society. In 1888, Lord Bryce suggested that there had been, to that time, three identifiable stages in the development of public opinion:

We have distinguished three stages in the evolution of opinion from its unconscious and passive into its conscious and active condition. In the first, it acquiesces in the will of the ruler whom it has been accustomed to obey. In the second, conflicts arise between the ruling person or class, backed by those who are still disposed to obedience, on the one hand, and the more independent or progressive spirits on the other; and these conflicts are decided by arms. In the third stage, the whilom ruler has submitted, and disputes are referred to the sovereign multitude, whose will is expressed at certain intervals on slips of paper deposited in boxes, and is carried out by the minister or legislature to whom the popular mandate is entrusted.[1]

.

1 *The American Commonwealth* (London: Macmillan & Co., Ltd., 1888), II, 220.

Bryce then declared that

A fourth stage would be reached if the will of the majority of the citizens were to become ascertainable at all times, and without the need of its passing through a body of representatives, possibly even without the need of voting machinery at all. In such a state of things, the sway of public opinion would have become more complete, because more continuous, than it is in those European countries which, like France, Italy, and England, look chiefly to parliaments as exponents of national sentiment. The authority would seem to remain all the while in the mass of the citizens. Popular government would have been pushed so far as almost to dispense with, or at any rate to anticipate, the legal modes in which the majority speaks its will at the polling booths; and this informal but direct control of the multitude would dwarf, if it did not supersede, the importance of those formal but occasional deliverances made at the elections of representatives. To such a condition of things the phrase "Rule of public opinion" might be most properly applied, for public opinion would not only reign but govern.[2]

Bryce believed that the "machinery for weighing or measuring the popular will" continuously, comprehensively, and in detail was not likely to be invented. Nevertheless, he feared that intolerant majorities would run roughly over minorities, and that the leaders would abandon leadership to become the mere cat's-paws of majority pressure in a society undermined by a "belief in the wisdom of numbers." However, anyone may, as Shakespeare said about the devil, "cite Scripture for his purpose"; and if Bryce is to be quoted, it is only fair to point out that he was apprehensive even of the idea that a measurable majority should make policy through pressure on legislators. He failed to discuss the evils in the speculative fourth stage only because he thought it an impossibility. But, quoting Bryce, some of the early pollsters seemed to claim, in their moments of greatest exhilaration, that the fourth stage had been reached, and that it made possible a system of policy making by nationwide polls.

Like Bryce's "fourth stage," the opinion-policy process in direct democracy presumes that popular opinion is turned directly into governmental policy. When sampling techniques become perfect (or nearly perfect)—or so the argument goes—opinion polling will be equal to referenda. Instead of all the people, making policy, as in a plebiscite, a perfectly representative sample can do so; thereupon, legislatures may be reduced to rule-making and constituency-service agencies—or, ultimately, abolished. Such a system, while as yet practically unattainable, has a certain superficial appeal in theory.

We may call this kind of direct democracy *opinion-sample majoritarianism,* to distinguish it from the face-to-face majoritarianism of town-meeting democracy. No pollster has ever quite declared that majority

2 *Ibid.,* pp. 220–221.

opinion, as measured by sample surveys, ought to be translated directly into policy.[3] But some pollsters have implied that opinion-sample majoritarians might be found among them if the necessary opinion-measuring machinery could be created.

Gallup, at times, has been incautious in the claims he has made for public opinion polls. For twenty years he has been enamored of certain themes which seem to indicate support for direct democracy. One such theme is that the judgment of the masses is fundamentally sound and often better than the judgment of legislators. For example, in 1948, he said, "people tend to judge wisely when they have the facts. There is a veritable mountain of evidence to prove that the basic tenets of democracy are sound."[4] Gallup reaffirmed this faith in popular opinion in 1960, when he said,

poll findings have lent great comfort to those who have faith in the common people. The collective judgment of our citizens has been found to be extraordinarily sound. The people, in fact, have been ahead of their representatives on a great number of the major issues of this period.[5]

Gallup has made other claims for public opinion polling:

Public opinion polls constitute almost the only check on the growing power of pressure groups. . . . The claims of pressure groups presuming to speak for millions can be tested by the polls.

Polls have uncovered many areas of ignorance. . . . A major service which they perform is that of finding out what the public knows about the issues that confront government.

Polls have helped administrative departments of government make better decisions.

Polls speed up the process of democracy by accurate and swift reporting on public opinion.

Polls help define the mandate of the people in national elections.[6]

Gallup's more careful statements—for instance, in testifying before

---

[3] Although one, in his peroration in a wartime book, came close, in writing: "We must improve the methods whereby the public makes felt its will. For the conduct of national and international affairs we cannot go back to the town meeting. But we must, if we are to survive as a democracy, recapture more and more of its spirit. What makes democracy is people. The mandate from the people must be heard, must be heard constantly." Jerome Bruner, *Mandate from the People* (New York: Duell, Sloan & Pearce, Inc., 1944), p. 227.

[4] George H. Gallup, "Public Opinion and Foreign Policy" in *Conference on the Citizen's Participation in Public Affairs* (New York: New York University School of Law, 1948), p. 19. In fairness to Gallup, it should be noted that he also said in this speech that "the public often reveals an amazing lack of interest and knowledge."

[5] Foreword to John M. Fenton, *In Your Opinion* (Boston: Little, Brown and Co., 1960), p. ix.

[6] "The Case for Public Opinion Polls," *New York Times Magazine*, February 27, 1949.

congressional committees—indicate that he is aware that opinion polling is only one technique, and hardly the most significant, for facilitating and understanding democracy. He performs a disservice, however, to his craft and to his audience when he approvingly repeats Samuel Stouffer's statement that "polls represent the most useful instrument of democracy ever devised."[7]

7.2 Opinion Measurement and Minority Rule

At the opposite extreme from direct majoritarians are avowed minoritarians, who believe that policy ought to reflect the views of elite groups who for special reasons of birth, wealth, intellect, or tradition are "fit" to govern the masses. To minoritarians, the opinions of large publics are of no concern, except as they may be manipulated by "superior" groups in the struggle to control governmental policy.

Earlier minoritarian theories of government, referred to by the Greeks as monarchy and aristocracy, are no longer viable in the Western world. (Perhaps it is safer to say that such theories are not now publicly expressed, for the fascism of 1923–1945 was a form of aristocracy, and one cannot say that it could not happen again, no matter how frightening the prospect.) Nevertheless, the most powerful nondemocratic societies today are governed by explicitly minoritarian systems. The stated objective of the Soviet and its satellite governments is a majoritarian system; but in the early, so-called "communist" stages of the system's development, their theory calls for a dictatorship of the few Communist Party members over the many nonmembers. In such circumstances, it is not just coincidence that the Communists say that public opinion research in the capitalist state is a stratagem by which the masses are hoodwinked into believing that they have influence and political power.[8] The Communists, therefore, are explicitly minoritarian in their views—at least during the early stages of what they choose to call the development of the "socialist society." But it is not without interest that they use the vocabulary and espouse the goals of democracy while they reject popular elections and opinions; it seems to indicate that the attractions of majoritarian ideals are so great that even those groups that do not believe in majority rule have to pretend to do so.

[7] In Fenton, *In Your Opinion* (see footnote 5), p. x. For a more recent suggestion about direct democracy through opinion polling, see Stuart C. Dodd, "Ascertaining National Goals: Project Aimscales," *The American Behavioral Scientist*, IV (1961), 11–15.

[8] A. K. Vledov, "Public Opinion as the Subject of Social Science Research," *PROD Translations*, III (February 1960), 21–31.

Although we should not ignore the dangers to democracy of both right- and left-wing minoritarianism, we need do no more at this point than to note the existence of such views, and to suggest that the relationship of public opinion to minoritarian government is quite simple: if public opinion does not threaten the government, it is ignored; if it threatens the government, it is corrected; if it supports the government, it is patronized and rewarded.

7.3   Qualified Majoritarianism and Public Opinion Polling

For our understanding of the meaning of public opinion in democracy, the important spectrum of beliefs on the majority-minority continuum may be called *qualified majoritarianism.* Qualified majoritarianism (sometimes called *mixed government,* or *mixed democracy*) shows essentially three subtypes: democracies adhering to qualified majority rule may subscribe to the doctrines of (a) concurrent majorities, (b) mandated majorities, or (c) coalition majorities.

The idea of *concurrent majorities,* as first expressed by John C. Calhoun in his famous *Disquisition on Government* (1849), and subsequently supported by many who emphasize the states-rights side of federalism, is simply that central policy must command a numerical majority in each of the major subgroups which together make up the central society or government. Thus, national laws in the United States, according to this doctrine, can be made constitutionally only if a majority in each state favors the laws. It is apparent that, under such a system, each unit (or state) would have a practical veto on central policy making. It is also apparent that concurrent majorities would result in as many arenas of public opinion formation as there are political areas or groups to claim this veto. If the doctrine is applied to the United States, the public opinion implications—no matter what the other implications—are merely that the national opinion-policy process becomes a simple summation of the results of the process in each of the states. Concurrent majorities, conceived on a state basis, would mean, quite simply, state sovereignty within a confederate league; and the important public opinion would therefore be the opinion that shapes the policy process in each of the states.

It is possible, however, to apply the doctrine of concurrent majorities to political elements other than state and local governmental units. Broadly speaking, central governments must command the support, or at least the acquiescence, of the major sectional, economic, and cultural elements within their boundaries. It may therefore be argued that the great regions ("the South," "the West") or major economic segments (management, labor, farmers), in effect, ought to be given a veto over central government action that they strongly oppose. In this larger and admittedly fuzzier sense, concurrent majorities would not mean a league of sovereign states but a sovereign central government, which grants a veto power in extreme cases to its major social and economic elements.

The theory of *mandated majorities* lies at the base of party government. In essence, this view requires the political parties to appeal to the electorate on the basis of general and identifiable principles (and sometimes on the basis of specific issue positions), and requires the winning party to translate these principles and issues into public policies. The successful party has a mandate, renewable or retractable at the next election, to put its program into operation as law and governmental decisions. Under such a theory and practice, the political parties become the most important groups, and other groups and individuals recede in influence; party opinion takes on greater significance, as does opinion and policy formation within the parties.

The third subtype of qualified majoritarianism can be called *coalition majoritarianism*. Although it is something of an oversimplification, we may say that the United States national government, in theory and in practice, observes coalition majoritarianism. Within a complex and highly fractionalized governmental framework of federalism and separation of powers, policy is made by temporary and ad hoc coalitions of groups and individuals.[9] There is a presumption—although it is only a presumption, because the reality is immeasurable—that a popular majority (or something near it) is represented by the coalitions which are successful in making policy on particular issues. Under these conditions, the opinion-policy process is very much like that described on pages 120–126 above. When policy is made by coalition majorities in the United States, the coalitions do not consist of internally disciplined parties, as is usually the case in Continental Europe, but of political individuals and groups (including party groups) with various strengths, goals, and access to the decision-making process.[10]

7.4   Public Opinion Polling and Mixed Democracy

Among believers in the American system of mixed democracy (or coalition majoritarianism), there is both agreement and disagreement about the place and the significance of public opinion polling. After thirty

[9] J. Roland Pennock, "Responsiveness, Responsibility, and Majority Rule," *American Political Science Review*, XLVI (1952), 790–807.

[10] See David Truman, *The Governmental Process* (New York: Alfred A. Knopf, Inc., 1951), for the best analysis and defense of rule by coalition majorities.

years of agitation and controversy, it appears that pollsters and critics agree that most public opinion polling serves some intelligence function for policy makers—it gives them information that may influence their understanding or beliefs—and that skillful polling may give them certain kinds of information that cannot be obtained in any other way.

Beyond this, however, agreement is less frequent and conflicting points of view more common. On three matters, especially, there seems to be considerable disagreement between pollsters and critics.

7.41   Should All Opinions Be Known?

A basic question—and one on which some students of democracy differ from the pollsters—is whether all opinions on public issues ought to be known, even if techniques are available to make them known. The pollsters say that all views should be known, because even if simple notions of plebiscite majoritarianism are not accepted, the policy makers ought to have as complete as possible an understanding of what popular feeling and thinking happens to be on each issue.

Some writers have suggested, however, that this view of the importance of polling is too simple. Wilfred Binkley took issue quite early with the pollsters' contention that their reports constituted an important contribution to democratic practice. His comment illustrates the point of view of those who consider concurrent-majority doctrines important to the proper functioning of democracy. Our democracy, Binkley seems to say, does not operate on the basis of some simple national majority, and the pollsters' projection of poll results into gross national figures is misleading, because it presumes a kind of democracy that we do not have:

It is to be doubted whether the American people want national issues decided on the basis of national referenda which opinion polls suggest. . . .

A feasible national policy rather represents the net result of the concurrences and balances of the dominant interests of the sections, states, and congressional districts. . . .

Perhaps our opinion polls might turn their attention more to discovering these concurrences than confining their investigations so much to the pattern of simple national referenda. Thus might they approximate the reality of the process by which national policy is formulated.[11]

Another critic argues that the activities of pollsters—especially the way they report their findings and the way these findings are accepted (interpreted) by newspaper-reading Americans—constitute a "disservice to democracy." The essence of democracy, according to John C. Ranney, lies

11 Wilfred E. Binkley, review of Jerome S. Bruner, *Mandate from the People* (see footnote 3), in *Public Opinion Quarterly,* VIII (1944), 428–429.

in an endless discussion of issues and policies. Such a dynamic, ever changing, and always open dialogue among individuals and groups is, as we have seen, the heart of the opinion-policy process. Ranney declares that the danger in public opinion polls is that the participants in this critical dialogue may take the polls to be more important than they are.[12] To the degree that poll results are assumed to be the last and, in a sense, authoritative word on any public issue, to that extent the opinion-policy process becomes slowed, rigid, and inoperative—and, to that extent, democracy has been ill served.

There is little evidence, however, to indicate that poll reports have significantly slowed or interfered with the opinion-policy process. It may be partly a result of the limits and inherent errors in polling—demonstrated from time to time (as in 1948) and admitted by the more careful pollsters—that the published results of polls have not noticeably rigidified the opinion-policy process. So many elections are determined within the 6 per cent range that pollsters allow themselves for error, and so many issues depend on the unpollable factors in the opinion-policy process, that the participants in the dialogue have found that poll results cannot be the sole or even the major determinant of their behavior. If the pollsters could claim 100 per cent, or near 100 per cent, accuracy, their pronouncements might have the result that Ranney fears. But, as long as their admitted margin of error is greater than the margin that usually determines the important elections, there seems no likelihood that the political controversy upon which democracy depends will be stopped or even appreciably slowed.

Although this speculative danger does not seem to be imminent, Ranney at least implies that perfect measurement of public opinion would be a disservice, because cross-sectional readings of the opinion of the moment would be substituted for an understanding of the opinion-policy process as a dynamic, never ending phenomenon. This is a profound and stimulating criticism, and one upon which it is not too extreme to say that those who understand democracy can be separated from those who do not. But whether or not we make it the test of one's understanding of democracy, it goes, for our purposes, to the heart of the matter of how opinion polling is related to democratic government.

If all opinion could be known at any given moment, this measurement would not, except in the most doctrinaire and theoretical sense of majority rule, be the sole basis for policy making. Despite the way pollsters used to talk, no one believes that other factors should be excluded from policy making. Above all else, policy makers have to be prospective. They must think about tomorrow. Aside from the possibility that opinion may be wrong, nothing is more certain than that opinion will change. De-

12 "Do the Polls Serve Democracy?" *Public Opinion Quarterly*, X (1946), 349–360.

cisions must be made on many grounds, involving many facts, judgments, and plain old hunches. In one profound sense, what the people think today is not so important to political actors as what the people will think tomorrow, especally if tomorrow happens to be election day. The politician who takes the momentary measurement of opinion—however accurate—as his sole criterion for decision making is not only a man unfit for public office in a democracy, but, from the point of view of his own political career, an ignoramus. If the perfect measurement of opinion had the effect of making large numbers of policy makers follow public opinion slavishly, democracy would indeed suffer a disservice. It is hard to believe, however, that even perfect measurement would induce any number of political actors to be so simple-minded in their understanding of the opinion-policy process.

What if the belief, or fact, of perfect measurement encourages the *electorate* to reduce the amount of testing, weighing, and discussion of public policy? If this occurred, we could again agree with Ranney that the polls would be doing a disservice to democracy. But it seems no more probable that knowing what people think today will determine what people will think tomorrow than that it will determine what decision makers decide today. The political nonelites are, after all, influenced by public officials and other opinion leaders just as the reverse is true. The opinion-policy process is a two-way street, and as long as significant numbers of the public recognize the complex nature of this interplay there would seem to be little danger that the polical dialogue will be slowed or ended. The leaders of interest groups will continue to attempt to influence opinion no matter how accurately it is measured. Some individuals and groups seem, in fact, to be more vigorous when they suspect themselves to be in the minority. Those who enjoy majority support know that when the count is taken again their happy position may be reversed or weakened, unless they continue to promote the democratic dialogue. Hardening of the arteries of public controversy is not likely to take place, regardless of polling accuracy. I think it is safe to assert that the dangers Ranney envisioned more than twenty years ago are now no more likely to take place than are the early pollsters' vastly more simple notions that polling heralded the last and perfect stage of democracy.

7.42   Democracy and the Accuracy of Polling

We have considered some criticisms of the methodology and the practical accuracy or inaccuracy of modern public opinion polling; now we turn to the importance of polling accuracy to the political life of a democracy.

One of the most vocal critics of polls in recent years has been Senator Albert Gore of Tennessee. Senator Gore's complaints about the polling brotherhood in 1960 seem to have been in part those of a Democrat responding to poll reports that the Democratic presidential candidate was *not* the people's choice. Candidates and friends of candidates who are reported behind in pre-election polls tend, quite understandably, to take a dim view of poll findings and poll managers alike. Their cause is strengthened in the campaign debate if evidence of inaccuracy can be found or presumed. Thus President Truman suggested that in 1948 there was a "concerted effort of the pollsters and the Republican-controlled press to drug the populace with their statistics and propaganda."[13]

Senator Gore's criticism in 1960 seems to have been, like President Truman's in 1948, a mixture of occasional political tactics and generalized doubt about the possible effects of inaccurate polling. The nonpartisan kernel of Gore's criticism is not that polling may be merely inaccurate, but that leaders and led may accept the inaccuracies as truth, and, acting upon them, may make serious mistakes. "Polls" he says, "may be grossly misleading and . . . their value, if any, is dubious, indeed."[14] Senator Gore seems particularly exercised about three sources of inaccuracy, which, according to him, create misleading impressions among politicians and voters: (a) the statistical presentation of poll results, (b) the effects of name familiarity on voter choice in pre-election polls, and (c) bandwagon effects from early and inadequately qualified "trial heats."

The controversy over how percentage error is to be calculated is an old one.[15] To a man, the pollsters figure their error as a percentage of the 100 per cent sample. Many critics contend that the proper error percentage is obtained by dividing the difference between the predicted and actual vote by the predicted vote. Thus, although Gallup claims that he missed the 1948 Truman vote by 5.4 per cent—he predicted 44.5 and President Truman received 49.9—Gore, Lindsay Rogers, and others assert that the percentage error in this case is over 12 per cent (5.4 divided by 44.5).

This debate may have some interest for partisan maneuvering and forensic effects. For our purposes, it is a quibble which we may deny ourselves. The pollsters' calculation recommends itself, because it involves simpler and more apparent arithmetic.

The possible misleading effect of name familiarity is a more significant matter for polling in a democracy. The argument is simply that respondents often give preference early in the campaign to potential

13 Harry S Truman, *Years of Trial and Hope* (New York: Doubleday & Co., Inc., 1956), p. 178.

14 *Congressional Record,* February 11, 1960, p. 2206.

15 See Frederick Mosteller, "Measuring the Error," *The Pre-Election Polls of 1948,* Social Science Research Council Bulletin 60 (1949), pp. 54–80, especially at pp. 54–58.

candidates merely because they know who these individuals are. Senator Gore suggests that a poll in which this effect is pronounced misleads the public as well as the potential or actual candidates. To test his view that name familiarity has an effect on pre-election responses (he need not have bothered—the literature is full of evidence that it does), in early 1960 he had his office staff poll 182 residents of Washington, D.C., using "an exact duplicate of Dr. Gallup's poll card except that we supplied the names of the persons on the card." The names on the Democratic card were:

1. Allen Dulles
2. John D. Eisenhower
3. Hubert Humphrey
4. Lyndon Johnson
5. Thomas Jefferson Jones
6. John F. Kennedy
7. Franklin D. Roosevelt, Jr.
8. Adlai Stevenson
9. Stuart Symington

Of the 120 respondents who took the Democratic card, Senator Gore reported that "25 per cent listed either Franklin D. Roosevelt, Jr., or John D. Eisenhower as their preference for either first or second choice."[16] Though neither of these persons was a potential candidate, one quarter of the respondents chose them over others who were announced or publicly assumed to be candidates.

Senator Gore queried both Gallup and Roper on, among other things, their views of the effects of name familiarity in pre-election polls. The question was: "Do you consider a poll on presidential candidates a measure of popular support? Or, in your opinion, is it a reflection of familiarity with a name or names, or is it a favorable or unfavorable reaction to a name or names?"[17]

Gallup's reply was equivocal, but Roper candidly replied that early poll results are "certainly much more a reflection of familiarity with names than anything else—until after the campaign itself has started."[18] "In a sense," Mr. Roper declared:

I share *some* of Senator Gore's misgivings, particularly about the effect of the polls on *nominations*. I have been dismayed to find many convention delegates exhibiting an obsessive and exclusive interest in finding a winner, dismayed at the weight given to preconvention polls which are in my opinion little more than a name-familiarity game, but which are often accepted as gospel evidence of the ability to win in November.[19]

---

[16] *Congressional Record*, February 11, 1960, p. 2206.

[17] *Ibid.*, p. 2203.

[18] *Ibid.*, p. 2204.

[19] Elmo Roper, "Polls and Sampling," *Saturday Review*, XLIII (October 8, 1960), 58. Italics in original.

Roper's sensitivity to the effect of name familiarity is further revealed by his comments about the timing of pre-election polls (and, incidentally, in his disclosure that the demands of the mass media may intensify the unfortunate effects of name familiarity):

We do not customarily start doing any research having to do with any aspect of the election until sometime during the year in which the election is to be held, and then we put more effort on trying to find out what might be described as the "general mood" of the people than we do on the "popularity contest" aspect of it—although naturally, in order to get any newspapers or television networks to sponsor us, we have to pay some attention to that.[20]

7.43 The Bandwagon Effect of Pre-Election Polls

The third complaint of many political critics relates to the alleged "bandwagon effect." It is said that undecided and apolitical voters tend to support an apparent victor simply because he is an apparent victor. People, it is said, like to back a winner.

There is little evidence that a bandwagon effect occurs. In the first place, the logic of the argument is not persuasive. People like to back a winner in matters to which they attach importance. But the bandwagon argument supposes that the voter is indifferent to the outcome. It could be argued, then, that the effect cannot occur, by definition, either to the indifferent or to the concerned voter. If the voter is indifferent, he will not care who wins nor whom he votes for—nor will he, at the moment of voting, have any memory of poll predictions; on the other hand, if he favors candidate A, he is not apt to vote for B simply because a poll predicted B's election.[21]

Beyond this argument, which is something of a definitional quibble, it is not at all clear that public faith in the pollsters is high enough after 1948, despite the good showings of 1960 and 1964, to warrant wide adoption of a bandwagon psychology. Roper's comment on possible bandwagon effect merits attention:

20 *Congressional Record,* February 11, 1960, p. 2203.

21 The alleged bandwagon effect in the case of the voter, as described here, is different from the partisan's attempt in a primary or convention to choose a candidate who can "be a winner." The nomination psychology quite properly takes win-ability into consideration; but the bandwagon effect is supposed to induce the voter, regardless of party and other factors, to support a candidate simply because he appears to be a winner. For a somewhat technical discussion of some problems in the measurement of possible bandwagon and "underdog" effects, see the essay "Bandwagon and Underdog Effects of Election Predictions," in Herbert A. Simon, *Models of Man* (New York: John Wiley & Sons, Inc., 1957), pp. 79–87.

I don't think there is much evidence that the polls directly influence the voters' preferences. If there were a "bandwagon effect," it seems to me that polls would always underpredict the margin of victory, since the whole theory of bandwagon is that more and more people jump on it, and there just has to be a week between the last poll and election day. As a matter of fact, surveys have overpredicted the margin of the winner at least as much as they have underpredicted it.[22]

7.44 Significance and Insignificance in Polling

The pollsters ask many questions of little or no political importance. Questions about the adventures of entertainment-world celebrities are only rarely of genuine public interest. But the critics who object to such questions fail to appreciate that the mass media which support the largest pollsters have commercial interests to satisfy as well as public responsibilities to discharge. As long as human-interest stories—even sensational human-interest stories—are sought by the consumers of mass media, the opinion column, whether it is the local "inquiring reporter" or the national Gallup poll, will have a certain fascination as casual reading of the kind that fills the coffee breaks and commuting rides with information that is welcome precisely because it is of no importance.

Jargonized questions, like the questions of no importance to political life, are also easy targets of the antipollsters. Jargon questions are perhaps more deplorable than trivial questions. They may encourage the plain-folks brand of anti-intellectualism that sees stuffily-worded poll questions as the product of "eggheads" who are as removed from the world of real language as they are from the world of real people. But jargon and academese on any subject may have this unfortunate effect, and it is difficult to single out the pollster from all the other abusers of language.

Beyond these two somewhat simple criticisms of the significance of polling are two related but more subtle points bearing on the matter of what is asked of whom.

As we have seen in Chapter 6, it is the unanimous judgment of the most thoughtful students of democracy that the people as a whole are not able to give specific policy direction, although the maintenance of popular government demands that the broad objectives and processes toward which and through which power is directed be approved by the masses. For example, one might say that it is necessary for the American people in general to approve the large-scale, continuous United States involve-

---

[22] *Congressional Record,* February 11, 1960, p. 2204.

ment in European economic and military life that began in 1947, but it is both unnecessary and naive to expect that large numbers of Americans will understand the operation of the European Common Market, or the Coal and Steel Community, or the structure and powers of the North Atlantic Treaty Organization.

Despite the repeated demonstration that a high level of public knowledge and thinking is neither necessary nor expectable (however much it is to be desired), the pollsters often ask questions that are inappropriate to all except a small percentage of the citizens of any society. The following question, aside from being semantically loaded ("to help prevent their going Communistic"), foolishly implies that the average respondent ought to have known how much the United States should spend on foreign aid in fiscal 1957: "During recent years Congress has appropriated about 4 billion dollars each year for countries in other parts of the world to help prevent their going Communistic. Should Congress appropriate the same amount this year or not?"[23]

Finally, it is said that the samples in political polling are sometimes as inappropriate as the questions asked. Herbert Blumer has argued that political polling ought to be weighted according to the political power of the subsamples.[24] This argument is old, and one we have considered earlier in this section, both as it relates to the matter of "effective" opinion in the opinion-policy process and as it bears on the question of whether or not all opinions ought to be known. Here it need only be said that political polling will be held to be significant or insignificant in part by what the report divulges about the persons whose opinions were polled. Each reader may judge for his own needs how significant the poll findings are. The apolitical housewife over her morning coffee may need no more than a dim sensation of someone supporting or opposing something, or agreeing or disagreeing with some opinion or attitude she holds herself. The highly politicized citizen, on the other hand, may subject the findings to a great variety of tests of significance. For the latter, it is important that the pollsters include in their reports all of the pertinent facts about their samples, interviewing techniques, and analysis. On this score, the pollsters' record is far from satisfactory. The comments of Ernst and Loth, in their otherwise somewhat peevish book about the 1948 election polls, are still very much to the point:

---

23 Gallup poll release (Associated Press), February 2, 1956, in the *Arizona Daily Star,* February 3, 1956, p. 10.

24 "Public Opinion and Public Opinion Polling," *American Sociological Review,* XIII (1948), 542–554, reprinted in Daniel Katz et al., *Public Opinion and Propaganda* (New York: Dryden Press, 1954), pp. 70–78.

. . . practically every genuine scientific document is divided into four parts: an introduction; the experiment; the discussion; and the conclusion. But the operators of the polls never gave us an inkling of the experiment. We got fed with a pretty good introduction, we were deluged with discussion, and certainly had conclusions thrown at us. But to this very time we are in the dark as to the experiment. We still don't know the techniques—that is, the interviewers in type, in number, in locale; the persons interviewed, in classes, in number of locations; the statistical compilations with adjustment, weighting factors, the possible variables, and, in fact, any of the bases for the discussion and the conclusion. Perhaps the measurement of public opinion never can be scientific in our present state of knowledge, but certainly a technique which fails to divulge its premises can have small claim to the adjective.[25]

7.5   Opinion Polling by Political Leaders

We have seen that political leaders in a democratic society must give unflagging attention to opinion measurement. Ear-to-the-ground is their common stance, as necessary to their own careers as it is to the maintenance of the channels of political communication. Traditional methods of opinion measurement may still be, at times, more valid than the scientific opinion survey. During the 1948 presidential campaign, when the major pollsters were predicting a Dewey win, Leslie Biffle, the secretary of the Senate and a political friend and aide of President Truman, after traveling through the Border and Western states in the guise of a chicken and egg buyer, reported that Truman would win.[26]

Though often valid, the "horseback" judgments of even the most seasoned politicians cannot match the reliability of scientific surveys. As opinion polling has gained greater respectability, and as its commercial and academic practitioners have developed a body of basic theory and technical skills—gradually overcoming the effects of enthusiastic friends as well as the dangers of attack—even the older politicians have slowly and reluctantly accepted this new technique.

The use of public opinion polling by party organizations, campaign groups, and candidates is a fairly new thing. On the basis of his experience with Democratic Party groups, including a period of eight months in 1952 as public opinion and election analyst with the Democratic National Committee, Lewis Dexter concluded that party organizations could

[25] Morris L. Ernst and David Loth, *The People Know Best: The Ballots vs. the Polls* (Washington: Public Affairs Press, 1949), pp. 143–144. Reprinted by permission of Public Affairs Press.

[26] Hedley Donovan, "How to Be a Political Prophet," *Fortune,* XLVI (September 1952), 192.

neither ignore the journalistic polls nor make much use of them. Dexter's argument was a good one. He declared that the nationwide sampling techniques were not closely related either to the political structures through which elections are conducted—single-member constituencies (often gerrymandered), plurality elections, and the electoral college—or to known patterns of voting behavior. To be useful in political campaigns, he wrote, polls must be specially designed to answer specific questions about strength and weakness; "this means that they must be designed with voting behavior and election statistics in mind."[27]

Since 1952, presidential campaign organizations have made increasing use of opinion pollsters. Greater amounts of campaign money are available in presidential than in other campaign years, and polls are among the frills that, through a cooperative trickle-down process, candidates for lesser offices may share. In 1960, the Kennedy strategists hired Louis Harris Associates to do a large number of specialized polls of candidate strength and issue interest in many states and among many voter groups. Claude Robinson, Inc., a Princeton agency using Gallup data, conducted many similar polls and analyses for the Nixon campaign.

Despite increasing reliance on professional, scientific pollsters, many political leaders remain suspicious and reluctant. Political polling is hardly the love child of the sociologist and the politician; it is more like the needed heir which the political king fathers for the good of the realm. Polling is, at least psychologically, an act of weakness for the candidate. There is, of course, a certain amount of so-called polling which is faked, wholly or in part, the predetermined results of which are eagerly taken and printed by a gullible press. This is all in the tradition of fairness in love and war, and is a matter of pride to the perpetrators.

But an honest poll is an admission by the candidate and his managers that they do not know their constituency. Before World War II, straw polls were newspaper vagaries of the human-interest type. There was no reason to believe that they were any better, as election predictors, than ancient ear-to-the-ground techniques. However, the development of scientific sampling just before World War II posed a new threat to the politician's monopoly of political skills. By the *Literary Digest* debacle in 1936 he was freed, probably forever, from the threat of the straw poll; and

27 Lewis Anthony Dexter, "The Use of Public Opinion Polls by Political Party Organizations," *Public Opinion Quarterly*, XVIII (1954), 53–61, quotation at 57.

The British parties did not make significant use of opinion polling until 1957, when the Conservatives first employed some surveys. According to one observer, the Labor Party was slower to appreciate the use of polling, and it is suggested that the parties of the left tend to be generally more distrustful of opinion surveys. Mark Abrams, "Public Opinion Polls and Political Parties," *Public Opinion Quarterly*, XXVII (1963), 9–18. See also, by the same author, "Opinion Polls and Party Propaganda," *Public Opinion Quarterly*, XXVIII (1964), 13–19.

he rejoiced in the news that James Farley, the politician's politician, had exactly predicted the electoral vote while the *Digest* was ludicrously in error. But 1936 carried a new and more real threat to the politicians. The nose of the scientific-poll camel was clearly inside the tent. Each of the three national polling organizations, with unbelievably small samples, had quite accurately predicted Roosevelt's landslide win. And for twelve years in national elections—few careful polls were done in state and local elections until after World War II—the pollsters maintained a record of accuracy in predicting presidential results.

Then came 1948 and the joy of the politicians who thought they had rewon their monopoly of the inside-dopester field with the downfall of the pollsters. The taunts of the politicians and of the press—which likes to be in on all kills, whether highway tragedies or the execution of celebrated criminals—have followed the pollsters ever since. One of former President Truman's favorite themes is that the pollsters had counted him out before the fight:

Almost unanimously the polls taken before the 1948 Democratic convention showed my popularity with the American people to have hit an all time low. . . .

I never paid any attention to the polls myself, because in my judgment they did not represent a true cross section of American opinion. . . .

The 1948 election proved the pollsters and forecasters so wrong and unreliable that to this day their reputations have not been fully restored and their influence is much reduced.[28]

It is doubtful whether even the remarkable accuracy of the pollsters in 1960 has rehabilitated them among the political scoffers. *Rehabilitate* may, in any case, be the wrong word. The pollsters have never enjoyed a comfortable relationship with the majority of politicians. Some politicians, however, have quite openly and successfully used public opinion polls for strategy purposes. Nelson Rockefeller has received some well-deserved publicity not only for his use of polls but for his bold acceptance of their findings.[29] In his planning and campaigning for the 1958 gubernatorial race in New York, Rockefeller ordered "the incredible total of 134 general and special public opinion polls and expert studies of other types."[30] Before the 1960 Republican national convention it was reported that he would decide, on the basis of public opinion polls whether to challenge

---

[28] Truman, *Years of Trial and Hope* (see footnote 13), pp. 177, 221.

[29] It is said that Rockefeller and Judson Morhouse, former New York State Republican Chairman, acquired their faith in the polls from former Governor Thomas E. Dewey. Leo Egan, "The Hunch That Paid Off for Nelson Rockefeller," *The Reporter*, XIX (November 27, 1958), 16.

[30] Joseph Alsop, column in the *Arizona Daily Star*, August 27, 1959.

Vice-President Nixon for the presidential nomination.[31] Rockefeller later denied that he would decide on the basis of the polls; but there is no doubt that he, and all other serious contenders for presidential nominations, rely heavily on opinion surveys.

But Governor Rockefeller and other presidential contenders are exceptional, not only because they freely use opinion polls but because they understand the value and limitations of polls and do not share the largely inarticulate fears of other politicians.

The aversion which many politicians have to scientific opinion polling seems to be a mixture of distrust born of their misunderstanding of the polling tool and of fear born of what they think might be the public reaction to their polling activities.

The first source of distrust has already been alluded to. It is hard for the politician to accept the aid of nonpoliticians, using nonpolitical methods, to procure that most crucial item of political information, the intention of the voter. The politicians, as Kriesberg puts it, "feel polls are challenging their prerogative of interpreting the public will."[32] Yet the politician also feels himself trapped, for the pollsters have demonstrated that they might have a contribution to make to his campaign and election.

Beyond the loss of his monopoly in the prediction of voting behavior, the politician who employs pollsters faces some mathematical and technical facts which look like legerdemain, gimmickry, or both. The politician cannot be expected, in general, to be much more knowledgeable than the average citizen about polling. At a 1959 meeting of the Democratic National Committee's Advisory Committee on Political Organization, three of the nation's top academic public opinion experts for more than one hour described how opinion research could be utilized by politicians. At the end of their presentation, the chairman of the Democratic Committee in one important state arose, obviously vexed and annoyed, and asked why, if there was so much of this "scientific" polling going on, hadn't he or any of his friends ever been asked their opinions. This is the oldest bromide, and the most unsophisticated (and perhaps most common) question asked of pollsters. The state chairman had sat through an hour's presentation with this doubt and question in his mind; he had obviously learned nothing about what the polls could or could not do for politicians.

The fault is not wholly the politicians'. They may be excused in part for not knowing which way to turn in the face of contradictory pressures. Uncertain of their own predictive abilities, yet resenting and dis-

---

[31] Homer Bigart, "National Polls Put Nixon Ahead," *New York Times,* August 5, 1959.

[32] Martin Kriesberg, "What Congressmen and Administrators Think of the Polls," *Public Opinion Quarterly,* IX (1945), 337.

trusting the predictive ability of others, they may understandably deflate the claims of commercial pollsters whom they suspect care more about their accounts (and cash) before election day than about the candidates' fate on that day. And they may misapprehend the often turgid or jargonized account of opinion polling given by academic advisers.

There is a need for some persons or agencies to make available to the practicing politician the findings of public opinion research. A number of political candidates and officeholders use opinion research with considerable regularity and skill; these tend to be the candidates or incumbents of high national or large-state offices. But great numbers of politicans use either no opinion research or that which is either deliberately or unintentionally biased. It has been suggested that governmental agencies—perhaps attached to state universities or private academic centers—be established to (a) collect the results of opinion research pertinent to electoral behavior and public policy; (b) arrange, summarize, and, in some cases, "translate" these results into usable forms for political and governmental leaders; and (c) actively disseminate these materials to those for whom they are produced.

In 1959, the Advisory Council of the Democratic National Committee felt these arguments keenly enough to bring George Belknap, a public opinion expert from the University of California, to the staff of the National Committee under the somewhat euphemistic title of "consultant in voting analysis." Belknap's study of crowd reaction, mentioned in Chapter 2, was just one of his assignments from the Democratic National Committee in 1959–1960.

"Simulmatics" is the most recent technique by which opinion research is made usable for political strategists. Large-scale computer programming was first done by the Kennedy organization in 1960. Social scientists from M.I.T., Yale, and Columbia made use of a complex of data-processing machines to analyze probable public opinion on various strategies which the presidential candidate might follow. Data from sixty-six surveys, representing a total of more than 130,000 interviews with the American public from 1952 to 1959, were fed into the machines; on the basis of these data, it was possible to make forecasts of future electoral behavior. Newspaper columnist Roscoe Drummond called the Kennedy computer project a "People Predictor," able to "forecast public reaction to alternative possibilities in a way that makes public opinion sampling seem as slow and outdated as a horse and buggy. . . ."[33] The figure is misleading. The Simulmatics Project (an awesome name—"People Predictor" might indeed be better) is no different from public opinion sampling; it is merely the projection of opinion trends from a time series

[33] *New York Herald Tribune,* December 19, 1960.

of samples. But it is a new and potentially very significant way to use public opinion data.[34]

The use of funded poll data and computers to predict the possible effects of campaign strategy is not the only source of developing friction between traditional election procedures and the possibilities of modern technology. Simulmatics makes use of polling and election data about hypothetical people and states, and other computer operations handle data from bellwether or swing-voting constituencies—data which, because of their complex nature, can only be effectively analyzed by electronic means. But, just as such information before an election can be extremely useful in planning campaign strategy, so it can give us a basis for early prediction of winners after the votes in only a few such bellwether districts are counted.

Recognizing the possibilities of "scoop by computers," the major television networks, in 1964, employed sampling for the reporting of election returns. In the critical California Republican primary of June 1964, the Columbia Broadcasting System, using what it called "Voter Profile Analysis," predicted Senator Goldwater's victory on the basis of just 42 of the more than 32,000 precincts in the state. Moreover, that declaration of victory came with twenty-two minutes of the closing of the polls in Los Angeles, *and before the polls were closed, in some areas of the state.*

Many political leaders and others concerned with the protection of voting rights and procedures saw dangers in the possibility of computer prediction of election winners before all voters had cast their ballots. Some critics argued that people would be discouraged from voting if the results could be more or less confidently known before the polls were closed. Others argued that a bandwagon effect would occur in the last minutes of voting as persons switched to the apparent winner. Defenders of the television networks countered that the use of computers to speed up voting analysis is only an extension of similar predictions made by political pundits on the basis of key districts.

Yet the demonstrated accuracy of electronic devices gives greater importance to early computer predictions of victory. The premature computer reporting of election results could be most serious in national elections. In the summer of 1964, Midwestern and Western congressmen were quite properly concerned by "the serious possibilities for unduly influencing election results by telling the country how the vast cities and populous states of the East have made their decisions before millions of Americans

---

34 See Ithiel de Sola Pool, Robert P. Abelson, and Samuel L. Popkin, *Candidates, Issues, and Strategies: A Computer Simulation of the 1960 Presidential Election* (Cambridge, Mass.: M.I.T. Press, 1964); Ithiel de Sola Pool and Robert Abelson, "The Simulmatics Project," *Public Opinion Quarterly,* XXV (1961), 167–183; and P. Kugel, "Computers and Political Strategy," *Computers and Automation,* May 1962, pp. 11ff.

farther west have exercised their solemn duty of voting for the candidates of their choice."[35] Some members of Congress thought a simple congressional resolution would suffice to persuade the networks to exercise self-restraint in the announcement of computer-proclaimed victories. One senator proposed a bill to outlaw the broadcast of both *returns and predictions* until all polls had closed in the United States. Other senators moved to establish a uniform closing time for federal elections—one version would close the polls at 11 P.M. in the Eastern time zone and at 5 P.M. in the Bering time zone (the farthest west zone of the Alaska islands). Some combination of self-restraint and legislation will no doubt be found to protect the integrity of the ballots of late voters and at the same time maintain a large measure of freedom for the news media to report and analyze election returns.[36]

The State of Washington has taken some steps in the direction of servicing candidates and public officials with reliable and nonpartisan opinion research. In 1947, the Washington Public Opinion Laboratory was established, with public appropriations, at the state University and Washington State College. The following kinds of activity have been conducted by the Laboratory:

civic research—to find the facts and amplify the voice of the people on current issues and problems; *basic research*—to learn how to predict and guide social behavior; *technical research*—to improve methods of polling; and *personnel training*—to help build up a body of scientists thoroughly trained in social research.[37]

The Washington Public Opinion Laboratory may be only an extension of the information services already offered by the governments of many states to their citizens and political decision makers. On referendum questions, a number of states require the distribution of information pamphlets that typically describe the ballot items and present arguments by those who support and oppose the measures. Likewise, legislators in many states are given research facilities and aids to help them in deliberations

---

[35] Senator Karl Mundt (R., South Dakota), *Congressional Record*, August 12, 1964, p. 18485.

[36] Of 2,961 voters interviewed in forty Oregon precincts between 5 P.M. and the time the polls closed, November 3, 1964, nearly 60 per cent had heard Eastern election returns before voting. While only nineteen persons said they changed their votes because of early returns, the study director, from other evidence, suspected the number of changers was in fact greater. See "Returns Affect Few in Oregon," *Broadcasting*, November 16, 1964, p. 102.

[37] Stuart C. Dodd, "The Washington Public Opinion Laboratory," *Public Opinion Quarterly*, XII (1948), 118. Italics in original.

and decisions. Publicly supported opinion- and attitude-measuring agencies might be justified in the way that such research organizations have been. A combination of both public and private opinion survey agencies, it seems, would serve the interests of democracy better than either kind alone.

PART THREE

THE
ENVIRONMENT
OF OPINION

In Part Two we dealt with public opinion as an intangible but important ingredient of self-governing polities. We suggested a definition and examined the component parts of public opinion, and we explored the interactions of opinions and public policy formation.

The scope and objectives of Part Three are quite different. In the six chapters that follow, we shall consider the reasons why opinions tend to develop in recognizable and, within some limits, predictable patterns.

Social scientists, journalists, and other students of human behavior are normally concerned with *differences* of opinion. The sociologist may be interested in why (and to what extent) city dwellers hold opinions different from those of suburbanites, or why immigrants think differently from second- or third-generation Americans; political scientists may be interested in why and to what extent Republicans hold views different from Democrats; economists are concerned with differences between buyer and seller or manufacturer and distributor. Our mass media (insofar as they have direct social impact), our research and teaching postures at the college level, and our public policy-forming processes concern themselves with *dis*agreements. We focus our attention, quite properly, on the conflicts of opinion in society; for it is only through vigorous but regulated opinion conflict that vitality is maintained and adaptive change is possible.

At the same time, each person does share a large

number of opinions with all other persons—although the conditions that determine the vast amount of agreement in the community of man, and in all the subcommunities from nation to family, are seldom considered. The social scientists whose business it is constantly to analyze opinions either directly or indirectly—and the man on the street, when he thinks about opinions—realize that most people agree with most other people about most things. Stated so flatly, this may sound like an irresponsible assertion or an unimportant truism. It is neither. Rather, it is a profoundly important simplicity.

Thus, though our attention is drawn primarily to opinion conflict and disagreement, it is well to notice the existence and importance of the massive substratum of agreement within any society. The great bulk of facts and opinions that are shared and unquestioned by almost every person in every society—the familiar "submerged mass of the iceberg"—makes possible and supports the smaller and visible contention that is our major concern in the analysis of public policy and social change.

The body of opinion agreement, which may be called *consensus* (although we have seen that that term is itself subject to abuse and ambiguity), has a most important function as the guarantor of social stability. It also has significance for the individual.

The plain truth is that most opinions are determined not by an effort of personal reason or will but by events and forces over which the individual has little or no control. What we are, what we know, and what we believe are determined in very large degree by conditions we never made and influences we have little power to change—despite the fact that the range of theoretically possible opinions is almost infinite.

Most people know, for instance, that the world is a globe. Therefore, it is impossible for them to believe that anyone could reach the sun by traveling east in the morning. Yet a few thousand years ago, perhaps even a few hundred years ago, most people could and did believe precisely that. Some primitive people no doubt still believe that the world is flat; and related to their acceptance of that opinion is the fact that they are denied thousands of other beliefs about modern astronomy, geography, and physics. The flatness or globularity of the earth is not now an issue around which public opinion can cluster, although before the voyages of the fifteenth-century Mediterraneans (of whom Columbus was only one) it may have been.

Another way of stating this elementary but important point is that many opinions are both *cumulative* and *exclusive*. Almost every opinion (or knowledge of fact—which, for the moment, is not distinguished from opinion) makes possible additional opinions at the same time that it denies the possibility of still other opinions. If I believe that an object is 100 cubic feet in size, I know that it will not fit in an area of 10 cubic feet but will fit an area of 200 cubic feet. If I think that candidate A is a completely honest man, I cannot believe my neighbor's report that he has been bribed (or that he knowingly lied during the campaign or that he is capable of crime in office); but I can easily hold any number of opinions about him consistent with my pivotal belief in his integrity. If I accept the fundamental tenets of a religion, I can as easily believe all its ancillary and supplementary doctrines; but any belief in contrary religious dogma is most unlikely.

We should be careful here. It is obvious that individuals can hold, simultaneously, opinions which are contradictory and even mutually exclusive, just as social groups can contain individuals whose views are different from, and even incompatible with, the opinions of other group members. The point is only that there are powerful influences that produce (a) vast amounts of agreement in human opinion, (b) clustering of opinions among cultural groups, and (c) certain patterns of inclusive and exclusive opinions within the individual.

In Part Three, we suggest a way of thinking about the influences and factors that produce both the uniformities and the differences in opinion holding. We are concerned with the physical growth and limitations of the individual and with the world of his mind, with the cultural and social influences that create the environment in which opinions form, and with some of the dynamics of the opinion-forming process.

OPINION FORMATION: APPROACHES AND A MODEL

8

For our purposes, opinions are *expressed points of view* about matters which are *controversial* or *capable of controversy;* public opinions are distinguished from private opinions on the basis of how many people are affected by the issue in controversy.

At this point, we are dealing with opinions, both public and private, and we are asking the simple question: What is the process, and what are the factors influencing this process, by which we come to have any particular opinions at any particular time?

8.1 Various Approaches to the Study of Opinion Holding

We can approach opinion holding in a number of ways. The simplest, and most congenial to the intellectual traditions of the West, is the *rationalist* approach. Human reason, the rationalist would say, determines opinions. Man is a thinking animal—*the* thinking animal. By the exercise of his reason, man is able to form both fact and opinion.

Opinions may be deduced from facts (i.e., from observed physical reality) and from laws. Men hold different opinions, the rationalist declares, because men do not all understand the facts and the laws equally well; if all men thoroughly comprehended the laws (facts of the physical world are manifestations of the laws) and acted in accordance with them, human reason would be the perfect instrument for the social organization of the perfect world.

It would be inappropriate here to attempt a summary of the history of rationalism in the Western world. Inappropriate, presumptuous, and, fortunately, unnecessary. The rationalist tradition, however, has been dominant throughout most of our history since Plato—and even today it is probably as respectable, in the world of the intellectuals, as any other tradition; and, no doubt, it is widely accepted among the literate public. Christianity (especially Catholicism) has contributed greatly to the dominance of rationalism in Western thought. Theoretical and applied science, too, has appeared to most observers to strengthen the belief that the physical world, at least, is tidily organized by unchangeable laws which have only to be discovered by human reason.

It may be that the physical world *is* controlled and determined by laws that, in time, will be discovered in their entirety by scientific inquiry. Many rationalists, however, are more totalitarian in their claims for reason as authority. Some argue that divine law, though unknowable in its entirety, is the great source and encompasser of the moral law, the civil law, and all lesser laws. These rationalists hold that both faith and reason are means for knowing truth—although one is obliged to say that the content of faith and reason for them seems determined not so much by the individual mind as by the authoritative doctrine of hierarchical organizations.

Rationalist thought in America is influenced less by the scholastic rationalism of the Catholic thinkers than by the Protestant and humanistic rationalism of continental European philosophers of the seventeenth and eighteenth centuries. Descartes and Rousseau, especially, made significant contributions to the belief that "true knowledge is obtained by the use of certain absolute principles given with the mind and constituting the reason."[1] For Descartes (whose influence in the natural sciences has been especially strong), these "absolute principles" were mathematically formulated; for Rousseau, they were the "natural rights" of man (which largely explains his influence in Western political thought).

What has philosophical rationalism to do with the study of opinion holding? Simply this. Those who accept any of the various subtypes of systematic rationalism are inclined to think that people arrive at their opinions through the exercise of their powers of reason and that the truth or falsity of opinions consist in their correspondence with some ideal truth or nonhuman laws.[2]

---

[1] Hugh Miller, *An Historical Introduction to Modern Philosophy* (New York: Macmillan Co., 1947), Chap. 14, "The Romantic Philosophy of Modern Science," p. 268.

[2] For a brief modern statement of the traditional (i.e., eighteenth-century) rationalist view, which underlies much of American political theory, see *Religion and American Society: A Statement of Principles* (Santa Barbara, Calif.: Center for the Study of Democratic Institutions, 1961). For example, the American political "consensus . . . represents the product of human reason reflecting on experience"; it is possible because "men who are agreed on general principles are more likely to reach rational decisions. . . . The men who argue for consensus are ultimately dependent on their belief that there *are* truths, not merely of a scientific but of a rational, philosophic, and political kind, which are the product of human reflection, are accessible to all, and are 'objective' " (pp. 56, 58; italics in original).

Later, I shall return to the discussion of the place of reason and deliberation in opinion holding and opinion change. Meanwhile, the course of honesty is to admit that I do not think that human reason is the only or even the principal determinant of human opinions. There is, as I shall try to show, an important place for reason and intellectual calculation in what is for me a helpful theory of opinion holding; but no one can make wholly rational decisions on every issue, and most people find it impossible to do so on any issues at all. We have seen, in Chapter 6, that the recognition of the fact that there are large, nonreasoning elements in political life has necessitated the reformulation of democratic theory. Opinion holding and decision making, closely allied in the opinion-policy process, are both largely nonrational; every analysis which overlooks the pervasiveness of nonreason, and which assumes the consistent and thorough use of reason, is bound to raise more questions than it settles.

Psychologists, especially Freudian psychologists, offer us another approach to the study of opinion holding. Psychoanalysis (Freudian psychiatry) provides a basis for a number of fairly specific propositions about, and some would say a nearly complete explanation of, attitude and opinion holding. Oversimplified, the Freudian view is that experiences in infancy and early childhood determine the personality structure and attitude patterns of the adult individual; these in turn limit and shape not only his self-image but his social outlook and his views of political issues. His private and public opinions emerge, therefore, as a limited and usually distorted part of what is possible for the human mind to believe.

Probably the most ambitious attempt by Freudian psychologists to explain political opinion holding is the research done for and following the study of the authoritarian personality. A large amount of fairly systematic survey data was collected during the years 1944 to 1947 by a team of psychologists and other behavioral scientists. From the basic studies came a number of works, of which the most important, substantively, was *The Authoritarian Personality*.[3]

The authors of *The Authoritarian Personality* attempted to link the attitudes and opinions of individuals with the personality characteristics formed by their respondents' separate life histories. Personality, to these authors, is "an agency through which sociological influences upon ideology are mediated." Our opinions are, in large part, a result of the way we perceive and "internalize" social events and ideas.

Although personality is a product of the social environment of the past, it is not, once it has developed, a mere object of the contemporary environment. What has developed is a *structure* within the individual, something which is capable of

[3] T. W. Adorno, Else Frenkel-Brunswik, D. J. Levinson, and R. N. Sanford, *The Authoritarian Personality* (New York: Harper & Row, Publishers, 1950).

self-initiated action upon the social environment and of selection with respect to varied impinging stimuli, something which though always modifiable is frequently very resistant to change. This conception is necessary to explain the consistency of behavior in widely varying situations, to explain the persistence of ideological trends in the face of contradictory facts and radically altered social conditions, to explain why people in the same sociological situation have different or even conflicting views on social issues, and why it is that people whose behavior has been changed through psychological manipulation lapse into their old ways as soon as the agencies of manipulation are removed.[4]

Sociological analysis offers a different approach to the study of opinion holding, one that relies heavily upon the idea that opinions are shaped by the cultural traditions, social institutions, and group norms of the society in which every individual finds himself.

A great deal of evidence indicates that most persons take their opinions ready-made, from that stock of acceptable views nearest at hand, and tailor them only slightly in putting them on or taking them off as more current fashions come along. This evidence has accumulated from the studies of three disciplines that are not neatly distinct in their theoretical or professional foundations: social anthropology, sociology, and social psychology. Since W. I. Thomas's monumental work *The Polish Peasant in Europe and America* (1918), the study of what has come to be called personality-in-culture has illuminated many aspects of the relationship between the thought and behavior of individuals, on the one side, and, on the other, the cultural requirements or expectations which bear upon the individual in his relations with those about him. The anthropologists have found that the patterns and individual acts of human behavior are almost unbelievably varied. So much diversity, in fact, has been discovered in the rules (permissions and prohibitions) of human societies that lists of practices found in all cultures are invariably short.

But cultural compulsions are not the only social forces that shape individual opinions. Large-scale social organization further narrows the effective choices individuals may make; interests of class, caste, and secondary-group memberships (such as national citizenship, religious identifications, and professional affiliations) invariably reduce the alternative opinions that affected individuals hold on various issues. For instance, what is the landlord's opinion apt to be on rent-control laws, what the Roman Catholic priest's view on birth-control clinics, and what the Negro's view of segregated schools? It is important to remember, however, that secondary-group identifications, or any social or cultural factors, do not *determine* opinions. There are Negroes who favor segregated schools, landlords who support rent-control laws, and there may even be Catholic priests who favor birth-control clinics. We are concerned here with in-

[4] *Ibid.*, p. 6. Reprinted by permission of Harper & Row, Publishers. Italics in original.

fluence and probabilities. Influence is always more or less, and should be distinguished from causation. When factor A is solely responsible for action B, we speak of causation. When factor A combines with unknown or unenumerated factors to produce action B, we speak of A as having influence (along with other factors involved), and the total complex of factors as being the cause. Because we are talking about influence and probabilities—remember the discussion in Chapter 3 about the inability to predict single cases from mathematical rules of probabilities—we are dealing with the likelihood, not the certainty, that the sociological environment will be related to individual opinion in some way that is not simply a chance relationship. The large-group factors, like class, nationality, occupation, religion, and education patterns, have been, traditionally, the bailiwick of the sociologists; and we look to them for an understanding of how these factors bear on opinion holding.

But small-group factors are important too. Most of the evidence indicates that they are more important than the large-group factors. The study of the relationships of small numbers of people has produced the new, integrative discipline of social psychology. The psychologists, who began with the study of the individual as individual, have enlarged their province, while some sociologists have focused more closely on the person. The two areas of study have joined, rather uneasily and uncertainly, in social psychology. And it is social psychology, more than any other discipline or combination of disciplines, that has greatly added in recent years to our understanding of the why and how of opinion holding. Probably the most important contributions of the social psychologists have been made through the study of small-group relationships and through an improved understanding of role perception. We will consider these contributions in more detail later. For the moment, it is only necessary to point out that our opinions are strongly influenced both by the network of friends and acquaintances whom we see often, or who are important to us, and by the "images" we have of who we are and of what opinions we deem appropriate for who we are.

There is one other specialized way to study opinion holding. Of all the approaches, this is the least satisfactory and the most subject to intellectual attack in the Western world. It is the theory (sometimes called the philosophy) of economic determinism.

Despite the fact that economic determinism is now thought by non-Marxist thinkers to be not very useful in explaining or predicting human thought and behavior, it is nevertheless an important concept in the 1960s, (a) because large numbers of Western nonintellectuals *do* subscribe in considerable degree to this theory, (b) because the "official" doctrines of all Communist societies require their approved thinkers to espouse a theory of economic determinism, and (c) because there are, indeed, clear economic influences on the formation and maintenance of individual opinions.

Let's take the last point first. A few paragraphs back, we suggested that we could expect the large social category of "landlords" to oppose rent control, and we suggested that their shared characteristics (their being landlords) was related to this opinion. It is likely, however, that the influential factors are not social but economic. The implication that the social factor is related to opinion holding is probably a spurious relationship. The major influence in landlords' opposition to rent control is no doubt as economic as it is simple—rent control would reduce their incomes.

Although many opinions are influenced by economic factors, the relationship is seldom pure. Noneconomic factors are almost always present, and usually more important. Nonetheless, two forms of economic determinism are much admired today. One, popular in the Western world and of great significance in the United States, is the result of the theories of Manchester economics and free-enterprise capitalism. Now held in its extreme form only by a relatively small number of Americans (but in less extreme form subscribed to—at least at the verbal and sloganized levels—by millions), this view holds that costs and prices of goods and services are determined by the unregulated exchange of goods and services between buyer and seller. That this kind of economic order "determines" noneconomic elements of human life is evident from the morality associated with it (e.g., that the "good" man is a frugal, sober, hard-working lover of his individualism); from the political theory and practice it implies (a government of minimum powers, protecting property and freedom of contract); and from the social organization to which it tends (inequality of wealth and sharp class distinctions).

The other brand of economic determinism is the Marxist. To oversimplify again, this theory holds that (all) social relationships at any given period in time result from the forms of production dominant at that period. Thus, in a slave economy, all society is shaped by the economic relationships existing between slave and owner; in a feudal society, all is determined by the relation between serf and landowner; and in a capitalist society, all is determined by the economic relations between capitalist and worker. Like all simplistic theories—especially, perhaps, those that demand or suggest clear courses of action—this view has superficial appeal; and it has just enough historical substance so that, in the hands of a powerful thinker and writer like Karl Marx, it could become the ideological vehicle for vast revolutionary forces in the past hundred years. But wide acceptance does not make a theory true—although it does make it important. The importance of the Marxist version of economic determinism is, internationally, that the opinions of Communist officials are heavily influenced by this theory, and, domestically (by an interesting twist), that the social analysis of economic influence has been distorted and impeded by a pervasive and undiscriminating anticommunism. At precisely the moment in history when the relationships between economic and noneconomic elements of society ought to be most diligently studied, the attempt to do so has been condemned as giving aid and comfort to the ideology of the Soviet Union. To suggest, for instance, that the corporate form of modern capitalism may not be wholly compatible with democracy is to incur the censure of those for whom the slogans of a theoretical free enterprise have become the embodiment of eternal truth.

Although economic determinism, in short, is not a very useful theory for the understanding of political opinions, economic factors play an important and, on occasion, decisive part in the shaping of our opinions on issues. Any approach to the study of opinion holding must recognize this fact, and deal with it satisfactorily.

8.2   Needed—A Synthesis of Approaches to Opinion Holding

What is needed is a way of combining the relevant theories and evidence on physical growth, psychic development, sociological influence, economic factors, and reason. One needs an *organism-in-the-environment* approach. Nothing less will do. No single-factor explanation can suffice.

Now, it is easy to say that such a prescription is needed. It is easy for social scientists, singly and in convention, to remind each other that the factors with which they deal are manifold and cannot be reduced to what Gordon Allport calls the "simple and sovereign remedy."

But on the other side is the equally simple fact that *some* generalization is necessary. Common sense tells us that we cannot mark, measure, and explain every influence which may have played on every opinion. When we are dealing with a single opinion of a single individual, it is often easy to isolate a number of prior opinions or experiences that are related to, have influenced, or perhaps even "caused" the opinion in question. Other opinions and experiences of this person are considered irrelevant to the explanation of the opinion being examined—although, in the present state of knowledge, no one could *prove* that other opinions and experiences are irrelevant. Still, considerable agreement can be obtained among analysts of the opinions of individuals, and the libraries are full of books and theses explaining "the influence of X on Y," and "—istic thought as reflected in the writings of Lilen's novels."

It is difficult to explain single or related opinions of single individuals. More difficult is the attempt to generalize about the origins and formation of opinions. Although the exegesis of single opinions, or of the opinions of single individuals, may proceed in terms of simple fact and real experience, the discussion of opinion formation in general must necessarily proceed on the basis of projections of samples of real experiences, on the basis of judgments, and to a considerable extent on an accumulation of tentative conclusions, any one of which is open to question. Upon careful study, we can determine, for example, that Mr. Black's opinions about the Democratic Party result from his early home life with rabidly Republican parents, his experiences as an adult in a city controlled by an Irish-Catholic Democratic "boss," his distrust of Catholics in political office generally, his regular exposure to five strongly Republican newspapers and magazines, and probably a number of other specifically identifiable influences. But, to provide a framework for the analysis of opinion formation generally—or a theory, as it were, about the dynamics of opinion formation—we have to generalize these and other influences that the observation and study of many single individuals may lead us to believe play to some extent on all or most individuals. We may then suppose that these kinds and categories and types of influences are factors of greater or lesser importance in the formation, maintenance, and change of all human opinion.[5]

To say this is to say no more than that we employ the scientific method of observation, generalization, hypothesis formation, and testing. Our great problem, the one that makes the scientific study of human behavior so vastly more difficult than the study of the nonhuman environment, is that, for a number of reasons, we have (a) more factors ("variables," in technical language) to contend with, and (b) less opportunity to control these factors. Despite this major difficulty, common sense—in addition to experience with scientific techniques—tells us that in ordinary life we are generally successful in applying a theory of human behavior, and a theory about opinions, to everyday happenings. Scientific method is systematic common sense. Day by day we observe regularities in human behavior. We come, quite properly, to expect regularities in our own thought and action

[5] In the consideration of public opinion phenomena, we should try to keep clear in our minds that we operate on two levels of analysis. On one, we deal with group and statistical probabilities, where the mathematical language of sampling, percentages, and tests of significance may be employed; prediction on this level is always a matter of estimating how groups of individuals will divide in their opinions. On the other level, we deal with the individual who forms and expresses opinions. It is necessary in the discussion of public opinion to move smoothly and often from one level of discourse to the other. It is important, but not always easy, to make clear which level we are dealing with at a given point. Sometimes we need to view opinion phenomena from the perspective of the individual; sometimes our attention must be given to mass regularities or irregularities. In this chapter, we have focused primarily on the individual and have summarized the various approaches ("conceptual frameworks," if you like) to the study of why persons hold the opinions they do.

and in the behavior patterns of others. We respond in similar ways to similar situations, because the tendency to conserve our energies leads us into repetitious responses (habits), which do not have to be thought through each time they are made. It is therefore necessary for the individual to develop habitual responses, in order to avoid the wasted effort of repeated analysis of the same data. When we awake in the morning, we engage in a number of routine tasks; we do not stop to consider the arguments for and against each action on that particular morning, because, quite simply, it is easier not to. We have learned that it is generally less wasteful of energy and time to wash our face each morning than to make a careful examination of the reasons why we should or should not wash our face on any particular morning. Habits save our attention for dealing with situations which are less common and therefore less able to be successfully routinized.

Besides this psychological importance of habits, there is a vital social reason why routinization of behavior is essential. In order to live together at all, human beings must be able to predict with reasonable certainty the daily behavior of others. In order to achieve even the simplest objective, I must each day be able to depend upon a regular pattern of behavior by hundreds of other people. The network of habitual, interdependent human behavior is the primary social-psychological condition of society.

Although this statement is as simple and as obvious as it is profound, like other obvious and profound facts it deserves some attention. All social stability arises from this predictable network of repeated human responses to repeated situations of fact. The stability of opinion and the predictability of opinion response depend equally upon habitual responses to repeated fact situations. Therefore, not only can we count on regular and generally peaceful social interaction among large numbers of people, but also—and more important for our purposes here—we do not need to consider all the potential or conceivable factors that *might have* influenced the opinions of any given individual or group. If we know enough about the physical, cultural, social, and intellectual history of the individual or group, we can be reasonably sure that many opinions will not be held by the individual or group of individuals, and that other opinions are apt to be held with greater or lesser degrees of frequency and intensity.

To sum up this major point: There are important practical limits to the range of opinions (and attitudes) held by single human beings and by social groups. These limits are determined by (a) the habit principle, which minimizes individual exertion and makes social interaction possible; and (b) physical, cultural, and social factors that make certain opinions likely.

8.3 The Funnel of Causality:
a Model for the Analysis of Opinion Formation

A few pages earlier I suggested that the causes of specific opinions held by specific persons at a particular point in time might, with great care, be discovered. Generalizations cannot be made, however, to the effect that opinion X is always a result of factors A–*n*. I have said repeatedly—for it bears repeating—that the lone opinion cannot be predicted from a sample of opinions. But I have also suggested that some factors tend to be associated with creating, strengthening, or weakening certain opinions, while other factors tend to be associated with creating, strengthening, or weakening other opinions. Thus, although we cannot predict any specific relationships between influencing factors and opinion, we can (and do, in everyday life) think in terms of general and probabilistic relationships between influencing factors and opinion.

It may be helpful to analyze opinion formation and opinion holding in terms of what has been called the *funnel of causality*. The term was introduced to social science by Campbell, Converse, Miller, and Stokes. In *The American Voter*, they used the concept of the funnel of causality as a device for visualizing a chain of events and decisions that lead to a specific political act. Although these authors were concerned with voting behavior, the analogy of the funnel may be applied to opinion formation (for our purposes here, the casting of a presidential vote, and the events that lead to it, may be thought of as an example of the formation of an opinion).

Campbell and his collaborators are properly cautious about the usefulness of their funnel of causality as a way of thinking about the social psychology of decision making. "The notion of a funnel," they warn, "is intended merely as a metaphor that we find helpful up to a certain point, [but] like all physical analogies for complex and intangible processes, it becomes more misleading than clarifying if pressed too far." They describe their model, thus qualified, as follows:

> . . . the axis of the funnel represents a time dimension. Events are conceived to follow each other in a converging sequence of causal chains, moving from the mouth to the stem of the funnel. The funnel shape is a logical product of the explanatory task chosen. Most of the complex events in the funnel occur as a result of multiple prior causes. Each such event is, in its turn, responsible for multiple effects as well, but our focus of interest narrows as we approach the dependent behavior. We progressively eliminate those effects that do not continue to have relevance for the political act. Since we are forced to take all partial

causes as relevant at any juncture, relevant effects are therefore many fewer in number than relevant causes. The result is a convergence effect.[6]

The Campbell version of the funnel of causality attempts to set no theoretical starting point, as represented by the large end of the funnel; for the analysis of voting behavior, it is useful to think of the starting points as relevant historical events as far back in time as seems appropriate to the case under consideration. The large rim of the funnel and the sloping sides represent the area of relevance and the focusing effect on the final decision over time.

In Figure 8–1, the cross section of the funnel at the large end represents (as in the Campbell model) the moment in historical time that the

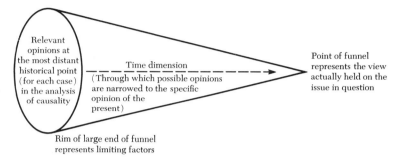

Figure 8–1. Funnel of Opinion Causality

analyst adopts (for whatever reasons) as a starting point. In order to broaden the theory of opinion holding—in an admittedly most tentative way—it seems wise to make the large end encompass all the possible opinions that may be held by the individual at the given point in past time. This assumption allows us a theoretical construct that has greater totality. To be more precise, it allows us the opportunity to consider *limiting factors*, as well as *influencing factors*, in the discussion of opinion formation. I think it important to warn, once again, that this model, like most models in the social sciences, is essentially quite simple and obvious.

The large end of the funnel represents the range and variety of all opinions which, on any issue, are capable of being held by the individual at the time chosen as the analytical starting point. Remember, for our purposes, an issue is a public matter about which controversy exists. The large end of the funnel represents the existing or possible points of view on matters of relevance to the issue under consideration. The limits of the large end are thus determined not only by what the individual knows,

[6] Angus Campbell, Philip E. Converse, Warren E. Miller, and Donald E. Stokes, *The American Voter* (New York: John Wiley & Sons, Inc., 1960), p. 24. Reprinted by permission of John Wiley & Sons, Inc.

and what he thinks about what he knows, but also by the physical and cultural facts or prohibitions that make controversy, and therefore *public* opinion, impossible. These are the *limiting factors* in public opinion formation.

Some examples will help us understand the way in which limiting factors set bounds to the area in which public matters can give rise to public opinion. Limiting factors are, we say, of two kinds: physical and cultural. In a very simple way, our knowledge about the physical world determines, at one extreme, what we can or cannot have public opinion about. We suggested earlier that public opinion about the flatness of the earth is now impossible; the gross shape of the earth is known beyond all controversy, and no sane people now believe the earth to be flat. Public opinion about the flatness of the earth was possible a thousand years ago, but it is no longer possible. It was then a cultural datum which might be encompassed, schematically, by the rim of the large end of the funnel; now it is not.

While some issues, such as the flatness or globularity of the earth, are removed as issues by the accumulation of physical knowledge, other issues are made possible. Before the development of the present level of rocketry, it could not be said that public opinion was possible on the question of how earthmen would use the moon. Today this is a matter of acute interest among scientists and military strategists, and public opinion is not only possible, it may even exist on certain more specific issues such as the wisdom of contacting the moon surface with germ-carrying earth vehicles.

Cultural *prescriptions* (things to be believed) and *proscriptions* (things not to be believed) may also determine the limits of what may become publicly controversial. These, like knowledge of the physical world, may be limiting factors. Seventy-five years ago, in the United States, polygamy was an issue about which an intense public opinion developed. Now it can hardly be said that polygamy is debatable, and the strongest evidence of the cultural prescription of monogamy among Mormons in addition to non-Mormons is the universal vigor with which the press and public officials condemned and prosecuted the polygamous deviants in the remote town of Short Creek, Arizona, in 1953.

In modern industrialized societies, there are few cultural requirements so strongly held that they constitute an absolute bar to the development of public opinion; the large end of the funnel of causation is very large indeed. Within the European-based Western culture of the 1960s especially, there are few requirements or injunctions so total as to make public opinion about them impossible. In the West, for example, one might suppose a certain basic respect for human life to be so strongly developed that the deliberate murder of thousands or millions of persons could never become a matter of public opinion or public policy. Yet, in Nazi Germany, the systematic killing of Jews as a governmental policy

was accepted by the great majority of non-Jews and was positively supported by many others. To repeat, then, the large end of the funnel—the
area within which controversy over public issues is possible—is very large
indeed in modern societies.[7]

The sloping sides of the funnel of opinion causality represent the
influencing factors in the determination of opinion. These are the conceptions, beliefs, events, and opinions that relate to the issue and in some
way influence the particular opinion being formed. The fictional Mr.
Black referred to earlier held opinions about the Democratic Party that
were in part a result of the following influencing factors: upbringing by
strongly Republican parents, experiences in a city controlled by a Democratic "boss," distrust of Catholics in public office, and regular exposure to
Republican newspapers and magazines.

Figure 8–2 is designed to represent the way in which influencing factors combine or are rejected in the opinion-forming process.

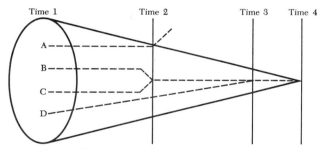

B and C are influencing factors that combine at Time 2

A is an influencing factor that becomes irrelevant at Time 2 as
a consequence of the combination of the B and C influences

D is an influencing factor that bears on the opinion at Time 3
late in the development of the opinion and just before its
expression at Time 4

*Figure 8–2. Influence Combination in the
Funnel of Causality*

As an example of the process illustrated in Figure 8–2, let us say that
the opinion (decision) under analysis is the partisan choice of a twenty-
one-year-old at the time of his registration for voting. Let *B* represent
the influence of his family (father and mother are both Republicans); let
C represent the influence of his fiancée, with whom he joins at *Time 2*

---

[7] The great increase in the number of personal and social alternatives in human behavior is one of the fundamental ways in which modern societies differ from primitive
societies. The implications of this fact can hardly be overestimated. For a perceptive
discussion of this matter, see Margaret Mead, *Coming of Age in Samoa* (New York:
New American Library of World Literature, 1949), pp. 133–137.

(at the age of 19) a college Young Republican group; let A represent the influence of his friends who, also at *Time 2* (which, let us say, is a presidential campaign), join the campus Young Democrats; and let D represent what our subject takes to be the prevailing pro-Republican influence among the upper management of the accounting firm where he gets his first job just two months (at *Time 3*) before his registration as a Republican.

We suspect that each person carries around in his head, so to speak, the raw materials for opinion formation on those issues of which he is aware. The way in which influencing factors are related to the end opinion is probably not given any conscious attention in most cases. There are many issues upon which the average person never has to formulate an opinion at all. Most Americans may know some things about U.S. immigration policy, but they will probably not have occasion to articulate anything that could be described as an opinion on the subject. Most Americans are never asked what they think about the quota system in the immigration laws, the oath of disclaimer that prospective immigrants have to make, or the provisions for naturalization or denaturalization of immigrants.

The point is that we are in danger of unrealistic thinking, and of abusing our model, if we believe that there is a ready-made and well-structured funnel of causality that can be extracted, so to speak, from every person on every issue. However, when individuals have in fact formulated opinions, or when they are asked to give an opinion in conversation or writing, then we can infer a funnel of causality from what we know about the other opinions and experiences of these individuals. It should be clear, of course, that our knowledge of the funnel of causality will always be incomplete—there will always be some influencing factors which are not capable of being taken into account. But this is merely to restate, in a particular context, an earlier point about the almost infinite number of variables that enter into the analysis of human thought and behavior.

In the chapters that follow, we take into account those influencing factors that seem to be most significant for the formation of public opinion. These include *social relationships,* especially relationships with primary and secondary groups, *economic considerations,* the *mass media* and other elements of the communication network, *intellectual calculation,* and *whimsy.*

The opinion-forming process in any specific case may be slow, or rapid, or suspended at any point. The limiting and influencing factors— the totality of facts, experiences, and judgments that are part of the making of an opinion—may occur in an almost endless number of combinations with various intensities and various results. There are, we know, powerful influences for sameness of opinion just as there are powerful

influences for diversity. In some cases, a single influence or a few reinforcing influences may overwhelm all others, narrowing the choices rapidly to
a strongly held point of view. The funnel will then be short and squat:

In other cases, the influences may be weak, or strong but contradictory,
and the ultimate choice difficult and long in being arrived at; this funnel
is deep and gradually sloping:

Finally, the process may be suspended for lack of information, or for
a lack of resolution of strong but conflicting influences; this is the case
when we say our mind is not made up:

THE PSYCHOLOGY
OF OPINION
HOLDING

9

The opinions that any individual holds are the products of his unique experiences as a person within an environment he shares with others. At birth, the individual's uniqueness is wholly, or almost wholly, a physical matter, determined by genes and chromosomes and a body chemistry that, in its essentials, still evades scientific exposure. But this is only true at birth. From the moment of his first breath, and at an increasing rate as he grows, the individual's unique endowments are modified by the effects of social life.

There is much talk about "native ability." Some of it arises from arguments about heredity versus environment—a sport that in academic circles is now as rare as it is useless. We know very little about the outer limits of intellectual ability; we do know, however, that some persons have physical (or chemical) impairments that prevent them from understanding abstractions, concepts, and sometimes even facts beyond a certain level of complexity. We assume, therefore, that all persons have limits (if unmeasured) to their ability to understand and learn. Some indication of the boundaries of the mind may be obtained from physical examinations, and from electrical, chemical, and performance tests; but our knowledge of the full potential of the human mind is hardly beyond the point where general medicine was in the early seventeenth century when Harvey discovered the principles of the circulation of blood.

For each person, the capacity for opinion holding is no doubt limited, then, by ultimate biological, or chemical, or electrical, factors of a physical nature. However, this is not of much concern as a practical matter for normal persons, because other limiting or influencing factors shape their opinions well within the range of what is physically possible. Other processes and needs, experienced by all persons—but particular to each individual in their manifestations—provide limiting and influencing factors of more significance to attitude and opinion study.

In this chapter, we shall consider opinion holding as it relates to the basic potentialities of the human equipment: to the development of intelligence and personality; to feeling, perception, cognition, and reasoning, and to the satisfaction of psychological needs. Such a survey will help provide a background for our consideration of the political significance of opinion holding.

9.1   Development of Opinion-Holding Capacity

In the prenatal period, a fetal organism develops a self-system that, with decreasing aid from its mother as birth approaches, integrates all of its physical parts and biochemical processes. During this period of rapid cell growth and differentiation, tissue damage can result from disease, bruises, or lack of nutriments (including oxygen), which may permanently impair the organism's abilities and set impassable limits to the capacity for thought. With most individuals, fortunately, no identifiable neurophysiological limits are set before (or after) birth, and the full and still unexplored range of human intellect is possible.

From the moment of birth, the individual is forced to be his own, wholly independent integrator of parts and processes. The birth trauma is vividly described by Strauss and Kephart:

> The infant organism is suddenly thrust into a strange new world. . . . No longer does the developmental process alone insure the proper outcome but this process must now be supplemented and elaborated by activities of his own. These new responsibilities must be assumed in the midst of a new environment. He must play the game of life on a field which he has never seen, with rules which he does not know. . . .
> Information about this world comes to him in peculiar forms: radiant energy entering his eye, sound waves impinging upon his ears, mechanical energy applied to his skin, chemical energy in his nose and on his tongue, etc. All of these forms of energy are new and strange. He must learn what they are about and what information they can transmit before he can use them to tell him what is happening in the world.
> His newly awakened senses at first only bombard him with impressions. They have no order; they have no plan. They are only a chaos of undifferentiated stimuli.[1]

---

[1] Alfred A. Strauss and Newell C. Kephart, *Psychopathology and Education of the Brain-Injured Child* (New York: Grune & Stratton, Inc., 1955), II, 47. Reprinted by permission of Grune & Stratton, Inc.

Very quickly, however, impressions begin to be differentiated. The child begins to identify certain objects as objects: his bottle, a blanket, the sides of his crib. He learns movement patterns as he is picked up or turned over. And he learns to associate comforts or discomforts with visual and tactile stimuli: he is moved, and the discomfort of wetness is changed to the comfort of dryness; or he sucks, and the comfort of eating replaces the discomfort of hunger.

He may be driven by instinct to some behavior, such as sucking, but all else is learned. To be sure, it is easy learning, and he has much help from other individuals; but insofar as the stimulations are accurately received and integrated by his sense receptors and his brain cells, he is ordering, interpreting, storing, and recalling stimuli in a systematic way. These actions are the basic subprocesses of learning.

9.2   Psychological Processes

One of the key (and unanswered) questions of behavioral scientists—as well as of medical scientists and philosophers—is the old one about the separation of mind and body. Are there clear distinctions between mental and physical parts and processes? Or, if there are no *observable* ways to differentiate mind from body, are there *qualities* of the mind (such as reason, sympathy, love, pride, or despair) that may be taken as symptomatic of real, if unobserved, differences between mind and body? Rivers of ink have been drained in speculation about this central question of the nature of man. No purpose could be served by an extended discussion of the matter here; it is enough to say that I have seen no evidence that the mind is empirically identifiable from the body. Something is known about the electrochemistry of perception, and, as we shall see, it does not indicate the separateness of a "mind." But that something that is known is still very little, and, in the future, "mind" may be physiologically distinguishable from body. For now, it needs only to be said that "mind," in the first sense, as something separate from body, cannot be proved.

The concept of mind may be used to describe a collection of qualities of which some are *normative* (that is, having aspects of "goodness" and "badness") and all are nonphysical. If we want to, we may employ the word *mind* to mean those particular capacities of reasoning and feeling by which men manipulate their environment and enter into social relationships. These qualities cannot—at least, not as yet—be explained on physical grounds alone; they distinguish men from all other known forms of life, and may, as a collective shorthand, be called *mind*—or even *soul*.

Now, although it may be perfectly satisfactory to use the term *mind* in this latter sense for the qualities, processes, and behavior that cannot be physically identified as some kind of energy, it seems preferable to me to discard the mind-body dichotomy. I would prefer to use, as consistently as possible, a phrase like *psychological processes,* in referring to instincts, drives, perception, cognition, reasoning, and feeling, and to divide these and their subprocesses and parts, when it seems appropriate, into the *neurophysiological* and the *nonphysiological.*

There is good authority for abandoning earlier (and still common) notions about the differences between mind and body. It is not too much of an exaggeration to say that all psychologists have done so. The great and never-to-be-forgotten contribution of Sigmund Freud was that he made us, as it were, conscious of the *unconscious.* As long as psychology was the study of reason and of the other "mental faculties" (as emotion and sense perception were quaintly called), it was possible to think of mind as separate from body, although having its locus within the organism. But when Freud made his early discoveries of unconscious suppression of feelings and their relation to (indeed, causing of) physical disability—when the evidence indicated that the unknown elements in the mind could have pathological effects on the body—then it was no longer possible to believe in the tidy separability of mind and body.[2] Since these discoveries of the 1890s, the idea of unconscious psychological processes has been verified repeatedly and unmistakably by general medicine and neurophysiology as well as by experimental psychologists and psychotherapists.

In the face of such evidence, the earlier, more or less complete separation of mind and body cannot be defended today. Freudian psychology first challenged the body-mind dichotomy in the 1890s; non-Freudian psychologists have been nearly unanimous in their acceptance of the importance of the unconscious. Moreover, the non-Freudian psychologists have been, in general, more concerned about the relationships between the psychological processes called perception, cognition, and reasoning, on the one hand, and, on the other, our knowledge of the electrochemistry of the body. Working with the neurophysiologists, the psychologists who may be grouped roughly as behaviorists have arrived at the beginnings of understanding about the way in which the human psyche receives, records, and analyzes sense data. One celebrated neurophysiologist implies that

---

[2] It is important to note that controversy has never been acute over the idea of the unconscious. The storm blown up by Freud, both among ninteenth-century puritans and among twentieth-century psychologists, was over the source of the unconscious processes that were the cause of neurosis and psychosis. Freud's troubles—the term is used to mean controversy, not necessarily error—were over sex rather than the idea of the unconscious. See Lancelot Law Whyte, *The Unconscious before Freud* (Garden City, N.Y.: Doubleday & Co., Inc., 1962).

mind may be wholly explained by body when more is known about the incredibly complex operations of the brain and nervous system:

> Is it likely that physiology will ever throw any real light upon the relationship between the brain and the mind? I believe that, working in conjunction with psychology, it will. I can only guess where present advances seem to be leading us. Think of a pattern. An atom is a pattern of electrons, a molecule is a pattern of atoms. There are patterns of patterns of patterns, and so on indefinitely. The most complicated patterns we know are in the brain. Not only are there twelve thousand million nerve cells out of which the patterns can be made, but nervous patterns exist in time, like a melody, as well as in space. If you look at a tapestry through a magnifying glass, you will see the individual threads but not the pattern: if you stand away from it you will see the pattern but not the threads. My guess is that in the nervous system we are looking at the threads while with the mind we perceive the patterns, and that one day we may discover how the patterns are made out of the threads.[3]

In the passage just quoted, Brain made a distinction between nervous system and mind. Mind, to him, seems to mean the patterned operations the human nervous system is capable of performing. These operations are what I prefer to call *psychological processes*. They depend on the electrochemistry of the nervous system, but are not (as yet) wholly explainable by the nervous system. They are *body*-plus.

Although we do not fully understand the nature of these psychological processes, there are some definitional agreements and experimental findings that help us to distinguish them one from another. Most phychologists distinguish perception from thinking and feeling; many distinguish all three of these psychological processes from a fourth, cognition. We may think of these as four (there may be more) different kinds of psychological operations, each using common elements of the nervous system (that is, having common electrochemical bases), but having characteristic modes of operation that differentiate them according to their dynamics and their end products.

One widely held view maintains that psychology as a scientific study has to do with those elements and processes that are intermediary between stimuli outside of the organism and observable physical response of the organism to the stimuli. In this formulation, known as *stimulus-response* (or S-R) *theory*, perception is part of the total process that produces re-

---

3 W. Russell Brain, *Mind, Perception and Science* (Oxford, England: Blackwell Scientific Publications Ltd., 1951), p. 30. Reprinted by permission of Blackwell Scientific Publications Ltd. This testimony of the mid-twentieth century is only slightly more guarded than the prophecy made by the Concourt brothers a century earlier (1853): "Every day, science swallows a piece of God. Probably the time will come when our thought processes will be explained in scientific terms as we now explain thunder." Quoted in John Nef, *Civilization, Industrial Society, and Love* (Santa Barbara, Calif.: Center for the Study of Democratic Institutions, August 1961), p. 11.

sponse after stimulation is applied to the human organism. Other possible psychological subprocesses are cognition, feeling, and reasoning. As the diagram below indicates, and as the following brief discussion explains, perception and cognition are necessary to all psychological activity; if the individual is even in the slightest influenced by or aware of the stimulus, he receives and holds in some way the impact of the stimulus. Feeling and reasoning are not necessary parts of every stimulus-response situation, although one may suppose that most conscious and voluntary responses of individuals to a single stimulus or to fields of stimuli are in some degree influenced by reason or emotion or both.

Perception, cognition, reason, and feeling are sometimes called the psychological variables intervening between stimulus and response. There are, of course, other ways of conceptualizing the field of psychology, but the S-R formulation is presented here both because it is widely accepted by psychologists and because its basic elements are easily understood and used by other social sciences.[4]

Perception may be defined as the way in which the organism takes account of the stimulus. Cognition is the way the organism gives meaning to the stimulus. Reason is the process by which the stimulus is related to other stimuli at the conceptual level of psychological activity. Feeling is the emotional connotation produced by the stimulus, either alone or in combination with other stimuli at the cognitive or conceptual level.

Consider the operation of these psychological processes in the farmer who, in the fable, was going home from market with a chicken, a fox, and a bag of grain. He rounded a turn in the road and perceived a river—that is, the light energy in his visual field created in his brain some electro-chemical action which he had learned to recognize as a river. But he also immediately recognized that the river was high—that is, the stimulus was classified as well as perceived, and cognition occurred as a concept (a high river), which took on meaning to the farmer.[5] At that point, the farmer

---

[4] For a good history and summary of S-R theory, see William W. Lambert, "Stimulus-Response Contiguity and Reinforcement Theory in Social Psychology," in Gardner Lindzey, ed., *Handbook of Social Psychology* (Reading, Mass.: Addison-Wesley Publishing Co., Inc., 1954), I, 57–90.

[5] Some psychologists would say that perception need not be distinguished from cognition; but the farmer, in this case, saw immediately a river with meaning, that is, a high river. This is a family quarrel, which we may leave to the psychologists. As a confessed nonpsychologist, I happen to believe the processes can be distinguished, and that it is normally helpful to do so.

had a problem and needed to use reason. (Consider for a moment why Humphrey, among others, has defined thinking as "what occurs in experience when an organism, human or animal, meets, recognizes, and solves a problem."[6] Other persons believe that there are several kinds of thinking, only one of which—reasoning—is problem solving.)[7]

But to return to the farmer. How to get the chicken, the fox, and the bag of grain safely across the river? Rather than being able to carry them all at once across the shallow ford as he expected, he found that he could carry only one at a time. If he took the fox first, the chicken would eat the grain before he got back. If he took the grain first, the fox would eat the chicken before he returned. If he took the chicken first, the fox and grain would be safe, but on the second trip he would have to leave either the fox or the grain with the chicken while he returned for the remaining object.

Being a clever farmer, as we all know, he associated the stimuli and concepts of the situation in such a way that he solved the problem by the use of reason. No feeling (emotion) was involved, apparently; but if he disliked chickens because they wakened him in the morning, or if they reminded him at some unconscious level of his henpecked existence at home, he might have let feeling interfere with reason and allowed the fox to eat the chicken.

In some cases, only perception intervenes between stimulus and response. The child draws his finger away from the hot stove without experiencing any of the psychological processes we have described as cognition, reason, or emotion. But most behavior, beyond the simplest reaction to intense pain or pleasure, is related to the more complex psychological variables between stimulus and response. Apparently, these psychological processes are seldom if ever separate in time from each other. Perception, cognition, reason, and feeling go on simultaneously, and much of what are called thinking, dreaming, imagining, fancying, studying, and the like, are combinations of perceptive, cognitive, rational, and affective elements.

From the perspective of the individual, opinions are products of (a) personal experience, as shaped by stimulations; (b) the meanings attached to these stimulations (their relation to classifications and abstractions); (c) the application of these meaningful stimulations to problem-solving situations; and (d) the pattern of emotional charges associated with the stimulations and their related classifications and abstractions. The kinds of opinions of interest to us—that is, views on matters of some significance

[6] George Humphrey, *Thinking* (New York: John Wiley & Sons, Inc., 1951), p. 311; see also Humphrey's footnote, pp. 311–312.

[7] See Robert Thomson, *The Psychology of Thinking* (Baltimore, Md.: Penguin Books, Inc., 1959), pp. 13–16 and 25–27.

to the small or large community—almost by definition refer to problems and problem solving. Reasoning is therefore most always in order, although it is not always evident in the expression of opinion.

Emotion alone may result in a person's opinion about certain issues, as when all matters of policy are reduced to a slogan, like "My country (or family, political party, or religion), right or wrong." But generally, we may suppose, an opinion that is significant for the study of public opinion is created in the individual by some more or less complex interaction of cognition, reason, and feeling.

9.3   Satisfaction and Fit in Opinion Holding

The last few pages, if they have demonstrated nothing else, have demonstrated that we know little about the details of either the biophysical or psychological processes of opinion formation and change. We know more, however, about the relations between opinions and the observable elements of personality and behavior. Some of what we know—or what we surmise—about these matters will be reviewed in later chapters, which deal with the effects of communication messages on individuals. Here we may only summarize two points related to the integration of an individual's opinions with his total personality, self-image, and effectiveness in small- and large-group situations.

The first point is that opinions must be at least to some degree consistent with observable reality. In large and common matters, a man's opinions must reflect a reasonably accurate understanding (or at least perception) of objective fact. A person may believe quite honestly that no slums exist in city A; but if on every criteria by which slums are measured it is clear that they *do* exist, this person has been unable to achieve a good "fit" between objective fact and subjective opinion. When such a fit is only mildly incongruous, we put it down, usually, to the person's indifference to fact or to his bad judgment; when the fit is notoriously poor, it may mean psychosis.

We must be careful, of course, not to overemphasize the need for opinions to square with fact. It is a matter of everyday observation that prejudice, personal interest, and opinions received uncritically as political (or religious or economic) ideology seem to produce in man an extraordinary capacity to ignore the most elementary facts. As Murphy and Likert put it:

One's immediate interests in a conflict issue are frequently discovered well enough with a minimum of technical information at hand, and all the learning in the world may have but little effect in changing one's sentiment. It is possible to argue that many of the value judgments expressed in . . . [this] survey are the reactions of ignorant people; knowledge would dispel them. But in reply, it may be said that factual education of this sort is notoriously incompetent to dispel attitudes based on deep personal sympathy or antagonisms, or attitudes which are rooted in self-interest. Primitive prejudices are a tough fiber against the scalpel of exact inquiry.[8]

The second point is that opinions must be, in some general and overall sense, comfortable to the individual. This consideration is partly a matter of the correspondence which the opinions bear to observable and measurable reality—most persons in reasonably good mental health will not be comfortable with opinions that contradict what they see and experience in the world about them. But it is more than mere fit with unambiguous experience, because most opinions worthy of being included in our definition of public opinion are about issues which cannot be resolved by reference to objective fact alone. In these cases, facts and experience are *not* unambiguous; they are capable of various and, indeed, often quite contrary interpretations. The opinions of publics cluster around matters about which honest men, honestly viewing the evidence, honestly disagree.

Consequently, except in extreme cases, opinions cannot be judged solely on their congruence with facts; the "facts" that give rise to public issues, and therefore public opinion, are not obvious, objective, and palpable. Except in extreme cases, where aberrant opinions are accompanied by aberrant behavior, it is hardly a good measure of the worth of an opinion to say that it is not in accord with the facts. Nor is it enough for the opinion holder himself constantly to test his views against the facts. It is important that he do so, of course, and that he beware of the rationalization processes which so often shape facts to opinions. But try as he may, no matter how candid his self-criticism, the test of fit is not sufficient when—as in all large public controversies—the nature of reality is so imperfectly known.

It is therefore, in a sense, as proper as it is inevitable that what we believe and hold as public opinion is to some important degree shaped by our personality needs and our self-image. Within the range of opinions that may adequately fit the facts—or the opinion area in which judgment, insight, creativity, and other individual traits are the decisive opinion producers—each individual selects the view that best suits his personal needs. There is some evidence, for example, that certain persons seem compelled to engage in scapegoatism; they seem to need out-group persons or symbols to blame for in-group troubles. It is characteristic of leaders and activists in American radical-right movements to find "bad guys," at

---

[8] Gardner Murphy and Rensis Likert, *Public Opinion and the Individual* (New York: Harper & Row, Publishers, 1938), p. 126. Reprinted by permission of Harper & Row, Publishers.

whose doors the problems of the "good guys" can be laid; as the Know-Nothings blamed the Irish and Popery, and the Ku Kluxers blamed Negroes and Catholics, so John Birch Society members blame the Communists for all difficulties.

The scapegoat mechanism is only one of several responses that may be shown by persons who display extrapunitive reactions to frustrating situations. Rosenzweig has argued that one dimension (or trait) of personality might be measured by reactions to frustrations; he observed that some persons in frustrating situations turned aggressively on others (these he called *extrapunitive*), some turned aggressively on themselves (*intrapunitive*), and some were able to ignore the situation (*impunitive*).[9]

Following Rosenzweig, Smith obtained, through depth interviewing, opinion and personality measurements from 250 adult American males. He found that "the 'extrapunitive' group were somewhat more likely than the 'intrapunitive' respondents to blame Russia for United States–Soviet disagreements and to support a 'tough' United States policy toward Russia." "This," he says, "is what one would expect if their attitudes were to be consistent with the rest of their personality tendencies."[10]

The authors of *The Authoritarian Personality* concluded that scapegoatism (or extrapunitiveness) is a significant trait of the authoritarian person.[11] Scapegoatism, and the attitudes and opinions associated with it, are used here only as examples of the relationships between personality factors and opinions. The reliability and validity of the measurements of these relationships are quite open to question; but one of the principal authors of *The Authoritarian Personality* argues that it is possible to predict some kinds of opinions that individuals will hold. She maintains that:

In a society in which alternative ideologies are offered, a prediction, from psychological data, of such social and political beliefs as liberalism or totalitarianism seems to offer good chances of success. . . . Certain personality scales correlate as high as .8 with fascist ideology.

The correlations of authoritarian attitudes with socioeconomic factors as such are much less pronounced.[12]

---

[9] S. Rosenzweig, "Types of Reaction to Frustration," *Journal of Abnormal and Social Psychology*, XXIX (1934), 298–300.

[10] M. Brewster Smith, "The Personal Setting of Public Opinion: A Study of Attitudes toward Russia," *Public Opinion Quarterly*, XI (1947), 520.

[11] T. W. Adorno et al., *The Authoritarian Personality* (New York: Harper & Row, Publishers, 1950), pp. 233, 409–411.

[12] Else Frenkel-Brunswik, "Interaction of Psychological and Sociological Factors in Political Behavior," *American Political Science Review*, XLVI (1952), 62.

It should be noted that the Frenkel-Brunswik assertion seems to refer to attitudes rather than opinions about specific policies or events. It is not wholly clear, in the original studies of ethnocentrism, authoritarianism, and prejudice, whether the conclusions linked personality factors with attitudes alone, or whether opinions too—which, in Doob's phrase, may only be "sharpened attitudes"—can be predicted to correlate highly with authoritarian personality traits. This uncertainty is only one of a number that surround the studies on the authoritarian personality; the studies have been attacked both methodologically[13] and substantively, and some of the larger generalizations made in and inferred from the studies are seriously open to question. Ferris has found, for example, that "jingoistic" attitudes and opinions seem to be associated more clearly with a sense of personal ineffectiveness ("political anomie," he calls it) than with authoritarian personality characteristics.[14] It seems likely that a sense of personal ineffectiveness may be related to and part of the make-up of the authoritarian personality, but such a sense may also turn out to be a distinct personality trait at least as important as the authoritarian personality type itself for the prediction and analysis of public opinion.

Other psychologists, following the work of Murray and his collaborators at Harvard, believe that much human behavior can be explained by the analysis of the numbers, intensities, and interactions of psychological and physiological *needs*. All persons, basically, have a need for maintaining their lives, for sex gratifications, and for social relationships. To these physiological needs, Murray and his associates systematically added a long list of psychobiological needs, which they experimentally measured. They investigated, among other things, the need for affiliation (in their terminology, "need affiliation" or "n-affiliation"), need nurturance, need play, need seclusion, and need understanding. The total personality, in the view of these psychologists, may be thought of as a result of the patterns and dynamic interactions of more than two dozen such needs.[15]

For our purposes, the application of Murray's personality theory is quite clear: personality needs, their intensities, their hierarchies, and the

---

13 See, among others, R. Christie, "Authoritarianism Reexamined," in R. Christie and M. Jahoda, eds., *Studies in the Scope and Method of the Authoritarian Personality* (New York: The Free Press of Glencoe, 1954), pp. 123–196; and Loren F. Chapman and Donald T. Campbell, "The Effect of Acquiescence Response-Set upon Relationships among the F Scale, Ethnocentrism, and Intelligence," *Sociometry*, XXII (1959), 153–161.

14 Charles D. Ferris, " 'Authoritarianism' as a Political Behavior Variable," *Journal of Politics*, XVIII (1956), 61–82; and "Selected Attitudes on Foreign Affairs as Correlates of Authoritarianism and Political Anomie," *Journal of Politics*, XXII (1960), 50–67.

15 Henry A. Murray et al., *Explorations in Personality* (New York: Oxford University Press, 1938); see especially Chap. 3, pp. 142–242.

ways in which they are met, all in some degree undoubtedly influence the kinds of opinions held by the individual. We believe, in part, what we find psychologically satisfying. What is satisfying is the fulfillment of our psychobiological needs. Opinions that tend to fulfill these needs tend to be held and cherished.

McClelland and his collaborators, exploring need achievement in experimental studies on motivation, produced a large body of reports, which suggest that what we think about public issues may be colored by the motivations and strivings that are temporarily or permanently most important for us if we are to become what we want to become or to maintain what we already feel we are.[16]

Of more general applicability, probably, than the work in prejudice and the authoritarian personality, or the experimental research on motivation, is the study reported by Smith, Bruner, and White in *Opinions and Personality*. These psychologists, with other collaborators, undertook a careful, comprehensive depth study of ten adult men in the spring and summer of 1947. They gathered a vast amount of information about the personality characteristics of these ten subjects, and the way in which the respondents obtained, held, expressed, and modified their opinions about Russia. The value of the Smith, Bruner, and White research is not merely that it points the way both to further efforts, using greater numbers of subjects, and to an ordering of further research priorities, but that it so effectively avoids an overcommitment to any psychological school or to any small number of influencing factors.

The rich accumulation of information and suggestions in *Opinions and Personality* may be illustrated by two short excerpts about the influence of temperamental qualities on opinions. "Mood tone" was found to be important:

Qualities such as optimism or pessimism, confidence or helplessness, buoyancy or resignation must be regarded on the whole as fairly stable and enduring features of personality, even though they are sometimes subject to great change. Three of our men were largely resigned to a personal fate that seemed full of heaviness. Hilary Sullivan expected little for his own life, though much for that better world order that would follow the historical demise of capitalism. Albert

---

[16] See, among others, David C. McClelland et al., "The Projective Expression of Needs III: The Effect of Ego-Involvement, Success, and Failure on Perception," *Journal of Psychology*, XXVII (1949), 311ff; "The Projective Expression of Needs IV: The Effect of the Need for Achievement on Thematic Apperception," *Journal of Experimental Psychology*, XXXIX (1949), 24ff; and *The Achievement Motive* (New York: Appleton-Century-Crofts, Inc., (1953). It has been suggested that McClelland's studies, many of which used projective techniques (the making up of stories or explanations around fictional events), lack validity and are unparalleled by responses evoked in real situations. Irvin L. Child, "Socialization," in G. Lindzey, ed., *Handbook of Social Psychology* (Reading, Mass.: Addison-Wesley Publishing Co., Inc., 1954), II, 676.

Rock was trying to make the best of an unhappy marriage and a burden of anxieties, confident of grace before his God. Clarence Clark had adapted himself to a narrow round of activities and interests, hoping a little apprehensively that his son would do better in life. Resignation did not, of course, produce uniform opinions about Russia, but we could scarcely claim to understand the opinions of these three men without taking into account the emotional coloring that appeared in all their behavior.[17]

Differences in "action level" were also found to be important:

> Upjohn was a man who habitually used action both to forward his own interests and to blow off the steam generated by his resentfulness and conflicts. . . .
>
> His preference for action was also responsible for his frequent self-contradictions. Thinking of each item about Russia with reference to its action possibilities, he often did not stop to consider the purely logical relationships among his various ideas. Kleinfeld, in contrast, showed in his opinions a clear intrusion of the passivity and sense of helplessness that characterized his general attitude toward people and problems of relationship. Although he disapproved of Russian expansion, he believed that the only hope of peace lay in giving no offense to the Russians.[18]

The many-sided sophistication of the Smith, Bruner, and White volume is apparent in the following longer excerpt from their discussion of the relationships among reality appraisal, cognitive processes, and personality needs:

> An opinion cannot be fully understood without taking into account its status as a hypothesis about the nature of the "real" in the person's social environment. Having an opinion about Russia is more than being "for" or "against" Russia: it is a way of "perceiving" or "knowing" Russia by inference from available information, and with reference to personal values, interests, and ongoing concerns. The selectivity of perception, inference, and memory, the reconciling of bias and evidence—all of these are considerations in understanding the status of an opinion in the functioning of a man's personality.
>
> Let it be clear, however, that emphasis upon the object-appraising function of an opinion is not a bid for the reinstatement of that admirable fiction, the "rational man." We are not proposing that the process is a kind of calculus of interest, wherein the person accurately appraises the relation of the world to his goal and decides his best line accordingly. Our insistence upon object appraisal as a cognitive activity stems from broader considerations. It is apparent, when one looks closely at a life, that the formation of an opinion does reflect a drive toward rational decision in terms of one's interests. We are rational according to our lights, but the lights may be dim indeed. The case material we have examined gives ample evidence of the highly selective ways in which Russia may be viewed and of the distorted manner in which inferences about her may be

---

[17] M. Brewster Smith, Jerome S. Bruner, and Robert W. White, *Opinions and Personality* (New York: John Wiley & Sons, Inc., 1956), pp. 257–258. Reprinted by permission of John Wiley & Sons, Inc.

[18] *Ibid.*, p. 258.

made. But, at the same time, there is also evidence of nicety, finesse, and reason. What is critical to emphasize is that opinions must also serve functions other than object appraisal. For, as we have repeatedly noted, opinions are also vehicles by which we orient ourselves to the social groups in our environment and a means whereby internal problems are externalized and acted out in the everyday world. Each of these functions limits and restricts the other.[19]

9.4　The Relation of Individual Opinion Holding to Public Opinion and Political Behavior

It may be useful to review the reasons why it is important to concern ourselves, in a book on *public* opinion, with the psychology of individual opinion holding. For instance, why has it been useful to consider both the neuropsychological equipment with which the individual forms and modifies his opinions *and* the personality factors that appear to be related (perhaps in some causal way) to the kinds of views the individual finds comfortable?

As I see it, the importance of this chapter is not merely the obvious fact that publics consist of individuals, and that the views of publics are therefore the collected views of individuals. This fact is important, to be sure, and if we are to avoid the mysticism of the "great being" view of the public, we must bear this fact in mind. But in the statistical study of the opinions of publics, the political sociologist may wholly avoid the organic fallacy of the public and at the same time ignore the individual as an individual. In fact, most of the modern study of public opinion is done in precisely this fashion. Thus, even the motivational analyses since 1952 of the Survey Research Center (in terms of party identification, issue orientation, and candidate orientation), which have been quite accurately described as making significant contributions to our understanding of voter behavior in general,[20] are not concerned with individual motivations directly but with the analysis of aggregate responses. Therefore, the description and study of public opinion does not require attention to the reasons why citizens X, Y, or Z hold the opinions they do. Indeed, it is somewhat unusual for the dimension of individual opinion holding to be given importance in the study of public opinion.

Nonetheless, it is of considerable, if secondary, interest to the study of public opinion to know something about the making and modifying of

---

[19] *Ibid.*, p. 265.

[20] V. O. Key, Jr., Foreword, in A. Campbell, G. Gurin, and W. E. Miller, *The Voter Decides* (New York: Harper & Row, Publishers, 1954), p. xi.

individual opinions. This interest was expressed by Murphy and Likert as early as 1938:

> Public opinion has been the concern of political scientists and of socioliogists, of historians and of social psychologists. Their investigations reflect their differences in interest. The study of public opinion has usually meant the examination of broad trends, in populations of considerable magnitude. The work is frequently descriptive, interpretive, and statistical. The causes making for changes in opinion may be fairly well known, as in the case of many propaganda studies; but the results necessarily hold only for an undifferentiated mass of people, or at least for some large social class.
>
> Another approach, which is a needed supplement, is the study of the individual. The individual's attitudes have indeed often been studied by the psychiatrist, but chiefly with a view to therapy; and the attitudes and feelings surveyed have related, for the most part, to highly personal and private matters. The result has been that these investigations have thrown little light on the nature of the individual attitudes on public questions.[21]

For the political strategist (and the student of political strategy), it is also important to know why some opinions more than others appeal to individuals. Much of the concern with political "images" seems to center on the most imperfectly understood appeals certain candidates have to voters. These appeals seem to be related, at least in part, to ideal types that voters want candidates to approximate (I once heard a clubwoman say she felt well protected when the late Louis Johnson was Secretary of Defense, because he was "such a large, strong man") and to basic personality needs that some candidate-policy combinations seem to satisfy better than other candidate-policy combinations. These matters, like so much else in political life, are far from being understood; but there is ample evidence that the investigation of individual opinion holding can contribute importantly to the political scientist's study of public opinion and political behavior.

9.5   Does Behavior Follow Opinion?

As is so often the case, one of the simplest questions which can be put to the analyst of public opinion is one of the most difficult: Does behavior follow opinion? Put another way, is there any reason to believe that people act consistently with their beliefs? Do people vote the way they think?—or the way they would like to?—or the way they say they are going to?

---

21 Murphy and Likert, *Public Opinion and the Individual* (see footnote 8), p. 3. Reprinted by permission of Harper & Row, Publishers.

Before we can answer these not merely rhetorical questions, we should rephrase them more systematically and a little more theoretically. We are asking, really, about the degree of consistency among three pattern variables, those usually designated attitudes, those designated opinions, and those designated behavior (or, more accurately, overt and measurable behavior). We are asking whether those dispositions toward action that we call attitudes are consistent with those expressions of views we call opinions, and whether both of these are consistent with what people actually do when they have to express attitudes and opinions in social situations.

Most social psychologists seem to accept the notion that there is a close and almost invariable relationship between attitudes and opinions. Attitudes, they say, are tendencies or dispositions, learned rather than inborn, toward objects, persons, or groups; these tendencies or dispositions are not specific to any particular set of facts or particular policy questions, but apply generally toward the objects, persons, or groups to which they relate. Opinions may be thought of as sharpened attitudes, specific to certain real objects, persons, or groups. A bigot may have *attitudes* toward Negroes, or Catholics, or Jews in general; but he has *opinions* about the Negro chairman of the N.A.A.C.P., about the Catholic candidate for political office, and about the Jew who runs the clothing store in his town. It would be a mistake, of course, to push too far this distinction based on the generality of attitudes and the specificity of opinions, for what we have called private opinion may have considerable overlap with attitude. However, if one accepts our working definition of public opinion as necessitating (a) an issue, (b) publics affected by that issue, and (c) an expression of views, then an opinion may be usefully thought of as a sharpened, *object-specific* attitude. Nevertheless, some writers prefer to use *attitude* and *opinion* interchangeably.

The literature of opinion and attitude study almost invariably assumes that, barring lies and views stated under duress, opinion is always consistent with attitude. This is probably an accurate assumption, so far as it goes. But it is subject to the qualification that lies and views stated under duress are quite common occurrences in attitude and opinion measurement. Racially bigoted persons often give verbal responses (recorded as opinions) quite different from the bigoted attitudes they hold. There are other examples of social pressure to conform to widely held norms and ideals; these may be thought of as problems in the measurement of opinion and, since they were alluded to briefly in Chapter 3, will not be reviewed here. It is enough to point out that recorded opinions are not, in fact, always consistent with attitudes, although it is conceptually proper and operationally satisfactory, in most cases, to assume that they are.

It is of greater importance to inquire whether attitudes and opinions are *followed* by behavior. Earlier writers seem to have assumed that behavior was consistent with attitude and opinion; but in a classic experiment in the early 1930s, R. T. LaPiere dramatically demonstrated a difference between attitudes and behavior. He traveled nearly 10,000 miles across the United States twice, and extensively on the West Coast; he was accompanied by a young Chinese couple, man and wife. They were served in 184 eating places and accepted at sixty-six different establishments offering sleeping accommodations. They were turned away at only one place, and even there it was not clear whether they were rejected because two of the three persons were Chinese. Following these travels, LaPiere sent questionnaires to all the places he visited; one of the questions was: "Will you accept members of the Chinese race as guests in your establishment?" One hundred and twenty-eight questionnaires were returned; and, of those responding, *over 90 per cent of the lodging and eating places which had served the Chinese couple said they would not serve Chinese, and only one respondent said Chinese would definitely be served.*[22]

What does this mean? One explanation is that a certain set of social and economic pressures acted on the respondents when they were answering an impersonal questionnaire and that another, quite different set acted on them when they were faced with potential lodgers or diners. Their written refusal to serve Chinese may have been prompted by their own prejudices, by social and economic pressure from their friends and fellow businessmen, or by personal bias and local pressures. When confronted by prospective paying guests, they were under pressure to respect the ideals of equality and brotherhood and to accept the income from the rooms and meals (it may be significant that the experiment was conducted during the depression).

Hartley and Hartley explain these pressures, and their effect on the respondents of this study, in terms of role orientations:

> The discrepancy in responses seems to indicate that behavior in the presence of other people is defined by role orientations different from those of behavior in the presence of a questionnaire. . . . Since roles are defined in part by relationships and interaction, the roles activated in the two types of situations must patently be different. The role of the respondent is defined and directed in part by the very presence and behavior of the persons who act as stimuli.[23]

Whether the inconsistencies among attitude, expressed opinion, and behavior are due to role orientations or to responses to felt social and

---

22 Richard T. LaPiere, "Attitudes vs. Actions," *Social Forces,* XIII (1934), 233–234.

23 Eugene L. Hartley and Ruth E. Hartley, *Fundamentals of Social Psychology* (New York: Alfred A. Knopf, Inc., 1952), p. 549.

economic pressures (there seems to be little real difference in this case), it
it obvious that we do not always act according to our beliefs. It is no doubt
true that some limits must exist to the amount of dissimulation which
the healthy personality can tolerate. We could not always, or even most
of the time, behave in ways contrary to our feelings and opinions. We need
to feel that, in general, we speak and do as we honestly think and believe.
But this basic sense of personality integration and consistency can be
achieved, for most people, at the same time that a good deal of conscious
and unconscious dissembling goes on. For, in the first place, our attitudes
and opinions are not always clear and uncontradictory; conflicting attitudes make room for conflicting behavior. In the second place, there is a
wide social tolerance, even expectation, for the use of white lies, acceptable
phrases, circumlocutions, and other forms of behavior that are inconsistent
with real attitudes and opinions.

It may be argued, then, that political life allows—perhaps even demands—a greater amount of dissembling at every level of involvement
than do other human-activity areas. Whether this is true or not, it is
important to bear in mind that, although both common sense and theories
of personality point in the direction of a general correspondence between
beliefs and behavior, there are many occasions when behavior will not be
consistent with attitudes or opinions. The study of public opinion must
therefore be paralleled by and compared in every possible way with the
study of political behavior.

CULTURE AND OPINION HOLDING

10

An individual's opinions are limited and conditioned by physical and chemical reactions within himself, and by the unique experiences of his own development. Though much is known about mental capacity and mental process, debate rages over many key questions, these among others: the effect of genetic variations on psychophysiological abilities; the nature of the processes by which we perceive, store, and recall sense impressions; the basic psychological and biological drives and needs; and even, indeed, whether mind can properly be distinguished from body.

All of these matters are important to the thinking processes, which in turn are basic to the holding of opinions (including public opinions as we have defined them). Nevertheless, we have no reason to believe that the resolution of these psychophysiological questions must be achieved before we can begin to understand the social and political implications of the uniformities and diversities of opinion. For the kinds of problems with which the political scientist and political sociologist deal, many workable, if not provable, assumptions may be made. We may assume that individual opinions are shaped by forces which, in most cases, do not need to be analyzed medically or experimentally. Although a case can be made for the study of politically influential psychopaths,[1] and for the importance of personality types in making or implementing public policy, it is important to note that the focus of our interest is sociopolitical rather than strictly psychological. Hitler may have been an acute paranoid; but this fact (if it is a fact) is important to us only insofar as it relates to the social environment that could raise him to great power and as it relates to the policies tolerated or supported by the leaders and citizens of Nazi Germany.

---

[1] For example, see Harold L. Lasswell, *Psychopathology and Politics* (Chicago: University of Chicago Press, 1930).

For our purposes, the key processes are social rather than psychophysiological; they relate to the interactions among men rather than the interactions within man.

The immediate importance of culture as a limiting factor, and the only distant importance of psychophysical limits, is summarized by one biologist as follows:

> Comparisons of the human brain with mechanical computers suggests that we may be justified in treating man's potential for thought combinations as practically infinite; that is, we need not be much concerned with physical or biological limitation in this regard. On the other hand, man's thought cannot be separated from his cultural history, and here we may look for limitations. It can hardly be denied that the course of man's cultural development has channeled his mode of thinking. Every revolution in scientific thought, whether great or small, reveals that we have not been viewing a particular problem properly because of the restricting effects of ideas from the past. Every superstition, every taboo, every incorrect scientific hypothesis or philosophical concept that persists for any length of time, places some limit on human thought.[2]

Much of our attention throughout the remainder of this book is given to matters that are unmistakably sociopolitical. We are, and will be, concerned largely with the patterned interpersonal relations that affect the character and distributions of opinions—with the ways in which social institutions and group relationships influence agreements and disagreements over public issues.

This chapter is an introduction to, and an overview of, theories, concepts, and evidence of the cultural anthropology of opinion holding. Its intention is to create a background for, and a framework for thinking about, the ways in which collective life molds shared opinions.

10.1   The Concept of Culture

The discovery and elaboration of the concept of culture is one of the few genuine breakthroughs in the social sciences. It is probably impossible to overemphasize the importance of the idea of culture. It is, as Cuber declares, "fundamental to the understanding of the human being and of groups. Most of the other social science ideas grow out of it or are dependent on it."[3]

---

[2] Harold F. Blum, "Time's Arrow and the Evolution of Society," *Princeton University Magazine*, Summer 1961, p. 13; excerpted in *Current*, December 1961, pp. 44–45. Reprinted by permission of *Princeton Alumni Weekly*.

[3] John F. Cuber, *Sociology*, 2nd ed. (New York: Appleton-Century-Crofts, Inc., 1951), p. 65.

Many definitions of culture could be cited. They all agree that it is the whole pattern of learned social values, myths, and traditions, along with the physical products of man's labors, created and shared by the members of a society. It is the whole man-made environment of human life.

Culture is learned. Very little of our day-to-day behavior is forced upon us biologically. Though certain bodily functions must, of course, be performed, even here the details and rituals of eating, elimination, and sex are culturally required (or expected) and prohibited (or discouraged). There are, as Gillin points out, three kinds of evidence that almost all behavior is learned:

First, we have the investigations on new-born infants, which indicate the extreme paucity of inborn goal-directed activity patterns of any type. . . . Our second type of evidence consists of various carefully controlled studies of identical twins who have been reared apart from each other and have grown up developing different custom patterns. In these cases, the individuals were identical in inheritance and differed only in the type of experience and training accorded them. If they grew up to exhibit different culture patterns, we can hardly assign the culture to heredity.

Finally, and perhaps most convincing for anthropological purposes, we have the evidence of the variability of human culture itself. We have already seen that all qualified experts agree that the species is one, biologically speaking. Yet the cultures practised by diverse groups within the species vary enormously among themselves. Likewise, there is no uniformity or regularity in the types of culture to be found within a single race or other subgroup of the species. . . . When we are acquainted with the great variety of cultures, it is impossible to believe that culture is carried in the germ plasm. There are only two other alternatives: either it descends upon people in some mysterious, unknown fashion, or it is learned. The first hypothesis has no data to support it, while the second seems to fit the facts.[4]

It should be clear from the examples Gillin gives, and from the most rudimentary observations everyone can make, that much (probably most) culture is learned, as it were, inadvertently. That part which we learn through our conscious imitation of our cultural teachers, or through the intended pedagogy of those with whom we associate as infants, children, and adults, is no doubt smaller than that which we quite literally grow into as we are socialized: basic eating and clothing habits are not taught in any formal sense, no matter how much the minutiae such as spinach eating may be impressed upon the small fry. The boy does not have to be urged to emulate his father, or the girl her mother, in the gross behavior that marks the development of the "little man" or the "young lady." This is not to say, of course, that the consciously learned subcultural dis-

[4] From *The Ways of Men* by John Gillin. Copyright, 1948, D. Appleton-Century Company, Inc. Reprinted by permission of Appleton-Century-Crofts, p. 191.

tinctions of social class—and especially of the acquisition of skills (which is so much a part of the formal schooling of the child and young adult)—are not important; it is only that the learning of culture in the broadest sense is in a large degree not self-conscious and intentional.

That culture is not alone a matter of deliberate learning is a consequence of the second fundamental characteristic of culture, that *culture is pervasive*. We are figuratively and literally immersed in our culture. Semantically, we find a clue to the total pervasiveness of culture if we consider the use of the term *culture* in the biological sciences. The culture of a micro-organism, of bacteria, for example, is the medium in which it lives and thrives. So it is with the human organism. We could not live without the culture that makes possible not only our social intercourse but every vital act of our individual existence.

Is this too strong a statement of the pervasiveness and indispensability of culture? I think not. There is, for example, some evidence that the existence and perception of ideas themselves depends on the most basic ingredient of culture, language. The argument for this point of view is too complex and lengthy to be set forth here, but some psycholinguists believe that concepts cannot exist unless they are expressive in language.[5] And, note well, language is the creature of culture.

But, it may be asked, cannot individuals exist alone, without society at all? Can there not be Robinson Crusoes? The answer is that there have been, no doubt, Robinson Crusoes. But, like the fictional character, they took their culture with them; the hut they built, the food they gathered, the clothes they improvised—and even the institution of "Man Friday" slavery—were cultural phenomena that washed ashore with them, and without which they would have wandered aimlessly on the beach until death.

Even the celebrated "wolf boy" of Lucknow was immersed in culture. If, as is thought by some, he was indeed raised by wolves, he shared in the culture of the wolves, and he learned from that culture to run on his deformed arms and legs and to bare his teeth when approached by his human captors.[6]

One consequence of the pervasiveness of culture is the likelihood that we cannot completely know ourselves, because objectivity, in the sense of noninvolvement, is impossible. Despite the most exhaustive attempts to "deculturize" themselves, the anthropologists have been unable to view

---

[5] For an excellent summary discussion of this and other evidence of cultural pervasiveness, see Clyde Kluckhohn, "Culture and Behavior," in Gardner Lindzey, ed., *Handbook of Social Psychology* (Reading, Mass.: Addison-Wesley Publishing Co., Inc., 1954), II, 921–976, especially 931–940.

[6] Paul Grimes, "India's 'Wolf Boy,'" *New York Times Magazine*, October 30, 1960, pp. 35ff.

alien cultures (or their own) with complete detachment. I do not suggest by saying this that cultural anthropologists are unable scientifically to study what they aspire to study—or even that the most able among them are very seriously inconvenienced by their own cultural cages. It is a matter of the first importance, however, that we recognize and, insofar as we can, guard against the danger of proclaiming as "truth" that which is only a culturally colored observation, measurement, or judgment.

Besides being learned and pervasive, *culture is patterned*. The elements of culture, the thousands of objects, values, techniques, and behavioral prescriptions, do not exist unrelated to one another. Few if any cultural phenomena are devised or maintained in isolation; rather, they are systematically related. One of the most important books to be published in this century, Ruth Benedict's *Patterns of Culture*,[7] makes this point not only in its title but in all the descriptive and interpretive accounts of the societies she examines. The internal relatedness of cultural traits had been remarked by many anthropologists before Benedict, and some had even noted that the patterns were often unobserved by the culture carriers themselves. Thus, Sapir, pioneering in what we now call the field of personality-in-culture, observed as early as 1927 that "normal human beings, both in confessedly social behavior and often in supposedly individual behavior, are reacting in accordance with deep-seated cultural patterns . . . not so much known as felt, not so much capable of conscious description as of naive practice."[8] Sapir's point ties together both the patterning and the pervasiveness of culture.

Please note that the statement that cultural elements exist in patterned relationships to each other says nothing about the goodness or badness of these patterns or about the functional or dysfunctional consequences of patterning. All cultures are constantly undergoing the reshaping of their patterns. The dynamic unmaking and remaking of cultural patterns is evident, to some extent, in even the most moribund cultures; in social aggregates experiencing rapid demographic, technological, or ideological change, the repatterning may proceed so swiftly as

---

7 (Boston: Houghton Mifflin Co., 1934.) Benedict's book is important both because it was a provocative challenge to her fellow social scientists and because, as an early best seller of the paperback age, it made the culture concept familiar to tens (probably hundreds) of thousands of students of the 1940s and 1950s. I think it is of interest, at least to political scientists, that some criticisms made of Benedict's book, by social scientists, and others as well, were essentially political criticisms. For instance, it was said that she had exaggerated the competitiveness of the Kwakiutl Indians and the cooperativeness of the Zuni in order to make a disguised attack on free-enterprise capitalism.

8 Edward Sapir, "The Unconscious Patterning of Behavior in Society," in David G. Mandlebaum, ed., *Selected Writings of Edward Sapir* (Berkeley: University of California Press, 1949), p. 548.

to defy even the measurement of its change. Only in the years to come will we be able to assess with accuracy the revolutionary cultural changes currently taking place in parts of Asia and Africa. This dynamic process is the meaning of the technologically induced telescoping of historical development stages in all of the societies being modernized: the old cultural ways are being modified or replaced at such a rapid rate that no person, group, or policy is able even to take account of the change, much less guide it into desired forms.

Whether cultural patterns are undergoing revolutionary change, as in modern Africa, or whether they seem static and immobile, as during long centuries in feudal Europe, there is a constant tension in every culture between the factors making for change and the influences for the maintenance of the status quo. Innovation is the great progenitor of change—innovation of ideas and applied technology. On the other side, habit and the convenience of regularity (of the certainty of anticipatory response) are the great forces underlying the stability of cultural patterns.

The modern era, which we usually consider to have commenced in the sixteenth or seventeenth century, is characterized everywhere by increased intracultural tensions and by greater change, in general, than any previous historical epoch. While we are unable to chart or predict the details of these changes within any given culture or any brief time span, a case can be made that in the middle of the twentieth century we are experiencing two vast secular tendencies in cultural-pattern change: intracultural diversity is increasing and intercultural diversity is decreasing.

10.2   Increasing Diversity within Cultures

The evidence of social anthropology appears to indicate that there are generally, within any given culture, fewer prescriptions and proscriptions than there were fifty, one hundred, or five hundred years ago. The patterns of values and behavior are less rigid; fewer things "must be done," fewer "cannot be done." The behavioral choices for the individual are in most places vastly increased.

One hears a great deal today in the United States, and in the Western world, about conformity. It is a *bad word* for many educators (especially in the humanities and the social sciences), political moralizers, editorial writers, and other preachers, lay and cleric. There is a sense, of course, in which the wide acceptance by adolescents, for example, of faddish peer-group styles or activities, or the adult worship of the symbols of money income, is unfortunate, stultifying to individual personality, and perhaps harmful to society. But the "conformity" of mid-twentieth-century America must be distinguished from the conformity of twelfth-century Britain or nineteenth-century New Guinea. It is the difference between having choices and not using them and not having choices at all.

Conformity in feudal Europe tended to inhere in the more rigid cultural characteristics of fixed obligations to and by the land-holding and ecclesiastical classes. Most of the people (and even to some considerable degree the nobility and higher gentry) were not free to choose their places of residence, occupations, mates, their duties to kinfolk and neighbors, or their belief-value structures. These were all given them by accident of birth; these were all provided by cultural patterns. The cultural imperatives, to use our terminology, tended to be limiting factors more than influencing factors in the determination of opinions and behavior. In many cultures, the institution of slavery alone deprived thousands of people of the right to any self-directed opinion or behavior at all. Serfdom allowed somewhat more, but relatively little, by modern standards.

Margaret Mead has described the cultural totalitarianism of the Balinese as she observed it in the 1920s. The Bali native did not depend on anything which could be called a public opinion process—even when defined, most narrowly, as consideration of an issue leading to small-group behavior. The individual was not expected to have an opinion; his group and role involvements all so tightly circumscribed his thinking that an issue, as we might understand it, could hardly arise. When an unusual matter arose, the facts were unemotionally laid before a leader, whose role it was to determine, within the traditions, what decision should be made.[9]

Modern cultural patterns are vastly more permissive. In the Western world, and with increasing rapidity in the non-Western world, the masses are allowed to make, each individual for himself, all the basic choices denied their ancestors of a thousand years ago. This, of course, is not universally true; some occupations, some mates, and some residential areas are still denied to members of minority races and religions, even in the United States. Some cultural *musts* and *cannots* remain outside the formal legal structure,[10] but there can be no doubt that the cultural requirements and denials have greatly descreased in number, while the cultural possibilities have multiplied many times over.

The transformation from cultural patterns of compulsion to patterns

---

[9] "Public Opinion Mechanisms among Primitive People," *Public Opinion Quarterly,* I (1937), 5–16.

[10] One of the concomitants of the transition of cultures from less to more freedom of choice for the individual is that the cultural *requirements* tend to become codified into the legal structure, so that the distinction between law and mores (or customs) becomes much more explicit. The common law gives way, also, to statutory law.

of permissiveness has been brought about largely by technological and ideological innovation. To say so, however, is to say something by now as trite as it is important; it is enough to observe that modern cultures are without exception more varied and rich in choices for most individuals than were previous cultures. There are still persons in our society for whom the cultural choices are not varied and rich enough to satisfy either the promise of the human spirit or the ideals of the good society. For both these objectives, we need to pursue the further enrichment and variation of our cultural patterns, and to increase the available choices for every individual. But the long trend is clearly in this direction. Intracultural diversity is, so far as one can tell, everywhere increasing.

10.3   Decreasing Diversity among Cultures

As intracultural diversity increases, intercultural diversity diminishes, for the same reasons that individual choices increase within cultures—because of technological and ideological innovations. It is an old story that the missionaries who brought the Bible to the South Sea Islanders were followed by traders and soldiers who brought radios, wrist watches, K rations and syphilis. For better or worse, the Papuans' culture became increasingly rich and varied, and increasingly like that of the West. In little as well as larger ways, among subcultures as well as across strikingly different cultures, intracultural variety increases and intercultural diversity disappears; the British adopt American refrigerators and quick-frozen foods, while gin and tonic becomes a standard American drink.

The possible implications and consequences of these long-run cultural tendencies make interesting speculation:

1. Within cultures, opinion and behavior become less the direct consequences of the requirements of culture and more a matter of the interplay of the voluntaristic social institutions and more or less free choices of individuals.

2. Law, as the codification of the remaining compulsory elements in the culture, becomes more clearly distinguishable from morals and mores. Government, as the agency that possesses officiality and a monopoly of coercive power, becomes more clearly differentiated from such unofficial, noncoercive power structures as the economic and religious.

3. Among cultures, the more striking differences tend to disappear. It seems likely that, as this intercultural uniformity increases, the "hard" facts of various levels of technology, education, and literacy, plus modes of production and urbanization, will have increasingly similar influences on public opinion, culture for culture. Thus, enough intercultural con-

sensus might be forthcoming, in time, to support a genuine world opinion. This uniformity is also related to the economic interdependence of the nation-states and to the hope of those who may be described as functional world federalists that political union and world public opinion may follow the economic integration of nations.

One cannot hope that the possible salutary effects of diminishing intercultural differences will be either rapid or profound. The causes of international conflict and war have not often been found in cultural diversity, and the history of man is more that of like peoples fighting one another than that of likes fighting unlikes. Still, it has been said that one hope for the democratization of the Soviet Union (leading, presumably, to a decrease in Soviet–U.S. tensions) is that a society with high levels of technology is compelled to permit increasing freedom of information and individual choice. If so, and if there are other evidences that the cultural patterns of the U.S. and Russia tend to converge, we may be somewhat more optimistic about the resolution of conflicting opinions and policies.

10.4   Culture as a Limiting and Influencing Factor in the Formation of Opinion

It may be useful to sum up the foregoing discussion of culture and recent cultural tendencies in terms of our model of the opinion-forming process. If we think of culture as a limiting factor, and, for a moment, as the only limiting factor of concern to us, then cultural requirements define the large end of the funnel of opinion causality. In the tightly culture-bound society, the possible opinions that may be held on any issue are few. The press of cultural imperatives—the limiting factor—is close upon the individual, and the funnel of causality is small (see Fig. 10–1).

In modern societies, the increasing intracultural diversity and the change of many cultural patterns from requirements to influences may be

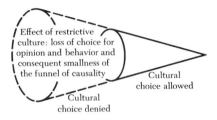

Figure 10–1. Funnel of Causality: Choice Restricted in Primitive Societies

represented as pushing choice further back into the funnel. By contrast to primitive patterns, modern cultural patterns *require* fewer opinions; but they *permit* many more. Still, they help to define at some point, along with the other limiting factors, the large end of the funnel of causality.

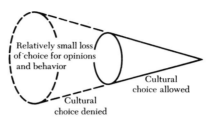

Figure 10–2. Funnel of Causality: Choice Enlarged in Modern Societies

10.5   The Study of Political Culture

An examination of the sources of public opinion should take note of the cultural patterns related to the processes of governance. For our purposes, the technological state of the society, the institutionalization of large economic and social forms, and the artifacts of the people are only important as they relate to the government and the social conflicts that are thought to be properly treatable by public authority. We are more interested in what might be called the *political culture,* namely, those thought and behavior patterns that are especially valued or devalued by the society and have to do more or less specifically with political leadership and the handling of political conflict.

Such a narrowing of interest from general cultural patterns to more specific patterns of governmental activity is exemplified by the conceptual framework adopted in the pioneering work of Gabriel A. Almond and Sidney Verba, *The Civic Culture: Political Attitudes and Democracy in Five Nations.* Noting the rapid decrease of intercultural diversity. Almond and Verba declare that the emerging world culture will be determined in its *social* organization by technology and rationality. But of its *political* orientation only one thing is clear: the mystique of popular participation will be pervasive. Though the common man will everywhere be expected to participate, the mode of his participation is uncertain:

The emerging nations are presented with two different models of the modern participatory state, the democratic and the totalitarian. The democratic state offers the ordinary man the opportunity to take part in the political decision-making process as an influential citizen; the totalitarian offers him the role of the "participant subject."[11]

The Almond-Verba study is an investigation of the political cultures of five nations: the United States, Britain, Germany, Italy, and Mexico. The political culture, as defined by these investigators, consists of

the ways in which political elites make decisions, their norms and attitudes, as well as the norms and attitudes of the ordinary citizen, his relation to government and to his fellow citizens. . . . They have the more diffuse properties of belief systems or of codes of personal relations, which the anthropologists tell us spread only with great difficulty, undergoing substantial change in the process.[12]

From their matched interviews with about one thousand persons in each of the five countries, Almond and Verba found some striking differences in the political cultures of the five countries. Comparisons are made on such criteria as knowledge and awareness of government and politics, political emotion and involvement, sense of political obligation and competence, and social attitudes and experiences in other authority contexts.

Differences in political culture will demonstrably influence the kinds of attitudes and opinions held by the citizens of various nation states. For an understanding of the genesis, stability, and importance of national opinion patterns, these factors of political culture may be critical. For the determination of larger questions of international politics, differences due to political culture may be less important—in view of the fact that policy-making elites tend to be most cosmopolitan and least susceptible to the blinders of culture.[13]

[11] (Princeton, N.J.: Princeton University Press, 1963), p. 4.

[12] *Ibid.*, p. 5.

[13] See Bernard C. Hennessy, "Psycho-Cultural Studies of National Character: Relevances for International Relations," *Background: Journal of the International Studies Association*, VI (1962), 27–49.

FAMILY, RELIGION, AND OPINION HOLDING

11

In the previous two chapters, we considered the psychology, and what might be called the cultural anthropology, of opinion holding. Now we come to the sociology of opinion holding. The question we ask in this chapter is fundamentally this: What are the probable effects on opinion, in terms of individual cases and statistical modalities, of family, religion, and other more or less enduring forms of collective life?

In considering this question, we are concerned almost wholly with influencing rather than limiting factors. Social institutions create powerful ideological channels and exert significant pressures on the individual as he forms and modifies his opinions; but in the relatively democratic community, social institutions will not alone determine, or require, that the individual hold some opinions rather than others. It should be clear from this statement that we are restricting our consideration to democratic societies. Furthermore, I do not pretend that anything like a comprehensive survey of the influence of social institutions on opinions can be given in this chapter—or in this book—although later, and in somewhat different contexts, I propose to take up in more detail the importance of certain forms of social organization, such as the mass media and governmental agencies.

11.1 Influence of the Family on Opinions

"Blood is thicker than water." "As the twig is bent so grows the tree." "Like father like son."

With these and many other sayings, the unknown historians of folk wisdom testify to the importance of the family in the shaping of opinion and behavior. One of the ways in which the rigid cultural patterns of the past bore most heavily on the individual was in the imposition of strict role and status responsibilities on each member of the family. In learning these responsibilities, and the related folklore of the tribe, the children learned to accept the views of their elders as proper and unchallengeable.

In modern America, the child does not have to accept uncritically the opinions of his parents; before he is very old, he has access and exposure to other views, which are often different from and sometimes incompatible with those of his parents. Nonetheless, though he does not have to accept his parents' views, he is very likely to do so; for his parents' influence is central and pervasive, at least in the first ten or fifteen years of his life, whereas his exposure to conflicting views is apt to be fleeting and tangential. Some attitudes and opinions, like most of the individual's personality characteristics, seem to be fixed before the child is ten years old. Modification of family-shaped opinions usually takes place very slowly and, in most cases, only under the pressure of strong extrafamilial social influences or of overwhelming evidence of fact or theory. Therefore, within the family there is a high order of agreement on economic, social, and political issues. This agreement is largely a result of three sources of influence.

Consciously and unconsciously, parents indoctrinate their children. What is good and bad, what is right and wrong, what is naughty and nice, what is proper and improper—by direct command and advice, and by indirect references and by setting examples, parents shape children to their own values and beliefs. This process is an inevitable and necessary part of socialization, of making little humans fit to live in a sort of social close-order drill with other humans little and big. It gives stability to the culture, predictability for day-to-day social relations, and—not least importantly—tranquility to family life.

Children imitate their parents. Like parental indoctrination, childhood imitation is both conscious and unconscious. To use the terminology of the sociologist, the ideal role model for the daughter is almost always her mother; for the son, his father. There is some evidence that the influence of the parental model decreases as the child grows older and he finds other models from among his wider social contacts; but the importance of the parent as a person to be imitated almost never wholly disappears, and it is strongest when the child's opinions and personality are the most malleable.

Members of a family are influenced by the same environmental stimuli. This fact is an important cause of the similarity of opinions within the family, although it is apt to be overlooked if we focus too attentively on the interpersonal influence within the family. All the family is influenced by the same neighbors and neighborhood, by the same friends (who usually share with the family such social characteristics as class, religion, and ethnicity), and by the same economic forces of the area and of the father's occupation. The family members read the same newspapers, attend to the same radio and TV programs, listen to the same preacher and other local opinion leaders, gather the same gossip, and hear the same stories. Exposed as they are, day in and day out, to identical, similar, and convergent stimuli, it is no wonder that families exhibit a marked uniformity of opinion.

There is much evidence of the tenacity of family influence on the political views of children, adolescents, and adults. Hyman reviewed a great many studies of parent-children political attitudes and opinions. His summary of findings strongly supports the common-sense observation that family influence is high (but that there are other important influences), and raises a caution about the psychoanalytic view that child opinions are frequently evolved in opposition or rebellion to parental opinions:

> These and other studies establish very clearly a family correspondence in views that are relevant to matters of political orientation. Over a great many such correlations from the different studies, the median value approximates .5. The signs, almost without exception, are *never negative*. The only negative findings bear on the area of war, where we might expect the larger social climate to be powerful, and these are but two correlations out of a total of perhaps one hundred. The import is clear. While influence might conceivably flow from child to parent, what is much more likely is that parents are the agents who transmit politically relevant attitudes to their children. The almost complete absence of negative correlations provides considerable evidence *against* the theory that political attitudes are formed *generally* in terms of rebellion and opposition to parents.[1]

Much attention has also been given to the transmission of political party preferences from parents to children, to voting similarities, and to other evidences of family influence on political *behavior* (as distinguished from political opinions). One of the earliest of these studies was made by Gordon W. Allport of the attitudes of Dartmouth undergraduates toward the presidential election campaign of 1928. He found that only 43 out of 361 voted or would have voted differently from their fathers.[2] Fay and Middleton found in 1932 that of their students 77 per cent of the fathers were Republican and 67 per cent of the students favored Hoover; 21 per cent of the fathers were Democratic and 30 per cent of the students favored Roosevelt.[3]

[1] Herbert Hyman, *Political Socialization* (New York: The Free Press of Glencoe, 1959), p. 72. Italics in original; footnotes omitted.

[2] "The Composition of Political Attitudes," *American Journal of Sociology*, XXXV (1929), 233.

[3] Paul J. Fay and Warren C. Middleton, "Certain Factors Related to Liberal and Conservative Attitudes of College Students: Father's Political Preference; Presidential Candidates Favored in the 1932 and 1936 Elections," *Journal of Social Psychology*, XI (1940), 112.

In their study of the 1948 election, Berelson and his colleagues found that, over-all, 75 per cent of first voters cast their ballots as their fathers did. Perhaps more interesting is the fact that among adults in families living together, and among those who had made up their minds in October, over 90 per cent agreed in their voting intentions.[4] This fact is interesting, yes, but it is hardly surprising either that there should be very high agreement among adults of the same generation, or of several generations, when they choose to remain together as a family unit, and that there should be high (but not quite so high) agreement between parents and children for whom the parental ties have become loosened. Families living together are almost certain to show higher agreement of attitudes and opinion than are families living apart. Note that there is no causal implication here; living apart may be cause or result of or have no relation to differences of opinion. The point is merely that, although distance *may* make the heart grow fonder, it is *almost certain* to weaken the influences that produce like opinions among families and strengthen those that produce unlike opinions.

Within families, disagreement of opinion comes primarily from cross pressures that result when stimuli are not shared equally by all members of the family. Perhaps the most important of these pressures are the effects of different levels and types of education within a family. Children *learn* to disagree with their parents; and the disagreements tend to be more profound if this learning involves not just new information but new values and life styles—as when the children of newly arrived immigrants go to American schools, or the son of the Southern hill farmer attends an Ivy League college. Like-mindedness within families is weakened by differences in economic stimuli, as when the son "graduates" from his father's haberdashery to the big department store, or when he leaves the farm to become a railroad brakeman. Differences in social status seem to be important, as when the daughter of the shoemaker marries the local physician or the newly rich oil driller joins the country club. Finally, changing family roles tend to create opinion differences, as when a daughter becomes a mother and follows the advice of Dr. Spock rather than that of her mother. Each of these clusters of influence—educational, economic, social status, and role—will be considered separately, albeit briefly, below. Here it is enough to say that they interact with—sometimes reinforcing, sometimes weakening—opinion agreement within families.

---

4 Bernard Berelson et al., *Voting* (Chicago: University of Chicago Press, 1954), pp. 89, 92. Factor analysis in a panel study of value climates in ten Illinois high schools indicated that the nuclear family influence explained 68 per cent of the variations in the party preferences of the students. See Martin L. Levin, "Social Climates and Political Socialization," *Public Opinion Quarterly*, XXIV (1960), 515.

11.2   Religion and Opinion Holding

Although a *religious feeling,* however defined, may exist in the individual without the aid or direction of social organization, such an unnurtured feeling is so uncommon that it is of little significance in the making and remaking of public opinion. When we talk of the influence of religion in public life, we are talking about the influence of religious organizations—we are talking of churches and synagogues. There may be elements of the individual conscience and of personal ethics that relate *self* to cosmos and provide sanction for behavior, but these elements, too, will depend mainly on church doctrine, cultural norms, legal prescriptions, or perhaps on all three.

For this overview of the sociology of opinion holding, it will not be too great a distortion to think of religion in the United States as organized Christianity and Judaism. Our concern is primarily with the patterns and probabilities of influence, in the group and statistical sense, although we intend not to overlook the importance of religiously based reinforcement or conflict for the individual opinion holder.

11.21   The Importance of Organized Religion in American Society

There are many ways of measuring the religious influence in a society. The simplest, and by no means the least important, is by the number of organized bodies and individual adherents. Recent copies of the *Yearbook of American Churches* report that there are more than 120,000,000 members in over 250 religious bodies in the United States. Protestant sects claim a total of about 67,000,000 members, or something over a third of all Americans. The major Protestant groups, in order of size, are: Baptist, Methodist, Lutheran, and Presbyterian. Roman Catholic membership is reported to be about 45,000,000, or 24 per cent of the total population.[5] Jews number something over 5,500,000, and Eastern Orthodox Churches claim over 3,000,000 members.[6]

Numbers alone are inadequate to assess religious influence. For a variety of reasons, members of the Jewish faith (about one thirtieth of

[5] Catholics count all persons baptized; most Protestant groups base membership figures on persons thirteen years of age and older.

[6] Figures taken from the *New York Times,* January 15, 1965.

the American people) have greater political and social importance than an equal number of Protestants or Catholics. The members of the Church of Jesus Christ of Latter-day Saints (Mormon) have also, no doubt, influence in American politics beyond their mere numbers. In some regions, and in some policy areas, other Protestant denominations may have considerable impact on public opinion and public policy; it might be argued, for example, that the Unitarians, the Christian Scientists, and the Jehovah's Witnesses, have each contributed more to the American elaboration of individual rights and civil liberties than have most other social groups of equal size.

Of basic importance is the fact that Jewish and Christian doctrines are a large part of the culture of the Western world. The norms of our everyday behavior and the ideals we profess as a society are obtained from the sacred books and the exegetical writings of the saints and teachers of organized religions. Not only that, but millions of church members draw much of their counsel and advice for daily decisions from contemporary religious leaders of every level. The fabric of our society is interwoven with the threads of religion and the religious. A recent study of religion and sociopolitical attitudes made the point in these terms:

> . . . it is clear that religion in various ways is constantly influencing the daily lives of the masses of men and women in the modern American metropolis. More than that: through its impact on individuals, religion makes an impact on all the other institutional systems of the community in which these individuals participate. Hence, the influence of religion operates at the social level as well as at the personal level.[7]

The significance of religion in political and social decision making is perhaps greater than is appreciated academically. Take two examples, one minor, the other at least notorious and possibly significant. First, a congressman, recently extending his sympathies on the death of a very undistinguished colleague, reported that the deceased had been a leader of a rather sizable group of congressmen who met weekly at lunchtime for a religious and prayer session. Two, following the Supreme Court's decision declaring unconstitutional the "official" prayer of the New York State Board of Regents,[8] the hue and cry from civic and political leaders was everywhere vociferous and in some places heartfelt. Although criticism of the Court has become a regular sport for certain conservative groups, many political leaders—whatever their position on the liberal-conservative scale —may feel that they need to make occasional proreligious statements. But

---

[7] Gerhard Lenski, *The Religious Factor* (Garden City, N.Y.: Doubleday & Co., Inc., 1961), p. 289.

[8] *Engel v. Vitale,* 370 U.S. 421, 1962.

no further point is intended; widely shared views that are essentially religious are important in the making of public policy. The policy makers themselves need not have religious views that are relevant (or are thought to be relevant) to the issues; it is enough that their behavior is influenced by such views held by their constitutents.

If the influence of religion and religious doctrine sometimes appears to be inadequately appreciated by the academician, it may be that the academician projects his own values and procedures on the world. The person skilled in the use of scientific method (or at least what passes for scientific method in the social sciences) is not apt to be heavily influenced by religious doctrine or by articles of religious faith. Uninfluenced by these things himself, he may tend to see the world as uninfluenced by them.

The presidential election of 1960 was a lesson for political scientists—in addition to its being a larger lesson in the patterns and limits of religious influence in the political life of the United States—for, in 1960, religion *did* make a difference to millions of Americans. Many Catholics seem to have voted for Senator Kennedy because he was a Catholic; many Protestants seem to have voted against him for the same reason. Though various motivations and vote influences have not been and cannot be fully explained, the most careful analysis seems to show that Senator Kennedy, had he not been a Catholic, would have been elected by a two-party majority considerably greater than the 50.1 per cent he received.[9]

11.22   Religion and Sociopolitical Attitudes

Organized religion in the United States in the 1960s may be an important factor in the maintenance of conservative values and the political and economic status quo—especially insofar as Protestantism is the predominant religious current in America. The historic tie in the theory and practice between Protestantism and capitalism has been stated most energetically and with considerable persuasiveness by Weber and Tawney.[10] Their evidence and arguments cannot be repeated here, even in summary fashion; it may only be noted that, historically, many theories

[9] Philip E. Converse, Angus Campbell, Warren E. Miller, and Donald E. Stokes, "Stability and Change in 1960: A Reinstating Election," *American Political Science Review*, LV (1961), 269–280.

[10] Max Weber, *The Protestant Ethic and the Spirit of Capitalism* (New York: Charles Scribner's Sons, 1958); and R. H. Tawney, *Religion and the Rise of Capitalism* (New York: Harcourt, Brace and World, Inc., 1926).

and opinions of the early modern period—the importance of freedom of choice for individuals, the philosophy of salvation through work, the religious and economic colonization of newly discovered land, and the breakdown of restrictions regarding money and credit—hastened and reinforced the growth of capitalism and Protestantism alike.

Two caveats are in order. First, the Weber-Tawney argument is historical, reflecting Protestantism from the sixteenth century to World War I; it says little explicitly about the Protestantism of mid-twentieth century. Second, capitalism was initially a form of economic radicalism; and, although it is no longer radical in the West, it can hardly be described as having been a conservative doctrine during most of the period about which Weber and Tawney wrote.

Furthermore, there are elements in many Protestant sects (and in Catholicism—which is not so monolithic as some Protestants think) that are highly critical of the status quo. Childs and Cater summarize the liberal strain in contemporary Protestantism as they see it reflected in the policies and positions of the National Council of Churches:

> One important part of our modern Christian heritage is the institutions which grew up as a result of the Social Gospel. In 1908, thirty denominations came together in Philadelphia to establish the Federal Council of Churches. From the outset . . . the Federal Council displayed a strong sense of social responsibility, fighting *against* the seven-day work week, child labor, unhealthy working conditions for women; fighting *for* healthy industrial conditions, old-age insurance, the right of employees to organize, and a living minimum wage. . . .
> The social conscience of the Church, awakened by the pioneers of the Social Gospel in the late nineteenth century, has not returned to slumber. . . . [T]he quest for a Christian approach to the major economic problems of our time continues. Church leaders have shed the easy optimism of the early Social Gospel and reexamined some of the fundamental precepts. . . . There is no tendency toward an easy acceptance of complete laissez faire or complete socialism.[11]

The more liberal elements of the Catholic Church may be seen in the policy resolutions of the National Catholic Welfare Conference, in the articles and editorials of the Jesuit journal *America,* and, far over on the left, in the romantic near-anarchy of the Catholic Worker movement.

Despite the historical changes since early Protestantism, and the liberal contemporary currents, there is still reason to believe that the net effect of organized religion is a conservative one in American public life. One content analysis of *The Christian Century Pulpit,* a monthly magazine of sermons, concludes that "a movement away from the 'social gospel'

---

11 Marquis W. Childs and Douglass Cater, *Ethics in a Business Society* (New York: Harper & Row, Publishers, 1954), pp. 149–150; italics in original. Reprinted by permission of New American Library of World Literature, Inc. The Federal Council of Churches was one of the constituent groups of the National Council of Churches, founded in 1950.

with the introduction of a note of social pessimism seems observable in the preaching of American Protestant ministers during the period from 1929 to 1940."[12] More recently, Lerner, after reviewing the social teachings of the major Protestant theologians of the 1950s, concludes that:

> A reaction has . . . set in against this humanist emphasis [of the social gospel]. Increasingly the young American intellectuals have been turning not to a social religion but to a new theological intensity which is at once radically pessimist in its premises about human nature and social possibility, and also a return to some of the old Calvinist themes. Theologians like Paul Tillich and Reinhold Niebuhr, while affirming a deep interest in contemporary social struggles, put their chief stress on the corruption of the human enterprise, the limits of human will and action, the difficulties of spiritual growth as well as of social struggle.[13]

The Roman Catholic Church (though teaching that private property is a God-given right) has never been wedded to strong free-enterprise positions. Considerable welfare-state activity, even some forms of cooperative and socialist organization, are quite consistent with the encyclicals and messages of recent Popes.[14] On the other hand, in Spain and Latin America, individual freedoms have been denied by the Church and by Church-supported governmental policies; here at home, the witch-hunts conducted in the early 1950s by Senator Joseph McCarthy and others had strong support from lay Catholics and some high officials. Thus, the history of modern Catholicism has been such that one is compelled to doubt the depths of its dedication to civil liberties. Likewise, some fundamentalist Protestants, whipped up by what appears to be a coalition of fanatical anticommunists, money-making evangelical preachers, and frightened free-enterprisers, appear to have accepted the fanciful (not to say reactionary) notion that a return to the America of 1900 would do away with the Soviet Union, the income tax, and industrial unionism all in one sweep.[15]

It appears to be the case, therefore, that there are powerful conservative influences within the Christian churches. The conservatism of

---

[12] Thomas Hamilton, "Social Optimism and Pessimism in American Protestantism," *Public Opinion Quarterly*, VI (1942), 280. Hamilton argues that the study of sermons may be significant, "since the pulpit is of some importance in the formulation of public opinion."

[13] Max Lerner, *America as a Civilization* (New York: Simon and Schuster, Inc., 1957), p. 709.

[14] See, for examples, Leo XIII, *Rerum Novarum* (1891); Pius XI, *Quadragesimo Anno* (1931); and John XXIII, *Mater et Magister* (1961). The last of these encyclicals summarizes and adds to the other two.

[15] In the early 1960s, the Protestant far right seems to have been concentrated in the Christian Anti-Communist Crusade, headed by the Rev. Dr. Fred C. Schwarz, and in The Christian Crusade, run by Oklahoma evangelist Billy James Hargis.

the Protestant ethic tends to support rugged individualism and an economic order in which social welfare is conceived of as a private rather than a public function. The conservatism of the Roman Catholic hierarchy and institutions, and of a significant and perhaps growing portion of Protestant fundamentalists, is that of inadequate regard for the civil liberties of political nonconformists and dissenters.

There are, no doubt, many sources of political conservatism in the Christian churches of twentieth-century America. First, to the extent that religious organizations depend on group acceptance of certain fundamental doctrines that are considered absolute (that is, right, eternal, and incontrovertible), and to the extent that this absolutism becomes a way of thinking about beliefs and behavior, to that extent the churches and their members tend to lose sight of and patience with the relativistic nature of democratic society. It can hardly have been a matter of chance that that part of the Christian world in which democracy has been least successful is precisely that part—Mediterranean Europe and Latin America—in which the most doctrinaire branch of Christianity has had the most power. Nor can it be wholly fortuitous that the most doctrinaire Protestant sects have been strongest in those areas of the American South and Midwest (primarily) where anti-Negro and anti-Catholic feeling has been the most virulent and accompanied by the most frequent denials of civil rights and civil liberties. Lerner nicely sums up the basic and persistent conflict between the spirit of democracy and that of revealed religion:

Democracy is the policy of individual choices and of majority consent; it can be run effectively only where there is a habituation to hard choices. Those who are certain of the simplicity of revealed truth make the initial choice of submission and do not have to make any subsequent choices; they do not furnish a fertile soil for the democratic seed. Those who expect miracles will not take the risk of dissent. Those who are sure of dogma given to them will not make the arduous effort of winning the slow and gradual victories of an always unfinished society. Finally, those who suffer no conflict within the arena of their own minds will not generate the needed dynamism to transcend the conflict and resolve their conscience.[16]

Second, religious organizations seem to become more conservative, with regard to their economic, social, and welfare doctrines, as they become more "successful." Success means membership and material wealth, and the fact is that radical groups, almost by definition—except in revolutionary circumstances—have little of either. There is a natural history of successful protest movements—and all religious groups have their beginnings in protest—that is one of change from small militant membership

---

16 Lerner, *America as a Civilization* (see footnote 13), p. 706. Reprinted by permission of Simon and Schuster, Inc.

out of step with their time to large, more or less apathetic membership accepting, and accepted by, the dominant social forces of their time. In American political history, this pattern is perhaps best seen in the rise and the taming of the grangers to the Grange, of the One Big Union to the AFL-CIO, and of the suffragettes to the League of Women Voters.[17]

It probably cannot be said that the acquisition of wealth is alone an important factor in the conservatism of church groups. That argument is sometimes made—indeed, it will be made in this book—to explain in part the political opinions of persons associated with big business, and especially with big mass media. But wealth by itself is not an important factor in producing conservatism in church doctrine and among church leadership. There are at least three reasons for this: (a) the doctrine of clerical poverty is widely enough held, even among Protestant sects, that individual wealth among church leaders offers no temptation to find reason and fairness in the economic status quo; (b) the wealth of church groups tends to be used for reformist ends—charity, teaching, and conversion—that daily remind these groups not only of their own limited resources but of the almost unlimited need for reform; and finally (c) one practical result of church immunity from taxation is that church resources are not reduced, as are those of wealthy individuals and corporations, by expensive government welfare policies.

Although it seems unlikely that wealth alone may tend to make churches conservative, size of membership, by itself, may have an important relationship to the organization's social and political opinion structure. It is doubtlessly not just chance that the smallest doctrinally identifiable churches in America (to distinguish them from personality-centered, local, or fundamentalist splinter groups) are also the least tolerant of the sociopolitical status quo. The Quakers, Unitarians, Brethren, and Jehovah's Witnesses are all (though in different ways) quite critical of mass social and political values in modern life; they remain small in numbers. Roman Catholics and the larger Protestant denominations seem to be on much better terms with those values. This fact is not a surprising point, however, since an organization that is generally supportive of the dominant and majority values of a society will by definition be supportive of the status quo, and will therefore gain many adherents, as long as access is not restricted and personal needs are met by membership. Conformity, in such cases, feeds on conformity, and the status quo is unchallenged.

The evidence for the claim that church influence in mid-twentieth-century America is predominantly conservative does not come alone from

---

[17] For an excellent summary of the natural history of protest movements, with specific illustrations from the history of American political interest groups, see V. O. Key, Jr., *Politics, Parties, and Pressure Groups*, 4th ed. (New York: Thomas Y. Crowell Co., 1958), pp. 46–50.

the analysis of doctrine and the official pronouncements of church leadership or policy. Attitude and opinion studies, on the whole, bear out the conservative image of churches and churchgoing. In the three-way breakdown of Protestants, Catholics, and Jews, only Jews are consistently found to express liberal opinions on social and political questions.

In their analysis of six Gallup surveys of 1945 and 1946 (a total of over 12,000 interviews), the Allinsmiths found that among Christian groups the Catholics were the most supportive of welfare-state activities, followed by Protestants in this order: Baptist, Lutheran, Methodist, Episcopalian, Presbyterian, and Congregational. This order is precisely inverse to the socioeconomic-status order of these groups, and the authors quite properly conclude that this finding "is a clear demonstration that economic role rather than religious affiliation is the important determinant of this politico-economic opinion [i.e., that of state-guaranteed welfare versus individual enterprise]."[18] More to the point, and of more import (for it was hardly a discovery that Catholics and fundamentalist Protestants tend to be poor and, like the poor of every sort, are apt to endorse economic equalitarianism), was the Allinsmiths' suggestion that on measures of noneconomic liberalism, such as support for civil liberties and for U.S. international involvement, the high-status Christians would score above the low-status Christians. These analysts found, indeed, that on one question, dealing with relations with Russia, the liberalism order was almost exactly opposite that derived from welfare-state questions alone. On relations with Russia, the high-status, high-education religious-group members (Congregational, Presbyterian, and Episcopalian) were much more liberal than were those low-status groups on the other end of the scale (Baptists and Catholics).[19] The Allinsmiths found Jews to be liberal,

18 Wesley Allinsmith and Beverly Allinsmith, "Religious Affiliation and Politico-Economic Attitude: A Study of Eight Major U.S. Religious Groups," *Public Opinion Quarterly*, XII (1948), 383. See also, for a recent confirmation of the Allinsmith findings, Benton Johnson, "Ascetic Protestantism and Political Preference," *Public Opinion Quarterly*, XXVI (1962), 34–46.

19 *Ibid.*, pp. 386–387. Although considerable sophistication has been achieved since 1948, there is still a great deal of confusion and superficial thinking among social scientists about the nature of liberalism and liberalism measures. Some social scientists prefer to define liberalism as a willingness to use governmental power to maximize individual welfare, bearing in mind that this view represents, historically, a near about-face from the attitudes of eighteenth- and nineteenth-century liberals; see, for example, Angus Campbell et al., *The American Voter* (New York: John Wiley & Sons, Inc., 1960), pp. 193–194. Others look for a noninstrumental definition relating to the basic personality or attitude set of the individual; thus Francis Carney argues that the distinguishing characteristic of the liberal personality is "intellectualism." He says:

"By intellectualism I mean simply the conviction that man, through his unaided reason, can have complete knowledge of himself and his world, and through knowledge can conquer his problems. Thus, there has ever been an affinity for science in the

regardless of individual economic status, on all measurement indexes; this finding, too, is a fact of considerable importance and will be returned to.

Stouffer's findings confirmed, in large measure, the Allinsmith study. Stouffer and his collaborators analyzed data gathered from 4,939 persons in a nationwide probability sample and from 1,533 community leaders in 123 cities in randomly selected sampling areas. Stouffer was concerned with measuring public toleration for political nonconformity in the context of the real and perceived internal and external Communist threat of 1954. He reported that churchgoers are more intolerant of political nonconformity than are nonchurchgoers, in the national sample, whether the results are controlled for sex (that is, when the factors of greater churchgoing by women and greater intolerance by women are taken into account), for education, for age, for degree of interest in issues, or for differences in the perceived dangers of internal Communist threat.[20] There is some inferential evidence from responses in the South that Protestants in that region may be less tolerant of political nonconformity than are Catholics; but this is not to be inferred about the North. Stouffer concludes that

> Regular church attenders are less likely than other people to be tolerant of the kinds of nonconformists or suspected nonconformists about whom we are inquiring. . . .

---

liberal outlook, a confidence in the accessibility of a science of man. Too, there has been generally a Utopian element in liberalism, a penchant for doctrines of perfectibility. The old liberals, wedded to their egoistic psychology and beguiled by a formal individualism, espoused political and economic programs that would free the individual to usher himself and society into a life without terror and misery and benightedness. Modern liberalism, freed of the twin incubi, have viewed man's problems as social or collective in nature and in their political and economic programs have sought engines whereby mind could be pitted against those collective problems. The modern liberal has looked upon government as a most formidable engine for the mobilization of mind and seeks to use government as eagerly as the classical liberals sought to confine it for the menace to individual choice and action that they deemed it to be." Francis M. Carney, "Is There a Liberal Party?" (Paper read at the Meeting of the American Political Science Association, September 1960).

Whether liberalism is defined in terms of receptiveness to governmental activity or in terms of more general personality or attitude patterns, the measurement of liberalism is a difficult conceptual and practical matter. Measurement techniques ought to eliminate the element of personal advantage from scales that are supposed to weigh general political orientation. The view of a "have not" on economic-redistribution policies is not an acceptable measure of his liberalism; but the view of a "have" may be highly significant. An unemployed man who favors unemployment compensation is not necessarily a liberal, nor is a Negro who champions equal rights for Negroes; but a wealthy white who is for both is a person on whom the label might be placed with a reasonable degree of confidence.

[20] Samuel Stouffer, *Communism, Conformity and Civil Liberties* (Garden City, N.Y.: Doubleday & Co., Inc., 1955), pp. 146, 148, 155, 203, 205.

There would appear to be something about people who go to church regularly that makes fewer of them, as compared with nonchurchgoers, willing to accord civil rights to nonconformists who might be Communists, suspected Communists, or merely Socialists.[21]

The authors of *The Authoritarian Personality* found that subjects who professed some religious affiliation were more prejudiced than those who did not: "There seems to be no doubt that subjects who reject organized religion are less prejudiced on the average than those who, in one way or another, accept it."[22] By sects, they found that "there are no differences of any significance between Catholics and Protestants . . . [and] among the Protestant denominations which have been classed as 'major,' only one group distinguishes itself: the Unitarians have a lower mean score than any of the others."[23] When subjects were grouped into church attenders and nonattenders (whether formally affiliated or not), those who said they never attend scored "very notably lower" on the prejudice tests; "once again, it appears that those who reject religion have less ethnocentrism than those who seem to accept it."[24] The psychological nexus of religious practice and the authoritarian personality is summed up in the following excerpt:

It seems that we can approach an understanding of the relations between religion and ethnocentrism by paying attention to what the acceptance or the rejection of religion means to the individual. When the problem is approached from this point of view, the psychological factors which appear as most important are much the same as . . . conformity, conventionalism, authoritarian submission, determination by external pressures, thinking in ingroup-outgroup terms, and the like, vs. nonconformity, independence, internalization of values, and so forth. The fragmentary data on religious ideology afforded by the [F] scale items lend themselves to the same mode of interpretation. An attitude of complete submissiveness toward "supernatural forces" and a readiness to accept the essential incomprehensibility of "many important things" strongly suggest the persistence in the individual of infantile attitudes toward the parents, that is to say, of authoritarian submission in a very pure form.[25]

The Jews are the only religious group which, in every study and measurement, are more liberal than the American norm. Stouffer classified 79 per cent of the Jewish males (N = 76) and 68 per cent of the Jewish females (N = 82) as "more tolerant" on his scale, as compared with 31 per

21 *Ibid.*, p. 142.

22 T. W. Adorno et al., *The Authoritarian Personality* (New York: Harper & Row, Publishers, 1950), p. 209.

23 *Ibid.*, p. 210.

24 *Ibid.*, p. 213.

25 *Ibid.*, p. 220. Reprinted by permission of Harper & Row, Publishers.

cent of the whole national sample so classified.[26] In October 1954, the
Survey Research Center obtained information about political attitudes
and voting patterns of Protestants, Catholics, and Jews (Table 11–1).
There were no important differences between the Protestant and Catholic
responses on U.S. involvement in world affairs or on the need for more
domestic social legislation, but the Jewish respondents were significantly
more internationalist and supportive of social legislation. Attitudes toward Senator McCarthy reflected his Catholicism and the Roman Church's
strong anticommunism; nonetheless, the liberalism of the Jews was
marked.

Table 11–1. Attitudes toward Internationalism, Social Legislation, and Senator McCarthy by Major Religious Groups, October 1954

	PROTESTANT	CATHOLIC	JEWISH
1. U.S. Involvement in World Affairs			
Too much involved	42%	44%	24%
2. Attitude toward Social Legislation			
Need more social legislation	24	29	41
Need less social legislation	10	8	0
3. Attitude toward Senator McCarthy			
Pro-McCarthy	9	21	6
Anti-McCarthy	39	24	53
	(N=857)	(N=217)	(N=34)

Source: Angus Campbell and Homer C. Cooper, *Group Differences in Attitudes and Votes: A Study of the 1954 Congressional Election* (Ann Arbor: Survey Research Center, University of Michigan, 1956), pp. 138, 142, 146.

After examining the Allinsmith work referred to earlier, a study by
Haveman and West of 9,064 college graduates, and his own survey work
in Jewish wards in Boston, Fuchs declared:

> The results of all of these studies show American Jews to be economic liberals
> —twentieth-century style—almost without regard to differences in class lines
> within the group, and despite the fact that Jews as a group are now perched near
> if not on the top of the economic class ladder.
> In foreign policy matters, the Jews have been internationalists.[27]

There has been much speculation about the sources of Jewish social
and political liberalism. Many commentators have seen it as a result of
centuries of Jewish minority-consciousness and of their oppression by non-
Jewish majorities. Historic underdogs themselves, they tend to take the

[26] Stouffer, *Communism* (see footnote 20), pp. 143, 151.

[27] Lawrence H. Fuchs, *The Political Behavior of American Jews* (New York: The Free Press of Glencoe, 1956), p. 107. Copyright 1956. Reprinted by permission of The Macmillan Company.

side of the underdog who needs collective help in material ways (social welfare) and who welcomes political and other kinds of change. Analyzing Jewish social attitudes as they relate to political opinions and behavior, Fuchs suggests that a cluster of more or less characteristically Jewish values underlie Jewish liberalism. "What are the distinctive values of America's Jewish subculture?" he asks.

To judge from a vast impressionistic literature and a growing systematic study of Jewish culture, those things most valued by Jews as Jews are: (1) Learning (Torah); (2) Charity (Zedakeh); and, for want of a better phrase or word, (3) Life's pleasures (nonasceticism). In probably no other American subculture is so high a value placed upon learning and intellectuality, or upon the helping of the poor by the rich and the weak by the strong, or upon living a good life upon earth in full use of one's body. These three values, taken together or regarded separately, have helped to guide Jewish political behavior in recent decades along what in the discourse of our times would be called "liberal lines."[28]

11.23   Religion and Political Action

In general, and almost always on matters thought of traditionally as "political" (e.g., elections, appointments, and party organization), clergy and parishioners alike seem to think that there ought to be a fairly clear separation of church and politics. In a study of the opinions of over fifteen hundred Episcopalians, Ringer and Glock relate that "few parishioners expect the church to stay out of politics altogether"; most think the minister should urge his church members to study the issues and to vote, but only one-fourth would allow candidates to speak in the church buildings, and fewer than one in ten would approve their minister's endorsing a candidate. In short, "the more the minister's activity would thrust him into the political arena as an active participant, the more hesitant are parishioners to voice approval."[29]

On the fringes of Protestantism are politicized clergymen, churches, and even whole sects. For many years, New York Congressman Adam Clayton Powell based his political career on the loyal and enthusiastic members of his Harlem church.[30] Evangelists Fred Schwarz, Billy James

---

[28] *Ibid.*, p. 178. Note the support here for Carney's view that liberalism is fundamentally related to intellectualism.

[29] Benjamin B. Ringer and Charles Y. Glock, "The Political Role of the Church as Defined by Its Parishioners," *Public Opinion Quarterly*, XVIII (1954), 338.

[30] See James Q. Wilson, *Negro Politics* (New York: The Free Press of Glencoe, 1960), especially Chaps. 2, 9, and 10; and David Hapgood, *The Purge That Failed: Tammany v. Powell* (New York: McGraw-Hill Book Co., Inc., Eagleton Cases in Practical Politics, 1962).

Hargis, Wayne Boucher, and other radio, TV, and circuit-riding stars of Protestant superpatriotism, may, for the most part, be regarded as "agitators"[31] rather than as political leaders. Although the organization "Christian Citizen" vowed "to develop party workers and candidates and make it possible eventually for evangelical Christians to control the local, state, and Federal Governments,"[32] its lack of success demonstrates again that religious groups as such do not become general political instrumentalities in the United States.

On special issues related to religious doctrine, churches may occasionally become militant and sometimes effective political agencies. The Eighteenth Amendment to the U.S. Constitution is a monument to the political power of the Anti-Saloon League and the other temperance agencies of American Protestantism.[33] In the same way, laws prohibiting the sale of birth-control devices in some states are tributes to the actual or latent political power of the Roman Catholic Church. Pacifism as a political movement in the U.S., and more strikingly in Britain, and the general antimilitary posture of Anglo-American society owes much to the leadership of the historic peace churches—and to the Methodists, especially, among the rest of Protestantism.

Though organized religion may become a direct political force on issues of high relevance to central church doctrine, the expectation of church member and nonmember alike is that the institutional separation of church and state will have its operational counterpart in a separation of church and politics. Religious influence in political life tends to be indirect, and to be exercised through attitudes and more generalized opinions, to which the political issues of the day can be related. This tendency makes religious beliefs (whether generalized precepts or sectarian doctrines) not less important, but more; in many cases, they become the touchstone by which rapid judgments can be made in the absence of facts or rational thought.

---

[31] Leo Lowenthal and Norbert Guterman, "Portrait of the American Agitator," *Public Opinion Quarterly*, XII (1948), 417–429. See also Arnold Foster and Benjamin R. Epstein, *Danger on the Right* (New York: Random House, Inc., 1964).

[32] John Wicklein, "Christian Group Aims at Politics," *New York Times*, February 1, 1962.

[33] See Peter Odegard, *Pressure Politics: The Story of the Anti-Saloon League* (New York: Columbia University Press, 1928).

EDUCATION AND OPINION HOLDING

12

Although the influence of formal education is much investigated, little is known about the ways in which schools create or re-create opinion. However—as is often the case in the analysis of opinion correlates—though we fail to trace the labyrinth of detail, some large patternings of influence may be observed.

After the family, the school is perhaps the most powerful institution of the society in its impact on what is thought by whom on what issues. The average school cannot re-form the opinion network of the average child; this is too certainly determined by the family and its environment. But the extraordinary school (there are a few) and the extraordinary teacher (there are many, though never enough) can sometimes re-form the opinions of the average child. What is more important, such schools and teachers (and, sometimes, even ordinary schools and teachers) can shape the opinions and often the whole life of the above-average child.

In the schools, whether public or private, the creation of opinion leaders begins. This is a sociopolitical function of the schools which, so far as I know, has been little remarked—perhaps because it is as obvious as it is significant.[1] In the public schools, the child for the first time is systematically exposed to as great a variety of people and opinion as his school district affords. The narrow world of his family, his playmates, and his parents' church (by which he is deeply marked at the age of six) is supplemented by a routinized but deliberately innovative social institution that not only tolerates but increasingly encourages opinion variety. One of the distinguishing

[1] I think there are other reasons also; important among them is the shallow understanding of democracy held by our progressive educators, for thirty years the masters of American public education, who discouraged the recognition of intellectual excellence, one mark of which is the evolution of both specialized and general opinion leaders.

and most significant characteristics of the American public school is that it is the first occasion for the nonvoluntary exposure of the individual to persons with whom he may have little in common except membership in a political community. This exposure constitutes the first direct impact of the polity on the individual. Until he enters the public school, he contacts the public (through government) only indirectly; but on his first day of class, and thereafter for ten, twelve, sixteen, or twenty years, he is obliged to follow some rules, to take note of some differences (and similarities), and to engage actively or passively in social controversies big and little. Parents start the socialization process; but at least one importance of the public schools is that, by virtue of the greatly expanded sociopolitical exposure, the socialization process is enlarged by a quantum leap.

Now, it should not be thought, just because the scope of community influence on the child is significantly expanded upon his entering the public school, that this influence will radically alter or conflict with the values and habits that his family and preschool environment have endowed. The schools may in some ways conflict with home conditioning, but the conflicts are usually not many or starkly presented. The hand of the state is on the child for the first time; but it is the gentle hand of a local school board and of local teachers, who are least aware of their political nature—and who, since they define politics in the traditional but narrow sense of party antagonisms, in fact deny their political nature (which is, perhaps, just as well). The major thrust of the schools is thus, at least in the early years, the reinforcement of family attitudes and family opinions; for although the social heterogeneity of the child's environment is significantly expanded, he is shielded from the full effect of this heterogeneity by a curriculum that attends mainly to common fact-gathering and superficial (if, at this stage, important) social graces. Primarily, he learns numbers and letters and simple words; he learns to work with a group, to respect nonfamily authority; and to behave by rule and time. Moreover, as a developing personality, he is probably intellectually and emotionally unable to absorb the wider implications of his new environment. He is thus protected by, and he protects himself from, his expanded environment, especially if his family is not socioeconomically extreme.

American public schools, for many reasons, tend to shape their wards to middle-class patterns. Both underprivileged and overprivileged children experience greater impact from new opinions in the public schools than do the average children of average families. Slum children have to learn obedience, self-discipline and, sometimes, simple cleanliness in the public schools. Wealthy children may have to learn some of the same things, but more often their lesson is one of learning *toleration*. Children who are culturally and intellectually overprivileged (a small but important group that the public schools are only now beginning to recognize) may have the hardest learning of all—to be humble, to be supportive of others, and often to be just plain bored.

12.1   Schools and the Indoctrination of Community Values

The importance of the public school system in forming, reinforcing, and altering social and political opinions may be seen in a controversy that took place in a small Wisconsin town. The symbolic implications of this minor contretemps (which would have been comic except for its significance as an index of the times) were not lost on the press or public commentators. In 1961, the school board of Twin Lakes (population 1,497), Wisconsin, voted four to one to require the use of the nineteenth-century classic *McGuffey's Reader* in all eight grades of its 225-student school. Under the threat of a taxpayers' suit and after a direct order from the state education authorities to abandon the book because of the sectarian nature of some of its readings, the school-board members pasted over the more objectionable pages and continued to use the books until required by court action to discard them.

The school-board majority in Twin Lakes argued that *McGuffey's Reader* taught phonetic reading and "wholesome Americanism." Since other, modern books encourage reading by the phonetic method, the controversy, only partly disguised, was primarily over the kinds of social and political values that should be taught in the public schools.

According to one analyst, the conservative majority of the Twin Lakes school board was correct in believing that *McGuffey's Reader* taught self-reliance, hard work, thrift, and other virtues associated with free-enterprise individualism. These famous books, selling over 120,000,-000 copies between 1837 and 1941 (not counting the 225 for Twin Lakes in 1961), emphasized the morality of acquisition:

There is no trace in McGuffey of virtue for its own sake; on the contrary, virtue *pays*. Those who practice these virtues—honesty, industry, charity, piety, and the like—received very tangible rewards in return.[2]

Furthermore, the *McGuffey Reader* taught not only the morality of acquisition but the virtues of a simple nationalism and of religiosity ("not so much a doctrine as an attitude").

The intention (or at least the effect) of thousands of local school

2 D. A. Saunders, "Social Ideas in McGuffey Readers," *Public Opinion Quarterly*, (1941), 584.

boards of the nineteenth century, and of the Twin Lakes board in 1961, was to use the public school system as a vehicle of indoctrination and reinforcement of predominant middle-class values. The results were no doubt impressive; for, during the McGuffey era, the readers did not compete with other printed (or electronic) media for the attention and value direction of the child:

McGuffey's social teachings slipped in unnoticed by the child, who absorbed them in the most formative years of life. The printed page itself was more respected in homes where often the only companion volume of the McGuffey *Readers* was the Bible.[3]

Generally, the conclusions of Charles Merriam on the origins of civic cohesion are still valid. After studying techniques for the development of loyalty in seven countries, Merriam emphasized the special importance of schools:

The fact is that in all cases the school system is the basic factor in the development of civic interest and loyalty, and the chief instrument for that purpose. Whether the use of the schools for mere indoctrination is the most intelligent method is another question. . . . In modern civilization, the school tends to take the place of force and fear in the earlier regime, and of religion, the family, and the army in the later, and it succeeds to all the rights and privileges as well as the power and prestige of the ecclesiastical group. In the scheme of civic education, it looms largest in the series of techniques employed to develop civic feeling and allegiance.[4]

Three years later, Merriam noted that conditions peculiar to the United States make it likely that the U.S. school system will be a more influential opinion-forming institution than the European school system: (1) the influence of the home is weakened by the migratory character of our people and (2) the influence of religion by the variety of competing systems of religion, which weakens the force of any one of them. Because of these conditions, it might be assumed that the influence of the school in America would be *pro tanto* greater than that of the school in Europe, and, to some extent, this is true.[5] These characteristics of American society, with their probable effect on the importance of the schools as value-forming institutions, are as significant in the 1960s as they were when noted by Merriam some thirty years ago.

I wish to emphasize, however, that I am talking about the general values and the basic attitudes that the school and the community share

---

[3] *Ibid.,* p. 589.

[4] Charles E. Merriam, *The Making of Citizens* (Chicago: The University of Chicago Press, 1931), p. 98.

[5] Charles E. Merriam, *Civic Education in the United States* (New York: Charles Scribner's Sons, 1934), p. 77.

in considerable degree. Though the process at the beginning, and in the early grades, is one of learning and reinforcing the simplest and most fundamental skills, what is learned as the level of schooling goes up increasingly becomes a filling in of the meanings of values, the relations of these values to the "real" world, and a greater specificity of attitudes and attitude constellations—along with a greater storehouse of fact and evidential material related (often in very simple ways) to value and attitude. Generally, what we hold in our minds of ideas, things, and persons changes through the educational process and institutions from fuzzy to less fuzzy. Like the infant's early learning of shapes and colors, the later educational process is one of increasingly subtle differentiation; things and ideas become more clearly distinguished from other things and ideas. Accompanying this differentiation is the increasingly more subtle ability to reintegrate things and ideas in ways that have wider meaning.

The process of learning, with its attendant fuzziness, only gradually sharpening through age and more complex stimuli, is vividly demonstrated by Harold Isaacs in the stream-of-consciousness technique used in his books *Scratches on the Mind* and *Emergent Americans*. The following excerpts catch the residue of moods and attitudes that young adults carry into their world from church and school:

In our interviews we asked our Crossroaders [college students who participated in an African work-camp project] to scrape their memories for some of these early acquisitions, and here, in their words and phrases, bunched together from the answers of many different individuals, is how they located and described what they had seen or heard about Africa in their younger years.

At *church* or in *Sunday school* . . .

. . . missionaries, . . . voodooism in interior Africa; heard about Egypt in Sunday school; about Schweitzer; Sunday school lessons about converting the heathen; Africa a vast jungle, . . . the primitiveness, illiterate savages, tribal wars, witch doctors; terrible sanitary conditions, people needing medicine and Christianity. . . .

At *school* . . .

. . . little or nothing, a little geography, Africa on the world map, the slave trade, some names of countries and rivers, Livingston, Stanley, Rhodes, the Nile, the Sahara, something about the Congo; British and French and Belgian colonies; jungles, tribesmen, primitive people with bones through their noses, head hunters, pygmies, a dark continent full of savages, animals, torrid zones, minerals, huge and unexplored; Bartholomew Diaz going around the Cape, Vasco da Gama; pictures of people carrying rubber trees; life of a boy, happy-go-lucky in the jungle; in high school I heard of Ghana's independence; heard about the apartheid situation in South Africa. . . .[6]

[6] Copyright © 1961 Massachusetts Institute of Technology. Reprinted from *Emergent Americans: A Report on "Crossroads Africa"* by Harold R. Isaacs by permission of The John Day Company, Inc., publisher. Pp. 38–40.

These impressions are not opinions, but they are the stuff of which opinions, public and private, are made. It is fuzzy stuff and background stuff, and it only becomes sharp and foreground in the context of a particular time, event, or question. It is all in the funnel of opinion causality, put there by chance and by the deliberate efforts of self and others acting within social institutions and social values. The schools are one such social institution—shaping, suggesting, and influencing the convergence in the funnel—behind every opinion of those individuals whose aggregated views comprise public opinion.

12.2 Opinion Change and Indoctrination of Values in the Schools

Social and political indoctrination, conscious and unconscious, clearly exists in the public schools. Some such indoctrination in the values of a democratic society is necessary—for "fair play" in school becomes due process in law, and "citizenship" becomes protection of minority rights. Other kinds of values no doubt impede the search for truth that educators everywhere profess to be their goal.

How much of this indoctrination "takes" and how long does it last? The effects of indoctrination depend on the receptivity of the student, the importance that he attaches to the matter, and the presence or absence of confirming or conflicting forces.

Political opinions are of little concern, generally, to precollege students. Except in the immediate context of a major campaign, school children—even of high school age—are largely indifferent to politics. Insofar as political questions do interest the high school student, he is more apt to be influenced in his thinking by his parents and other adults than he is by his schoolmates.[7] Thus, it is reasonable to suppose that political opinions might be easier to inculcate in schools than are other kinds of opinions.

Experimental studies of indoctrination in the schools bear out the common-sense view that the pupils are influenced by one-sided arguments. In 1938, Remmers summarized several experiments on the amount and permanence of induced opinion change. On deliberate attempts to change social and political attitudes, he declared:

[7] H. H. Remmers and D. H. Radler, *The American Teenager* (Indianapolis: Bobbs-Merrill Co., Inc., 1957), p. 222.

. . . a high school teacher is likely to obtain the kinds of attitudes which are consciously set up as educational objectives and striven for as such. And it appears that unless some specific effort is made to change attitudes they are not likely to change.[8]

Remmers' investigations were followed about a decade later by a comprehensive series of experiments at Yale. The results of the Yale Communication and Attitude Change Program will be summarized at a later point. It is enough to point out here that, in general, the Yale studies corroborated the findings of the earlier work. Other things being equal, exposure is followed immediately by considerable change in the direction indicated by the content of the message; over a short period of time, much of the effect of a single exposure wears off; but there remains a net and lasting (in the absence of countering information) change in the expected direction. The experimental studies indicate that

a class period or two of directed social-stimulus material is quite sufficient to bring about appreciable changes, and these changes, except for a very powerful counter stimulation, tend to result in persisting attitudes. Such attitudes are learned, and apparently the forgetting curve drops certainly no more rapidly than it does for measured achievement in conventional high school subjects . . .[9]

Repeated, confirmatory, and ego-satisfying stimuli are much more likely to occur in school experience than is a single experimental stimulus of no special interest to the student. Under normal exposure conditions, the schools reinforce the modal values of a community; at the same time, however, they risk the development of nonconformity through at least a feigned (and often real) dedication to freedom of thought.

12.3   Effects of Education on Opinion Holding, Political Confidence, and Political Involvment

Education helps a person to think. The more a person knows, the more he is able to free himself from the restricting viewpoints of his own self and his own experiences. This is perhaps the cardinal sense in which, as the cliché goes, "education makes broader horizons." The individual who knows a good deal about other persons, places, and ideas is able more effectively to relate his own existence to his social and physical environment. Opinion surveys reveal, almost without exception, that college

[8] H. H. Remmers, "Propaganda in the Schools—Do the Effects Last?" *Public Opinion Quarterly,* II (1938), 202.

[9] *Ibid.,* p. 207.

graduates have more opinions on more issues than do high school graduates, and high school graduates have more opinions than do grade school graduates. For example, in a study of the relation between information and opinion holding in Pittsfield, Massachusetts, Hastings reported the distribution of opinion levels by education as demonstrated in Table 12–1.

Table 12–1. Distribution of Opinion Level by Education on Thirteen Questions Asked in Samples of Pittsfield, Mass., Adults, 1952

EDUCATIONAL LEVEL	0–5 ITEMS CORRECT ($N = 43$)	6–10 ITEMS CORRECT ($N = 199$)	11–13 ITEMS CORRECT ($N = 120$)
Grades 1–8	53%	27%	20%
Grades 9–12	37	49	43
Part or All College	—	18	30
Other*	10	6	7

* Meaning not explained.

Source: Philip K. Hastings, "Level of Information and Opinion Content," *Political Science Quarterly*, LXIX (1954), 236.

In 1956, the Survey Research Center study found, as one would expect, a strong positive relationship between education and familiarity with a battery of foreign and domestic issues. This relationship is shown in Table 12–2.

Table 12–2. Relation of Education to Familiarity with Issues, 1956

FAMILIARITY WITH ISSUES	NO FORMAL SCHOOLING TO COMPLETION OF 8 GRADES	HIGH SCHOOL: SOME OR COMPLETION	COLLEGE: SOME OR DEGREE
High	21%	31%	50%
Medium	37	47	44
Low	42	22	6
	100%	100%	100%
Number of Cases	543	890	331

Source: Angus Campbell et al., *The American Voter* (New York: John Wiley & Sons, Inc., 1960), p. 175.

Using the same data, Key demonstrated that the better educated have more opinions regardless of occupation. His analysis suggests that those with less education may be unwilling or unable to express opinions on foreign issues or complex questions of domestic policy, but are as capable as those with more education of answering questions about economic policy that affects them as individuals. Thus, on the question of govern-ment guarantees of job security, only about 10 per cent of those who had eight or less years of school refused to give an opinion. The form of the question made it very easy for them to do so, and thus the sociopolitical expectancy of omniscience (see Chapter 3) was controlled; on more com-plex questions of regulation of business, electric power and housing policy, and aid to neutral countries, about 40 per cent of all grammar school graduates expressed no opinion—as compared with less than 15 per cent of those who had college education.[10]

A number of analysts have suggested that every person's political behavior is heavily influenced by the confidence he has in the political system of which he is a part. The authors of *The Voter Decides* define this quality as a sense of political efficacy: it is, they say, "the feeling that individual political action does have, or can have, an impact upon the political process, i.e., that it is worth while to perform one's civic duties."[11] They further report that, "as was expected, education is highly related to the efficacy scale; one-half of those respondents who attended college rank high on this scale, as compared with only 15 per cent of those who have completed no more than grade school."[12] Later, in *The American Voter,* Campbell and his collaborators point out that this sense of political effi-cacy is in part a function of income and high-status occupation; but, they declare, the fact that it is "more strongly related to education than to other dimensions of status that may symbolize equal strength in the power structure suggests that education contributes to the attitude in a more direct way."[13]

The generalization that the highly educated show more confidence in the political system is supported even more strongly by a study of 779 Oregon adults in 1959. On a six-point Guttman-type scale of "political cynicism," it was found that "the highly educated are much more politi-cally trusting than the least educated. . . . The politically trusting out-number the political cynics by five to one among the highly educated, while the ratio is 1:1 among the least educated."[14] When the results were controlled for income and occupation, the educational factor was still overwhelmingly important; the "data show clearly that within every in-

10 V. O. Key, Jr., *Public Opinion and American Democracy* (New York: Alfred A. Knopf, Inc., 1961), pp. 333–335.

11 Angus Campbell, G. Gurin, and Warren E. Miller, *The Voter Decides* (New York: Harper & Row, Publishers, 1954), p. 187.

12 *Ibid.*, pp. 190–191.

13 Angus Campbell et al., *The American Voter* (New York: John Wiley & Sons, Inc., 1960), p. 280.

14 Robert E. Agger, Marshall N. Goldstein, and Stanley Pearl, "Political Cynicism: Measurement and Meaning," *The Journal of Politics,* XXIII (1961), 484.

come level, the higher the level of education, the lower the proportion of political cynics. The relationship here is both strong and consistent."[15] The highly educated were also found, in this study, to possess a greater sense of "political potency,"[16] which corroborated the findings of earlier studies on this dimension of political confidence.

The effects of educational levels on opinion holding are deftly summarized by Smith in his study of the shifting views of social aggregation on world affairs between 1946 and 1956. After reviewing the literature and presenting his own data from AIPO polls, Smith suggested three types of patterns with regard to opinion quantity, stability, and confidence:

> Composed of the executive and professional and college groupings, the first international public enjoys an impressive degree of opinion homogeneity on a variety of issues. It exhibits a consistently high level of information and concern about world affairs, reacts quickly and appropriately to events, and evidences more opinion stability than do other publics. . . . While any label will be imperfect, the present set of groupings and opinions clearly approximates Almond's "attentive public"; but all things considered, the term "engaged public" seems more apt, for it adds the connotation of an active effort to keep informed and to influence policy, an important distinguishing feature of this public. . . .
>
> At the other end of the international scale we find a second public, composed basically of the grammar-school-educated and unskilled workers; farmers usually, and skilled workers frequently, are also in it. This public is characterized by low levels of international information and concern, sluggish opinion reactions to events, and unstable and exceedingly pessimistic appraisals of foreign affairs. With little true comprehension of world circumstances, persons in this public rely on stereotypes and prejudice for guidance; their abiding but ill-defined sense of insecurity is amplified to frustration and anxiety by international events compelling their attention. . . .
>
> The third international public, comprising the white-collar, high-school-educated, and sometimes skilled-worker groupings, exhibits a poorly defined membership-opinion profile. Both the white-collar and skilled-worker segments show distinctive attitude sets of their own, plus puzzling internal inconsistencies; the former often joining the engaged public while the latter erratically tends toward the irresponsible. . . . Hence, while defying categorization, this public may be considered "attentively passive" toward world affairs.[17]

---

[15] *Ibid.*, p. 487.

[16] The Oregon investigators divided the notion of political confidence into political trust and political potency. Political trust is a positive evaluation of politics and politicians as being relatively clean, no more selfish than most persons, and generally desirable. The sense of political potency is the feeling that individual action is of some use—i.e., it is what the Survey Research Center scholars call *political efficacy*. Though a person might be politically trusting at the same time that he has a sense of political impotence (or be cynical and feel politically potent), the Oregon study found, as one would expect, that cynicism and impotency were usually found in the same person, just as trust and a sense of potency were found together.

[17] Paul A. Smith, "Opinions, Public and World Affairs in the United States," *The Western Political Quarterly*, XIV (1961), 709–713. Reprinted by permission of the University of Utah, copyright owner. Footnotes omitted.

Smith notes the importance of the educational factor among the several associated with these opinion-types: "The high-school-educated may be taken as the core of this third public, just as the college-and-grammar-school-educated are of the engaged and irresponsible publics, respectively."[18]

Without laboring the matter, it may be observed that the Smith analysis and those cited earlier in this section offer no conclusive evidence that political behavior is consistent with attitudes. There is no need to repeat our earlier general discussion of the correspondence among attitudes, opinions, and behavior; what evidence we have indicates that behavior is generally consistent with attitudes, though surprisingly large inconsistencies can be tolerated under some circumstances. It is clear, too, that education is positively related to community and opinion leadership.[19] Whether education is more or less important than income and occupation as an indicator of political participation is not apparent as yet. After reviewing much of the literature, Lane concludes:

> Perhaps for a simple conventional act such as voting, income is more important, while more complex forms of participation are more dependent upon qualities associated with education. Occupation is hard to grade along a similar, single dimensional continuum, but from inspection of the 1952 Survey Research Center data, it is apparent (for what it is worth) that differences among standard occupational classifications are smaller than differences among the educational or income classifications.[20]

In view of what we know about the correlations of education with information holding, sense of efficacy, and participation in the opinion-policy process, it is tempting to believe that social improvements might be understood and welcomed by the masses if they only knew more. It is part of the liberal mythology that "education" is a way to get rid of wars, economic dislocations, social injustices, political conflicts, and most of the real and imagined evils attending the human adventure. We have seen enough, even in this brief overview, perhaps, to conclude that the sim-

---

[18] *Ibid.*, p. 713.

[19] See, for example, Robert E. Agger and Vincent Ostrom, "The Political Structure of a Small Community," *Public Opinion Quarterly*, XX (1956), 81–89, especially Table I, pp. 87–88; George Belknap and Ralph Smuckler, "Political Power Relations in a Midwest City," *Public Opinion Quarterly*, XX (1956), 73–81, especially 79; and Elihu Katz and Paul F. Lazarsfeld, *Personal Influence* (New York: The Free Press of Glencoe, 1955), pp. 272–275.

[20] Robert E. Lane, *Political Life* (New York: The Free Press of Glencoe, 1959), p. 222. Copyright 1959. Reprinted by permission of The Macmillan Company. The authors of an early study concluded that "education and SES level seem to have about equal importance in creating and maintaining political interest." Paul F. Lazarsfeld et al., *The People's Choice* (New York: Columbia University Press, 1944), p. 43.

plistic notion of education as a panacea for social ills is, like most simplistic notions, a fraud. In the first place, a good deal of what is labeled
education is no more than public relations—which, as Almond points out,
will not do:

> It is a great temptation to attribute these differences in political attitudes
> which are associated with income, occupation, and education to "lack of informa-
> tion" or "areas of ignorance." The policy implications of such an interpretation
> are clear and simple. Lack of information can be remedied by more information;
> and "areas of ignorance" can be dispelled by civic-minded campaigns of public
> education. In actuality, the problem runs a great deal deeper. A discriminating
> analysis of the evidence suggests that a large sector of the lower-income, poorly
> educated majority of the population is incapable of assimilating the materials of
> informational campaigns. Its basic apathy is a consequence of emotional and
> social conditions. Its intellectual horizon tends to be quite limited, and its
> analytical skill rudimentary. It will take a great deal more than public relations
> to remedy such a situation and produce the degree of involvement and activism
> which is characteristic of the upper-educational and -income groups. Actually, no
> one has proposed a solution to this basic problem which is not transparently in-
> adequate or obviously Utopian.[21]

Although statistical opinion differences exist among adults with various educational backgrounds, the size and importance of these differences
are apt to be exaggerated. A college graduate can score high in most
opinion or attitude surveys by having only a modicum of information—or,
indeed, by being more adept at verbalization. It is a question of no small
importance whether the differences shown in the studies mentioned above
should be interpreted as demonstrating the total ignorance and indifference of the lowest groups or only the qualified ignorance and indifference
of the highest. Such a question prompted the authors of *The Authoritarian Personality* to end their report on ethnocentrism and education
with these words:

> We may tentatively conclude that ethnocentrism shows a slight negative corre-
> lation with amount of education. It is likely, though far from a demonstrated
> fact, that college graduates are less ethnocentric than high school graduates, who
> are in turn less ethnocentric than those who did not complete high school. It is
> not clear which is more important: that the correlation is greater than zero, or
> that it is at best not far from zero. To those who urge education per se as a
> kind of panacea, the smallness of the correlation ought probably to be stressed.
> But this is not to deny the importance of education. It is rather to emphasize that
> our educational system, college as well as public school, is still far from realizing
> its potential strength as a social force in the service of democratic values. The
> reasons for this are outside the scope of the present research. It may also be

---

[21] Gabriel A. Almond, *The American People and Foreign Policy* (New York: Frederick
A. Praeger, Publisher, 1960), p. 130. Reprinted by permission of Frederick A. Praeger,
Publisher.

pointed out that, even under the best educational conditions, *exposure* to the classroom is not enough, and that motivation to learn and receptivity to new ideas provide the only psychological soil in which democratic education can develop effectively.[22]

Finally, we have little evidence that even small numbers of people can be brought suddenly and lastingly into the ways of righteousness through the influence of formal and institutionalized education. Mass opinions or behavior cannot be changed in any short period of time; educators can be only slightly in advance of the society which they must reflect as they help to re-create. Change is slow. Nonetheless, there is some change, and some of that is due to the fact that education does widen horizons, and to the fact that in America ever greater numbers are obtaining ever greater education. The attentive public is increasing, not just absolutely, as the population grows, but relative to the size of the inattentive. This changing ratio means not only that policy issues may receive more discriminating consideration, but that the pool that produces opinion leaders and decision makers will be correspondingly larger. Talent for creating and leading public opinion is thus being saved and produced.

22 T. W. Adorno et al., *The Authoritarian Personality* (New York: Harper & Row, Publishers, 1950), p. 287. Reprinted by permission of Harper & Row, Publishers. Italics in original.

ECONOMIC ORGANIZATION AND OPINION HOLDING

13

"Tell me where a man gets his corn pone, and I'll tell you what his 'pinions are." In these words, Mark Twain, no economic determinist of any school, expressed the common observation that opinions arise in large part from economic circumstances.

Opinions can, indeed, be bought and sold like shoes and ships and cabbages—or like votes and other things of political value. More often, however, opinions of individuals are influenced and determined not by market transactions but by less direct and more subtle economic forces. Some opinions serve better than others the immediate or long-range economic needs of each individual. The farmer believes in sales or income taxes rather than property taxes; the small tradesman believes in local regulation of business (if in any regulation of business at all); the southern box and crate manufacturer strongly opposes minimum-wage legislation; and the trade-union leader detests the idea of the open shop. It would be difficult to find any public issue on which all opinions were free from the influence of economic factors. Even simple local ordinances with no specific impact, such as dog-leash laws or the manner in which the streets are named or numbered, are apt to provoke economic fears or hopes from homeowners or businessmen.[1] No doubt some matters of public policy are wholly free of economic factors; but these are surely infrequent and almost never important. In a democracy, the public's business, at least in part, is an economic business.

[1] The businessmen of New York City's Third Avenue recently began a campaign to change its name to "Avenue of the Promenades," to offset the unfavorable image associated with the old elevated tracks (now removed) and the Bowery.

13.1 Economic Organization as an Influencing Factor in the Funnel of Opinion Causality

The term *economic organization*, as employed in this section, means the way in which demands for goods and services are met. It includes all the processes and social forms by and through which physical things and services are identified, created, transferred, and preserved for the satisfaction of human needs and desires. It seems to be, and is, the broadest kind of term. But the definition is meant to *exclude:* (a) psychological factors that influence opinion and behavior; (b) social institutions that are primarily religious, recreational, educational, and ideological; and (c) that part of the physical environment that is not exploited in the production of goods and services. Moreover, by *economic organization* is meant not only the goods and services themselves but the relationships among the individuals and groups involved in the creation, transfer, preservation, and consumption of goods and services.

Like most attempts at categorization and definition in the social sciences, this meaning of the term *economic organization* is fuzzy around the edges. For example, it is difficult to know whether some relationships are primarily religious rather than economic (the selling of relics and indulgences), recreational rather than economic (moviegoing by an individual or by the members of a community), or educational rather than economic (the college degree as a symbol of learning or of earning power). Perhaps, in the end, it is wisest only to speak of the economic aspects or perspectives of human relations. Moviegoing is largely an economic matter for actors, producers, managers, ushers, and others whose jobs depend on it. For the individual who attends once a week or once a month, its economic impact is slight, probably negligible—although an economic component is present, inasmuch as the admission price may be spent in other ways.

13.2 Economics and Politics in American Life

Calvin Coolidge once said, "The business of America is business."
Less bluntly, many Americans and foreign visitors have observed that the private pursuit of private wealth has marked our society from the beginning. In a most insightful chapter of his commentary on the political life of America in the 1830s, De Tocqueville described and speculated about

the economic drive he found in the United States. He said that "the desire of acquiring the good things of this world is the prevailing passion of the American people,"[2] and he linked this economic drive to the prominence of the middle class, to the appearance of a great restlessness and a search for novelty, and to a parallel capacity for religious and political passions.

Others have stressed the relation (often, the transferability) of economic power to political power. The interconnections of economic and political power in America have been ably reviewed by Alpheus T. Mason. "Our Founding Fathers," Mason wrote, "inherited from James Harrington's *Oceana* of 1656 the maxim that 'power always follows property.' 'This I believe,' John Adams commented, May 26, 1776, 'to be as infallible a maxim in politics, as that action and reaction are equal, is in mechanics.' "[3]

Whoever is able to set the terms of the economic order is able, in large manner, to set the terms of the political order. It is likely that the organization of economic life in every society is the most powerful determinant of political life and, either directly or through the mediation of the family or other social institutions, the most persuasive molder of opinion.[4] A strong case could be made for the revealing name by which the study of political science was known in the nineteenth century— *political economy*.

Nevertheless, the classical liberals of the eighteenth and nineteenth centuries overemphasized the importance of economic forces in individual and collective behavior. Human felicity, domestic tranquillity, and international peace cannot be achieved through the "unseen hand" of private economic enterprise. And, as was earlier pointed out, a major theoretical weakness of Marxism is that it adopts a near identity of economics and politics within a framework of pseudoscientific determinism. The state is much more than, as Marx described it, the "executive committee of the capitalist class."

The social-contract theorists (Hobbes, Locke, Rousseau) were perhaps the first to overemphasize the dependence of politics on economics. If the economics-politics relationship was ill understood from the seventeenth

---

2 Alexis de Tocqueville, *Democracy in America*, ed. Henry Steele Commager (London: Oxford University Press, 1946), p. 403.

3 "Business Organized As Power: The New Imperium in Imperio," *American Political Science Review*, XLIV (1950), 324.

4 Mason succinctly puts the case for politics over economics in the democratic state: "To escape anarchy, politics must be dominant over economics. Official, politically responsible government must insist on monopolizing coercive power, as against any and all private aspirants for such power. It must do this, not because there is special virtue in established authority, or because government is or can be omniscient, but because this is the only way of avoiding chaos, the only way, as Locke's men discovered in his state of nature, to prevent individuals and groups from taking law into their own hands" (*ibid.*, p. 342).

to the twentieth century, it was perhaps because the break up of the long-stable political economy of feudalism necessitated new economic forms, new political forms, and new relationships between them. Capitalism, it could be argued, was never achieved in anything like its pure theoretical form, because the economics of extreme individualism are simply not compatible with the idea of politics, which is necessarily a collective human enterprise.

The last to overemphasize the dependence of politics on economics were the post-Marxists of the 1930s. These men—Charles A. Beard, Harold Laski, and others—were too sophisticated for the simple determinism of Marx, but not yet prepared to admit the limits of a theory that made acquisitiveness the major motivation of both production and governance.

From Machiavelli to Harold Lasswell may seem like a long time for Western society to go without a proper understanding of the relations between economics and politics. I do not suggest that this has been the case, for there have been political thinkers in every age[5] who have resisted the simple view so conveniently exemplified by Adam Smith and Karl Marx. But we may note the tendency of the politics and the economics—that is, the political economy—of the period when capitalism rose and flowered and aged: the tendency was to forget the basic fact, which Machiavelli clearly saw, and Lasswell clearly saw again—that politics is a struggle for wealth *and other forms of power*. According to Machiavelli:

When men are no longer obliged to fight from necessity, they fight from ambition, which passion is so powerful in the hearts of men that it never leaves them, no matter to what height they may rise. The reason of this is that nature has created men so that they desire everything, but are unable to attain it; desire being thus always greater than the faculty of acquiring, discontent with what they have and dissatisfaction with themselves result from it. . . . The Roman people were not content with having secured themselves against the nobles by the creation of the Tribunes, to which they had been driven by necessity. Having obtained this, they soon began to fight from ambition, and wanted to divide with the nobles their honors and possessions, being those things which men value most.[6]

Honors and possessions. Not just possessions. Nor even possessions and honors—but honors and possessions. Like the American businessman

---

5 Montesquieu, for example, in *The Spirit of the Laws* (1748), Book XX, "Of Laws in Relation to Commerce Considered in Its Nature and Distinctions." In the nineteenth-century, George Cornewall Lewis wrote in *An Essay on the Government of Dependencies* (1841) that dependencies in some cases ought to be kept even if they are a net economic drain on the mother country (Oxford: Clarendon Press, 1891), p. 212; compare this with Adam Smith's view that dependencies ought to be abandoned if not paying propositions (*Wealth of Nations*, Book V, Chap. 3), and with the well-known Marxist view of the nature of capitalist imperialism.

6 Niccoló Machiavelli, *The Discourses* (New York: Random House, Modern Library Edition, 1940), p. 208.

of the nineteenth century, Marx was never able to see that, having to choose between the two, many will consciously prefer honors over possessions. Men give up their wealth daily for love, pride, patriotism, safety, comfort, and all kinds of objectives that are mainly noneconomic. Beyond some minimum level of physical comfort, men seek wealth primarily because it is considered a means to nonphysical ends. As Hagen has pointed out in a series of brilliant articles, the psychological and social elements are often much more important than the resource factors in economic growth. For example, even in the most marginal and primitive economies, some wealth is systematically diverted to nonproductive religious purposes, though it might, given different motivation patterns, go into capital accumulation.[7]

13.3 Effects of Economic Status

Before the introduction of survey-research techniques, the consideration of the economic basis of opinion holding was largely a matter of generalization from scattered testimony or observation, and of hypothetical (but largely unverified) statements derived from theory. Machiavelli had seen that the rulers of Renaissance Italy sought wealth as avidly as they sought power. From these observations came his generalization that "a man will suffer the loss of his father easier than he will suffer the loss of his patrimony." Marx developed a theory that insisted that capitalists, individually and as a class, were driven solely by economic considerations. He could then describe the bourgeoisie as having "pitilessly torn asunder the motley feudal ties that bound man to his natural superiors, and left remaining no other nexus between man and man than naked self-interest, callous 'cash payment.' "[8]

Beyond the broadest generalizations of political philosophers, what we know about economic influences on opinion holding is almost all of fairly recent origin. When public opinion as we know it first began to emerge, and as it became important in the determination of policy, there was at best only a very limited knowledge of the distribution of opinions by social class, occupation, and income. What was known was mainly speculation based upon "common sense," primitive notions of motivation,

[7] Everett E. Hagen, "Economic Development: Principles and Patterns," *World Politics*, VII (1955), 448–460. See also his articles "Population and Economic Growth," *The American Economic Review*, XLIX (1959), 310–327; "How Economic Growth Begins: A General Theory Applied to Japan," *Public Opinion Quarterly*, XXII (1958), 373–390.

[8] Karl Marx and Frederick Engels, *The Communist Manifesto* (New York: New York Labor News Co., 1945), p. 11.

and theories of social organization. Much of the speculation was no doubt accurate enough: financiers, money lenders, and eastern manufacturers were properly alarmed at what they took to be the temper of debtors and inland farmers who voted Jacksonian democracy into states and nation in the 1820s and 1830s; the Chartists and Anti-Corn Law Leaguers accurately saw the economic nexus between the views of the landed class and the protective tariffs of England during the same period; the leaders and militants of the early labor movement recognized, quite generally, the extent to which capitalist views had been written into public policy by 1890.

Nevertheless, "common sense" and theory in the absence of facts led to some very wrong judgments about opinion holding and economic organization. The Marxist view of the pervasiveness and the ever increasing polarization of class consciousness is an outstanding example of how fact-free theory misleads; and another example is the belief, cherished until World War I by all socialists, that the brotherhood of class is stronger than the fatherhood of nation. Equally misleading is the "common-sense" notion of classical free enterprise that the motivation of workers is entirely or mainly a matter of money incentives. Although the course of history demonstrated the fallacy of the socialist views of ever sharpening class consciousness and of "international solidarity," the belief in the omnipotence of money incentives was not shaken until the coming of social-science research in the 1930s.

13.31 Types of Issues in Which Economic Status Affects Opinion

Whatever sophistication we now possess in understanding the economic basis of opinion holding has been gained, not at the expense of the fundamental proposition that economic factors produce distinctive opinion patterns, but in the elaboration of what kinds of factors tend to be associated with what kinds of opinions and with what significance. A sample of survey results from 1935 to 1946 will illustrate the contributions to more accurate knowledge made by cross-sectional studies of adult American opinion. The data that follow are all taken from the 1951 compilation of opinion poll results *Public Opinion 1935–1946*.[9]

---

[9] Hadley Cantril and Mildred Strunk, eds., *Public Opinion 1935–1946* (Princeton, N.J.: Princeton University Press, 1951). Polls collected in this volume are inconsistent in their use of indexes of economic status. The AIPO seems to have used "class" before 1940 and "income" after that date when presenting opinion distributions; the *Fortune* Poll avoided the dilemma by using neither—an unfortunate imprecision, for the meanings ought to be differentiated.

In the following cases, the economic factor is shown to relate to opinion distribution in expected ways:

1. Should employees of industries working on defense contracts have the right to strike if their protests are not taken care of? (AIPO, Jan. 1941)

	YES	NO	NO OPINION
Upper income	17%	76%	7%
Middle income	27	64	9
Lower income	30	51	19

2. Do you think government spending should be increased to help get business out of its present slump? (AIPO, Jan. 1938)

	YES	NO
Upper class	23%	77%
Middle class	32	68
Lower class	57	43

3. President Roosevelt proposes a 28% (about one-fourth) reduction in federal government spending for relief. Do you approve or disapprove of this cut? (AIPO, Feb. 1940)

	APPROVE	DISAPPROVE
Upper income	79%	21%
Middle income	67	33
Lower income	38	62

4. There have been all sorts of ideas suggested for things we should do in this country after the war, and we'd like to know how you feel about some of them. Do you think it is a good idea or not such a good idea to give labor unions more say about the way companies are run? (*Fortune* Poll, Aug. 1945)

	GOOD IDEA	NOT SO GOOD	DON'T KNOW
Prosperous	6.8%	86.5%	6.7%
Upper middle	7.8	82.3	9.9
Lower middle	16.5	70.1	13.4
Poor	26.7	48.3	25.0

5. In California, a pension plan has been proposed to pay thirty dollars every Thursday in script money to every person fifty years of age and over who is not employed. Would you favor the adoption of this plan in this state? (AIPO, Oct. 1938)

	YES	NO
Upper class	9%	91%
Middle class	26	74
Lower class	54	46

6. In order to help pay the cost of the war, should the federal government put a national sales tax of 2% on everything you buy, in addition to taxes now in effect? (AIPO, Dec. 1941)

	YES	NO	NO OPINION
Upper income	58%	34%	8%
Middle income	48	46	6
Lower income	43	50	7

Issues in which the economic impact is simple and clear are those on which economic status turns out to be an influencing factor in opinion holding. This correlation is hardly to be wondered at; but, in the above examples, what is surprising is that, on question 2, 43 per cent of the poorer respondents opposed federal spending, and, on number 3, 38 per cent approved a major reduction in relief expenditure. It might be supposed that these data represent a cross-class reluctance to use the federal government—or state government (see question 5)—for wealth distribution or regulation of the economy. Speculation on such matters is inviting, but often fruitless.

Determining one's own economic interest is not easy. In their excellent study of businessmen's attitudes toward tariff policy, Bauer, Pool, and Dexter point out that:

The theory of self-interest as a complete and all-embracing explanation of behavior breaks down when we realize that self-interest is itself a set of mental images and convictions. Whose self-interest does a man see it as his role to serve —his own as a physical individual, that of the corporation for which he works, or that of some other unit? If the corporation is the unit, who does he perceive as constituting the corporation? Over what period of time is he seeking a maximum—the short or the long term? What values does he pursue—solely money, or also respect and other values? The role businessmen played, the communications that impinged upon them, their ideology—all influenced their definitions and perceptions of their self-interest.[10]

Even if self-interest could be adequately defined, the question of alternative ways of maximizing this self-interest remains. Self-interest and opportunity are not always equally matched. The authors of the above quotation point out that the most important determination of what messages went from businessmen on tariff questions was "neither self-interest nor ideology, but the institutional structures which facilitated or blocked the production of messages."[11] Thus, behavior and attitudes about what is proper to think and do about the economic aspects of political opinions

[10] Raymond A. Bauer, Ithiel de Sola Pool, and Lewis Anthony Dexter, *American Business and Public Policy* (New York: Atherton Press, 1963), p. 226.

[11] *Ibid.*, p. 229.

are influenced not by naked self-interest alone, but by considerations of role, access to information, and support or nonsupport of the environment.

13.32   Economic Status, Levels of Knowledge, and Opinions

Attempts to show the relationships between economic factors and patterns of opinion distribution often reveal the effects of differences in levels of knowledge. Though the correlation of income (or other economic indexes) with education is far from precise—as college professors frequently lament—the two are related closely enough that the level of knowledge, as a variable, enters the analysis of opinions by economic status, as it enters the analysis of opinions by education. The generalization is clear: Those of lower economic status usually have no knowledge or no opinion (the two are often, but not always, the same) and therefore fail to appreciate where their economic advantage lies. In the two examples that follow, the increase in "no opinion" probably results from lack of knowledge or understanding of the economic consequences of the proposed policies.[12]

1. If the government needs to increase taxes, which would you personally prefer: to increase the withholding tax on your salary; or to put sales taxes on all things you buy? (*Fortune* Poll, Nov. 1943)

	INCREASE WITHHOLDING TAX	SALES TAX	DON'T KNOW
High	25.1%	66.7%	8.2%
Upper middle	34.3	57.7	8.0
Lower middle	34.4	52.6	13.0
Low	34.5	43.6	21.9

2. If you were a member of the incoming Congress, would you vote yes or no on a bill to reduce federal spending to the point where the national budget is balanced? (*Fortune* Poll, Mar. 1939)

[12] The political importance of economic status is probably a function of how voters compare the personal consequences of social-welfare measures with other influencing factors, in their vote decision. War and the personalities of candidates appear to be factors that reduce the support given to social-welfare considerations by low-income voters (as in the increase of the lower-income Republican vote in 1952 and 1956). See Robert Alford, "The Role of Social Class in American Voting Behavior," *Western Political Quarterly*, XIII (1963), 180–193.

	YES	NO	DON'T KNOW
Prosperous	76.3%	11.1%	12.6%
Upper middle	67.1	17.8	15.1
Lower middle	62.2	17.8	20.0
Poor	54.8	18.3	26.9
Negroes	40.2	19.5	40.3
Unemployed	57.5	20.0	22.5

13.33 Types of Issues in Which Economic Status Does Not Affect Opinion

As one would expect, issues that have no readily apparent, personal economic implications for respondents usually produce answers quite independent of economic status. The potential economic impact of foreign-policy decisions, for instance, is often too subtle to be detected in gross figures:

Would you like to see the United States join a league of nations after this war is over? (AIPO, May 1941)

	YES	NO
Upper	53%	47%
Middle	48	52
Lower	49	51

Likewise, the economic implications of shifting populations are not revealed in the aggregation of individual responses to this question:

If there were nothing to keep you from living wherever you wanted to, in what kind of location would you choose to live? (N.Y. *Herald Tribune,* April 1946)

	A LARGE CITY	A SMALL CITY	SUBURB	SMALL TOWN	IN THE COUNTRY	DON'T KNOW
Prosperous	14.3%	15.2%	44.2%	3.1%	21.9%	1.3%
Upper middle	13.8	19.3	40.2	3.4	22.6	0.7
Lower middle	14.7	18.9	36.6	3.4	25.0	1.4
Poor	15.6	14.8	29.1	4.0	31.2	5.3

Some questions that refer to potential economic policy are so unclear when stated as generalizations that they produce no pattern of response by economic class. The uncertain prospects of compulsory mediation in labor disputes produced this distribution of opinion in 1939:

Would you favor a law requiring employers and workers to submit their differences to a federal labor board before a strike could be called? (AIPO, May 1939)

	FAVOR MEDIATION	OPPOSE MEDIATION
Upper class	84%	16%
Middle class	87	13
Lower class	85	15

When the question of compulsory mediation can be set in a specific environment, when respondents are alerted to the existence of the issue and have more particular knowledge of the views of those who might mediate, the anticipated differential effect on economic classes may be reflected in poll questions. The Labor-Management Act of 1947 (Taft-Hartley) provided for compulsory mediation and a sixty-day "cooling-off period" upon presidential order. Thereupon, the labor unions began a campaign for a repeal or a major change of the Taft-Hartley Act. In a climate of heightened awareness, the economic-class implications became obvious, and the polls began to show an opinion distribution such as the following:

Many businessmen and Republican leaders think that the Taft-Hartley Law has worked well and should be kept pretty much as it is. Do you agree or disagree? (AIPO, April 1949)[13]

	AGREE	DISAGREE	NO OPINION
National total	43%	38%	19%
Union members only	22	66	12
BY OCCUPATION			
Professional & business	62%	26%	12%
Farmers	51	27	22
White collar	43	39	18
Manual workers	33	47	20

A specific question brings to the surface economically significant opinions patterns that are not apparent in the absence of particular meaning to respondents. In 1939, compulsory mediation was not felt to be of more or less advantage to employers or employees; in 1947, in the midst of a general antilabor swing of the public mood and a swarm of labor-regulation bills before Congress, the class meaning was apparent.

Considerations of loyalty, patriotism, or other whole-group ideals also blur the potential difference in economic impact that may be implicit in policy change. The question of labor mobilization in 1942 gained almost identical support among persons of high, middle, and lower incomes:

After finding out what each person can do, should the government have the power to tell each citizen what to do as his part in the war effort and require him or her to do it? (AIPO, Feb. 1942)

13 *Public Opinion Quarterly*, XIII (1949), 353.

	YES	NO	NO OPINION OR UNDECIDED
Upper income	62%	34%	4%
Middle income	61	33	6
Lower income	60	30	10

13.4 Economic Status and Opinion about Democracy

Issues with clear economic implications for various income or occupation groups display opinion distributions consistent with the economic biases of the grouped respondents. It is not at all strange that more than half of the poor favor a state pension plan for those over fifty and unemployed. What is surprising—and more significant for the study of human motivation—*is that almost half (46 per cent) of the poor did not support the idea.* Similarly, as we have seen, more than one-third of the lowest-income group approved a proposed major reduction in federal relief spending. People do not always vote their own economic interest even when it is plain to see. More than two-thirds of the states have general sales taxes, many of them approved by a majority of low-income voters whose own interests call for a graduated income tax instead.

However interesting may be the surprisingly imperfect fit between economic interest and popular opinions on public policy, the matter is of less importance than that of whether economic status affects opinions about the values of the democratic order. Or, more simply stated: Do economic and economic-class factors relate significantly to a belief in democracy? There are theories that the very rich and the very poor are less attached to democratic views than those with middle incomes. To be sure, these theories rely on criteria of class stratification more complex than income alone; but the economic dimension of class is undeniably basic, no matter how it may be qualified by other social and psychological variables.

By themselves, economic factors seem to have only a small influence on anti- or prodemocratic opinions and behavior. The very poor may, because of their poorness, have to devote themselves entirely to economic efforts at the expense of all prodemocratic sentiment. If so, the poor man may be indifferent to democratic values, and, indeed, he may have anti-democratic values—but they will probably result from factors other than his poorness. Lipset has documented the "realization that extremist and intolerant movements in modern society are more likely to be based on the lower classes than on the middle and upper classes."[14] The influences

[14] Seymour Martin Lipset, "Working-Class Authoritarianism," *Political Man* (Garden City, N.Y.: Doubleday & Co., Inc., 1960), p. 97.

that produce working-class authoritarianism do not seem to be directly economic, but the *by-products,* so to speak, of insufficient material resources. The characteristically authoritarian behavior of the lower classes seems almost wholly due to social disorganization (e.g., lack of family stability), personality deprivations (e.g., inordinate punishment, tension, and aggression in childhood), and narrow, rigid, attitude sets resulting from lack of education and repeated ego denials. Unquestionably, this cluster of characteristics is related to economic scarcity; but the economic scarcity seems less a direct than an indirect influence on the antidemocratic posture of the lower classes. What little evidence exists indicates that income alone—other variables being held constant—does not seem to correlate strongly with pro- or antidemocratic views. Some poll data of the period 1938–1941 produced the following mixed results:

1. Do you believe the government should own or more closely control the newspapers? (*Fortune* Poll, Aug. 1939)

	OWN	MORE CLOSELY CONTROL	LEAVE ALONE	DON'T KNOW
Prosperous	1.4%	5.9%	87.4%	5.3%
Upper middle	1.7	7.3	82.9	8.1
Lower middle	2.8	10.5	76.2	10.5
Poor	4.6	11.1	67.3	17.0

2. Do you think that in America anybody should be allowed to speak on any subject any time he wants to, or do you think there are times when free speech should be prohibited or certain subjects or speakers prohibited? (*Fortune* Poll, Feb. 1940)

	ANYBODY, ANY SUBJECT, ANY TIME	PROHIBIT SOME	DON'T KNOW
Prosperous	47.5%	51.6%	0.9%
Poor	52.1	38.7	9.2

3. Do you think membership in the Communist Party in this country should be prohibited by law? (AIPO, May 1941)

	YES	NO	NO OPINION
Upper income	70%	28%	2%
Middle income	71	24	5
Lower income, including those on relief	72	16	12

4. [Asked only of those familiar with the "Dies Committee for investigating un-American activities."] Do you think its findings have been important enough to justify continuing the investigation (AIPO, Nov. 1938)

	YES	NO
Upper income	77%	23%
Middle income	73	27
Lower income	74	26

Economic factors are evidently related to political activity and inactivity. They have been shown to be significant variables, though often mediated by related noneconomic variables, such as education and group memberships. On a scale of "political relatedness," which measured both sense of political responsibility and sense of political efficacy, Eulau and Schneider found the distribution by income groups that is indicated in Table 13–1. The authors of this study found evidence for the view that

Table 13–1. Distribution of Respondents on Index of Political Relatedness by Income

INCOME	POLITICAL RELATEDNESS				N
	HIGH	MED-HIGH	MED-LOW	LOW	
$5,000 +	31%	40%	24%	5%	339
$2,000–4,999	13	39	34	14	639
$2,000–	8	39	32	21	147

Source: 1952 National Sample, Survey Research Center

income and other economic factors are not as directly important as education, which "seems particularly relevant in a study of political involvement."[15] A study of local political participation produced the same results; scores on a participation index ranged from 1.64 to 4.75 by income levels, and from .75 to 5.77 by educational levels.[16]

Income is obviously not the only index of the economic order and how it may relate to individual opinion holding or to statistical patterns of opinion holding. Opinion analysis by occupation categories is common and often contributes to our understanding. Generally, occupation, like income, as a single variable, is less significant than education in the explanation of opinion variation on public questions. A widely cited study by Centers, based on a national sample of 1,092 adult males, gathered opinions on the following questions: role of women in society, importance of religion, confidence in technology, why some people succeed economically and others do not, sympathies and antipathies toward other occupational classes, and racial and ethnic prejudices. Results were largely what one would suspect from common-sense predictions of occu-

[15] Heinz Eulau and Peter Schneider, "Dimensions of Political Involvement," *Public Opinion Quarterly*, XX (1956), 132.

[16] Robert E. Agger and Vincent Ostrom, "Political Participation in a Small Community," in Heinz Eulau et al., eds., *Political Behavior* (New York: The Free Press of Glencoe, 1956), p. 139.

pational-class opinions—except that all persons, even those of lowest economic status, seemed to believe that being poor and unsuccessful was basically the fault of the individual. Occupational differences on values related to the maintenance of the democratic society do not appear to be significant in Centers' study; here again education was shown to be more important than occupation:

> Our findings with regard to prejudice tend only in a general way to agree with the theories of Otto Klineberg, which account for prejudice on the supposition that there is something, usually economic, to be gained by it, or hold that it is due to the need for a scapegoat on the part of persons who are economically disadvantaged. Caution is advised with respect to this interpretation because of the large differences in prejudice that are found between groups of persons of different educational levels, and which make it appear that prejudice is to a considerable extent a function of lack of education.[17]

13.5 Economic Influence Modified by Personality Factors and Group Memberships

In the funnel of opinion causality, economic factors, as measured by income, occupation, or other indexes, interact constantly with noneconomic factors. Psychological factors relating to self-image, world view, and success or failure in the integration of personality and environment—all these are important and have been briefly and generally alluded to in earlier chapters. More specific to the matter of the influence of economic factors on opinion is the way in which these factors may be mediated by psychological characteristics. Glimpses of many of these psychological characteristics can be obtained from Lane's depth studies of businessmen and workers.[18] From Lane's 1954 work, Dahl summarizes one example of how psychological forces mediate economic factors and opinions on political issues:

> . . . to businessmen . . . the economic costs of regulation were relatively low; but the psychic costs were high. Regulation challenges the businessman's ideology, damages his self-image, generates frustrations by depriving him of customary choices, and creates anxieties by introducing new uncertainties into an already

[17] Richard Centers, "Attitude and Belief in Relation to Occupational Stratification," *Journal of Social Psychology,* XXVII (1948), 185.

[18] Robert E. Lane, *The Regulation of Businessmen: Social Conditions of Government Economic Control* (New Haven, Conn.: Yale University Press, 1954); "The Fear of Equality," *American Political Science Review,* LIII (1959), 35–51; and "Fathers and Sons: Foundations of Political Belief," *American Sociological Review,* XXIV (1959), 502–511.

unpredictable environment. . . . It follows that among the important conditions for effective regulation of business are means for minimizing damage to the businessman's ego and changing businessmen's attitudes.[19]

The effects of economic factors on opinion holding are further mediated and modified by organizations. Commitments to party membership, to group ideology, to role expectations of leaders and followers, and to other aspects of group behavior will often significantly distort the more directly economic influences on opinion holding. In this way, wealthy socialists and liberals will support high-spending policies that bear heavily on them as individual taxpayers; or debt-ridden junior executives, for the sake of their attachment to free enterprise, will oppose federal aid to their local schools at the cost of continued overtaxation of their suburban tract homes.

Studies of the political opinions of union members and nonmembers demonstrate the effect of group membership in modifying views presumed to have important economic sources. In its study of the 1952 presidential vote, the Survey Research Center found that labor-union members and their families "did not differ from the rest of the population in the extent of their concern with parties or candidates, [but] they were clearly more likely to be concerned with issues."[20] Moreover, union members thought of themselves (as a group) as being significantly more Democratic in vote intention (as indeed they were) than did other persons of the same economic stratum.[21] All studies of the matter indicate that union members vote more uniformly Democratic than do nonmembers. Their political opinions (assuming that expressions of vote intention and actual voting performance reflect opinions) are quite clearly strengthened by group membership. The Elmira study revealed that

in each occupational category, *non*union members and their families vote Republican about half again as much as union members. Nor is this simply a reflection of different class status; in each broad socioeconomic category (and in more detailed classification too, for that matter) union members are more Democratic. In fact, no matter what additional characteristic is controlled—education, age, class identification, religion, father's occupation or father's vote, even satisfaction with job or with management—union people are consistently more Democratic than nonunion people of the same kind.[22]

19 Robert A. Dahl, "Business and Politics: A Critical Appraisal of Political Science," *American Political Science Review,* LIII (1959), 30.

20 Angus Campbell, Gerald Gurin, and Warren E. Miller, *The Voter Decides* (New York: Harper & Row, Publishers, 1954), p. 154.

21 *Ibid.,* p. 214.

22 Bernard Berelson et al., *Voting* (Chicago: University of Chicago Press, 1954), pp. 46–47. Italics and parentheses in original.

As final evidence that economic factors do not determine political opinion (or even relate to them in predictable ways), consider the fact that political parties in America are not ideological parties based on economic class. Tradition, party history, the decentralized structure of government, which results in discrete and overlapping party objectives, and a mobile society that allows (even encourages) an individual to hitch the wagon of his political opinions to the star of his aspirations rather than to his present economic state—all these factors and more combine to render fatuous any view of a simple correspondence between economic forces and political opinions as reflected in party membership. Whether political parties ought to be more closely based on economic class is a question of interest and concern; but the fact that in America they are not is a testimony that contradicts Mark Twain's aphorism, quoted at the start of this chapter.

There are, of course, some "corn-pone opinions." On some matters, economics presses hard on politics, and political opinions are determined by the appearance or reality of the getting and spending processes. But on most matters of public concern, the relations between the economic and the political are much too subtle to be captured by any determinist prescription, and much interwoven by other social and psychological forces.

PART FOUR

DYNAMICS
OF PUBLIC
OPINION

In the preceding chapters, we have been concerned with the nature, the sources, and, in a sense, the ingredients of public opinion. First, we dealt with the measurement of public opinion, its meaning for democracy, and some problems of the use and abuse of polling in the free society. Next, we suggested a model (borrowed from other social scientists) for the opinion-forming process and considered briefly how culture and some of the larger psychological, sociological, and economic forces act as limiting and influencing factors in the shaping and reshaping of opinion.

In Part Four, we focus more narrowly on the specialized communications techniques and interpersonal relationships that are (in most cases, at least) consciously used for the making and remaking of opinions. In place of the macroscopic view of the funnel of opinion causality, we shall undertake now a more microscopic examination of the organization and techniques of opinion creation and transmission—though candor requires me to repeat what you must already be perfectly aware of: namely, that we have, at this time, only the most incomplete knowledge of the dynamics of opinion holding and opinion change.

We are still dealing with public opinion—with views expressed by significant numbers of persons on issues of public importance—but, for maximum clarity of exposition and understanding, we shall have to move back and

forth from the aggregate to the individual levels. Thus, in our analysis of
opinions and voting, we shall consider the low frequency of voting among
the lower-economic classes (expressed in probabilities and percentages)
and its possible partial cause in their low sense of political efficacy (expressed in terms of individual psychodynamics). In our analysis of the
mass media, we shall consider such group phenomena as the correlation
of newspaper exposure to issue opinions and candidate choice, and to the
study of why individuals read what newspapers and what parts of newspapers. We shall try to understand how and why the individual holds
what opinions on public questions, and to determine in what proportion
the various points of view on an issue are shared by the members of the
public created by that issue.

Our concern may be summarily represented by the following diagram:

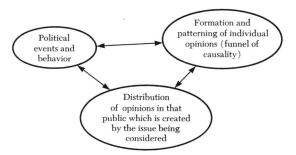

We want to explain political events and behavior. To do so, we need
to know something about the politically relevant opinion held by the
individual (its cause, intensity, and relation to other opinions); and we
need to know about the distribution in the mass (i.e., in the public or
publics involved) of that opinion.

In Part Four, we focus on the ways in which face-to-face and mass
communication between opinion leaders and opinion followers shape and
reshape both individual views and mass distributions.

COMMUNICATION
AND OPINION

14

According to Colin Cherry, communication is "the establishment of a social unit from individuals, by the use of language or signs. [It is] the sharing of common sets of rules, for various goal-seeking activities."[1] At another point, he says communication "is essentially the *relationship* set up by the transmission of stimuli and the evocation of responses."[2]

Human communication needs to be distinguished from animal communication on the basis of its flexibility, its adaptiveness, and its ability to deal with concepts such as space and time. The coinage (more technically, the stimulus) of communication is the "sign"; and signs may be—still in Cherry's terms—languages, codes, or logical-sign systems.

For our purposes, we may say that communication is *the meaningful use of signs to establish social relationships*. In most cases, we may narrow our consideration to language as the stimulus (sign), since, except for the use of gestures and symbols in politics, the currency of communication is the spoken or printed word.[3] Over three thousand languages and dialects are spoken in the world today. Many of these do not have written forms—i.e., they do not have conventional visual symbols that represent the sounds of speech and the ideas these sounds convey— and it is likely that there are no more than seventy-five to one hundred languages of importance. But even this number testifies to the flexibility of human invention and the variety of social custom. Chinese is the language spoken by most people, although English is the language most widely spread over the world.

[1] *On Human Communication* (New York: Science Editions, Inc., 1961), p. 303.

[2] *Ibid.*, p. 7. Italics in original.

[3] I do not mean to suggest here that national or party emblems, flags, music, salutes, and the like, have been infrequent or unimportant in the shaping of public opinion.

In this book, we deal very largely with communication through language, and with the relationship between small and large communication networks and the holding of opinions on issues of public importance.

14.1 Communication Networks

Communication creates social meaning through mutually understandable signs. The simplest form is that of individual A initiating a sign, which is more or less understandable as A intended it, to individual B. Thus:

A —————▶ Sign —————▶ B

Let us assume that A is a sentry. He becomes aware of B, and calls, "Halt." B is then aware of A, and he is aware that he must stop or run the risk of being shot. A simple communication network has been established. The network becomes a conversation when B returns his name to A's next query, "Who goes there?" A meaningful social relationship exists, a product of communication.

But instead of speaking, perhaps A levels his rifle at B; B recognizes the meaning of A's movement (the sign) and raises his arms; then a meaningful social relationship has likewise been created through communication. Spoken or written language, though usual in communication, is not essential.

The simplest communication network consists of two individuals exchanging meaningful signs. The primary diad is not only the simplest, but in all probability the most important network for the making and remaking of opinions—public as well as private. The husband-wife, parent-child, friend-friend, employer-employee, co-workers—all these common two-person relationships inform the private and public opinions of each of us. The simple two-person communication net constitutes (a) a powerful form of direct influence on individual opinions and (b) the basic structure for more complex communication patterns.

It is now common to distinguish *primary-* from *secondary*-group relationships. Each of these has its own communication networks, with characteristic and differential effects on public opinion.

14.11 Primary Groups and Primary Communication Networks

The sociologist Charles H. Cooley was perhaps the first to recognize the basic distinction between primary and secondary human groups. In

1909, he described primary groups as "those characterized by intimate face-to-face cooperation and association."[4] Homans, a latter-day student of small-group behavior, explicitly added the element of *frequent communication* to the definition of the primary group, which, according to him, is "a number of persons who communicate with each other often over a span of time, and who are few enough so that each person is able to communicate with all the others, not at second-hand, through other people, but face-to-face."[5]

The common definition of the primary group today is *a collection of persons who interact as individuals who are distinguishable, as individuals, from one another.* The diad, or two-person interaction, is the simplest of these. Work groups, bridge clubs, school classes, and dozens of other ordinary human interactions also constitute primary groups. Cooley's requirement of the members' being face-to-face need not be taken too literally; it is not necessary that the members of a primary group see each other or be in each other's presence. A conference telephone call produces a primary group—and a primary communication network— though the persons may be thousands of miles apart and, except for that particular interaction, total strangers. The only essential ingredients of the primary group, and of the primary communication network, are that the individuals who comprise it shall be recognizable as individuals and that there should be some concerted (probably goal-directed) pattern of activity among them.

Primary groups, and the communication networks established by them, may vary greatly in function, objective, membership, and degree of formality. Some may be wholly and permanently apolitical, some wholly and permanently political, and many with some actual or potential political implications activated at different times and in different degrees.[6]

14.12 Secondary Groups and Mass-Communication Networks

All group relationships in which the members are not recognizable as individuals may be described as *secondary groups*. Categorical groups— for example, all twenty-year-olds or all left-handed males—are one type of secondary group, normally of little concern for anything other than

4 *Social Organization* (New York: Charles Scribner's Sons, 1909), p. 23.

5 George C. Homans, *The Human Group* (New York: Harcourt Brace and World, Inc., 1950), p. 1.

6 See Sidney Verba, *Small Groups and Political Behavior* (Princeton, N.J.: Princeton University Press, 1961), especially pp. 3–60, for an excellent statement and overview of the importance of primary groups and politics.

statistical convenience. Our main interest here is what Truman calls *institutionalized groups,* both primary and secondary. Institutionalized groups—the family, organized religion, corporations, civic and fraternal clubs, to give only a few examples—show a rather high degree of formality, uniformity, and generality. Institutionalized groups not of the face-to-face variety are what we choose to call secondary groups.[7] In the analysis of public opinion, we shall use categorical, institutional, and associational secondary groups, in addition to the primary group.

In the marchland between clear-cut primary and secondary groups are some types of human interaction in which individuals may be identifiable as such, with names and significance as persons at some times, but at other times with the individuals lost or merged into the collective whole. The *crowd,* the *assemblage,* and the similar but often distinguished *mob* are ways to conceptualize situations in which the individual, as an individual, may be either visible or submerged in the interaction patterns.

Secondary communication networks can be distinguished from primary communication networks the same way that secondary groups are distinguished from primary groups. Secondary communication networks may be described as mass-communication systems, or simply as *mass communication.*

Wright points out that "mass communication is a special kind of communication involving distinctive operating conditions, primary among which are the nature of the audience, of the communication experience, and of the communicator."[8] The audience, he says, is distinguished by its large size, its heterogeneity, and its anonymity; the communication experience is characterized as "public, rapid, and transient"; and the communicator "tends to be, or to operate within, a complex organization that may involve great expense."[9]

The common mass-communication media—the press, radio, television, and the movies—meet all the basic requirements of anonymity, publicness, and institutionalization. They are also more or less rapid and transient, although some parts of each may require considerable time for preparation (e.g., magazine articles and movies), and may in some instances be designed for semipermanent use (e.g., the periodic reissue of old movies). Nevertheless, they are clearly more rapid and transient than such specialized communications as textbooks and scholarly publications,

7 David B. Truman, *The Governmental Process* (New York: Alfred A. Knopf, Inc., 1951), pp. 26–27. Truman's attention is focused on political-interest groups, and especially on "associations," which he describes as groups that grow out of "tangent relations" with institutionalized groups (pp. 33–41).

8 Charles R. Wright, *Mass Communication: A Sociological Perspective* (New York: Random House, Inc., 1959), p. 13.

9 *Ibid.,* pp. 13–15.

which, at least in theory, have value over an indeterminate span of time.[10]

It will not be profitable for us to try to define each form of communication—especially of printed communications such as pamphlets, newsletters, and memoranda—as mass communication or nonmass. Some may be public, transient, and addressed to a large heterogeneous audience. Polemical pamphlets and "open letters" to public officials probably should be thought of as mass communication; a diagnostic pamphlet issued by a medical society probably should not. As in all attempts at categorization, some items may not be readily identifiable as mass communications, and can be handled only as they appear. Despite the overlap in practice between mass communication and nonmass forms, the general distinction is important conceptually and has been useful in empirical research.

14.2 Communication and Direct Observation as Sources of Opinion

Opinion formation or change is not necessarily and always the result of communication. Instinct and unaided learning through individual experience may produce some kinds of attitudes and views about some matters. But, as we saw in Chapter 8, there can be no opinions worthy of that name without *learning,* and none but the most limited kind of learning without the social relationships that can be established only through communication. Thus, communication is essential to the formation and re-formation of those kinds of opinions with which we are concerned.

Members of society get almost all their knowledge of public issues through communication. Each person witnesses directly only a tiny part of the facts and opinions that make up what he knows and thinks about public matters. He sees and hears from others meaningful signs (words and pictures) that help him form or change attitudes and opinions. Some of these messages come from the members of his family, his friends, and others who communicate more or less directly to him; the rest of the messages he receives through impersonal media.

10 Some scholars define mass communication as all "impersonal transmission regardless of the size of audience . . . radio, movies, books, newspapers, and magazines are included in this definition, but those involving personal address, the drama, and other face-to-face communications are excluded." See Carl I. Hovland, "Effects of the Mass Media of Communications," in G. Lindzey, ed., *Handbook of Social Psychology* (Reading, Mass.: Addison-Wesley Publishing Co., Inc., 1954), II, 1062–1063. Hovland's definition would include textbooks and, apparently, all printed material except that circulating only among known individuals. A play in a book would be mass communication; a play performed would not. The definition has the advantage of being tidy.

Communication interacts with personal observation. Although very few persons can form or change their opinions about public matters without some communication with others, direct observation may supplement, confirm, or disconfirm the meaning of communicated information. Many opinions, formed through communication, are thus tested by personal experience. Information received from primary or mass-communication networks may have convinced medical students A and B that more extensive public welfare services are desirable in their community. As doctors, however, A and B may have very different experiences. If A has many indigent and low-income patients, his experience will no doubt confirm and strengthen his opinion on this issue. If B's patients are drawn largely from persons who can afford private welfare services, B's experience will probably disconfirm his earlier view, and may lead to a change of opinion.

There are many ways, at both the individual and group levels, to reduce the conflict and dissonance of communication and observation. Alone, or in groups, we tend to see and hear what we want to see and hear; thus, communication tends to be identical or at least similar to observation. Nevertheless, the interaction of communicated information and directly perceived information, and especially the reconciliation of communication-observation experiences, is an important part of the dynamics of opinion formation and change.

Most opinions are based upon facts or upon other opinions, which are not learned first-hand but communicated by other individuals. Few opinions are based wholly or, possibly, even in part on direct observation. Moreover, those few that are observation-based are often made possible by conditions that are established by prior communications. When persons think some events or behavior are important, or when they are especially sensitive and watchful for clues that may give meaning to certain events or behavior, we say these events have *attention salience* for them.

What establishes attention salience? One observation may lead to another or still more observations in a chain of observation: salience—new observation—new salience. If Benjamin Franklin's accounts of his own life are to be wholly credited (a matter of controversy among scholars), it was something like this chain that led him from the observation of a kitten's fur to glass-and-wool experiments to the key on the kite and finally to a theory of lightning. The isolated scientist would have no other way to proceed than through ever more well-defined observation-salience-observation cycles. But the progress of science is possible precisely because scientists are not isolated; communication intervenes, and makes possible great leaps of information accumulation.

So it is also, to a large extent, with all opinion creation and change.

Attention salience is created by communication. We learn sometimes by communication what we should, perhaps, be learning by observation.[11] Doctors A and B read in the paper that the President has sent to Congress a proposal for expanded health benefits for the aged. They then pay special attention to need and inadequacy, or to no need and adequacy, as real cases appear in their own practices or in the practices of their fellow physicians. Communication—mass communication in this case—creates for them a saliency that leads to direct observation. Or, to take another case, the mythical Mr. Black, created some pages back, has strongly Protestant parents who first raise his attention-salience to Catholics in politics; he subsequently looks for, and finds, a Catholic party boss in his city. In Black's case, primary communication in his family rather than mass communication first triggers his concern. Or, as a final case, John Henry North, our first mythical creation, through books and scholarly pursuits became aware of some of the social and political problems he observed and then emphasized in his campaign. What created salience for him (books and academic study) was not clearly either primary or mass communication, but something of both.

[11] For some stimulating, and even quite revolutionary, propositions about the human capacity to gain and hold knowledge, see Michael Polanyi, *Personal Knowledge: Towards a Post-Critical Philosophy* (Chicago: University of Chicago Press, 1958); and, by the same author, *The Study of Man* (Chicago: University of Chicago Press, 1959).

PRIMARY GROUPS, PERSONAL INFLUENCE, AND PUBLIC OPINION

15

A series of studies, employing laboratory and field investigations that cut across several disciplines, have emphasized anew the importance of primary groups and of primary communication networks in making and changing opinions. Our understanding of the behavior and opinion interaction of individuals has been much extended and clarified especially by two significant research developments in the past thirty years: small-group studies and scientific sample surveys.

In this chapter, we shall consider some of these primary-group studies, and try to understand interpersonal influences on opinion within the context of communications networks. Our interest here is in the following variant of the prime question for political analysis: Who, in face-to-face or otherwise close situations, influences whom, how, and with what political consequence? A further question, to which we turn at the end of this chapter, has to do with the relationships between primary and secondary communications networks—i.e., between face-to-face communication and mass communication.

15.1 The Creation and Maintenance of Group Norms

Members of self-conscious groups tend to distinguish themselves from nonmembers. Sometimes human groups are formed on the basis of the physical characteristics of their members (men or women, black or white); by place of residence (X community or Y community); by age (under thirty, over sixty-five); by ancestry (Irish, Italian, Mayflowerites); or, most often, probably, on the basis of *shared opinion*. Whatever it is that determines group membership, those who belong have at the outset, or very quickly develop, what Cooley called "we-feeling" and "they-feeling."

Related to we-feeling and whatever common history

may exist, and often binding the members together in behavior patterns, are the intangible rules for group identification. These rules are what we know as *group norms*—values, and hierarchies of values, plus behavioral expectations, all frequently unwritten but by no means unimportant in obtaining group objectives and minimizing intragroup conflict. Even the simplest groups possess norms; norms develop in the very act of the creation of a group. They are, in a sense, the unacknowledged and informal codification of the interactions that make group consciousness (we-feeling) possible.

One of the earliest systematic investigations of group behavior was conducted in the Hawthorne, Illinois, plant of the Western Electric Company, makers of telephone equipment. For a rather long period of time, a team of social phychologists observed the Western Electric employees under various experimental and nonexperimental working conditions. Of the many studies in this series, the experiment of the Bank Wiring Observation Room, briefly described, may illustrate best the way in which group norms may be created—and illustrate the difficulty of predicting group norms from wholly rational premises.

The Bank Wiring experiment was designed to test some incentive plans based on the view that workers would work harder for extra pay. The workers whose behavior was being studied had been put together in a special room with an observer whose reputed function was to "keep the records." Under varying conditions of extra-pay incentive—much to the investigators' surprise (and contrary to an earlier experiment in which, on reexamination, the psychological variables were quite different)—the workers' production was not significantly changed.

What had happened? Under the circumstances, a special kind of we-feeling had been created among the workers. An informal group had emerged, a group with norms about production output and quotas. This new primary group had evolved a very real understanding, only partly verbalized but, nonetheless, generally accepted. The behavior norms thus created prevented the faster workers from producing more (from being "rate busters") for fear that management would then reduce the piecework rate. Likewise, the norms included the expectation that each person would do his share of the work, and that each member would protect these informal agreements from being learned and dealt with by management.[1]

In the Hawthorne studies, group norms had much greater influence, in general, on individual behavior and opinions than did the variables of pay and working conditions, which were directly manipulated by the investigators. Other studies have revealed the importance of the group in

[1] For the Hawthorne studies, see F. J. Roethlisberger and William J. Dickson, *Management and the Worker* (Cambridge, Mass.: Harvard University Press, 1939).

the establishment and maintenance of rules of rightness and wrongness and of behavior for members of the group.[2]

15.11   Opinion Similarity within Groups

Depending upon the importance of the group to the individuals who comprise it, the group norms will strongly or weakly influence the shared opinions. The importance of the group to its members will be the result of many personal propensities, views, and judgments. Importance may be measured by various tests of cohesion or integration, one frequent element of which is an index of sameness of opinion among the group members.

Much of the study of political behavior depends on the similarities and dissimilarities of opinion and candidate preference within and among groups. In our consideration of the sociology of opinion holding, we discussed the influence of family, religious, and economic groupings. It was no surprise to find clusterings of political opinions significantly related to group membership; indeed, large-scale analysis of public opinion would be nearly impossible if it could not be demonstrated that people who share group membership tend to hold similar political views.

The extent to which members of groups are aware of the sameness of their views appears to depend on the size of the group, the intensiveness of group interaction in the past, the relevance of the issues for group functioning, and on the centrality or marginality of the individual whose judgment is under consideration. In general, and as would be expected, leaders and centrally located members of small, long-established groups are able to assess very accurately the opinions of the group on issues of salience to the group.[3]

15.12   The Influence of Group Norms on "Objective" Judgments

No one will be surprised that studies of group behavior show group members to have consistent similarities of opinion. It may be of some

---

[2] See, for example, William F. Whyte, *Street Corner Society* (Chicago: University of Chicago Press, 1943); and George C. Homans, *The Human Group* (New York: Harcourt, Brace and World, Inc., 1950).

[3] For a helpful summary of findings, see Harold H. Kelley and John W. Thibaut, "Experimental Studies of Group Problem Solving and Process," in G. Lindzey, ed., *Handbook of Social Psychology* (Reading, Mass.: Addison-Wesley Publishing Co., Inc., 1954), II, 768ff.

interest, however, that group members, under certain conditions, tend to agree with one another on judgments that appear to be purely objective—even when such judgments are erroneous in fact.

The social psychologist Muzafer Sherif discovered that perceptions, as well as opinions, of individuals are influenced by group norms. He was investigating the *autokinetic effect*—the fact that a stationary point of light, viewed through a totally dark box without any visible referents except the light itself, *appears* to oscillate. He found that reports of the amount of light movement, given by individuals in a group setting, tended to converge around a group norm. Individuals who first reported greater or lesser movement when alone, tended after discussion to agree with the median reports.[4]

Asch, elaborating on Sherif's methods, systematically varied the intensity and division of opinions with the use of "stooges." He found that the "naive" subjects in a large majority of cases yielded to group pressures to converge on the norms established by the "stooge" subjects at the will of the investigator. He found, among other things, that the "majority effect" attained full strength when three out of four subjects agreed, and that the tendency of a single minority member to yield to the majority position was not changed by increasing the majority.[5]

15.13 Group Norms and Opinions on Public Issues

A word of caution is perhaps in order. The pioneering studies of Sherif and Asch, like others carried out in the laboratory, are very dramatic. They illustrate well what is important for our purposes here, namely the influence of group pressures and expectations on individual opinions. Nevertheless, there is a danger in overestimating these evidences of the influence of group norms. Olmsted summarizes the dangers of laboratory experiments as:[6]

1. *Generalization from too little information:* "It is evident that these experiments make no claim to have investigated all the possible effects of the group on the individual . . . our knowledge can hardly be said to be very systematic or exhaustive."

2. *Transference from unreal to real situations:* "It is . . . important

---

4 Muzafer Sherif, "Group Influences upon the Formation of Norms and Attitudes," in Eleanor E. Maccoby et al., *Readings in Social Psychology* (New York: Holt, Rinehart and Winston, Inc., 1958), pp. 219–232.

5 Solomon E. Asch, "Effects of Group Pressure upon the Modification and Distortion of Judgments," in Maccoby, *Social Psychology*, pp. 174–183.

6 Michael S. Olmsted, *The Small Group* (New York: Random House, Inc., 1959), p. 76.

to ask whether behavior observed in the laboratory and that observed in the 'real' world are the same in fact or in name only. . . . The sort of experimentation described above is only in the broadest sense a study of groups at all. These groups—or more accurately, aggregates of subjects—have very little interaction and almost no organization or structure."

3. *Temptation to explain all behavior in terms of the influence of groups:* "Third is the danger that 'group norms' become an explanation for everything. Further exploration of group behavior can too easily be smothered by the apparently wise but actually trite explanation that this or that happens because of a group norm."

Bearing in mind the dangers of overgeneralization from too little or unreal evidence, the discovery and elaboration of the importance of small-group–individual relationships is one of the most significant developments of modern social science. The influence of small groups on individual members is not, for public questions, that of direct and explicit norms that are essential to the operation and survival of the group and that the individual is constrained to observe. Opinions on issues that can be called public are ordinarily not critical to the smooth functioning of primary groups. Many families, work groups, and social clubs include members whose views on public issues differ widely from the average opinion of the group—this is clearly true; but it is equally true that there are influences on both the group and the individual whenever there is even the slightest indication of these opinion differences. One important reason for these influences is the fact that individuals respond to what they *believe* to be group norms; opinions are formed or held in accordance with what might be called the *anticipated pressures* from the group. To test this proposition, Steiner interviewed a national sample and a local (Michigan) sample for opinions toward the economic and political power of big business and for the norms these respondents assumed to be held by their closest friends. He concluded "that perceived primary-group pressures can have considerable effect on attitudes even when there is reason to doubt that group norms and sanctions are operating."[7]

Whether group norms are known or presumed, it is likely, as Verba points out, that the pressure to conform will be greater, not less, in social and political than in other matters. The pressure to conform to the opinions of those around us is strong

even when there is a clear objective referent for our opinions, but it is more the case with those political and social opinions for which there is no clear and easy test except comparison with the opinions of our fellows. In such testing situations, there is pressure on the individual to change his opinion if it differs from

[7] Ivan D. Steiner, "Primary Group Influences on Public Opinion," *American Sociological Review*, XIX (1954), 267.

the opinions of others around him. These pressures come both from the individual himself and from the other group members, since the condition of dissonance will be unpleasant to both the deviant and the other group members.[8]

15.2   Role Differentiation in Primary Groups

All members of groups do not perform, for the group, the same kinds of tasks, nor behave, in group interaction, in identical ways. Individuals in groups have various roles to play. Although there is considerable disagreement about the nuances and specialized meanings of *role* and *role behavior*,[9] one useful and fairly typical statement defines a social role as "an organized pattern of expectancies that relate to the tasks, demeanors, attitudes, values, and reciprocal relationships to be maintained by persons occupying specific membership positions and fulfilling definable functions in any group." In their definition of role, these authors place emphasis "on expectancies rather than behavior, because the role is defined by what others expect of the person filling it. Behavior refers to actual performance—how a person fills his role."[10]

There may be *natural* roles, determined by sex and generational differences, as in the obvious examples of the mother and father roles in the primary family group. In formally organized groups, specialized officers may handle *functional roles* (that is, behavior for facilitating the attainment of group purposes), such as presiding over meetings (the president or chairman), handling group finances (the treasurer), or taking care of group communications (the secretary).

All of these role differentiations are simple—or at least obvious. What is less obvious is that role differentiation takes place even in informal groups—and that this role differentiation may be very important for the determination of opinion. What we think about private or public issues is inevitably influenced by what we believe is appropriate for us to think, depending upon who we are and what others expect of us. In discussion and problem-solving groups, in laboratory and real situations, functional-role categories can be identified and differentiated. Thus, one team of

---

[8] Sidney Verba, *Small Groups and Political Behavior* (Princeton, N.J.: Princeton University Press, 1961), pp. 23–24. Verba cites Leon Festinger, *A Theory of Cognitive Dissonance* (Stanford, Calif.: Stanford University Press, 1957).

[9] See Lionel J. Neiman and James W. Hughes, "The Problem of the Concept of Role —A Re-Survey of the Literature," *Social Forces*, XXX (1951), 141–149.

[10] Eugene L. Hartley and Ruth E. Hartley, *Fundamentals of Social Psychology* (New York: Alfred A. Knopf, Inc., 1952), p. 486.

investigators observed several roles, including: "information seeker" (or "information giver"), "initiator," "energizer," "evaluator-critic," and "harmonizer."[11]

More important to us than the kinds of roles that exist is the evidence that social roles influence opinions about political issues. Many wives find in their wifely role the reasons, or at least the rationalizations, for their disinterest and lack of information about public affairs—"Oh, my husband does the political thinking in our family."[12] It is a belief among junior corporation executives "on the rise" that their role requires them to be inactive in politics and without opinions (at least, without *expressed* opinions) on issues of public concern.[13] Clergymen will not ordinarily express highly political opinions; and even the Pope, whose leadership role for Roman Catholics is broadly defined, speaks infallibly only on matters of faith and morals.

In situations of more highly concentrated politics, social roles heavily influence the nature of opinion creation and exchange. The candidate role carries with it expectations absent from (or even incompatible with) the role expectations of the elected legislator—or, a fortiori, the elected judge.[14]

The separation of powers, at least in the United States, where it is institutionally so imbedded, appears to have strengthened role differentiations associated with the functional behavior of legislators, executives, and judges. At news conferences, the President often tells his questioners that "it would be inappropriate" (for a person in the presidential role) to comment on this or that topic; and the Supreme Court has developed a whole inventory of "non justicible questions," that is, matters with which the justices, in their role as judges, will not concern themselves.[15]

---

[11] Kenneth D. Benne and Paul Sheats, "Functional Roles of Group Members," *Journal of Social Issues,* IV (1948), 41–49.

[12] Angus Campbell et al., *The American Voter* (John Wiley & Sons, Inc., 1960), pp. 490–492.

[13] Andrew Hacker, *Politics and the Corporation* (New York: Fund for the Republic, 1958), p. 9. See also the comments of Preston E. Peden, of the Chicago Association of Commerce and Industry, and Ernst A. Dauer, of Household Finance Corporation, in James A. Gathings, ed., *Politics and the American Businessman* (Lewisburg, Pa.: James A. Gathings, 1960), pp. 65, 77.

[14] Personality as well as role considerations enter here; Adlai Stevenson seems to have disliked campaigning and to have been, generally, as ill suited to it as he has been well suited to small-group diplomacy.

[15] It should not be thought, however, in these examples especially, that role considerations are the sole or even the primary causes of presidential or judicial self-restraint. Frequently, such restraint is sheer political strategy, though cast in role-appropriate terms. The President or the Court may find that some situations require less restraint than others; President Truman found no role inhibitions in castigating

At less lofty levels, and throughout the opinion-policy process, role considerations bear on the existence and intensity of public opinion. On public finance questions, the bankers are listened to closely; the views of the "Mothers Committee of Public School 310" are given special attention on education matters; almost any "older businessman" is respected by his younger colleagues when public issues are discussed. In all groups (but in primary groups especially), role considerations bear on opinion formation and change; in some group relationships, role may be insignificant, or nearly so, whereas in others it may be of central importance.

15.3   Personal Experience and Personal Influence

It is apparent that role is related to experience. The leader has led, the expediter has expedited, and the inside-dopester has acquired inside dope. Conceivably, one could fill a role without gaining experience in the practical matters and specialized knowledge associated with that role; role behavior, to continue Hartley and Hartley's distinction, could be irrelevant to role efficacy. In general, however, there should be a fairly close correspondence between influence associated with role and influence associated with experience. In simple societies—and to some extent in those not so simple—the village elder has a large-group social role as patriarch, which is in turn related to genealogical fact and to his personal experience. His experience supports his role, and his role makes possible an increase in his influence as a leader of opinion.

Role is thus quite obviously related to specialization of labor. Both social role and labor specialization create the presumption of opinion expertise. Plato believed that philosophy, or the study of truth, was a matter of specialization like the study of medicine; his antidemocratic bias is in large part traceable to his view that the philosopher-king is the expert in governing, whose opinions, based upon special study and experience, ought to be law.

Plato seems to have assumed that some people have expert training, skills, and competence and others have none. Whatever the case may have

---

the Republican-controlled 80th Congress as "Do Nothing" and "the worst in history," whereas President Kennedy, hoping to extract his program from a reluctant House peopled by former colleagues and controlled by his party friends, was most considerate of legislative prerogatives in 1961 and 1962. Likewise, the Supreme Court Justices found it inappropriate for them, as judges, to look for unconstitutional legislative motives in a margarine-tax law they agreed with (*McCray v. U.S.*, 15 U.S. 27, 1904) but quite appropriate in a tax law repugnant to their own economic views (*Bailey v. Drexel Furniture Co.*, 259 U.S. 20, 1922).

been 2,500 years ago in Greece, a more modern view of society would recognize that specializations—and roles and experience based on special-izations—are spread very widely. In the nineteenth century, George Corne-wall Lewis went beyond the mere fact that specialization of roles and experience means that expert knowledge (and, therefore, reliable opinion) is divided unequally in society. "In considering the seat of authority," Lewis observed, "it should be borne in mind, on the one hand, that no man is a competent judge on *all* subjects; and, on the other, that every man is a competent judge on *some*."[16] The evidence of some recent field studies indicates that Lewis was right. Specialized interest and specialized experience create specialized opinion leadership. Among their more than seven hundred women respondents in Decatur, Illinois, Katz and Lazars-feld found very few "general" leaders—so few, in fact, that those found might have been the product of interviewing error or dishonest re-sponses.[17] Younger, single women, in the Katz and Lazarsfeld study, had their opinions sought by other women on matters of clothing style and fashion; married women with larger families were sources of general marketing advice; in public affairs, the specialized opinion leaders seemed to be those higher in social status and gregariousness (an index of non-neighbor contacts and group membership).

Thus, it appears that Plato was wrong or naive about the possible creation of generalized opinion leaders. As Will Rogers put it, "We are all ignorant, only on different subjects." Nevertheless, the dynamics of repre-sentative government require political executives to assume the appear-ance, if not the substance, of generalized opinion leadership.[18]

Though there are few generalized opinion leaders, it seems equally true that not everyone is a specialized opinion leader. Even the most influential are uninfluential on some matters. But some are uninfluential on every matter—at least every *public* matter.

---

[16] George Cornewall Lewis, *An Essay on the Influence of Authority in Matters of Opinion* (London: Longmans, Green, 1875), p. 114; italics in original. The work was first published in 1849.

[17] Elihu Katz and Paul F. Lazarsfeld, *Personal Influence* (New York: The Free Press of Glencoe, 1955), p. 334. However, a reassessment of Katz and Lazarsfeld's material led two scholars to the conclusion that generalized opinion leaders existed among the Decatur women. See Alan S. Marcus and Raymond A. Bauer, "Yes: There Are Generalized Opinion Leaders," *Public Opinion Quarterly*, XXVIII (1964), 628–632.

[18] Proper staffing, of course, may provide the political executive with specialized opinion leadership which, through the device of ministerial responsibility, results (or may result) in the functional equivalent of generalized opinion leadership. For example, the President may become, in effect, a generalized opinion leader by pooling the talents of expert assistants, each of whom is limited in his expertise. Legislative bodies rely in the same way for over-all competence on the interdependent expertise of their individual members.

15.4 Personal Influence on Public Opinion Formation and Change

Political scientists and sociologists have only recently rediscovered the importance of person-to-person contact in opinion formation and change. Despite the early writings of Cooley, Mead, and other sociologists, and the significant work of Mayo and other industrial psychologists, it was not until the 1940s and 1950s that the wider implications of primary-group interactions became apparent.

Retrospectively, it seems clear why the effects of primary communication networks were not understood and acknowledged until recently. Before the age of scientific sample surveys, what we knew (or thought we knew) about political behavior was largely gained deductively from "general principles" of human action or empirically from the observation of atypical individuals and groups. In particular, our understanding was limited by two conceptions, which we now believe to have been inaccurate or oversimplified. One was, and is, the old bugaboo of "the rational man," the implications of which we have considered at earlier points in this book. We need not repeat here the warnings and dangers of believing that reason and logic control human behavior. We need only say, in this context, that habit, faith, avoidance of commitment (i.e., indifference and apathy), and the other nonrational sources of human behavior often depend on informal—perhaps even unrecognized—person-to-person influences. It is an interesting question, in this age of what Riesman calls "other-directedness," whether the influence of nonrational factors is greater than it was in earlier periods of "inner-directed" social ethic. In any case, reason is only one—and often one of the least important—of the elements that create opinions. Our earlier model of the rational man was too simple; and its simplicity made it easy for us to ignore other influences —among which are the influences of casual friends and neighbors.

In addition to the overemphasis of reason, our earlier views of opinion formation and change presumed that the mass media provided the individual with facts and opinions he absorbed directly, without the aid of mediation or translation by other individuals. The influence of the mass media was thought to be immediate, direct, and more or less equal in its impact. "In short," as Katz and Lazarsfeld say, "the media of communication were looked upon as a new kind of unifying force—a simple kind of nervous system—reaching out to every eye and ear, in a society characterized by an amorphous social organization and a paucity of interpersonal relations."[19]

---

[19] Katz and Lazarsfeld, *Personal Influence* (see footnote 17), p. 16.

The influence of the mass media is not so simple. Not all persons are equally or randomly exposed to mass media, and people therefore receive different messages. Programming varies from medium to medium and within each medium—another factor accounting for variety in what individuals receive from mass communications. Furthermore, individuals who receive the same messages find different meanings in them, depending upon what they are or are not looking for and upon what information and skill they have in relating these messages to other messages.

These disturbing complexities led a number of analysts to differentiate individuals (to take them out of the "mass") according to the roles they played in the flow of information and opinions. The authors of *The People's Choice,* first among survey researchers, "discovered" that some people are, in Orwell's celebrated phrase, "more equal than others" when it comes to determining the way votes will be cast. Personal influence, they found, was probably more important than formal media in determining voting decisions. Personal contact is apt to reach persons not exposed to media messages; "on an average day, at least 10 per cent more people participated in discussions about the election—either actively or passively —than listened to a major speech or read about campaign items in a newspaper."[20] Not only is personal influence more extensive than mass-media political influence, but, as the authors of this pioneer study point out, personal influence has the following psychological advantages:

1. *It is nonpurposive:* "politics gets through, especially to the indifferent . . . because it comes up unexpectedly as a sideline or marginal topic in a casual conversation."

2. *It is flexible when countering resistance:* "can counter and dislodge such resistance . . . can make use of a large number of cues . . . can choose the occasion at which to speak . . . can adapt [the] story to . . . the other's interests and his ability to understand."

3. *It offers immediate reward for compliance:* "When someone yields to a personal influence in making a vote decision, the reward is immediate and personal. This is not the case in yielding to an argument via print or radio [or television]."

4. *It allows the individual to put his trust in a known and intimate source:* "The doubtful voter . . . can trust the judgment and evaluation of the respected people among his associates. Most of them are people with the same status and interests as himself. Their attitudes are more relevant for him than the judgments of an unknown editorial writer."

5. *It allows for persuasion without conviction:* "Personal influence, with all its overtones of personal affection and loyalty, can bring to the

---

[20] Paul F. Lazarsfeld et al., *The People's Choice,* 2nd ed. (New York: Columbia University Press, 1948), pp. 150–151.

polls votes that would otherwise not be cast or would be cast for the opposing party just as readily if some other friend had insisted. [It] differs from the formal media by persuading uninterested people to vote in a certain way without giving them a substantive reason for their vote."[21]

The power of personal influence to induce *behavior* for what are essentially irrelevant reasons is unparalleled in the mass media. Behavior may indeed be induced by the mass media for what are *in fact* irrelevant reasons (as when "Charlie" buys Wildroot Hair Oil because he believes the jingle which says girls will therefore like him), but the reasons are *thought* to be relevant. Most of the strength of personal influence lies in the willingness of individuals to think or do things simply because their friends want them to.

The Erie County study of 1940 dealt mainly with voting intentions. Since then, a number of researchers have investigated the way influence flows more generally in the formation and re-formation of public opinion. A number of categorization and classification schemes have been developed. Almond suggested a helpful stratification of opinion leadership. Within the wide, "general public" he recognized an " 'attentive public,' " which is informed and interested in foreign-policy problems, and which constitutes the audience for the foreign-policy discussions among the elites." Smaller and more influential than the attentive public is the stratum he designates as the "policy and opinion elites," which he describes as "the articulate policy-bearing stratum of the population, which gives structure to the public, and which provides the effective means of access to the various groupings."[22]

Elmo Roper developed a typology of leadership and followership with more categories than suggested by Almond. He illustrated the stratification by a series of concentric circles, from the small numbers of "Great Thinkers" in the center circle to the large numbers of "Politically Inert" in the outer ring (see Fig. 15–1).[23]

James Rosenau divides the American opinion public on foreign-policy issues into three major strata. Seventy-five to 90 per cent of the adult population at any given time are members of the *mass public,* "composed of opinion holders who have neither the opportunity nor the inclination to participate in the opinion-making process." Perhaps 10 per cent of the population comprise the *attentive public* of persons "who are inclined to participate but lack the access or opportunity to do so." At the very top of influence are the members of the *opinion-making public,*

21 *Ibid.,* pp. 152–156.

22 Gabriel A. Almond, *The American People and Foreign Policy,* 2nd ed. (New York: Frederick A. Praeger, Publisher, 1960), p. 138.

23 Elmo Roper, "Who Tells the Story-Tellers?" *Saturday Review,* July 31, 1954, pp. 25–26.

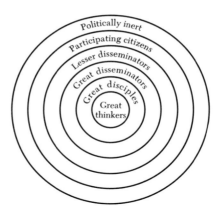

*Figure 15–1. Elmo Roper's Conceptualization
of Relative Numbers and Importance of
Opinion Leaders and Followers*

whom Rosenau further subdivides into *local* opinion makers (either single-issue or multi-issue) and *national* opinion makers (either single-issue or multi-issue).[24]

In all these conceptualizations and stratifications, the flow of information and influence is from the smaller groups of knowledgeable, active persons to the larger groups of less knowledgeable, less active persons. Both knowledge and activity are qualified, of course, by many other considerations, of which socioeconomic status, education, personality characteristics (e.g., gregariousness), role, and ego-involvement are important. But the over-all pattern appears to be that of multidimensional networks of opinion giving and opinion taking in which the opinion givers are (a) *many*—although some never seem to have their views sought, nor accepted if volunteered; (b) *specialized*—although "general" opinion leaders may exist in some communities and at some social levels; and (c) *effective* (insofar as they are effective) to some considerable degree through informal and unself-conscious techniques of conversation and example-setting.

Much remains to be learned about influence and the transfer of opinions through primary- and small-group communication. It seems probable—although the evidence is not yet available—that the essentially private matters studied by most sociologists in small-group research (and to a large degree by Katz and Lazarsfeld in their interviews with the women of Decatur) are heavily influenced by the primary-group contacts

[24] James N. Rosenau, *Public Opinion and Foreign Policy* (New York: Random House, Inc., 1961), pp. 33–34, 50–52.

each person experiences in day-to-day living. An individual's opinions about public questions seem to be less influenced by his peers than by the strata of people immediately above him, to whom he turns for information and (perhaps, more often) conclusions that square in some general way with (a) his own basic attitudes and (b) the values of those primary groups to which he feels allegiance. For public questions, the governmental and group leaders, the managers and producers of the mass media, and others who are visible or powerful in the hierarchies of social institutions (churches, schools)—these people, whom Almond, Roper, and Rosenau describe, will be more important sources of opinions than mere friends and acquaintances. It is to these larger leaders, and their use of mass-communications media, that we now turn in the next chapter.

MASS COMMUNICATION
AND PUBLIC OPINION

16

To this point we have considered some of the important factors, causal and influential, that shape opinions in individuals and, through individuals, in groups. We have considered the influence of culture (patterns of thought and behavior that are approved and disapproved), and of larger social institutions, such as family, religion, and economic organization. Now we shall deal with the way human communication binds individuals together and makes possible meaningful opinion interaction in a social context. Here we are concerned with *mass communication*.

According to the sociologist Charles R. Wright, mass communication may be most usefully defined in terms of "the nature of its audience, of the communication experience, and of the communicator." Mass communication, he says, "is directed toward relatively large, heterogeneous, and anonymous audiences; messages are transmitted publicly, often timed to reach most audience members simultaneously, and are transient in character; the communicator tends to be, or to operate within, a complex organization that may involve great expense."[1] Not all these characteristics will be true of all examples of mass communication; and many examples of communication neither clearly "mass" nor clearly personal (or individual, or private) may be found: marginal cases would include political rallies, religious sermons, newsletters, and scientific monographs. Nevertheless, the general distinction is clear and useful: mass communication is always directed to an anonymous and varied audience; it is public; and it is created within and transmitted through complex impersonal channels.

Mass communications are made through the mass

[1] *Mass Communication: A Sociological Perspective* (New York: Random House, Inc., 1959), pp. 13, 15.

media.[2] The mass media, in order of importance for public opinion, are: the press, television, radio, and movies. By the press I mean, first, newspapers, and, second, news and opinion journals. So-called family magazines such as *Saturday Evening Post*, women's magazines such as *McCall's* and *Ladies Home Journal*, picture magazines such as *Life* and *Look*, and other periodicals of fiction and entertainment are, of course, part of the American press. No doubt, articles in a popular potpourri like *Reader's Digest* have some influence on the underlying predispositions of American voters, and, unquestionably, some editorials in *Life* or the *Post* are taken into account—or at least noted—by political decision makers.[3] For the most part, however, the printed word that is important in American politics appears in the newspapers and in a few weekly or monthly journals such as *Time, Newsweek, U.S. News and World Report, Harpers, Fortune,* and *Atlantic,* and in a few smaller journals such as *Commentary, America, National Review,* and *The New Republic.* In this chapter, we shall not concern ourselves much with the part of the press that has only little or indirect impact on controversial opinion related to public policy. But we bear in mind that normally apolitical journals sometimes become politicized (as did the publications of the various medical associations in the fight over national health programs for the aged) and exert measurable influence on policy making, and that sometimes a single book may have important political consequences by illuminating a policy matter and affecting the opinions that count—as, in 1963, Rachel Carson's *The Silent Spring* so effectively warned of the dangers of the indiscriminate use of herbicides and insecticides.

16.1   Major Influences of the Mass Media on Public Opinion

One of the elements of American political folklore is that the mass media, especially the newspapers, have great influence over the course of

---

2 *Media* is plural for *medium*—and it is one of those Latin plurals not yet naturalized into American English, probably because pedants give it continued visitor's status by writing footnotes about it. A *mass medium* really ought to be a *mass medium of communication,* since a *medium* (Webster) is "that by or through which anything is accomplished"; but the whole phrase *mass medium* (or *media*) has come to mean that by or through which mass communications are accomplished.

3 A case in point is *Life* magazine's massive documentry story (August 16, 1963) on congressional pork-barrel projects, "Now See the Innards of a Fat Pig," which was widely reprinted and discussed, in Congress and elsewhere, but seems not to have reduced the number of rivers-and-harbors bills.

elections, legislation, and executive decisions. This bit of "common knowledge" is especially cherished by defeated candidates and reformist interest groups who find some comfort in the identification of scapegoats for the failures of their causes. But winners and status-quo organizations also subscribe in large measure to the view that the mass media can move political mountains.

There are some valid reasons why the mass media are felt to be powerful influences in the political dialogue and in the political resolution of social conflict. One is that the mass media do, indeed, influence political decisions—by giving, or withholding, publicity (and, sometimes, endorsements) to candidates and promoters of policy, and (through their editorializing) by helping a small number of people make up their minds about issues. Another reason the media are politically important is quite simply that political decision makers often *think* they are important. If enough people whose collective influence is great think that the *New York Times* editorials are important, or that the CBS "White Papers" are powerful expressions of concern and of popular value judgments, then these media presentations do become influential—but more because of what they are thought to be than because of what they are.

In part, this escalator of importance occurs with regard to the mass media because there are so few ostensibly impartial indicators of what people think about public policy. Special-interest pleading there is aplenty; but there are not many ways for the attentive decision maker to find out "what the people *really* think." The tendency is for political actors to believe that the mass media somehow have special insight into the "public mind" (an illusion carefully nurtured by the self-image of the press—especially as being "vigilant" and "searching"). Cohen, among others, notes this overreliance on the newspapers:

> . . . lacking any other *daily* link to the outside, any other *daily* measure of how people are reacting to the ebb and flow of foreign-policy developments, the policy maker reaches for the newspaper as an important source of public opinion, as the instrument of "feedback." In fact, many officials treat the press and public opinion as synonymous, either explicitly equating them or using them interchangeably.[4]

Despite their giant-killing reputation among politicians, the mass media are not powerful and merciless defenders or destroyers of the good society. Their influence is, in most cases, less than overwhelming, never monolithic (an important point, to which we will return in a later chapter), and often inconsequential.

---

[4] Bernard C. Cohen, *The Press and Foreign Policy* (Princeton, N.J.: Princeton University Press, 1963), pp. 233–234. Italics in original.

16.11   Most Mass Media Are Not Very Political

To keep a perspective on the political significance of the mass media, we should bear in mind that the media are, to a very large degree, apolitical—if not antipolitical.

Why do newspapers, TV and radio stations, movies, journals, and mass-circulation books exist? For one thing, they exist to make money for their owners and producers—another important matter to which we shall return later in this book. From the perspective of the consumer, however, the mass media provide three main functions: (a) entertainment; (b) a guide and orientation for daily living; and (c) a source of information and opinion about public events. Of these three functions, it is undeniable that the third is least important for the majority of media consumers. Much of the intellectuals' criticism of the mass media misses this simple point: *most mass-media consumers neither want nor appreciate the subtleties of political discourse.* Moreover, for those who are politically aware and active, the mass media provide only a part of the environment of influence.

16.12   Some Media Are More Political Than Others

Great differences exist in the way media spokesmen interpret their public responsibilities. The history and traditions of the medium tend to shape the self-image of its social function. The late Eric Johnson, for many years the chief public speaker for American movies, was fond of telling congressional committees that Hollywood's job was to entertain people, not to teach them civic virtues or political philosophy. "Many motion pictures," he said in 1947, "are produced very frankly to entertain and do no more than entertain; to make people happy; to bring them a pleasant hour or two of complete relaxation—a vital necessity in a complex, wearing, worrisome world."[5] In 1961, Johnson was still describing "the motion picture theater . . . as the center of fine entertainment for persons of all ages and a wide variety of tastes,"[6] but he promised moviegoers that the 1961 pictures would be "invigorating, stimulating, and challenging entertainment." The well-known Motion Picture Production Code, in its 1956 revision as in the original 1930 edition, straightforwardly says that "the-

[5] "The Motion Picture as a Stimulus to Culture," *The Annals,* CCLIV (1947), 101.

[6] *Arizona Daily Star,* January 6, 1961.

atrical motion pictures . . . are primarily to be regarded as entertainment."

Television and radio spokesmen have tended to view their media in much the same apolitical way that Johnson and movie manufacturers see Hollywood's responsibilities. But the history, and therefore the traditions, of public accountability in radio and TV are somewhat different from that of movies. Movies do not depend, as do TV and radio, on a scientific fact which from the very beginning made regulation of the airwaves a matter of public necessity. The materials for making and showing movies are widely distributed and practically unlimited. But only a small number of radio-transmission bands exist, and their rational use required early and continued governmental regulation at the national and international levels. Yet radio and TV—regulated by government because they were, in the words of Chief Justice Waite, "affected by a public interest"—nevertheless resisted political involvement; only a minority of TV or radio stations editorialize, even though they have been free to do so since 1949.

16.13   Audiences Do Not Want the Media to Be Very Political

Audiences, too, resist the "public-service" programming required of TV and radio stations. As television became available to more and more families from 1947 to 1957, it gradually replaced radio and the movies as the major source of entertainment for almost all categories of Americans. By the end of 1957, three-fourths of a national sample declared television their main source of entertainment. The electronic media are seen as part of the "fun" of the ordinary day—like the comic strip of the newspaper and the lunchtime chatter of bench- or officemates. As Alfred Hero says, "It appears that television and, to a declining extent, radio, are accepted as part of the daily routine, a reward of pleasure built into daily cycles of work and relaxation. At the end of a day's labor, most citizens seek entertainment, not the additional work involved in absorbing new information and ideas."[7] About 85 per cent of the content of commercial TV and radio stations consists of entertainment or of advertising related to an entertainment program. Even more illuminating is the estimation that 97 per cent of audience man-hours are given to entertainment and commercials.[8]

---

[7] Alfred O. Hero, *Mass Media and World Affairs* (Boston: World Peace Foundation, 1959), p. 110.

[8] *Ibid.,* p. 111.

16.2 The Common Denominator in Mass-Media Programming

Although the mass media generally do not regard themselves as political phenomena—and although audiences do not want them to be or become such—political leaders (for reasons we have hinted at and are soon to develop further) *think* the mass media to be (a) highly political, and (b) politically very important. These are, for our purposes, the two most significant characteristics of the mass media.

However, there are other characteristics that have importance for the opinion-policy process. Some of these have to do with the fact that the audiences of the mass media are unknown, in the most complete meaning of the word *unknown*—they are without personality; they are nonpersons, except in a statistical sense.[9] Consequently, mass-media programs cannot focus beyond the most general interests—or, perhaps a better way of saying it, beyond the average audience member's tolerance either for specificity or abstraction. Thus, "situation comedy," as the phrase goes, is the most popular kind of TV fare; and the dramatic immorality of celebrities makes the best newspaper copy; but a real-life account of a housewife's shopping trip or of drunkenness and lechery on the Bowery is of no more general interest than a talk on Boolean algebra. Mass appeal has its price; namely, programming pitched to an anonymous audience, whose common characteristics can be assumed, and catered to, but whose special interests can neither be known nor served.

To counter this disability, the media make many efforts to "personalize" their content, using colloquialisms, first-person address, and ego associations with fictional characters ("Dobie Gillis," "Beaver," "the country editor," and the like), who are, indeed, typical in their thought processes, but unusual in their dialogue, since they appear clever beyond all commonness. The most successful TV commentators of the intimate genre, men like Dave Garroway, Jack Paar, and Steve Allen, build up large followings of viewers who sense that these actors, though still actors and still commercial, in some ways and to some degree cut across the common

---

[9] An appreciation of the nature of this anonymity in the mass media will help us understand why statistics, and quantification generally, have become so important to the economic well-being, to the nature of "research," and to the self-images of the mass media. With an audience necessarily consisting of "unpersons" (in the stark language of Huxley's *Brave New World*), "success" is measured by numbers of listeners, readers, or viewers (sometimes broken down by statistical subsets to show that program X or paper Y reaches, for example, more families with greater purchasing power), and "research" consists primarily of counting noses in the field (or as a congressional committee discovered in 1963, of making arbitrary guesses in an office—see *New York Times,* March 13, 1963).

denominator.[10] Such talents, however, have not been used with avowedly political intentions (with the possible exception of David Susskind's "Open End" program); and it is doubtful that even the most winningly personalized approach would make television useful for the direct shaping of the political opinions of persons who are generally indifferent to public issues.[11] We can expect, therefore, that, despite the efforts of the mass media to strike "plain folks" and ego-involving postures, most of the opinion formation of the majority of apolitical citizens will result from person-to-person relationships rather than from direct media-to-person relationships.

16.3   Mass Media and the Funnel of Causality

It may be helpful to place the points made so far in this chapter into the model of opinion formation described in Chapter 8. The model compared the progressive focusing of interests and narrowing of opinions in each individual with a funnel, into the large end of which come various stimuli relevant to the developing opinion. These stimuli are played upon by other stimuli within the funnel as time passes and as thinking and opinion formation proceed. The consequence is an opinion on an issue—as well formulated as it needs to be to meet the level of articulation demanded from the individual by his own conception of the issue or by others with whom he interacts.

In the funnel of opinion causality represented in Figure 16–1, A is a point in time when an issue becomes significant for an individual. The issue may be, for example, the building of a new school for which his tax money will be used or which his children will attend. There may be many stimuli of relevance to this issue; but, for illustrative purposes, we put them in three clusters: cultural predispositions or pre-existing attitudes; personal influence or leadership-followership relations; and knowledge (facts and impersonal opinions). Directly from the mass media, the person may receive knowledge relevant to the question of the new school. Indirectly from the mass media, say, through his personal acquaintances, he may receive additional stimuli that help him form an opinion. The mass media will not influence the pre-existing attitudes except in the broadest and most indirect ways. These and other stimuli, in which the mass media play some part, will mix over a period of time and may come down to an

[10] Consider the similar success, with children and mothers alike, of "Captain Kangaroo."

[11] During the heightened salience of major, close campaigns, however, a candidate's "winning TV personality" might be the cause of the decisive majority.

opinion that may be acted upon—in a bond election, for instance. But perhaps, when the opinion has been formed, at point *B,* new stimuli of relevance are experienced by the individual. To the extent warranted by the new stimuli, or to the extent that the new stimuli reopen earlier uncertainties, the funnel of causality is widened again, as Figure 16–1 indicates, and the resolution process may be carried again to an opinion—the same or a different opinion.

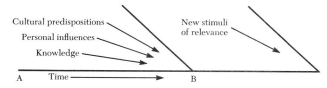

Figure 16–1. Funnel of Opinion Causality: Elements That May Be Influenced by the Mass Media

16.4 Cultural Predispositions and the Mass Media

In Chapter 10, we considered the effects of culture on opinions and commented on the fact that opinions are limited by the generally accepted standards of good taste, fairness, and the humanistic traditions of Western culture. We also observed that industrialized societies tend to be characterized by a great diversity of values and behavior standards and that, in contrast to premodern societies, the cultural restrictions of the United States in the 1960s are small indeed. Except for the myths that relate to nationalism and patriotism, almost all cultural commands and injunctions can be safely questioned; the range of potential opinion is great; and the limits of public opinion are not to be found so much in cultural prescriptions or proscriptions as in the deficiencies of imagination and in the ego needs that make conformity attractive and nonconformity painful.

Nevertheless, there are some cultural proclivities in twentieth-century America that have importance for the mass media. For one thing, there is a lingering belief that the citizen *ought* to have an opinion on all matters of public policy. The ideal of the omnicompetent citizen has filtered deeply and widely throughout American society, the evidence of which may be found in the answers of survey respondents who say "yes" or "no" when they should say "I don't know," and in the deep contradictions of the New Haven workingmen interviewed by Lane, who were very badly informed but who refused either to blame others for their ignorance or to turn to others for advice. This phenomenon, which Lane has aptly called "the parthenogenesis of knowledge," is a characteristic observed by De Tocqueville in the 1830s and is related to fears of being influenced, as well as to the idea of the "rational" man that is so pervasive in American culture.[12]

Persons who believe—yet not too strongly—that they *ought* to have opinions tend to look to the mass media for help. But because in most people the motivation for opinions on public issues is weak, as the facility for the ordering and assessing of relevant facts also is weak, the help sought from the mass media is in the nature of clues that make public events simple and consistent with pre-existing values and a conventional world view. The mass media are consequently obliged to simplify, dramatize, and emotionalize the reporting of events at the same time they cater to the need for personalization. The reader has his cake and eats it too when he reads a headline that tells him (without his having to be influenced by another person, friend or stranger) briefly and simply that a public event or issue may be thought of within the context of an already existing opinion or set of opinions. Cooper and Jahoda found that persons introduced to ideas contrary to existing attitudes adopted a number of compensatory and rationalizing devices to make the new data compatible with (or irrelevant to) those attitudes.[13]

Within the media, important differences exist between sources believed by the audience to be suspect and those considered more objective. A message may be widely accepted when it appears in a source thought to be trustworthy, but the same message may be rejected when it is printed in a periodical thought to be untrustworthy.[14]

People generally give greater credence to the electronic media than to the printed word. Greater authority somehow attaches to facts or opinions expressed by TV and radio. A 1954 summary of survey findings indicated that "several opinion surveys during the last fifteen years have seemed to show that people had a great deal of faith in the trustworthiness of radio news as compared with newspapers."[15]

[12] See Robert E. Lane, *Political Ideology: Why the Common Man Believes What He Does* (New York: The Free Press of Glencoe, 1962), pp. 373–377.

[13] Eunice Cooper and Marie Jahoda, "The Evasion of Propaganda: How Prejudiced People Respond to Anti-Prejudice Propaganda," *The Journal of Psychology*, XXIII (1947), 15–25.

[14] For some experimental findings on this point, see Carl I. Hovland and Walter Weiss, "The Influence of Source Credibility on Communication Effectiveness," *Public Opinion Quarterly*, XV (1952), 635–650.

[15] Wilbur Schramm, ed., *The Process and Effects of Mass Communication* (Urbana: University of Illinois Press, 1954), p. 82.

Why the electronic media are considered more reliable and more fair than the printed media may be partly a matter of individual psychological processes; but it seems probable that much of the difference may be attributed to the histories of the two kinds of media. Newspapers and magazines in the Anglo-American tradition have always been political, and contentious, if not downright cantankerous, in their politics; at least since the seventeenth century, political controversy has employed printed propaganda for reform and counterreform. The newspapers of the American Revolutionary period and the early years of our republic were unashamedly partisan, and engaged in diatribe and invective that today would be considered extremely ill-mannered if not libelous. Newspapers still sometimes express their editorial views with convictions unmatched in any other media; by comparison, television and radio handling of public issues is dull, standardized, dryly descriptive, and nonpartisan. This difference is known, or is sensed, by the consumers of the media.

The printed media are relatively unregulated by governments and are jealous of their freedom from regulation. The electronic media have a different history and posture in relation to governments; their tradition is one of close *technical* regulation, and of the popular presumption (although not the practice) of government regulation of content. This difference too is known or sensed by the users of the media; and their perceptions of the trustworthiness of the media are colored by the notion —as expressed in one survey response—that "the government wouldn't let the TV stations get away with lying."[16]

A number of investigators have studied the effects of mass media on the political behavior of Americans. Findings are reviewed in Lane's *Political Life,* where the major effects of the mass media on political behavior are summarized as follows:

Exposure to the media increases political discussion, and political discussion increases exposure to the media.

The reinforcement effect of the media is greater than the conversion effect.

While reading, listening, and viewing political material in the media are sometimes substitutes for civic or political action (narcotizing dysfunction), usually they are preliminary to such action.

While the media occasionally discourage political action by featuring the complexity of social problems, more frequently they oversimplify them, giving a

---

16 There is, of course, the possibility that regulation may mean control, and, in nations where governments enjoy little popular confidence, the regulated media might be considered *less* trustworthy than the unregulated. But this is not the case in the United States; here, apparently, governments are felt to be *more* trustworthy than large, nongovernmental economic and social groups (see, on this point, Lane, *Political Ideology,* p. 473–475). It may be a question of which are *distrusted* least, governments or private interests; in America, fortunately, the balance of confidence is in favor of governments.

(false) impression that the members of the public can devise their own solutions.

The media present more news and comment on public affairs than most of the public demand, thus politicizing rather than apathizing the public.

Failure of the media to establish ideological rapport with large sections of the public tends to discourage participation.

While the news sections of the media tend to give prominence to political figures, and, in this sense, confer status upon them and upon political activity, the fiction in the media fails to cast its heroes in governmental or political roles.

Fictional presentations in the media attribute evil and suffering to personal, not social or political . . . problems presented, thus distracting attention from the gains to be achieved through political participation.

Emphasis upon citizen duty in the media (to the extent that it is emphasized) serves to bring the widely recognized but private "do-nothing morality" closer to the official morality of the democratic dogma.

The tendency of media owners, advertisers, and segments of the media audience to dislike references to the roots of social conflict (class or ethnic) weakens the resonance of the media with the problems of the time and, hence, weakens the power to stimulate political response.

On balance, however, exposure to the media is associated with: (a) interest in politics, (b) higher turnout, (c) joining community organizations, (d) superior information, (e) stronger views, (f) closeness to the party position, (g) strong candidate preferences.[17]

In summary, the mass media—of which newspapers, magazines, television, and radio are politically the most important (probably in that order)—are not highly politicized, generally, and are not expected to be by their users. There are, however, differences in the self-images of the media, and in the expectations of media performance held by citizens of various levels of political interest and activity. Finally, most Americans feel obliged by cultural factors to "keep up with things," and this bedrock of demand for political news and views is satisfied mainly by TV and newspapers—with TV the most popular and most trusted source for the impressions and snippets of knowledge that pass for "keeping up" with public events.

[17] Robert E. Lane, *Political Life: Why People Get Involved in Politics* (New York: The Free Press of Glencoe, 1959), Chap. 19, "Mass Media and Mass Politics," pp. 275–298; quotation from pp. 288–289. Copyright 1959. Reprinted by permission of The Macmillan Company.

TELEVISION
AND RADIO

17

There is much controversy about the social and political effects of the electronic media.[1] For the last thirty years, beginning with the widespread use of home radio receivers and the proliferation of local broadcasting stations, various reformers (with preachers and professors leading the pack) have indicted the radio and television industries for everything from indifference to modern art to the destruction of children's personalities.

The social charges can be summed up in two ideas: (a) the media have failed to reflect the rich and abundant culture of America and the world, and (b) they have wasted the opportunity to instruct and uplift the masses through programs of substance. The psychological, or social-psychological, complaints of the critics have to do mainly with the feared (but in no instances fully demonstrated) effects of the media on the personalities and behavior of children.[2] It has been alleged that

sadism is . . . the bulwark of 90 per cent of popular entertainment. . . .

Television is a wasteland, and much of this wasteland is given over to sheer senseless brutality. To take a typical example of the wasteland, Richard Boone in a very recent "Have Gun, Will Travel" mowed down three 15-year-old boys, justifying this massacre by saying that boys shouldn't play with guns.

This, as I say, is typical of television entertainment. Of television's 73½ hours of prime time, that sort of sickening violence is on the air most of the time. Every year it gets worse and there gets more of it. We are, in a sense, teaching children

---

[1] It is an interesting, if trivial, illustration of the power of habit that when the two wireless electronic media are mentioned together radio always precedes television. This is a tribute to history and primogeniture, but a clear case now of the less important before the more important.

[2] For a recent, and reasonable, consideration of these matters, see Wilbur Schramm, Jack Lyle, and Edwin B. Parker, *Television in the Lives of Our Children* (Stanford, Calif.: Stanford University Press, 1961), especially pp. 169–188.

debauchery, brutalizing their instincts 73½ hours a week in prime evening time.[3]

The heady criticisms of TV content were endorsed in another idiom, with authoritarian overtones, by the Reverend Dr. Robert J. McCracken, minister of New York's famed Riverside Church, who is reported to have told his congregation that "the test of a true democracy is to give the public what it 'ought to want.' " "You can't blame a child for preferring to see The Three Stooges," Dr. McCracken argued, "but you have to do more than cater to his preference. . . . His tastes and preferences have to be educated, elevated, refined. God help America if it rears the rising generation on mediocrity and trivia."[4]

But the clever, pious complaints of publicists and preachers were mere echoes of the explosion set off by Federal Communications Commission Chairman Newton T. Minow in his widely quoted speech to the convention of National Association of Broadcasters, May 9, 1961. He invited the broadcasters themselves to watch a full day of television programming:

> I can assure you that you will observe a vast wasteland.
> You will see a procession of game shows, violence, audience-participation shows, formula comedies about totally unbelievable families, blood and thunder, mayhem, violence, sadism, murder, western badmen, western good men, private eyes, gangsters, more violence, and cartoons. And, endlessly, commercials—many screaming, cajoling, and offending. And most of all, boredom. True, you will see a few things you will enjoy. But they will be very, very few. And if you think I exaggerate, try it.[5]

Some of the criticisms of the electronic media have to do with the functions they perform—or, as the complaints are ordinarily phrased, that they do *not* perform—in the opinion-policy process. It is said that the media have a responsibility to search out the facts on important issues; to make these facts available quickly and thoroughly to the public; to provide a forum for the discussion and consideration of these facts (and of all the opinions that might be relevant to the facts—or to the problems to which the facts are germane); and to subordinate to such programming (a) the commercial interests that finance such efforts, and (b) the desire for fame or affluence that motivates the individuals involved in the media.

[3] From a column by John Crosby, entitled "I'm Against Rape," scheduled to be printed May 17, 1961, but suppressed by Crosby's paper, the *New York Herald Tribune,* and printed subsequently, on June 12, 1961, in *Congressional Record,* p. 9341, by Senator Ernest Gruening of Alaska.

[4] "McCracken Fights TV Majority Rule," *New York Times,* February 12, 1962.

[5] *Congressional Record,* Appendix, May 11, 1961, pp. A3302, A3303.

17.1 "Culture," Mediocrity, and the Electronic Media

We are interested in politics, and in opinions of importance to the political processes in America. Except indirectly, through basic values and educational levels, the social criticism of television and radio is not very relevant to our interest. However, since the subject is so inviting, a few comments may be made about the social and cultural responsibilities of the electronic media—then we may move quickly to the political responsibilities and problems.

It is said that the mass media, especially television, encourage bad taste, pander to mediocrity, glorify violence and crime, and do not take advantage of their many opportunities for educating the public. What the critics fail to recognize is that mass audiences in all places and in all recorded times have had bad taste (according to the critics' standards), have been mediocre, have delighted in violence and crime, and have resisted education. Taking this theme, Max Wylie, an advertising-agency executive, argued in 1961 that "what television is doing right now is about right for right now . . . an honest projection of what America is like, is interested in, is doing; what America wants to hear about, or object to, or support." Mr. Wylie resists the critics' attempts to impose their "culture" on the mass media, pointing out that crash programs for mass culture always follow the "law of raspberry jam: the wider you spread it, the thinner it gets." As for violence in TV entertainment, Wylie contends that

Violence of the most extreme kind, tortures of the most diabolical have the instant endorsement of Mr. Crosby's purity league . . . [when] these villainies are committed by a sweating tenor in a pair of tight pants, singing in French; that's quite all right, because it's opera. But it's all wrong for these villainies to be committed in a pair of tight levis and in English, because then it's a western.[6]

In further explanation, if not in defense, of TV mediocrity is the fact that great art (violent or not) simply cannot be produced in large enough quantity to fill an eighteen-to-twenty-hour broadcast day for three major networks and several hundred individual stations. There is not that much artistic talent in America, and there is no general evidence (despite some clear individual cases) for the charge that mediocrity, pressures, and discrimination keep people of excellence out of the television industry and its productions.

[6] "What's Wrong with Our Critics," *Television Age,* 1961, reprinted in *Congressional Record,* April 20, 1961, pp. A2693–5, from which these quotes are taken. Wylie also cites, tellingly, the plots of *Macbeth, Titus Andronicus, Rigoletto,* and the great classic fiction of Poe, Hawthorne, Hardy, Conrad, Kipling, Scott, and Dickens as examples of the entertainment value "of alarms and shipwreck, murder in the dark, of beheadings, trials, insanity, of grave robbing, infidelity, and cannibalism, war, thirst, and suicide."

Even the most extreme critics acknowledge that there are some excellent television programs; but they want more of what they consider excellent and less of what they consider bad or mediocre. What the critics fail to acknowledge is that (a) there is a great deal of choice (and, more importantly, public-service choice) in American television; (b) a program-production system based on private, profit-making enterprise cannot afford to "elevate" its audience's taste at the cost of losing viewers; and (c) when offered a choice between what the critics consider "high-taste" and "low-taste" programs, the American public will usually (though not always) choose the "low-taste." In early 1962, it was said that

During any given week, the U.S. public has more total hours of free choice of discussion, talk, forum, education, news, farm information, and so-called public service programs than is available to the public in any nation of the world. . . . [And during each year] the three American networks devote more money, manpower, know-how, and total telecast hours to education, talks, discussion, and public affairs than all the nations of the world combined.[7]

The critics admit that there is some variety in American TV programming, and that if they are willing to turn dials and shop around the channels, they can be informed and uplifted to some extent. The charge is that there are not enough good programs, and that what is available tends to be concentrated into Sunday-afternoon and early-morning oases in "the wasteland." The industry argues that the good, small-audience programs are made possible under conditions of private enterprise only by the large-audience mediocrity to which the critics object. According to an NBC-TV spokesman:

Wagon Train, Perry Como, and Dinah Shore carry the NBC opera, which has been sponsored for only 11 of 60 performances since 1950 and has cost us nearly $6 million. The profits from mass-appeal shows enabled us to absorb a loss of $11 million in 1960 on informational programs.[8]

17.2   Public-Service Programming

Since the exposures of fraud on the television shows "Twenty-One" and "$64,000 Question" in 1959, and since the 1961–1962 campaign of Chairman Minow of the FCC (who lost his fight in Congress for greater regulatory authority and resigned his office in early 1963), television is probably less a wasteland, and the networks have strengthened their

---

[7] Richard P. Doherty, "By What Standard Should U.S. TV Be Judged?" reprinted in part in *Congressional Record*, February 19, 1962, pp. 2174–2175.

[8] Robert W. Sarnoff (as told to Stanley Frank), "What Do You Want from TV?" *Saturday Evening Post*, July 1, 1961, p. 14.

public-service programming. Public-service news coverage of international events, space launchings, and presidential politics is more than adequate, technically superb, and attracts large audiences. Smaller audiences are found for discussion and issues programs such as "Face the Nation," "Meet the Press," "CBS Reports," and "NBC White Papers."

In September of 1963, *New York Times* TV critic Jack Gould was optimistic enough about the future of public-service programming to declare that he had seen "a turning point in TV's journalistic evolution."[9] His extravagant statement was elicited by a three-hour-long, prime-time, NBC special, "The American Revolution of '63," depicting the Negro struggle for full civil rights. In several ways, this NBC documentary *was* a first: never before had so much of the most heavily watched time been given to a public-service program. The regular sponsors for NBC documentaries did not underwrite the program, fearing adverse economic consequences; as a result, the network lost an estimated half-million dollars for its decision to show a "balanced, thoughtful, and penetrating treatment of what is unquestionably the most important and most controversial domestic problem of our time."[10]

The point is simply that the electronic mass media offer the American viewer and voter more pertinent facts and opinions than he is ever likely to need in discharging his citizen responsibilities. That he is not generally interested enough to attend to these facts and opinions, nor intellectually trained to make them meaningful, is another story—though hardly one that makes democracy impossible, however much simplistic Jeffersonians may call for a society of omnicompetent citizens. The electronic media may be, at times, trivial, banal, and full of chaff that does nothing more than stimulate the juvenile id. But at other times—and, I think, in nearly sufficient quantity—it offers good wheat for the mills of the opinion-policy process. We cannot expect it to be the great teacher of civic virtue or more than one of several raw-material sources (and part of the mixing process) for the funnel of opinion causality.

17.3   Special Responsibilities in the Opinion-Policy Process

In recent years, television and radio, we have asserted, have been about as good, in variety and coverage of public-service programming, as

9 *New York Times*, September 3, 1963.

10 Richard Elden, "TV Nets Pick Up Some Big Costs," *Chicago Sun Times*, September 3, 1963, reprinted in *Congressional Record*, September 3, 1963, p. 15423. Elden also pointed out that all except a small portion of the four-to-five-and-a-half-hour coverage, by all three networks, of the August 28, 1963, civil-rights "March on Washington" was unsponsored and thus very costly to the television industry.

the economics of the industry and the tastes of the audience will bear.

Nevertheless, there are matters of special responsibility for the electronic media, if they wish further to improve their ways and to maximize their contribution to the American polity. Some of this special responsibility has to do with the everyday procedures and standard operational rules of the networks and stations: primarily, the tendency toward sponsor and advertising-agency pressure on the *political* content of programming should be at all times resisted, as should the tendency toward network domination of individual stations.

I do not believe that either of these tendencies is presently out of control or even acute—although I think there have been times (such as the McCarthyism period of the early 1950s) when the electronic media, like much of our public life, suffered seriously from fear, suspicion, and lack of confidence in civil liberties generally. Such times may come again.

Meanwhile, pressures toward conformity and the avoidance of controversy continue to be reported—and one may assume that the reported instances of network, sponsor, or advertising-agency pressures are only a small fraction of those that go unreported. Pressure from the Ford Motor Company and from Chrysler Corporation kept Ed Sullivan and Jack Benny from participating in the 1957 "Emmy" award show, because that gala was sponsored by General Motors.[11] Much more important from the point of view of the country's political dialogue was the disclosure, on the same day that Sullivan and Benny were reported being withheld by their sponsors, that the Columbia Broadcasting System had "killed" Eric Sevareid's program of February 6, 1957, for his attempt to "editorialize" and had reproved Edward R. Murrow for the same sin.[12]

Networks can, if they choose, intimidate both member stations and independent stations by threatening to buy or sell them or their competitors,[13] by requiring packaged deals, and by preempting time for certain network shows.[14] Network pressure can also run backward, in the course of TV programming, to the producer of the program; one Hollywood producer of TV shows complained to a senatorial committee in 1961 that the television networks "had more power than the seven members of the

[11] *New York Times,* February 13, 1957.

[12] Jack Gould, "Radio: Matter of Opinion," *New York Times,* February 13, 1957. Editorials were then, and are now, allowed by FCC rules; however, "editorializing," in this context, was a euphemism for a difference of opinion in which the commentators took a view that was critical of U.S. foreign policy, and the networks were scared.

[13] See the *New York Times* story, April 18, 1960, about NBC's manipulations of TV stations KRON and KTVU in San Francisco.

[14] See Lawrence Laurent, "Ol' Network Dominance Raising Corporate Head," *Washington Post,* February 4, 1961, reprinted in *Congressional Record,* February 9, 1961, p. 1861.

Federal Communications Commission" and that the three network presidents had "virtually complete control over the airwaves."[15]

Resisting the tendencies to provincialism, timidity, and economic selfishness, whether these tendencies have their origin in networks, sponsors, or advertising agencies, is only the negative side of the political responsibilities of the electronic mass media. Equally important are the positive obligations of communications channels: primarily, to continue to provide ready opportunities for minority points of view—and, to put the matter most plainly, this does not mean the reluctant airing of less-popular views only when FCC rules seem to demand it, but the constant searching out of important issues and the encouragement of integrity and conviction by owners, managers, producers, and commentators. Similarly, advertisers are obliged to support public-service programs, recognizing that sponsorship does not commit the advertisers and their regional business outlets to the endorsement of the views expressed on the program. Fortunately, some sponsors have already had the courage to support documentaries and programs of political comment. Bell and Howell, Gulf Oil, International Telephone and Telegraph, and Richfield Oil Corporation have been willing to risk the possibility of adverse audience reaction; their number are few as yet, but they may be increasing.

17.4 Special Responsibilities in Political Campaigns

During political campaigns, the electronic media, and especially television, have additional obligations. The importance of television and radio in modern campaigning is attested both by the numbers of citizens who can be (and sometimes are) reached by political programs and by the large proportion of campaign budgets devoted to television and radio coverage. In 1960, an estimated 115,000,000 persons watched one or more of the presidential "Great Debates." These pioneering confrontations of presidential candidates before a national television audience—however good or bad they may have been, and however important for the outcome of the election—were only the first of hundreds of smaller debates in 1960, and each general election since, between senatorial, gubernatorial, congressional, and even city and county candidates. For such joint appearances (which are usually made at station or network expense) and for thousands of more traditional campaign programs, not to mention tens of

---

[15] *New York Times,* July 29, 1961. In 1965, the FCC opened what promised to be a long fight by proposing, in a 4-to-2 vote, to limit network control of prime television time to two hours a night—see the *New York Times,* March 23, 1965.

thousands of film clips and spot announcements, candidates for the highest state and national offices will spend, typically, a third to a half or more of their campaign budgets. In early 1961, FCC Chairman Frederick W. Ford estimated that $14,550,000 had been spent on television and radio campaigning by all candidates in the 1960 general elections; $7,500,000 by Republicans, and $6,750,000 by Democrats. In addition, 430 TV stations gave 1,250 free hours to Republicans and 1,253 free hours to Democrats.[16] Total *reported* political broadcasting expenditures by candidates in 1960 were 44 per cent greater than in 1956, with "some estimates [putting additional] cost to the industry as high as $15 to $20 million if allowance is made for convention coverage, election-night coverage, newscasts, and special programs, as well as for free time provided the candidates during the presidential campaign."[17] The precise figures for television and radio campaign costs are unobtainable; but, quite clearly, the totals are going up year by year—and a high and increasing proportion of these costs go for television rather than radio.

The television and radio industries, networks and individual stations alike, should be expected (and required by the FCC, if necessary) to provide special opportunities for candidates during campaigns. To avoid hardship to the television and radio broadcasters, and to keep within the tolerance level of the apolitical portion of mass audiences, free or reduced-rate political time should be limited to a short period (say, thirty days) before the election. During this period, free time, or combination of free and reduced-rate time,[18] should be made available in a general election to all candidates running in a constituency that is greater than some minimum geographical size. For example, the law (or FCC ruling) might say that TV or radio stations must give thirty minutes of free time to general-election candidates in all constituencies that equal half or more of the broadcast area. Free time would thus be available only to candidates for major offices. To limit the free-time period to general elections would avoid the intricacies of defining candidacy and the burden of providing time for large numbers of primary aspirants in some areas; it would also have the salutary effect of encouraging the minority party to field candidates, and thus speed the development of two-partyism generally.

In addition to free time for the major, general-election candidates,

16 *New York Times*, February 1, 1961.

17 Herbert E. Alexander, *Financing the 1960 Election* (Princeton; N.J.: Citizens' Research Foundation, 1962), p. 35.

18 So far as I know, reduced-rate time has never been given or even considered for campaign programs. Most paid political time is sold at a *higher rate than regular advertising, for cash in advance.* Such an arrangement is not only a disability for the democratic dialogue but an insult to candidates, and it should be prevented by FCC ruling or by statute, even if nothing else is done to facilitate political broadcasting.

reduced-rate time might be required for other candidates within the broadcast area. It is not desirable, of course, that *all* candidates be given reduced-rate time; a sound policy would be to discourage, rather than encourage, political broadcasts over a large area of which only a small fraction is in the constitutency of the candidate; the citizens of twenty-four wards of a city should not be required to suffer the compulsory loss of a TV channel so that the councilmanic candidate of the twenty-fifth ward can appeal to one twenty-fifth of the potential viewers. Obviously, any requirement of free or reduced-rate time must be sensible in its coverage and applied with good judgment.[19]

Besides the provision for free campaigning time, television and radio stations ought to take positions on issues and candidates. Since 1949, individual stations have been free to editorialize, but few have taken advantage of the opportunity. Indeed, it was not until October 27, 1960, that an American radio station endorsed a candidate for president of the United States. On that evening, at 10:35 P.M., WMCA, New York, declared itself for John F. Kennedy, and declared that it would take its "public responsibility seriously, even when it means running risks of being ahead of the times." That WMCA was ahead of the times is not to be doubted, for less than one-third of American television and radio stations seem to be editorializing. But the number is growing—sixty-two stations (almost all radio) editorialized for or against candidates in 1960, and one hundred forty-eight did so in 1962.[20] There is, as yet, no evidence that the stations that editorialize have been harmed by the practice.

The final responsibility of the electronic media, especially of television, to the opinion-policy process is one that is shared by parties, candidates, and opinion leaders of all kinds. It is the responsibility never to lose sight of the instrumental nature of the mass media in the political processes of democracy. The media and their products must never be thought of as ends in themselves, but always in terms of whether they

---

19 I do not discuss here the "equal-time" provision (Section 315) of the Communications Act of 1934. The earlier, ridiculously strict interpretation of the equal-time requirement was changed by Public Law 86–274 (September 14, 1959), and there is reason to believe that the present requirement for equal time to minority parties and "nuisance" candidates (waived by Congress in 1960 for the presidential campaign, but not, unfortunately, in 1964) will soon be adjusted. Such a modification ought to give bona fide third parties, proportionately to votes cast, a share in the free or reduced-rate broadcast time which, in my view, ought to be required of each radio and television station. For discussion of a bill to require free television time for presidential candidates, see *Congressional Record*, March 10, 1960, pp. 4792–4795. See also *Broadcasting*, January 18, 1965, pp. 76–77, and subsequent issues of that journal for contemporary developments in the equal-time controversy.

20 *Broadcasting*, July 29, 1963, p. 46. For a good discussion of the growth and problems of TV editorializing, see John E. McMillin, "New Voices in a Democracy," *Television Quarterly*, III (1964), 27–52.

facilitate or impede representativeness, comprehensiveness, fairness, and openness in the making and remaking of public policy.[21]

In a sharp attack on the "Great Debates" of 1960, historian Henry Steele Commager argued that such confrontations on television "do not fulfill the most elementary political purpose of permitting the candidates to explore and clarify the vital issues." Worse, he said, they are more conducive to questions and responses "guaranteed to produce headlines" and "to provide sensations." And worse still, according to Commager, they are "not designed to discover in candidates those qualities really needed for the conduct of the Presidential office . . . patience, prudence, humility, sagacity, judiciousness, magnanimity." "What we want in a President," Commager asserted, "is the ability to think deeply about a few matters of great importance; what television questions encourage is the trick of talking glibly about a great many matters of no particular importance."[22]

Commager's are serious charges. Almost exactly two years after they were made, New York Times TV critic Jack Gould, without mentioning Commager's article, dealt with a number of these criticisms from a point of view generally sympathetic to television and optimistic about its good influence in politics. Gould's rambling essay consisted of impressionistic comments about the television styles of contemporary American politicians, with the insertion, here and there, of a proposition about television campaigning. His general theme seemed to be that there is indeed a tendency to posturing, artificiality, and irrelevance in television campaigning, but that, in the long run, naturalness pays off, because "if a TV viewer boasts unrivaled skill in anything, it is in knowing how to separate the good guys and bad guys on television."

Aside from this quixotic faith in the powers of audiences to divine good people from bad people, Mr. Gould's defense of television campaigning is hardly a defense at all. He concedes Commager's points about superficiality and personalism: "These encounters [the debates] have the admitted weakness of not delving into issues as deeply as they might and of putting a premium on personality for its own sake." But the tendency for

---

21 An example of the possibly deleterious kind of influence that the television industry may have on American political processes is the transformation of the national nominating conventions into great, quadrennial, television circuses. An industry publication glowingly reports: "When the Democratic and Republican parties pull the wraps off their national conventions next summer, the nation will find that the historic nominating machinery has been streamlined more than ever for the television and radio audience." Broadcasting, September 9, 1963, p. 86. Those who saw the maneuvering and posturing of candidates, delegation leaders, and delegates in the conventions of 1952, 1956, 1960, and 1964 are aware that more and "streamlined" coverage could well be dysfunctional for the nominating process.

22 "Washington Would Have Lost a TV Debate," New York Times Magazine, October 30, 1960.

such debates to require quick and simple answers, which Commager takes to be the greatest danger, is applauded by Gould: "Their virtue is that they have moved the dialogue of politics in the right direction, by requiring candidates to speak more to the point." Nonetheless, Gould's capacity for contradiction is marvelous, and he says in the same article that the candidates should not take recourse in "oversimplifications of the complexities of government, [because] the viewer also hungers for more reality in political TV performances." There may be, as Gould's discussion of Richard Nixon as a television campaigner suggests, a rough winnowing and sifting—by chance and irrelevancies, if not by the viewer in whose judgment Gould professes such confidence. Nixon, said Gould, "saved his career with his superemotional justification of the Nixon fund in 1952; in the first debate of 1960 he got caught in the wrong format and missed out on the Presidency."[23]

A much more careful and plausible answer to Commager's charge that televised debates result in a superficial treatment of issues was made in 1962 by Stanley Kelley. The 1960 debates, Kelley says, required the candidates to admit that they were in agreement about most of the basic goals of public policy and prevented them from adopting the pretense so common in solo performances that they alone have concern for the problems and needs of society: "Thus debates may help to identify for the voter those issues on which rival candidates do not disagree, making it easier for him to center his attention on those issues on which they do." Moreover, "both candidates specified their program intentions in the debates on a greater number of issues than they did in their televised speeches. . . . Thus the debates seem to have had some tendency to overcome the inclination—often remarked—of campaigners to say little about method and much about goals." Kelley found also that "the debates brought out the other side of a number of issues that remained one-sided in the speeches." Finally, Kelley's analysis of the total presidential-campaign coverage in 1960 convinced him that the debates were superior, in pertinency and the airing of differences, to the interviews and panel programs presented by the networks.[24]

To make a tentative assessment of the importance of television and radio for opinion formation during a campaign period, we have to distinguish between the specific use of novel formats, such as the debates of 1960, and the total patterns of exposure and influence the electronic media may be expected to manifest over time. Roper found that after all

[23] "Candidates on TV—The Ideal and Others," *New York Times Magazine*, October 28, 1962.

[24] Stanley Kelley, Jr., "Campaign Debates: Some Facts and Issues," *Public Opinion Quarterly*, XXVI (1962), quotations from 360, 361, 362.

four television debates in 1960, 44 per cent of his respondents said they had been influenced by the joint appearances, and 5 per cent said they made up their minds on the debates alone; if these findings are even close to accurate, Kennedy's winning margin is attributable to the debates.[25] And, despite the imponderables in this kind of evidence, it supports the presumption, shared by media experts and politicians alike, that the debates were influential enough in the close election of 1960 to elect Senator Kennedy and defeat Vice-President Nixon. But, in such a close race, many other factors were probably equally important and equally determinative of the outcome.

Television is clearly of great importance as a campaigning medium. It seems probable that joint appearances and other dramatic devices will become common campaign features of the major races of the future—and will lose some impact by becoming common. Angus Campbell's summary of television's influence on political campaigning is probably accurate: "Television has no doubt succeeded in making a sizable part of the electorate direct witnesses to episodes in recent political history, but the effect of this exposure remains a question. . . . It has greatly extended the purely visual dimension of political communication; the public no doubt finds it easier to form an image of its political leaders."[26]

Unquestionably, television has given the electorate a better opportunity to make superficial judgments of candidate "sincerity" (a much-prized characteristic in our "other-directed" society, according to David Riesman), warmth, and articulateness under pressure. But has it, as CBS Vice-President Sig Mickelson confidently proclaimed in 1958, "created a better-informed, more sophisticated public—a public better equipped to pick its elected officials"?[27]

Mickelson said his statement was "indisputable"; it is, in fact, very disputable. Campbell's conclusion is that television

seems neither to have elevated the general level of political interest nor to have broadened the total range of political information. . . . If there is one dependable law in the world of mass communication, it is that those most likely to seek

[25] Richard S. Salant, "The Television Debates: A Revolution That Deserves a Future," *Public Opinion Quarterly*, XXVI (1962), 341.

[26] Angus Campbell, "Has Television Reshaped Politics?" *Columbia Journalism Review*, I (1962), 10, 12. For one of the few attempts to measure the effects of television on campaigns, see Herbert A. Simon and Frederick Stern, "The Effects of Television upon Voting Behavior in Iowa in the 1952 Presidential Election," *American Political Science Review*, XLIX (1955), 470–477.

[27] Speech before the Indiana Broadcasters Association's Conference on Hoosier Politics, quoted in the Democratic National Committee's mimeographed broadside "Campaign Publicity Tips for 1958," October 15, 1958.

information are already the best informed. Thus, we find that the people who follow the election campaigns most closely on television are precisely the same ones who read about them in the newspapers and magazines. . . . Rather than adding an important new dimension to the total flow of information to the public, [television] seems largely to have taken over the role of radio."[28]

[28] Campbell, "Has Television Reshaped Politics?" (see footnote 26), pp. 12, 13.

THE PRESS AND
THE OPINION-POLICY
PROCESS

18

The short history of American newspapers is that of eighteenth-century publications which depended on politics, and how they became twentieth-century publications upon which politics depends. This statement, like all epigrams, exaggerates its message: newspapers were never wholly political; and only in a few places in this century can it be said that politics depends on newspaper influence. Yet the general historical change in American newspapers is clear: they were once thoroughly political; but their political interests are now apt to be vague, occasional, and of no great importance to their own economic life. Although newspapers remain the most consciously political of the mass media—reflecting both their traditions and the expectations of their readers—the pervasiveness of politics, characteristic of early newspapers, has generally given way both to moderation in tone and to a physical separation of news from political advice (i.e., from *editorializing*).

In our early national period, newspapers were important weapons of the fight between Federalists and Republicans. The contest between John Fenno's *Gazette of the United States,* subsidized by Hamilton and the Federalists, and Philip Freneau's *National Gazette,* supported by Jefferson and the anti-Federalists, was marked by the bitter, no-quarter style characteristic of the early American press. The editors delighted in trading such epithets as "fawning parasite," "blackguard," "crackbrain," "jackal of mobocracy," and "salamander."[1]

The first of the large-circulation, inexpensive news-

---

[1] See Samuel E. Forman, "The Polit'cal Activities of Philip Freneau," *John Hopkins University Studies in Historical and Political Science,* Series 20, Nos. 9–10 (September–October 1902), pp. 473–569. Forman says that "in the [*National*] *Gazette,* Jefferson's opinions were reflected as in a mirror" (pp. 529–530). He also quotes John Adams' confession that "the causes of my retirement are to be found in the writings of Freneau, Markoe, Ned Church—and other troublesome newspaper men" (p. 539).

papers of the 1830s and 1840s, the *New York Sun,* the *New York Herald,* the *Philadelphia Public Ledger,* and the *Baltimore Sun,* were not direct organs of partisan rabble-rousing; the *New York Sun,* established in 1833, emphasized police reporting, crime, sex, and disreputable advertising. But, as Mott says, whatever may be said of the enterprise and success of the penny press—and however important its part may have been in the news revolution—the fact remains that up to the time of the Civil War, it was not the independent penny press but the partisan political press that dominated American journalism.[2] Newspapermen of the middle and late nineteenth century were often colorful propagandists, outspoken individualists, and capable of great passion. Henry Adams said that in 1866

the press was still the last resource of the educated poor who could not be artists and would not be tutors. Any man who was fit for nothing else could write an editorial or a criticism. The enormous mass of misinformation accumulated in ten years of nomad life could always be worked off on a helpless public, in diluted doses, if one could but secure a table in the corner of a newspaper office. The press was an inferior pulpit; an anonymous schoolmaster; a cheap boarding school.[3]

Most American newspapers are still political to the extent that in editorials, and occasionally in their selection of news to report, they may support or attack public figures and public policies. But the age of moderation, gentility, and the soft sell has come to newspapers, and only rarely does one encounter highly emotional or *ad hominem* political journalism—except for a few syndicated columns written by men whose stock-in-trade is extremism.

There are many differences between the older style of politicial journalism, as practiced by Greeley, Dana, Pulitzer, and Hearst in the nineteenth century, and modern political journalism. The political journalism of the last century was personal; in this century, it is institutional. Editorial pages are increasingly the products of groups of men, editors and managers, who do not make the policy of the paper. The late Col. Robert R. McCormack was probably the last of the great owner-publisher-editors who could say on the editorial page what he damn well pleased, because the policy of the *Chicago Tribune* was what Col. McCormack damn well pleased. There are still, perhaps, a few other such papers, smaller but of some local fame—for instance, William T. Evjue's *Capital Times* in Madison, Wisconsin, and William R. Matthews' *Arizona*

2 Frank Luther Mott, *American Journalism,* rev. ed. (New York: Macmillan Co., 1950), p. 253.

3 *The Education of Henry Adams* (New York: Random House, Inc., Modern Library Edition, 1931), p. 211.

Daily Star in Tucson—but the fate of the large dailies has been almost uniformly that of the *New York Times'* transfer from Henry J. Raymond to the Sulzberger family, and of the *New York Herald Tribune* from Horace Greeley to the Whitney family, and of others from venturesome founding editors to stable corporations. It should not be thought that the large American newspapers are worse for their change from personalism to institutionalism. They are unquestionably better in their service to the balance, judiciousness, and moderation that, in any well-ordered society, must be central to the opinion-policy process.[4]

Not only are editorials of the major newspapers joint endeavors, which, like all products of committees, must respect the law of the lowest common denominator, but what passion remains is syndicated, nationalized, and mailed-in. Westbrook Pegler writes his fulminations from his winter home in Arizona, Drew Pearson writes his political gossip from Washington, and their indignation is muffled by the time lag between the writing and the reading in a hundred local dailies and by the requirement that a national audience must be fed commentary on national (and thus, for most people, less interesting) events. Victor Riesel's attacks on Jimmy Hoffa's empire of the Teamster's Union cannot match the emotional impact for New Yorkers that the *Times* created in 1871 by its exposure of corruption in Mayor Tweed's City Hall.

Sheer size, too, has contributed to the increase of blandness on the editorial pages of our newspapers. A mass-circulation paper cannot support extreme political journalism—the model newspaper reader is not an extremist. A highly partisan paper may please those who are highly partisan; but such readers are too few to support large papers. When the 882,000-circulation *New York Daily Mirror* folded in the fall of 1963, it sold its "name, goodwill, and other intangible and physical assets" to the *New York Daily News* (which had a circulation of over 2,000,000). If the *News* is to keep the old *Mirror* readers, it may, among other things, absorb the politics of the defunct paper. Thus mass circulation begets moderation.

Finally, the politics of moderation has a clear benefit not found in the extremely partisan papers of earlier times. Moderate papers will air controversy and opposing views within the limits of the moderate middle. During the period of the most sensational political journalism, a paper that supported, let us say, the vigorous pursuit of Latin American and Pacific imperialism, under the banner of the "white man's burden," would allow no suggestion in its pages that the anti-imperialists had an argu-

---

[4] Karl E. Meyer says of the modern Washington newspaperman: "He is far more competent than his predecessors, and far less colorful." See "The Washington Press Establishment," *Esquire,* April 1964, p. 73.

ment or two. During the Reconstruction, the Radical Republican paper would admit no word for the indigenous white leadership in the South. Now one can find a variety of views—few of them, to be sure, very extreme—in the editorials and signed columns of the large American dailies. Most of us, unless we are of the small minorities at the radical or reactionary ends of the political continuum, can find both agreement and disagreement on the editorial pages of our major papers. Mass circulation may bring moderation, but mass circulation plus a sense of responsibility will also bring (at least to our better newspapers) a pertinence of materials and a reasonable exchange and confrontation of varied opinion. To find the right balance of conflict and consensus about the issues that really count is no easy task, and one that is not always undertaken, nor hardly ever achieved; but one that is at least a possible objective for political journalism in the 1960s.

18.1   Biases of the American Press

American newspapers are generally conservative, jealous of their independence from governmental regulation, and presumptuous, but probably our most important safeguard against the manifold evils to which any large public might fall prey.

The characteristic biases of the American press are all displayed at the annual meetings of the American Newspaper Publishers Association. At one recent gathering of the ANPA, committees advised the world generally that (1) newspapers, "along with food and utilities," are "an indispensable daily service in the home"; (2) publishers should resist regulation of child labor, because "the training of a newspaper boy was one of the country's strongest deterrents to juvenile delinquency"; (3) the national government was withholding news and imposing censorship; (4) the national government should improve its second-class mailing service, revise its rules on the taxability of institutional advertising, and reduce its rates on shipment of newsprint through the St. Lawrence Seaway; and, oh, yes, (5) the government should get rid of its " 'deep-rooted attitude' against the peoples' right to know about public affairs." At the same meeting, the ANPA declared that it would continue its practice of "accrediting" journalism schools and departments—and that forty-six schools had already been blessed with the seal of approval of this self-interested private group.[5]

5 All examples and quotations are from the *New York Times,* April 28, 1960.

The presumptuousness especially of newspapers need hardly be documented—it is apparent at all times. The usual American newspaper coverage of prisoners charged with lurid crimes is so prejudicial to their rights of due process of law as to be unacceptable to even the most minimal standards of fair play—and to be illegal in countries that follow the British practice.[6] A central part is played by the press in the public condemnations, prejudgments, vilifications, and horror (real and pretended) of alleged murderers and rapists. The most celebrated case of journalistic justice in modern times is doubtlessly that of Lee Harvey Oswald, the alleged assassin of President Kennedy, who had been resoundingly tried and convicted by the nation's newspapers (and by the Dallas police department) several hours before he was "exterminated" by an irate citizen whose passion had been inflamed both by the assassination and the accounts of the supposed assassin.

One can understand—though hardly condone—the reporter's desire for a quick story or the editor's passion for a sensational lead, or even the publisher's view that a fastidious conception of due process need not stand in the way of increased sales. But the higher-than-law presumptuousness sometimes indulged in by newspapers is both incomprehensible and intolerable. Consider two cases, one general and one highly specific.

In the middle 1950s, many American newspaper editors and columnists became incensed by the State Department's total ban on travel to mainland (Communist) China. Secretary of State Dulles' interpretation of our nonrecognition policy was that the validation of any U.S. passports for travel to Red China might be construed by that government as an element of *de facto* recognition. Under the Dulles policy (long maintained by his successors), even news reporters were barred from travel to Red China. Hence, many newspaper publishers and editors were (or pretended to be) outraged by what they took to be an unwarranted restriction of their activities. But their argument was curious; it can only be explained if newsmen believe that they have special rights not possessed by other citizens. Thus, their argument was, in essence, that freedom to travel was a special case of freedom of the press, and, therefore, that reporters should be allowed to go to Red China. But no argument was made that others—scholars, representatives of nongovernmental groups,

---

[6] There seems to be a current encouraging willingness on the part of courts to face the thorny problems of balancing fair trials and a free press. The Philadelphia Bar Association overwhelmingly endorsed a code of good practice to be worked out with police and newsmen (*New York Times*, December 30, 1964); the New Jersey Supreme Court declared it would use its disciplinary powers if necessary to prevent prejudicial pretrial statements by police and attorneys; and in Massachusetts, twenty-six of forty daily papers voluntarily subscribed to a code drawn up by the bar (*New York Times*, November 22, 1964). For a collection of newspaper articles on free press and fair trials, see *Congressional Record*, February 25, 1965, pp. 3491–3495.

or just plain, interested tourists—should be allowed to go to Red China. In short, the newspapers wanted *special privileges.*

Now and then the presumptuousness of some newspapermen is exposed by one of their brothers. Thus, when Carl Rowan, a long-time correspondent for the *Minneapolis Tribune,* became a public-affairs officer in the U.S. Department of State in 1961, he found, from his new perspective, that he was nettled by "the pious assumption that the only people in this country who really care about the public's right to know are the newspaper and magazine people." He added that "a great deal of this so-called concern about the public's right to know is really concern about the fourth estate's right to make a buck."[7]

The second illustration of the newspapers' higher-than-law presumptions comes from a single paper, the *San Francisco Examiner.* It is admittedly a most extreme case (but it therefore has the heuristic value of all extreme cases that illustrate tendencies). In November 1963, a University of California coed disappeared from Berkeley under circumstances that strongly suggested foul play. The *Examiner,* long in a no-holds-barred race for subscriptions with the *San Francisco Chronicle,* offered a $1,000 cash payment to anyone who had information about the case *and who would supply such information to the Examiner before giving it to the police.* In a self-serving editorial, the *Chronicle* decried the *Examiner's* offer:

> Apparently the Examiner had constituted itself as a superdetective agency, independent from our own police agencies, apart from the lawful constabulary. . . . [This] is completely outside our comprehension of the canon of responsibility and decency of the free American press. We are not playing circulation games.[8]

That American newspapers have a high and exaggerated notion of their own importance is beyond doubt. But it is also beyond doubt that newspapers are important, indeed, indispensable elements in the public discussion and criticism that is fundamental to self-government. The foregoing critical comments should not be taken to mean that newspapermen should have any lesser view of their responsibilities and their importance, but only that they should be ever aware of the fallibility of their judgments, and of those tendencies (which they share with all of us)

---

[7] "Outspoken Ex-Newsman," *New York Times,* January 22, 1964. Frederick C. Irion recounts the efforts of newspaper publishers during the period 1925–1940 to restrict the free circulation of advertising handbills and shoppers' guides. Such activities, he says, "show how newspaper publishers tend to regard only newspapers as protected by the constitutional guarantee of freedom of the press . . . and illustrate the principle that newspaper publishers sometimes are blind to the real meaning of press freedom." *Public Opinion and Propaganda* (New York: Thomas Y. Crowell Co., 1952), pp. 107–111, quotation from p. 111.

[8] *San Francisco Chronicle,* November 13, 1963.

to mistake their own interests for the general interest. Precisely because they are so important in the opinion-policy process, newspapers should strive for *extraordinary* humility.

The biases of the American press have historic, economic, and political roots. The best newspapermen are acutely aware of the deep tradition of free inquiry in Western civilization, and of the importance of printing in the history of intellectual controversy. We can hardly overestimate the value of the printing press in the development of modern democratic societies. It is hardly debatable that Luther, who was born fifteen years after Gutenberg's death, was greatly advantaged in his reformism by the printing press, just as Luther's precursor John Wycliffe, who died 14 years before Gutenberg's birth, was disadvantaged by the lack of the printing press. The most able present-day American newspapermen have a deep commitment to the arguments of Milton's *Areopagitica* and a deep sense of participation in the honored profession of Peter Zenger and William Lloyd Garrison. C. D. Jackson, publisher of *Life* magazine, points out the important distinction between written and electronic journalism:

> Thoughtful writing in magazines, pamphlets, and newspapers goes back a long time; it goes back to an era of great courage and great thought and emotion. . . . There was no "show biz" element in writing in the old days. It was many times a life-and-death matter. Now today even the most irresponsible editor or publisher, the cheapest, tawdriest, cheeziest journalist, has had some of that old stuff of the tradition of journalism rub off on him, some of that tradition of integrity and valor which attached to the printed word. But television started off as pure show business and now they're trying to tack on to show business what journalism always had.[9]

The refusal of a small-town Minnesota editor to be stilled by the "gag laws" of his state (*Near v. Minnesota*, 283 U.S. 697, 1931), and the refusal of the august *New York Times* to be intimidated by a Senate committee's investigation of its employees,[10] are not the last times, we may be sure, when newsmen will remember that they are among the foremost attendants of the goddess of freedom.

Yet the goddess of freedom, like all interesting women, is complex and full of changing moods. It used to be thought that the conservative bias of the American press was maintained by a small and selfish group of wealthy investors and capitalists who prevented liberal reporters and "the common people" from expressing liberal or radical sentiments. Nowadays,

---

[9] *The Press*, interviews by Donald McDonald with Mark Ethridge and C. D. Jackson (Santa Barbara, Calif.: Center for the Study of Democratic Institutions, 1961), p. 32.

[10] The editorial writer of the *Times* produced on this occasion a ringing and masterful statement of what is best in American (or in any) journalism; defiant, uncompromisingly for integrity and fair play, yet humble with the knowledge of human limitations. "The Voice of a Free Press," *New York Times*, January 5, 1956.

the conservative bias of the American newspapers is usually attributed to more subtle factors, related to the nature of the industry. A major daily newspaper is a large business enterprise, having most of the characteristics of all large business enterprises. It usually has a corporate form, a large and expensive plant, and a management separated from its ownership (although the prevalence of "family" newspapers such as the Hearst, McCormack, Chandler, and Cox empires, to name only a few, complicate the neat owner-manager dichotomy made famous by the Berle-Means study and its progeny).[11] Gerald W. Johnson calls this management-ownership separation the "quandary of the editors":

> How can the editor of a big-city newspaper be at once politically liberal and financially honest? Consider his position. He is practically never the owner of the prosperity he controls, but he is its custodian. The paper usually represents an investment of many millions of other people's money, and a conscientious agent is not going to take chances with other people's money, even in circumstances under which he might gamble his own.
> To put an honest man in charge of $10 million or $20 million or $50 million worth of highly perishable property belonging to other people and then expect him to lash out boldly in defense of what is right but unpopular is to subject human nature to an unbearable strain.[12]

That large newspapers tend to be conservative in their economic and political views may be, in part, the natural conservatism of big and middle-sized business in America, and one hardly needs to seek an explanation for newspaper conservatism in Marxist and anticapitalist ideologies.

It used to be said, also—another variant of the anticapitalist argument —that newspaper owners and editors were intimidated by their large advertisers, and, in turn, intimidated their reporters to slant the news in a conservative direction. This argument seems to have little present validity. There are, no doubt, examples of advertisers' pressures on newspapers; but most of the documented cases occurred many years ago.[13] Economic reprisals by advertisers against editorial policies appear to be less common now than in former times (if only because papers are larger now, on the

---

[11] Adolf A. Berle and Gardiner C. Means, *The Modern Corporation and Private Property* (New York: Macmillan Co., 1939).

[12] "The Superficial Aspect," *New Republic*, May 2, 1955, p. 6.

[13] For an account of pressure on Philadelphia papers by brewers in the early 1900s, see Edward L. Bernays, *Crystallizing Public Opinion* (New York: Liveright Publishing Corp., 1961), p. 182; on the advertisers' boycott that destroyed the Valley City, North Dakota, *Times Record* in 1947, see Curtis D. Macdougall, *Understanding Public Opinion* (New York: Macmillan Co., 1952), p. 607; and for the account of a Chicago Negro newspaper that is said to have been bankrupted in recent years by the withdrawal of advertising accounts of white businessmen, see James Q. Wilson, *Negro Politics* (Chicago: University of Chicago Press, 1960), p. 143.

average, and larger papers are harder to destroy); and such reprisals as are attempted are more apt to be related to labor or racial conflict than to a newspaper's over-all policy. Some reporters may feel that managerial pressures limit their freedom to report objectively, but recent studies indicate that pressures toward conservatism and biased reporting are much diminished, or too subtle to be noticed. Of 273 Washington correspondents queried in 1962, only 7.3 per cent said that their stories had been "played down, cut, or killed for 'policy' reasons"; whereas over 55 per cent of a 1937 sample of Washington reporters had had such experience. When asked if they had experienced subtle pressures, 60 per cent of the 1937 sample (but only 9.5 per cent of the 1962 sample) answered yes.[14]

Whether or not reporters are subject to pressure from their editors and publishers to follow a "party line" is a function largely of the balance between the kinds of probias and antibias pressures that the newspapers' policy setters experience. The probias pressures are apt to come from the individuals and groups who are satisfied with the social and political status quo in the community—and this may include the newspaper policy setters themselves. The antibias pressures are apt to come from the individuals and groups who want to initiate change in the community— but we should bear in mind that those who seek social and political change may falsify reporting and deny freedom of expression in those arenas over which they have control as easily as those who want no change.

The major antidotes to bias and falsification in newspapers are (a) economic competition, and (b) governmental regulation. Of these two, governmental regulation is the less favored in America; it has been resorted to only in the more flagrant cases, such as libel and grossly misleading, subversive, or inflammatory publication.

As an inhibitor of press bias, economic competition is, first, a matter of alternative sources of news and opinions for the citizenry, and, second, a matter of what the employees of the paper and its readers will tolerate. It goes almost without saying that monopoly control of the dissemination of news and opinions gives the monopolist an opportunity for unlimited bias and distortion of truth. The rulers of a totalitarian society, by definition, have such a monopoly; but it seems unlikely that such control has ever existed in the United States—even in the smallest and most isolated company-owned mining town in the West—or that it would in the future be technologically possible (although the history of Nazi Germany warns us against assuming too much from our complex, modern nation-states).

---

[14] William L. Rivers, "The Correspondents after 25 Years," *Columbia Journalism Review,* I (1962), 5. Rivers compared his findings with those reported in Leo C. Rosten, *The Washington Correspondents* (New York: Harcourt, Brace and World, Inc., 1937).

In the United States today, many sources of news and opinion exist. Although there are fewer daily newspapers now than there were in 1900, there are important alternative news sources that did not exist in 1900. In recent years, much has been made of the fact that, through bankruptcy and mergers, many newspapers have closed in the past four or five decades, with a consequence that there are many one-newspaper cities. In 1915, there were 2,502 daily newspapers in America; and in 1955 there were 1,760. Since the middle 1950s, the number of dailies has remained nearly constant—there were 1,761 dailies as of January 15, 1962. Because of this rapid decrease in the number of papers through bankruptcies and mergers, it is often said that the monopolies enjoyed in one-newspaper towns encourage or at least increase the likelihood of distortion, slanting the news, irresponsible exercise of editorial power, and the like. These charges are heard most often from liberals and reformers, because it is they who feel most consciously the general conservatism of American newspapers. These days, however, the danger from newspaper monopolies and one-newspaper towns is not very great. There are some large cities— for example, Indianapolis and Phoenix—where none but narrow and biased papers are published; but persons in such cities may purchase out-of-town papers and newsmagazines and receive increasingly thorough television coverage of state and national news. Monopoly papers may report the local news unfairly (this is the major news-distortion problem in one-newspaper cities). But weekly papers and the publicity organs of community groups help to redress the balance; and a large city that cannot support a fair and responsible paper may ultimately be judged as a city that does not deserve a fair and responsible paper. With very few, if any, exceptions, the possibility for variety, fairness, and comprehensiveness of news reporting is as great as the readers' desire for variety, fairness, and comprehensiveness.[15]

If the American press is, on the whole, mediocre and intellectually unchallenging (and it is), the cause is hardly to be found in the decreasing number of daily papers, but in the fact that most producers and consumers of newspapers prefer mediocrity to intellectual challenge. There is a dearth of talent in American newspapers. A dearth of talented writers and a dearth of talented readers. It is, as Leo Rosten put it:

a woeful fact that despite several generations of free education, our land has produced relatively few first-rate minds; and of those with first-rate brains, fewer have imagination; of those with brains and imagination, fewer still possess judgment. If we ask, in addition, for the special skills and experience involved in

[15] For a summary of evidence that interested persons subscribe to quality out-of-town papers, see Alfred O. Hero, *Mass Media and World Affairs* (Boston: World Peace Foundation, 1959), pp. 84–85.

the art of communicating, the total amount of talent available to the media is not impressive.[16]

In sum, the general social and political biases of American newspapers are what one would expect, given the large-business and corporate perspectives of their policy makers, the imperatives of competition for recency and sensation—for the titillation of audiences that consist mainly of persons uninterested in public issues—and the endemic lack of journalistic talent to write and edit their millions of daily lines.

18.2　Newspapers and Partisanship

As one would also expect, in view of the conservatism of the American press, most newspapers support Republican Party policies and Republican candidates. At least such is the big generalization—which, like most big generalizations, does not take us far on the road to understanding. The pro-Republican tendencies of American newspapers are by no means simple or direct; we must have some information on three subtopics, in order to appreciate more clearly whether, or to what extent, a pro-Republican bias in newspapers is a matter of importance to the opinion-policy process. We need to know (a) how self-consciously pro-Republican American papers are (that is, how many newspapers intend to be pro-Republican in their editorial policy);[17] (b) how the biases are shown generally and at critical junctures in the governing process (e.g., in election campaigns and votes on public issues); and (c) how newspaper favoritism affects the outcome of electoral decisions.

Most newspapers adopt an official stance of nonpartisanship or political independence. The rhetoric of the free press places a high value on the word *independence,* so that even papers as notoriously pro-Republican as the *Chicago Tribune* or as notoriously pro-Democratic as the *New York Post* declare themselves as independents. Among those papers that, for historical reasons related to the papers themselves or to the sections of the country in which they are published, declare themselves to be either Democratic or Republican, the partisan balance may be about even.

16 "The Intellectual and the Mass Media: Some Rigorously Random Remarks," *Daedalus,* LXXXIX (1960), 335–336.

17 No statistical information could be expected on newspapers whose managers intend to be biased in their news coverage or advertising policy, simply because newspapermen will not admit to such intent. Data on disproportionately great or favorable coverage must be more inferentially come by—from content analysis, participant-observation, or educated guesswork—as is the case in the sources cited below.

Thus, in one sample of "principal daily newspapers" in 1960, out of 349 papers giving such information, 213 (61 per cent) described themselves as independent, while 68 (19.5 per cent) were "independent-Democratic" or Democratic, and the same number (68) were "independent-Republican" or Republican.[18] By an almost identical counting procedure, Mott found that there were about as many self-identified Democratic as Republican papers in 1944; of a larger sample, he found 25.5 per cent self-described as Democratic or independent-Democratic, 26.6 per cent as Republican or independent-Republican, and 47.9 per cent independent.[19] It is unclear whether the apparent increase of independency (13 per cent in a sixteen-year period) is to be attributed to sampling error or whether it is further evidence of the long-run trend away from partisan self-identification. The latter is probably the case, although the rate of change to at least a nominal independency may be subject to exaggeration in this measurement.

The probable decrease in the numbers of self-identified partisan papers seems to be a result of several factors. The many mergers among newspapers in the past few decades have increased the circulation and geographical coverage of the remaining papers, making readerships more apt to be heterogeneous and less likely to welcome partisanship in their papers.[20] Moreover, there may be a general long-run increase in independent voting among the population at large,[21] and the historic one-party areas in America (the Democratic South, and Republican New England and the North Central states) seem to be moving in the direction of two-partyism. In a 1926 count of partisan dailies, and again in the 1960 count, there was "a more positive tendency for states of unusually heavy Republican or Democratic majorities to have the bulk of its newspaper circulation listed as of the same respective party affiliation."[22] Newspaper publishers and editors may be trimming their overt partisanship to the changing winds of two-party registration in their circulation areas.

18 *The Working Press of the Nation* (Chicago: The National Research Bureau, 1960), pp. 47–165.

19 Frank Luther Mott, "Newspapers in Presidential Campaigns," *Public Opinion Quarterly*, VIII (1944), 366.

20 There is some evidence, for example, that the *Los Angeles Times* became more liberal when the *Mirror* and the *Examiner* (both of which had had more Democratic readers) folded. See Jack Lyle, "Audience Impact of a Double Newspaper Merger," *Journalism Quarterly*, XXXIX (1962), 151.

21 See, for example, Richard E. Neustadt, *Presidential Power* (New York: John Wiley & Sons, Inc., 1960), pp. 4, 187.

22 George A. Lundberg, "The Newspaper and Public Opinion," *Social Forces*, IV (1926), 714.

Another index of how partisan newspapers intend to be is their record of endorsements for public office. Because the only national election in the United States is that for president, the quadrennial score cards of newspaper support for major-party candidates will give us some idea of the preponderance of Republican support from American papers. In 1956, slightly over half of the dailies in the country endorsed one of the major-party candidates; 740 (80 per cent) supported Republican President Eisenhower and 194 (20 per cent) backed Democrat Adlai Stevenson.[23] In 1960, of the papers endorsing a presidential candidate, 731 (78 per cent) backed Republican Richard M. Nixon and 208 (22 per cent) endorsed Democrat John F. Kennedy. In 1964, using the same measurement, 349 (45 per cent) supported Republican Barry Goldwater and 440 (55 per cent) supported Democrat Lyndon B. Johnson.[24]

Very little study has been made of newspaper endorsements of state and local candidates. It is probably safe to assume that papers endorse more Republicans than Democrats, judging from the distribution of presidential-candidate endorsements and from the findings of the few state and local studies. In one analysis of statewide campaigns in Connecticut and Wisconsin, of the eleven dailies chosen in Wisconsin four supported the Republican candidates, two the Democratic, and four were neutral; in Connecticut, no one of the nine dailies supported the Democrats—but the authors unfortunately do not indicate how many of the nine papers were pro-Republican and how many were neutral.[25] In another study of newspaper treatment of partisan candidates and campaigning, this one in Pennsylvania, of twenty-six papers nine endorsed the two Republican candidates (for governor and U.S. Senator), three supported the two Democrats, four divided their endorsements, and ten papers remained neutral.[26]

Aside from self-admitted partisanship, and from the endorsement of partisan candidates, is there evidence that American newspapers show partisan favoritism in their treatment of news? If the newspapers have a genuinely conservative bias as a result of their owners' and managers' general identification with big business, might they not expose this bias in giving preferential treatment to conservative candidates generally and especially to Republican candidates? To argue that this is likely to be the

---

[23] *Arizona Daily Star,* October 28, 1960.

[24] *Editor & Publisher,* October 31, 1964, pp. 9–13.

[25] LeRoy C. Ferguson and Ralph H. Smuckler, *Politics in the Press: An Analysis of Press Content in 1952 Senatorial Campaigns* (East Lansing: Governmental Research Bureau, Michigan State College, 1954), pp. 65–71.

[26] James W. Markham, "Press Treatment of the 1958 State Elections in Pennsylvanvia," *Western Political Quarterly,* XIV (1961), 921.

case is not necessarily to ascribe conscious favoritism to the newspaper managers (though conscious favoritism is consistent with at least one tradition of American journalism); such favoritism might result from an accumulation of small advantages of news slanting or selection or placement in favor of the approved candidates. For information bearing on intended and unintended bias we must turn to content analyses of newspapers during campaigns. The author of one national study of thirty-five daily papers concluded that

there was slanting in the news columns during the 1952 election, but it was not as widespread as some critics have maintained. A majority of the newspapers in this study—eighteen—met the highest standards of fair news presentation, and a large number of newspapers—eleven—showed no significant degree of partiality that would warrant a charge of unfairness. The six newspapers found to have demonstrated partiality in their news columns constitute a minority.

It also is evident that newspapers which supported the Republican presidential candidate performed, on the whole, at a higher level than did the pro-Democratic newspapers.[27]

In another study, thirty-four of the thirty-seven Florida daily newspapers were reviewed during the 1952 presidential campaign, and a total of 5,240 news articles and 61,500 column inches of space scrutinized for evidences of treatment given the major party candidates. The avowed support for the Republican was impressive—twenty-one papers with 78 per cent of the circulation favored Republican Eisenhower, and eight papers with 16 per cent of the circulation favored Democrat Stevenson; 216 editorials supported Eisenhower, and 115 favored Stevenson. But on the question of which side was favored in news treatment (number and placement of references, positive or negative references, flattering or unflattering pictures, and the like), the Democratic candidate had the better of it by a small margin. Stevenson received a slight majority of all news stories and a slight advantage in picture usage, and twelve of the editorially pro-Eisenhower papers gave Stevenson better treatment in the news columns than they gave Eisenhower.[28] Another investigation found that only one of fourteen Wisconsin dailies sampled favored Stevenson in 1952, but that the two candidates received roughly equal treatment in quantity of coverage.[29]

In contrast to these findings are the conclusions of a study of news-

27 Nathan B. Blumberg, *One-Party Press?* (Lincoln: University of Nebraska Press, 1954), pp. 44–45.

28 Sidney Kobre, "How Florida Dailies Handled the 1952 Presidential Campaign," *Journalism Quarterly*, XXX (1953), 163–169.

29 Charles E. Higbie, "Wisconsin Dailies in the 1952 Campaign: Space vs. Display," *Journalism Quarterly*, XXXI (1954), 56–60.

paper handling of the Nixon and Stevenson "slush fund" stories in the 1952 presidential campaign. An evaluation of eleven days' treatment of this issue by thirty-one major American dailies evoked this summary:

> . . . with the possible exception of the *New York Times,* all papers—both Republican and Democratic—showed evidence of favoritism in their news columns in violation of their own accepted rules of conduct. . . . almost every example of favoritism in the news columns coincided with the paper's editorial feelings. . . . On the basis of the 1952 editorial endorsements of candidates, that would indicate that over 80 per cent of the nation's newspaper readers may be getting their news as well as editorials with some Republican flavoring.[30]

A study of fifteen major American dailies' treatment of the 1960 presidential campaign concluded that there was such good balance and equal coverage, quantitatively, that there must have been conscious efforts on the part of editors for a 50–50 treatment.[31] Finally, an imaginative comparison of newspaper treatments of the 1896 and 1952 presidential campaigns found a great difference between the partisan favoritism and distortion in the 1896 campaign and the much more nearly fair and equal treatment given the candidates in the 1952 campaign.[32]

To this point, our look at the partisanship of American newspapers reveals that most papers describe themselves as independent, and that of those admitting a partisan preference, the Democratic-Republican split is about even. However, as measured by endorsement of partisan candidates, the newspapers as a whole seem significantly Republican, by 60 to 80 per cent of the endorsements made in national and state elections (too little is known about newspaper endorsements in local elections for us to hazard even a tentative generalization). Measurements of partisan bias in newspapers indicates that, over-all, Republicans get more favorable treatment than do Democrats; but this finding seems to be significantly less true of the larger and more influential dailies. On the whole, the claims of some Democrats that America has a "one-party press" seem greatly exaggerated, although based on a kernel of truth.

Another, different, but at least equally important question is whether partisan favoritism by newspapers actually helps the favored candidate. Here again most of our knowledge is about presidential elections. The best historical study, reviewing two-party presidential campaigns since

---

[30] Arthur Edward Rowse, *Slanted News: A Case Study of the Nixon and Stevenson Fund Stories* (Boston: Beacon Press, Inc., 1957), pp. 127–128.

[31] Guido H. Stempel, III, "The Prestige Press Covers the 1960 Presidential Campaign," *Journalism Quarterly,* XXXVIII (1961), 157–163.

[32] Robert Batlin, "San Francisco Newspapers' Campaign Coverage: 1896–1952," *Journalism Quarterly,* XXXI (1954), 297–303.

1800, reported no evidence that newspapers unduly affect presidential races:

> In half of our comparable elections, candidates have won without the support of a majority of the newspapers, and losers have failed despite majority press support. There seems to be no correlation, positive or negative, between the support of a majority of newspapers during a campaign and success at the polls.[33]

But Mott's generalization refers only to presidential campaigns, which are so visible and played on by so many forces that one is not surprised to find no demonstrably great influence from newspaper endorsement. What of the thousands of more obscure state and local candidacies, often run in jurisdictions where only a few communications channels exist —are newspapers, under such circumstances, not more influential for election outcomes? The answer seems to be yes, although the evidence is too scanty to be conclusive. In an early study based upon the postelection recollection of Seattle respondents, Lundberg found that, on four referendum questions on which the local papers had taken positions, there was "no significant relationship between the attitude of the newspaper and the attitude of the reader on the questions investigated"; moreover, he found that the relation between newspaper support and Seattle voters "in the last [1924] presidential election appears to be entirely negligible."[34] But the Lundberg study, although local in setting, is not about local *candidates* and therefore is not quite pertinent to our question (despite his interesting finding on local ballot measures). In the study of Wisconsin and Connecticut statewide races mentioned earlier, all three candidates favored by the majority of the newspapers won their races; but the Pennsylvania study of 1958, for a variety of reasons, is inconclusive on the point.

A somewhat more impressionistic—but possibly more reliable—report stems from the experience of the *Toledo Blade*. A former editorial writer of the *Blade* declares that it "has a notable long-run record of supporting local candidates who turn out to be winners." "Generally speaking," he says, "strong editorial support of a candidate is believed by experienced Toledo politicians to be worth three or four thousand votes out of a total city vote of around seventy thousand to ninety thousand." The reasons for this influence conform to common sense and to the scattered observations of knowledgeable students of local politics:

> [W]hile some political veterans can undoubtedly win without *Blade* support, more obscure political figures, including younger men trying to get a foothold on the city's political ladder, are critically dependent on the *Blade's* favor. An edi-

[33] Mott, "Newspapers in Presidential Campaigns" (see footnote 19), p. 358.

[34] Lundberg, "The Newspaper and Public Opinion" (see footnote 22), pp. 710, 712.

torial or two lambasting or lauding a relatively unknown man can affect his fortunes crucially. . . . As for judicial candidates running on a non-partisan ballot, the *Blade's* verdict carries its heaviest punch in these contests.[35]

18.3 The Press, Government, and the Free Society

The mass media are vitally important to the maintenance of democracy in the modern world. No system of face-to-face communication could possibly provide a network for the exchange of information sufficient for a society larger than the Greek city-states or the historic New England town. We depend upon the mass media for the survival of self-government in the twentieth century.

Our judgment of how well the mass media are performing their indispensable function will depend on whether we expect them to lead their readers' tastes or merely to satisfy them, or whether we expect the media to be teachers as well as transmitters of news and opinions. If we cannot ask the media to be better than the communities they serve, then, it seems to me, we must conclude that they are now performing well. An astounding range of material is available to the American public by the printed and electronic media; there is hardly a hamlet left where a person may not get both the Beverly Hillbillies and a Shakespearian drama in the same week on his television set, where he cannot watch both Oral Roberts and the top American political figures on the same Sunday, where he cannot buy on his local newsstand or obtain at subsidized rates through the U.S. mail either the *Police Gazette* or the *New York Times,* where he cannot obtain *Playboy* or *The Atlantic.* In judging the media from this perspective, it is beside the point for intellectuals to argue that Walter Lippmann does not appear in the *East Overshoe Daily Bugle;* the fact is that East Overshoeians do not want Walter Lippmann, and if one is found who does, he may subscribe to the *Washington Post* or the *New York Herald Tribune.*

One may, however, ask the media to be better (in terms of one's own standards) than the communities they serve, and, thus, to be even better than they now are. One likes to believe—and, indeed, the evidence supports the belief—that the media have less trash, bigotry, selfishness, parochialism, and mediocrity than they had formerly. Yet, even greater re-

---

[35] Reo M. Christenson, "The Power of the Press: The Case of the *Toledo Blade,*" *Midwest Journal of Political Science,* III (1959), 235. For an excellent summary of what is known and knowledgeably inferred about the power of the press in urban political life, see Edward D. Banfield and James Q. Wilson, *City Politics* (Cambridge, Mass.: Harvard University Press, 1963), Chap. 21, "The Press," pp. 313–325.

sponsibility and public responsiveness may be expected of the media. For those who believe that the media should be instruments of *information and instruction,* one rule of thumb may be the simple question whether the media have as much instructional content as the traffic will bear. The owners and managers of the media may not fairly be asked to relinquish the support of their mass audiences to satisfy the more demanding tastes of their critics; but the question is whether they are attempting to meet the tastes of their critics (and whether they are acting as their own critics) at the same time that they retain their mass base of support. Mark Ethridge, publisher of the Louisville *Courier-Journal,* makes the point well:

There are certain features you've got to have; the public kills you if you don't have them. One of them is a medical column; every American is a hypochondriac to some extent. Ann Landers' column on dating and marriage is another very popular feature here. . . . And you are still not able to do away with comic strips. . . . We do carry a minimum of entertainment-type material. [Also] you've got to have the instant journalism, but you've got to have the elaboration of what happens. . . . In our "Passing Show" section we ask, "What does the news mean?" We have articles by our science reporters and political writers and men versed in international affairs.[36]

Beyond the canons of accuracy and the separation of news from editorial comment, there are improvements to be made in the mass media. In several aspects of their work, the mass media may be expected to be constantly on the alert for ways to improve their performance. The media have a responsibility to select—which means *to seek out—*events to be reported on. Especially, they should not let human laziness or archaic techniques stand in the way of their reportorial functions. Much of the controversy over "managed news" in Washington relates not so much to the willingness of bureaucratic press officers to hand out the news in amounts of their choice with prepackaged interpretations as it does to the willingness of Washington and hometown newsmen to accept what they are given. Bureaucrats are apt to use the weaknesses of others to further their own interests. Newsmen have a responsibility to go beyond the press release and the press officer—though I do not dismiss the "managed-news" problem so offhandedly, and shall return to it below.

Modern journalism suffers from the stultifying conventions that have to do with "newspaper style" and the demand for immediacy. The archaic rules of newspaper style require that a "good story" tell only what happened since the last issue of the paper and that the essential features of the story be summarized in a few crisp sentences in the very first paragraph. This requirement, of course, is absurd. Most of the important news of any day is not new at all, but a development of yesterday's news, as that news was a development of the news of the day before. The pretense that public events are discontinuous not merely distorts the facts, but exaggerates the ordinary citizen's tendency to envision the impersonal world of public affairs as episodic snippets of reality rather than as a flow of interrelated events. The best news media strive to place the events of the day in perspective, but there is still entirely too much effort to isolate, concentrate, and capsulate the news into "flashes."

Other conventions, especially some having to do with political reporting, are equally senseless—if not equally misleading. One is the use of anonymous attribution. Consider the following examples from the first 150 words of a *New York Times* story (with my brackets):

"Forecasts [by whom?] of a swelling neutralist coalition . . .

"Some [who?] of the Western delegations question . . .

"These delegates [which delegates?] see the action and observations . . .

"The point is made [by whom?] that Marshall Tito's drive . . .

"Thus, the Soviet leader would formally recognize the neutralist bloc, it was said here [by whom?]"[37]

Or consider the effects of a mechanically applied "fairness" doctrine that allows real events to be countered by pseudo events. In the first week in April 1963, for example, New York Governor Nelson Rockefeller made a trip and some speeches in the Midwest that, in view of his prominence then as a potential presidential candidate, were of reportable importance. Yet, side by side with the story of Rockefeller's trip, the *Times* printed an almost equally long story of an anti-Rockefeller statement released by Democratic National Chairman John M. Bailey from Washington. One can hardly blame Bailey's press assistant for taking advantage of an opportunity, but one may question the *Times'* editor's decision to create such an arbitrary balance.[38]

In their treatment of domestic public affairs, the mass media, especially the newspapers, may make a particular contribution to the administration of justice, to the maintenance of high ethical standards for public officials, and to the efficacy of the electoral process. Police brutality and denial of due process to indigent and minority-race defendants are all-too-common occurrences in America; the constant surveillance by local reporters and city editors over the administration of criminal justice is a service of great importance that any local newspaper can perform for its community—and a service for which there is celebrated precedent in the

[37] Jack Raymond, "West Questions Tito Neutralism," *New York Times,* September 26, 1960.

[38] Warren Weaver, Jr., "Rockefeller Gains on Midwest Trip," and "Bailey Hits G.O.P. on Economic Aims," *New York Times,* April 8, 1963.

history of journalism. Newspapers can also watch over the ever more complex ethical problems of conflict of interest of all public officials from governors to traffic patrolmen. In the courts, in the legislative bodies, and in the administrative agencies from the highest to the lowest, favoritism and the temptations to favoritism are so common—and so destructive of the public confidence on which democracy is based—that the alert newspaperman has no difficulty finding dragons to slay.

The press's right to criticize public officials was given momentous support in 1964 by the Supreme Court's decision in *New York Times and Abernathy v. Sullivan,* where a unanimous Court held that a public official cannot collect damages for published statements critical of his official conduct, even if such statements are false and defamatory, unless he proves actual malice. The mass media, and especially the newspapers as the political medium *par excellence,* can take new confidence from the Court's declaration that America has

a profound national commitment to the principle that debate on public issues should be uninhibited, robust, and wide open, and that it may well include vehement, caustic, and sometimes unpleasantly sharp attacks on government and public officials.[39]

Beyond the exposure of corruption, one might also ask—still within the context of prescribing for those newspapers that wish to lead opinion in their communities—that greater editorial conviction be taken and defended with regard to candidates and public issues. James Reston's comments are much to the point:

The newspapers themselves can do something about the Congress . . . if they will look at the . . . primary elections and tell the truth about the many dubs and incompetents who represent their states and districts on Capitol Hill. . . . the majority of men and women in the House and Senate are able and industrious public servants, but as the editors know, there is a minority of numskulls in the Congress whom no self-respecting editor would trust to cover the local City Hall.

It would be difficult to overestimate the damage done to the quality of Congress by the amiable goodfellowship of newspaper editors and owners. Usually they know their senators and congressmen very well, and often go on backing them long after age or sickness has impaired their usefulness. Lacking any lead from the papers, the voters do the same.[40]

Alert newsmen can usually find ways to discover the facts in local, state, and national news. Acting as the agents of "the people's right to know," a role in which newsmen like to cast themselves, they can ordinarily ferret out all the facts that the people need to know about domestic

---

39 *New York Times,* March 10, 1964.

40 James Reston, "The Press and the Congress and the Nation," *New York Times,* January 17, 1964.

public policy, even when information is withheld by government officials who feel threatened by such exposures. Reporters may not always be able to ferret out the facts from a source, but with the help of officials in other branches or levels of government (congressmen, state legislators, or attorneys general), the energetic press can well perform its responsibilities as critic and scrutinizer of the public's business.

The task of obtaining facts is not so easy, however, with regard to foreign and defense policy. The problems of unfamiliarity, complexity, geographical distance, and espionage (real and imagined) are so great in foreign and military affairs that even a minimum public consideration of national policy in these areas demands the closest cooperation and understanding between governmental officials and the news media. It is not surprising that, very often, officials and newsmen disagree about where the balance should be struck between secrecy and exposure. The late President Kennedy summarized the dilemma when he said that international tension

imposes upon our society two requirements of direct concern to both the press and the President—two requirements that may seem almost contradictory in tone, but which must be reconciled and fulfilled if we are to meet this national peril. I refer, first, to the need for far greater public information; and, second, to the need for far greater official secrecy.[41]

Governmental information policy with respect to sensitive material may range from complete exposure to complete manipulation. The ends of such a continuum are unrealistic, of course, because no nation under present or foreseeable international conditions is prepared to tell all it knows, and no country is totalitarian enough successfully to manipulate *all* information.[42] What is practical, however, even in a nation with strong traditions of an open and free press, is a policy that employs selective openness and closedness with regard to what the media are given by government officials. Public officials, like other human beings, prefer to have their work and their organizations well thought of:

Any government—whether city, state, or national—tries to maintain the most favorable image possible. Its news announcements and its answers to questions by the press will always be in this framework. This is old stuff, old as the Republic . . .[43]

When governmental officials have convinced themselves that the "national interest" requires it, they have withheld from the public some or all of the

[41] *New York Times*, April 28, 1961.

[42] Although Nazi Germany, under Hitler's Propaganda Minister Goebbels, attempted complete manipulation. See Leonard Doob, "Goebbels' Principles of Propaganda," *Public Opinion Quarterly*, XIV (1950), 419–442.

[43] George Chaplin, "Who Manages What?" *Honolulu Advertiser*, May 13, 1963; reprinted in *Congressional Record*, May 16, 1963, p. A3098.

news about events, or some or all of the explanations about policy. The historic complaint of newsmen (and congressmen) is that the administrative agencies do not tell all they know. In some cases, no information at all may be given about an event or policy; in other cases, selectively misleading or inadequate information may be given. Nimmo reported that fewer than half of the Washington newsmen he interviewed had ever found the withholding of information a problem. His informants seemed to agree that plain secrecy on the part of government officials (i.e., simply refusing to give information on a matter) was not regarded as serious unless the newsman was personally frustrated in his efforts to get a particular story. There was, as he put it, "a tendency for withholding to be accepted by newsmen until that moment when they were denied a story."[44]

Something more than mere withholding is implied by the notion of governmental "management" of the news. News "management" involves the deliberate creation of partial truths, or of outright falsehoods, in the furtherance of a governmental policy. An attempt at news "management" (in this case, unsuccessful) is illustrated by the official versions of the May 1960 flight of Francis Gary Powers over the Soviet Union in his U-2 reconnaissance plane. When it became apparent that Powers had been downed in Soviet territory, as the Soviet government claimed, both the State Department and the National Aeronautics and Space Administration gave out false (and different!) official stories—which both were forced to retract when the truth of the flights could no longer be suppressed. That "management" is used by Democratic as well as Republican administrations when they feel that the national security interests require it is attested by the bold-faced statements of Assistant Secretary of Defense Arthur Sylvester in October 1962. In the crisis over Soviet missiles in Cuba, the United States agencies involved found it expedient to plant several lies in the American press to mislead Cuban and Soviet officials. Sylvester put the matter starkly. "It is inherent in government," he said, "[to have] the right to lie to save itself when going toward a nuclear war. It's basic." The concept Sylvester laid bare is an old one; but he gave it a new name amidst some new frankness: "news as weaponry" means "in the kind of world we live in, [that] the generation of news by actions taken by the government becomes a weapon in a strained situation."[45] The use of

---

44 Dan D. Nimmo, *Newsgathering in Washington* (New York: Atherton Press, 1964), p. 177.

45 *New York Times*, November 1, 1962. See also, Bernard C. Cohen, *The Press and Foreign Policy* (Princeton, N.J.: Princeton University Press, 1963), pp. 198–202. Sylvester had Plato on his side, though he made no note of the fact: "Then if anyone at all is to have the privilege of lying, the rulers of the State should be the persons; and they, in their dealings either with enemies or with their own citizens, may be allowed to lie for the public good." *The Republic* (New York: Walter J. Black, Inc., 1932), p. 65.

outright lies by a democratic government is hardly ever to be tolerated, short of wartime or the brink of war—perhaps not even then. For a high official of the U.S. Department of Defense, himself a veteran newspaper-man, boldly to proclaim that the newsman has a responsibility, as Sir Henry Wotton once said about the diplomat, "to lie for his country" is a doctrine that is dangerously, perhaps even fatally corrosive of democracy itself.

Of the more subtle "management" of news—by special and flattering treatment of newsmen, or by the use of "leaks" and of "planted" stories that do not violate the broad definition of "truth" that the tactics of poli-tics require—a more cautious judgment must be made. It is the responsi-bility of the press not to be taken in by governmental officials. One must believe that the editors and publishers of the *New York Times* and the *New York Herald Tribune* were not duped, but convinced by high officials of the Kennedy administration, when they led the public acceptance of the President's decision to renew atmospheric nuclear testing in early 1962. On December 27, 1961, both these papers printed editorials deplor-ing the necessity (if the President should later proclaim such a necessity) of further pollution of the atmosphere by U.S. nuclear testing. On Febru-ary 28, 1962, James Reston, chief of the Washington bureau of the *Times,* made the same points; and on March 1, the self-fulfilling prophecy was fulfilled when *Times* correspondent E. W. Kenworthy reported that "Ken-nedy decides to renew atom tests in atmosphere: announcement is due in a few days." It is, as in this case, frequently unclear who leads and who follows when high governmental officials and the prestige press interact in making and enunciating policy.

Like all the great, abiding tensions that inhere in self-government, the conflict between the demands of secrecy and the right to know must be weighed anew with each decision and within the conscience and good judgment of each decision maker. We are committed to the maximum freedom of information; and when there is doubt, this conflict always ought to be resolved in favor of disclosure. A primary responsibility of the mass media, and particularly of the press, is to be what Thomas Jefferson called "the censor of the government"; though we should bear in mind the editorial admonition of the *Washington Post* (March 10, 1964) that: "As the area of freedom for public utterance, in our society, is great, so is the responsibility to use that freedom with care and discretion."

PART FIVE

DYNAMICS OF THE OPINION-POLICY PROCESS

In the first part of this book, we dealt with the problems of knowing what public opinion is and how it may be recognized—and, hopefully, how it may be measured with greater than guesswork accuracy. In the second part, we delineated some of the relationships between the opinions of publics and democratic systems of governance; we introduced the notion of an *opinion-policy process,* through which citizen interests, mediated by a variety of group and institutional interests, have influence on governmental policy and programs.

Part 3 dealt with the *environment* of public opinion —the cultural, social, and psychological forces that influence opinion formation, stability, and change. We made some distinction between *limiting* and *influencing factors,* and considered both the intrapersonal, or psychological, aspects of opinion formation and the effects of social organization. We adopted the *funnel of causality* to represent (although with severe limitations) the opinion-forming process in the individual.

In Part 4, we investigated opinion and communication networks, with primary-group relationships as the basic communication structures for the maintenance of psychological balance, ego identity, and cognitive meaning for the individual. (Many, probably most politically relevant opinions grow out of small-group relationships and those opinions that are not, so to speak, native born, but that arrive through mass channels and are quickly naturalized through mediation, conversion, partial incorporation, and other devices of reason and rationalization.) We examined the characteristic modes of operation and biases of mass-communications media for what that kind of exercise might tell us about why publics think as they do about policy matters.

In this, the final section, I propose to examine (a) the processes of opinion change, and (b) the interrelations of opinion change with political behavior and policy change.

Underneath public opinion lies private opinion. The expression of points of views on issues by significant numbers of persons—what we have called *public opinion*—is only possible if many individuals have preferences (however formed) that they are able and willing to make public (when they volunteer or are asked to do so). Therefore, although public opinion is a phenomenon of aggregate human behavior, our analysis of it cannot be adequate unless we have some understanding of how individuals make and remake their separate opinions. Daniel Katz has put the matter succinctly and clearly:

> The study of opinion formation and attitude change is basic to an understanding of the public opinion process even though it should not be equated with this process. The public opinion process is one phase of the influencing of collective decisions, and its investigation involves knowledge of channels of communiction, of the power structures of a society, of the character of mass media, of the relation between elites, factions, and masses, of the role of formal and informal leaders, of the institutionalized access to officials. But the raw material out of which public opinion develops is to be found in the attitudes of individuals, whether they be followers or leaders and whether these attitudes be at the general level of tendencies to conform to legitimate authority or majority opinion or at the specific level of favoring or opposing the particular aspects of the issue under consideration. The nature of the organization of attitudes within the personality and the processes which account for attitude change are thus critical areas for the understanding of the collective product known as public opinion.[1]

All this is old stuff; but it is repeated here because the relationship between private and public opinion is so fundamentally important. On this relationship depends the justification—indeed, the necessity—for our consideration of those processes in the individual that bring about new opinions and change old ones. But much more than understanding is involved, for the social fabric depends on individuals' being able to learn new attitudes, new opinions, and new behavior, and, in the process, to change and sometimes give up old attitudes, opinions, and behavior. Attitude, opinion, and behavior change is a cardinal fact for parents and

---

[1] "The Functional Approach to the Study of Attitudes," *Public Opinion Quarterly,* XXIX (1960), 163. Reprinted by permission.

teachers in the socialization of the child, and for special pleaders in the education or manipulation of individuals of every age.

Old opinions change, and new opinions are formed. But how? Under what circumstances, as a consequence of what forces, and with what political results? In the three chapters that follow, I raise some questions about how opinions change and about how these changes affect political life and public policy.

OPINION CHANGE: SOCIAL-PSYCHOLOGICAL PROCESSES

19

In this chapter, I will not ordinarily make a distinction between *attitude* and *opinion:* unless otherwise stated, each term may be substituted for the other. There are, of course, some dangers in this lack of discrimination; for *opinions,* we have agreed, are *sharpened attitudes* with more specific referents. Ordinarily, this is an important distinction; but in the consideration of the psychological processes of attitude and opinion change, we may generally ignore it—for simplicity's sake.

Opinions follow attitudes. An individual may hold conflicting and even contradictory attitudes and opinions; or an opinion may be influenced by many (complementary or conflicting) attitudes. Furthermore, individuals may falsify their expression of attitudes or opinions or both. Despite these sources of confusion and misunderstanding, our common sense tells us that a high general consistency must be maintained between a person's attitudes and his opinions—and, as we shall see, there is experimental and empirical evidence of such consistency.

19.1 The Study of Attitude and Opinion Change

Attitudes and the study of attitudes have been central to much of social psychology. In a historical survey, Allport says that

[attitude] is probably the most distinctive and indispensable concept in contemporary American social psychology. No other term appears more frequently in experimental and theoretical literature. Its popularity is not difficult to explain. It has come into favor, first of all, because it is not the property of any one psychological school of thought, and therefore serves admirably the purposes of eclectic writers. Furthermore, it is a concept which escapes the controversy concerning the relative influence of heredity and environment. Since an attitude may combine both instinct and habit in any proportion, it avoids the extreme commitments of both the instinct theory and environmentalism. The term likewise is elastic enough to apply either to the dispositions of single, isolated individuals or to broad patterns of culture (common attitudes). Psychologists and sociologists therefore find in it a meeting point for discussion and research. This useful, one might almost say peaceful, concept has been so widely adopted that it has virtually established itself as the keystone in the edifice of American social psychology.[1]

Generally speaking, the study of experimental psychology, of neurophysiology, and of comparative psychology was well advanced before any systematic attention was given to attitude *change*. Not until Pavlov's work on conditioned responses, and its popularization by Watson and other early behaviorists, was it clear that stimulus-response conceptualizations might be generalized to cover attitude change. If uniform stimuli produced more-or-less uniform responses in an organism, then it might be possible to isolate causal factors in attitudes and opinions, and to change attitudes and opinions by the selective manipulation of stimuli. It was a long road by way of laboratory and professional journals from Pavlov's crude stimulus-response formulation to Hullian learning theory, but it was only a short jump of the imagination from Pavlov's dogs to the education of children in Huxley's *Brave New World*.

Quite clearly, if one could control all the stimuli received at the integrative center of the human brain, one could control the attitude structure, personality, and behavior of the individual. Or, in terms of explanation rather than control, if we could identify the kinds and degrees of stimuli associated with the measured responses of an individual in a given set of circumstances, we would be able to say with a high degree of certainty why he behaved as he did. For prediction, we would have to have additional information based on patterns of usual behavior under similar circumstances.

Almost all study of attitude formation and change is based upon *stimulus-response theory*. Stimulus-response theory (or *S-R,* as it is often called) is, as Doob says, "the magic formula of most of modern psychology. . . . A stimulus is a change in the environment, including internal changes (like an accelerated heart beat), which affects the individual. A response is what the person actually does or does not perceive or do after being affected by the stimulus."[2]

The funnel-of-causality model that we introduced in Chapter 8, and have referred to a number of times later, is a simplistic device for demonstrating how opinions are formed over a period of time (short or long)

[1] Gordon W. Allport, "The Historical Background of Modern Social Psychology," in Gardner Lindzey, ed., *Handbook of Social Psychology* (Reading, Mass.: Addison-Wesley Publishing Co., Inc., 1954), I, 43. Reprinted by permission of Addison-Wesley Publishing Co., Inc.

[2] Leonard W. Doob, *Public Opinion and Propaganda* (New York: Holt, Rinehart and Winston, Inc., 1948), p. 14.

during which varied stimuli reach an individual who is (at the moment the analysis starts) uniquely the product of his physiological endowments and his past experiences. At the moment taken for the beginning of the analysis, an individual may be said to have certain attitudes and opinions, each of which is the product of earlier funnels of causality and each of which is more or less capable of being identified and measured. These are the *independent variables*—the factors that are given—and they may be described, in a shorthand that is often useful, as the *existing attitude structure*.

Our fictional Mr. Black of an earlier chapter, may be said to have had, as a part of his attitude structure when we introduced him, the following characteristics: (a) distrust of the Democratic Party, (b) a tendency to regard Republicans favorably, and (c) anti-Catholic feelings. Each of his attitudes may be thought of as a product of a funnel of causality that involved his earlier experiences and his personality needs. Each attitude is, in a sense, a long-lived response to various stimuli variously received, and his whole attitude structure is a *pattern* of his responses to various stimuli variously received.

Each attitude has two major aspects: (a) *cognitive;* and (b) *affective.*[3] The cognitive aspects of an attitude have to do with the intellect—they are descriptive and reasoned. The affective part of an attitude has to do with feelings, emotions, and values. My attitude toward dogs, for example, includes such cognitive aspects as animal, useful on farms, meat eaters, and capable of loud sounds; but it also includes such affective aspects as rambunctious, overly friendly, servile, and source of filth in cities. Cognitively, my attitude toward dogs squares pretty well with reality, insofar as reality is physical and testable; I know what a dog is. Affectively, my attitude is filled with subjective judgments and value preferences; I do not like dogs.

19.2   Models of Opinion and Attitude Change

As with so much else in modern psychology, Freud and his followers seem to have been the first psychological investigators to consider the possibilities—and to some extent the dynamics—of attitude change. Earlier, the study of psychology tended to be static, descriptive, and concerned with the nature of presumed "drives" such as egoism, or with the

---

[3] Meanings, as given by *Webster's Third New International Dictionary,* unabridged: *Cognition:* the act or process of knowing in the broadest sense; specifically, an intellectual process by which knowledge is gained about perceptions or ideas—distinguished from *affection* and *conation. Affect:* the conscious subjective aspect of an emotion considered apart from bodily changes.

pleasure-pain formulation. From the beginning, psychoanalysis had both the advantage and the disadvantage of being developed in the context of therapy and medicine. Freud's methodology, though very unscientific in many ways, had an empirical base; he dealt with real people who had real psychological problems. And, more important for the point being made here, his objective was to produce changes in attitudes and attitude structures (and in even deeper levels of the personality).

Unfortunately, the Freudian concern for attitude change is too limited and too narrow to meet the demands for generalization made in this book. The very features that moved the Freudians to concern themselves with attitude change—namely, a desire to reduce neurotic and psychotic conflicts in the individual—were also those that now limit the usefulness of Freudian conceptualization for the general study of attitude change. The attitudes of interest to psychoanalysts come about through conflicts of drives and training—conflicts that are unresolved but that in some way distort or repress emotions and, therefore, prevent satisfactory personal relationships. The Freudian concern for attitude change is therapeutic, the question being: How are unsatisfactory (i.e., dysfunctional) attitudes changed into satisfactory (functional) attitudes? For the study of political science, the lasting and valued contribution of psychoanalytic theory, especially as it has been brought to bear (in works such as *The Authoritarian Personality*) on the primary sociopolitical problem of our time, racial and ethnic prejudice, is that it demonstrates the direct policy implications of personality needs and identifies the psychological impediments to the realization of the democratic processes. For an understanding of how conflict-based attitudes agitate the human mind, prevent satisfactory interpersonal relations, and impede the peaceful resolution of social issues, Freudian thought is extremely helpful.

But the Freudians do not tell us the psychological *processes* by which attitudes are changed, nor even how such processes operate in psychoanalytic therapy. Thompson's statement of attitude change is essentially the same as that described in any problem solving: identification of problem, gathering of knowledge through trial and error, insight, and reintegration of meaning. "The test of the insight's validity," she says, "should be an effortless change of attitude."[4] This is all well and good—and helpful to the individual patients, if it works;[5] but it tells us nothing of general use about how attitudes change.

[4] Clara Thompson, *Psychoanalysis: Evolution and Development* (New York: Hermitage House, Inc., 1950), p. 240.

[5] Although it is not at all certain that psychoanalysis works any better than other forms of psychotherapy. See Bernard Berelson and Gary A. Steiner, *Human Behavior: An Inventory of Scientific Findings* (New York: Harcourt, Brace and World, Inc., 1964), p. 289.

There are two other and more general approaches to the study of opinion change: (a) *dissonance theory;* and (b) *functional theory.* We shall briefly describe each; but since the latter encompasses the former, the systematic statement of attitude change that follows the descriptions is in terms of a *functional* analysis.

Dissonance theory[6] is based on the proposition that the human organism needs and seeks a total configuration of beliefs, attitudes, and behavior that has (a) internal consistency and that (b) generally squares with the objective facts of the environment. Not all beliefs, attitudes, and behavior need to be regarded as rational, but rationality plays an important part in dissonance theory. The belief structure that is in balance, or in equilibrium, will reflect reason as well as irrational needs, the individual's state of knowledge or of ignorance, and a host of environmental factors of which cultural prescriptions and group pressures are among the most important.

If major perceived inconsistencies exist between the cognitive and affective aspects of an attitude, or between different attitudes, dissonance theory would predict some direct or indirect changes to bring the attitude or attitudes into greater consistency. For example, if our mythical Mr. Black finds himself in the presence of friendly, pleasant, likeable Catholics, he may sense the inconsistency between (a) what he observes as the facts of the moment (his *cognitions*) and (b) his general dislike (*negative affect*) for Catholics. Dissonance theory tells us that Mr. Black's attitudes (either the cognitive or the affective elements, or both) are apt to change under these conditions. It was, in fact, in studies of prejudice that some of the elements of dissonance theory were first brought to the attention of Festinger and others.[7] The basic, generalized proposition of the dis-

---

[6] I have adopted Festinger's use of the term *dissonance,* because I believe, with him, that the words *consistency* and *inconsistency* have some logical and evaluative connotations that social science should avoid as much as possible. But the adoption of his term should not mean that I find his formulation the most useful for students of public opinion and the opinion-policy process. As a matter of fact, Festinger's major statement provides inadequate attention to the affective elements of individual attitudes and to the nonrational capacities and devices to tolerate rational inconsistencies. See Leon Festinger, *A Theory of Cognitive Dissonance* (New York: Harper & Row, 1957). For a critical review of the work of Festinger and his students, see Natalia P. Chapanis and Alphonse Chapanis, "Cognitive Dissonance: Five Years Later," *Psychological Bulletin,* LXI (1964), 1–22.

[7] Those who wish to pursue the genealogy of ideas in the search for intellectual legitimacy or bastardy will find helpful the following comment from William J. McGuire, "A Syllogistic Analysis of Cognitive Relationships," in Milton J. Rosenberg et al., eds., *Attitude Organization and Change* (New Haven, Conn.: Yale University Press, 1960), pp. 65–66:

There have been a number of approaches to this modern version of the "rational man" concept. The earliest was probably Sumner's (1907) "strain of consistency,"

sonance theory of attitude change has been stated as follows:

> When the affective and cognitive components of an attitude are mutually consistent, the attitude is in a stable state; when the affective and cognitive components are mutually inconsistent (to a degree that exceeds the individual's present tolerance for such inconsistency), the attitude is in an unstable state and will undergo spontaneous reorganizing activity until such activity eventuates in either (1) the attainment of affective-cognitive consistency or (2) the placing of an "irreconcilable" inconsistency beyond the range of active awareness.[8]

The third, most general, and most integrating approach to the study of attitude dynamics is the *functional approach.* "The basic assumption . . . is that both attitude formation and attitude change must be understood in terms of the needs they serve and that as these motivational processes differ, so too will the conditions and techniques for attitude change."[9]

Katz has categorized the four major functions of attitudes as:

1. *The instrumental, adjustive, or utilitarian function:* "Essentially, this function is a recognition of the fact that people strive to maximize the rewards in their external environment and to minimize the penalties. . . . the dynamics of attitude formation with respect to the adjustment function are dependent upon present or post perceptions of the utility of the attitudinal object for the individual."

---

although present-day theories owe more to Heider's "tendency toward balance" [F. Heider, "Attitudes and Cognitive Organization," *Journal of Psychology,* XXI, 1946, 107–112]; the most complete statement of his position is to be found in his recent book [*The Psychology of Interpersonal Relations,* 1958]. Heider's line of descent may be separately traced to both Cartwright and Harary's "balanced structures" [D. Cartwright and F. Harary, "Structural Balance: A Generalization of Heider's Theory," *Psychological Review,* LXIII, 1956, 277–293] and to Abelson and Rosenberg's "balanced matrices" [R. P. Abelson and M. J. Rosenberg, "Symbolic Psycho-logic: A Model of Attitudinal Cognition," *Behavioral Science,* III, 1958, 1–13]. Closely allied to these is Newcomb's "stress toward symmetry" [T. M. Newcomb, "An Approach to the Study of Communicative Acts," *Psychological Review,* LX, 1953, 393–404]. While the "tendency toward increased congruity" postulated by Osgood and Tannenbaum [C. E. Osgood and P. H. Tannenbaum, "The Principle of Congruity in the Prediction of Attitude Change," *Psychological Review,* LXII, 1955, 42–55] may be less closely related to Heider's concepts, the behavioral implications of this postulated tendency are similar. A recent variant of the consistency point of view is Festinger's "cognitive dissonance" [see footnote 6]. All of the above approaches agree that there is a tendency for people to behave in ways which will maintain an internally consistent belief system. They differ, however, in their conceptions of consistency and the means by which it may be measured.

[8] Milton J. Rosenberg "An Analysis of Affective-Cognitive Consistency," in Rosenberg et al., *Attitude Organization and Change* (see footnote 7), p. 22.

[9] Daniel Katz, "The Functional Approach to the Study of Attitudes," *Public Opinion Quarterly,* XXIV (1960), 167. For much of what follows I am indebted to this thoughtful and illuminating essay by Katz. Quotations reprinted by permission.

2. *The knowledge function:* People, Katz says, "seek knowledge to give meaning to what would otherwise be an unorganized chaotic universe. People need standards or frames of reference for understanding their world, and attitudes help to supply such standards" by providing definiteness, distinction, consistency, and stability.

3. *The value-expressive function:* These attitudes "have the function of giving positive expression to [the individual's] central values and to the type of person he conceives himself to be." Such attitudes are in a sense the reciprocal of the ego-defensive attitudes; ego-defensive attitudes are designed to prevent damage to the self-image, whereas value-expressive attitudes enhance the self-image.

4. *The ego-defensive function:* The individual "protects himself from acknowledging the basic truths about himself or the harsh realities in his external world." Devices by which the individual defends his ego (his self-image) include those designed to avoid the dissonant elements entirely —denial, misinterpretation—and those, less incapacitating, which distort the dissonant elements—rationalization, projection, displacement.[10]

Although a great deal (perhaps most) of the attention given to attitudes and attitude change has been directed at understanding the way that attitudes contribute to the ego-defensive and value-expressive functions, it is likely that the utilitarian and knowledge functions are more important for the everyday life of the individual. This proposition is, doubtless, especially true for the *political* attitudes of the average American; the evidence is overwhelming that politics are not ego-related for most people —although we must bear in mind the relevance of *role* and *elite* factors. Most people do not construe public issues as capable of threatening or enhancing the self-image. The average citizen does not internalize political ideologies or controversies to the point where they matter at any other than the most superficial levels of consciousness. For political leaders, however, quite the reverse may be true; the ego-defensive and value-expressive functions may become so important that their satisfaction impedes the knowledge and utilitarian functions.

The process of opinion change, from the point of view of functional analysis, appears to operate somewhat as follows: the individual becomes aware of (perceives), ordinarily at the conscious level, a new stimulus (a *message,* in communication terms); if (a) the stimulus is seen as related to attitudes which serve one or more of the functions named above, and (b) the stimulus is internalized (cognitively or affectively or both) in such a way that dissonance is created in an existing attitude or attitudes, and (c) the dissonance is sufficiently disruptive, then (d) cognitive or affective

10 *Ibid.,* pp. 170–175.

(or both) aspects of the existing attitude or attitudes will be changed until the dissonance is reduced.

So stated, dissonance theory describes the process by which existing attitudes or attitude structures are changed, within a framework for explaining *why* attitudes are important (i.e., what attitudes do for the individual).

Smith, Bruner, and White, using a research framework quite similar to Katz's, suggest that functional analysis may be very helpful for an understanding of attitude and opinion change. Attitudes and opinion, these authors maintain, serve the following functions: (1) *object appraisal*, which is reality testing and is analogous, in part, to Katz's "knowledge" and "adjustment" and "value-expressive" functions; and (2) *externalization*, which includes part of Katz's "value-expressive" function and all of his "ego-defensive" function.[11] Smith, Bruner, and White sum up their research and insights in the following general statement of attitude and opinion change:

Why do attitudes change? . . . In no . . . instances can an answer be essayed simply in terms of a shift in the relation of the reality situation to personal interests and values, a change in social factors, or an alteration in the inner economy of personality. Each may be a precipitating factor, indeed the sole precipitating factor in attitude change. But the process of change involves a shift in the balance of all factors. Psychological comprehensiveness requires that all be taken into account.

Hypothetically, we can go farther than this in proposing a relationship between our threefold analysis and the conditions of change in opinions. People's attitudes on topics of public concern involve an admixture of the three sorts of determinants. But people presumably differ . . . in the extent to which one or another predominates in the basis for their opinions about a given topic. The thinking of people at large on various public issues may involve different weightings of the broadly realistic, social, and projective components, and these may differ on the same issue from one time to another. . . . These differences in the functional determination of opinions may be expected to have important consequences for the circumstances of their probable change.

To the extent that object appraisal predominates, the person tends to react rationally, according to his lights and according to the information at his disposal. In terms of this function, his interests and values stand to be advanced by flexibility on his part in assimilating the implication of new facts. Conventional educational campaigns rest heavily on the assumption that the attitudes to be affected are rooted primarily in object appraisal. The failure of some pro-

---

11 See M. Brewster Smith, Jerome S. Bruner, and Robert W. White, *Opinions and Personality* (New York: John Wiley & Sons, Inc., 1956), pp. 39–44. I use Katz's categories here, because the fine distinctions he makes between the knowledge, ultilitarian, and value-expressive functions seem to me to be more adaptable to political phenomena. But I would agree with Smith, Bruner, and White (as I am sure Katz would also) that "definitions are matters of convenience, and they attain high status only in the advanced stages of a science. In time, greater precision will come. In the meantime, we think that little is served by quarreling about definition in the abstract" (p. 34).

grams, for instance some attempts to reduce race prejudice by supplying information, can perhaps be attributed to mistakenness in this assumption.

To the extent that a person's attitudes are primarily rooted in his social adjustments, he is less oriented toward the facts than toward what others think. Probably the effective strategy for changing opinions serving this function is that of the propagandist who relies on "prestige suggestion"—creating the "impression of universality," drawing on testimonials, and discrediting the group support of opposing views. This strategy is often effective, but not always. It has been remarked that such techniques in the hands of the advertising man, while they may give competitive advantage to one product over equivalent ones, do not always transfer effectively to the "selling" of ideas. For opinions are imbedded in larger systems of value or belief that give them support, and one does not "change" a single opinion by invoking a reference group or figures of prestige without also providing the person with material for revised object appraisal.

To the extent that a person's attitudes serve to externalize inner problems, and are therefore embedded in his defenses against obscure and unresolved tensions, we may expect them to be rigid and not particularly amenable either to reason and fact or to simple social manipulation. Anything that increases his anxiety and sense of threat may be expected to heighten their rigidity. Reassurance and permissiveness are the conditions under which such attitudes are most accessible to change, while firm authority may supress one "symptom" in favor of another.[12]

It is clear from this statement of the process that opinion change will only take place if a number of conditions are met. Attitudes and opinions are remarkably stable—and necessarily so, for maintenance of the individual's mental health and for dependability in social interaction. Resistance to attitude change is ordinarily high; habit and stereotypical thinking satisfy most of the functional needs of most people; and messages may be quite easily distorted to fit into existing attitudes, thus eliminating the need for change.

As an example, we may consider a fictional Mr. Carter, a white voter in the delta country of Mississippi, who has a set of well-defined and strongly held attitudes toward Negroes. He regards Negroes as lazy, dirty, immoral, and of less native intellectual endowment than whites. This set of attitudes is one of long standing, having been created by the uncontradicted influence of parents, white peers, and social institutions during Mr. Carter's childhood and youth in the town where he was born and still lives. Nor has this set of attitudes ever been challenged by contradictory forces that Mr. Carter has had to take into serious consideration; although he knows there are others, outside of his circle of friends and acquaintances, who believe Negroes equal to whites in every way, such notions have never been of any significance to him.

One day Mr. Carter is told that a Negro minister is encouraging his congregation to register to vote. Whether this message has any meaning

---

[12] *Ibid.*, pp. 276–278. Reprinted by permission of John Wiley & Sons, Inc.

for his attitudes will depend on a number of factors: for example, the source and form of the message, how it is related to other attitudes or attitude structures, and what psychological devices he has for dealing with the message.

Mr. Carter's existing attitude structure is most easily protected if he does not believe the message about Negroes registering to vote. If the source of the message, the person who told him, is regarded as untrustworthy, it is easier to ignore the message completely;[13] in the absence of later, confirming information, Mr. Carter may simply not believe the message, and that will be the end of it—message disbelieved, no change.

But, if Mr. Carter thinks his source is credible, or if he has other messages supporting the initial one, he will no doubt believe that Negroes are, in fact, registering to vote or intending to register to vote. This is not an important message, however—even if he believes it—unless it is related to attitudes that serve one or more of the knowledge, utilitarian, ego-defensive, or value-expressive functions. This particular message is, no doubt, easily related to one or more (perhaps all) of these functions; and one would expect Mr. Carter to be in a state of dissonance from the moment he receives the message. He will probably relate the message to his understanding of the social structure of his community (if Negroes get the vote, they will want other evidences of equality, in education, public office, and so on), to his utilitarian needs (if Negroes improve their position in any way, they may compete with him and his white friends for jobs), to his ego-defensive needs (Negro men are said to be sexually more virile than whites), and to his value-expressive needs (as a Christian gentleman, one should be understanding and tolerant of Negroes, as long as they stay in their place).

Thus, the message may easily be related to important existing attitudes. Yet dissonance may be avoided or reduced if the message may be interpreted as insignificant or unthreatening. Mr. Carter may believe that the local Negroes are being stirred up by one or two home-grown or visiting agitators who will leave or become less militant, and that the Negroes do not really want to vote. Or he may believe that the Negroes will not be allowed to vote even if they do want to—that the white-dominated electoral machinery can be made resistant to Negro pressures. Or he may believe that only a few Negroes will register, not enough to make any difference in election outcomes. Or he may persuade himself that, even if Negroes vote, the other undesirable (from his point of view) social changes will not ensue. All of these and other forms of rationalization are possible; all allow Mr. Carter to interpret the message in such a

13 See, on this point, Carl I. Hovland and Walter Weiss, "The Influence of Source Credibility on Communication Effectiveness," *Public Opinion Quarterly*, XV (1951), 635–650.

way that it becomes less threatening to his existing attitudes, self-image, and values. With these devices, he may reduce the dissonance that the message would otherwise produce.

How Mr. Carter perceives and internalizes the message about Negro registration, and with what consequences for existing attitudes, will depend, as we have noted, on the source and form of the message and on how he interprets it. His general personality needs are also important, as are his impressions of how the message is interpreted by persons whose judgment he respects and whose goodwill he wishes to gain or keep. If Mr. Carter demonstrates a general rigidity in his thinking, if he has little tolerance for ambiguity, or if he shows other traits of the authoritarian personality, the message about Negro registration may be expected to be especially difficult for him to deal with. The authoritarian personality, according to Frenkel-Brunswik:

> displays both stereotypy and lack of differentiation—in short, an all-or-nothing approach. His opinions are "closed" and cannot be modified; new experiences are immediately viewed from the standpoint of the old set and are classified in the same way as the earlier ones.[14]

The inflexibility of the authoritarian personality is doubly disadvantageous for its adjustment to new stimuli. Any message not wholly consistent with existing attitude structures is disturbing because of its very strangeness, and the mental processes are too inflexible to develop new relationships, either by incorporation or association, between the incoming message and the older attitudes.

Rigidity of thinking and intolerance of ambiguity are often associated with a low evaluation of one's own abilities and a compensating high need to have one's opinions supported by experts or by a "gospel."[15] Thus the individual with a rigidly stereotypical mind will be disposed to harbor one-sided, simple, and unambiguous attitudes that resist change *unless* the source of the change-producing stimulus is thought by the individual to have special authority or competence. In short, if the

---

[14] Else Frenkel-Brunswik, "Interaction of Psychological and Sociological Factors in Political Behavior," *American Political Science Review*, XLVI (1952), 54.

[15] See Charles D. Farris, " 'Authoritarianism' as a Political Behavior Variable," *Journal of Politics*, XVIII (1956), 61–82; and Robert E. Agger, Marshall N. Goldstein, and Stanley A. Pearl, "Political Cynicism: Measurement and Meaning," *Journal of Politics*, XXIII (1961), 477–506. One study showed "persons of high self-esteem to be less susceptible to influence from persons of low self-esteem than vice versa" and that "individuals of high self-esteem were better able in general to protect themselves against unfavorable reactions from their social group and reacted less to any specific group expectations communicated to them"; but no uncontradicted relationships were found between persuasibility and other personality characteristics. See Carl I. Hovland, Irving L. Janis, and Harold H. Kelley, *Communication and Persuasion* (New Haven, Conn.: Yale University Press, 1953), pp. 230–231.

individual holds certain attitudes because of deep-seated feelings of insecurity and ineffectiveness, then (a) he is apt to hold these attitudes intensely and tenaciously; (b) they are apt to be simple and uncomplicated; (c) contradictory or modifying messages are apt to be regarded as threatening; (d) he will tend to reject or distort the threatening messages, in order to reduce the threat—unless (e) the source of the new messages is regarded as authoritative, in which case attitude change will take place.

If, as is likely to be the case, Mr. Carter's attitudes toward Negroes serve important ego-defensive and value-expressive functions, he is apt to hold simple but intensive attitudes that will be highly resistant to change unless the change-inducing stimulus is seen as being especially authoritative. Given the social structure and opinion leadership of Mississippi delta communities, it is doubtful that Mr. Carter's attitudes toward Negroes can be easily changed. Individuals and groups that are important to him, and serve to anchor his acceptance of what attitudes and opinions are authoritative, are likely to have strong anti-Negro attitudes similar to his own.[16]

If Mr. Carter's utilitarian and knowledge functions then, as well as his ego-defensive and value-expressive functions, are served by his simple, intense, and anti-Negro attitudes, (a) these attitudes will be highly resistant to change, and (b) one would not expect that opinions that have their bases in such attitudes would be easily changed in a pro-Negro direction. On the contrary, one would expect that the message about increased Negro militancy with regard to voting rights would *intensify* Mr. Carter's anti-Negro attitudes and simultaneously crystallize his negative opinions about the issue of Negro registration. Thus, any attitude or opinion change, under the conditions hypothesized here, would tend to change attitudes (if at all) only in their intensity, and opinions only in their specificity with regard to the registration issue. The message creates dissonance, (a) because it arouses utilitarian and knowledge conflicts, and (b) because it threatens ego-defensive and value-expressive needs; the dissonance is reduced only when Mr. Carter's anti-Negro attitudes are *increased*, and when he holds an even stronger opinion against the registration of Negroes.

Let us suppose, however, that Mr. Carter is not a native Mississippian, but that he was raised in Medford, Massachusetts, where he attended public schools and a college of racially and ethnically mixed students,

---

16 For an experimental study of the ways in which an individual's expressed attitude may be influenced by what he believes are his friends' opinions, see Raymond L. Gorden, "Interaction between Attitude and the Definition of the Situation in the Expression of Opinion," *American Sociological Review*, XVII (1952), 50–58. For a more general statement, see H. H. Kelley, "Salience of Membership and Resistance to Change of Group-Anchored Attitudes," *Human Relations*, VIII, No. 3 (1955), 275–289.

and then moved into a middle-income apartment house in New York City. He hears one day that a Negro family is moving into the apartment next door. Although he has associated with Negroes since childhood, he has never had any as friends and neighbors, and he is apprehensive, because most of those he has known have been poor dwellers in slums and blighted areas; he likes privacy, quiet, decorum, and cleanliness, and his casual experience has reinforced the stereotype that Negroes are noisy, indecorous, and untidy. So, he would prefer to have white neighbors.

But this Mr. Carter has been exposed to a different set of psychological and social influences from the Mississippian's. He believes that prejudice based upon physiology is immoral, destructive of the religious and democratic view that the human personality is the highest good, and he knows that the law in New York (which he supports in a general way) makes it a crime to discriminate against Negroes in a housing project supported or subsidized by state funds. Considering such cross pressures, we may predict that Mr. Carter's attitude about Negro housing will be in a state of imbalance, but that he will acquiesce in the new circumstances. We would also predict that he will experience new stimuli of relevance to the situation, with the likelihood that his attitude will change.

The second Mr. Carter's premessage attitude may have been positive toward Negroes living in Negro districts, and also positive toward equality of opportunity. Now, his attitude toward Negroes living next door is negative; but toward equality of opportunity he remains positive. His attitude structure is thus in an unbalanced state, and it can be balanced only by reducing the inconsistency—which means either a change in attitude toward Negroes living next door or a change in attitude toward equality of opportunity. Experimental and empirical field studies of racial bias indicate that reduction of anti-Negro prejudice usually (but not always) results from regular, day-to-day contact in a residential or work situation. White merchant seamen who had shipped with Negro crewmen were found to be much less prejudiced than those who had never worked with Negroes.[17] Another investigation found that white housewives in two integrated public housing projects had much more favorable attitudes toward Negroes, both cognitively and affectively, than did white housewives in two segregated housing projects.[18]

Rosenberg and Abelson speculate that the process of reducing attitude-structure imbalance occurs somewhat in this order: (1) a *"search for*

[17] Ira N. Brophy, "The Luxury of Anti-Negro Prejudice," *Public Opinion Quarterly,* IX (1946), 456–466.

[18] Morton Deutsch and Mary E. Collins, *Interracial Housing: A Psychological Evaluation of a Social Experiment* (Minneapolis: University of Minnesota Press, 1951).

balance-appropriate material"; (2) a *"reality test* of such material (does it 'make sense'? is it appropriate and realistic in context?)"; and (3) an *"application* of the material (attending to it, 'rehearsing' it) if it satisfies the reality test."[19] Applying this "microprocess" to the first Mr. Carter, we might find that he attributes the Negro registration to outside agitators (which is appropriate balance material); if there are or were outside integrationist leaders in his area, such an interpretation might pass the reality test; then he may easily apply this interpretation to reduce the dissonance in his attitude structure (when these outsiders go away, or are driven away, the local Negroes will stop their registration efforts). Similarly, the process may help to explain a possible reduction of dissonance in the attitude structure of the second Mr. Carter; he may believe that his new neighbor will be an educated, middle-class Negro (balance material); and if this turns out to be so (reality test), that fact, when incorporated into the cognitive elements of his attitude structure, reduces the dissonance.

It should be clear from the general statement of the problems in understanding opinion change, and from the examples given above, that the functional approach to the study of attitude and opinion change is directed primarily to the question of the uses the individual makes of attitudes and opinions, and of how change relates to these uses. The functional approach says, in effect, that attitudes serve needs of individuals, and that attitude change should be considered in terms of what change would mean for these needs. Dissonance theory (and other theories of attitude-structure imbalance) deals with the presumed psychodynamics of opinion change, both in terms of meaning (cognition) and emotion (affect). Highly oversimplified, we may say that functional theory is concerned with the *why* of opinion change, and dissonance theory with the *how* of opinion change. They are not, therefore, alternative or substitutable approaches; they are complementary, and they are applied in this chapter in a complementary way.

The process of attitude and opinion change of an individual in a social context is shown schematically in Figure 19–1. The change-promoting stimulus, or message, may be any fact or opinion that is perceived by the individual as related to but inconsistent with existing attitudes or attitude structures. Any perception that is recognized as inconsistent with existing attitudes, regardless of the intensity of the perception, may be thought of as a change-promoting stimulus—the question of intensity will be dealt with in a moment; it is sufficient here to have the stimulus recognized, no matter how mildly.

For analytical purposes, the whole stimulus situation may be quali-

---

[19] Milton J. Rosenberg and Robert P. Abelson, "An Analysis of Cognitive Balancing," in Rosenberg et al., *Attitude Organization and Change* (see footnote 7), pp. 159–160.

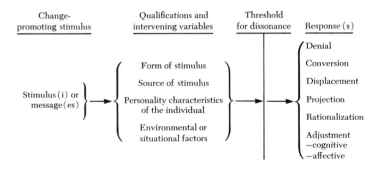

Figure 19–1. Stimulus-Response Formulation
for Attitude and Opinion Change

fied in terms of form, source, personality factors, and environmental conditions; these intervening variables must be taken into account for any satisfactory understanding of the process of attitude or opinion change. Stimuli which come in threat- or fear-arousing form may produce one kind of response, and less threatening or fearful forms may produce another kind.[20] Stimuli from trusted sources are more likely to change attitudes and opinions than are stimuli from untrusted sources.[21] Personality variables are mainly those having to do with the ego-defensive and value-expressive functions of attitudes and opinions. Messages related to significant personality needs of individuals are often dealt with in dysfunctional ways (denial, projection, rationalization), and are often exceedingly difficult to adjust into healthier and more realistic balance. Finally, the social context in which the change-promoting stimulus appears is highly significant for both the subjective responses made by the individual and for the overt expression or behavior it occasions.

The concept of *threshold for dissonance* is a necessary recognition that perceived change-promoting stimuli will not always produce responses. All persons are capable of withstanding some inconsistencies within attitudes and among related attitudes. Some people have very high tolerance for inconsistency. Attitudinal dissonance is a fact of life, a necessary part of realistic uncertainty, of trial-and-error living, of the scientific method, and, on the whole, of the adventure of human thought and feeling. "What is assumed," by dissonance theory, "is that for any

[20] Irving L. Janis and Seymour Feshback, "Effects of Fear-Arousing Communications," *Journal of Abnormal and Social Psychology*, XLVIII (1953), 78–92.

[21] Hovland and Weiss "Influence of Source Credibility" (see footnote 13). Although the major generalization of this study is as stated above, a much-noted subsidiary finding is that of the so-called "sleeper effect," namely, cognitive changes that result from messages given by untrusted sources when the source but not the message is forgotten.

particular attitude as held by any particular person there is some limit to the degree of inconsistency that he will be able to tolerate. If this limit, which may be conceived as an 'intolerance for inconsistency threshold,' is exceeded, the attitude will then be rendered unstable . . .".[22]

19.3   Effects of Attitude Change on Related Attitudes

The consideration of the threshold for dissonance leads to a related question—the final matter to be raised in this chapter—the question of the generalization of attitude change. A rational model of attitude change would lead one to expect that once changes had taken place in an attitude, related changes would take place in other attitudes. Theories of dissonance should (and do) suppose that the change or abandonment of one attitude will set up a chain of dissonance with other attitudes that are inconsistent with the change (or absence, or replacement) of the original attitude. Any change, in short, should not be confined solely to the changed attitude, but should bring about complementary changes in related beliefs and feelings.

Although, as Katz points out, "research evidence on the generalization of attitude change is meager . . . it is puzzling that attitude change seems to have slight generalization effects, when the evidence indicates considerable generalization in the organization of a person's beliefs and values."[23] Katz suggests three possible reasons for the apparently small amount of generalization of attitude change:

1. The over-all organization of attitudes and values in a personality is highly differentiated [and] the many dimensions allow the individual to absorb change without major modification of his attitudes.
2. The generalization of attitudes proceeds along lines of the individual's own psychological groupings more than along lines of conventional sociological cate-

22 Rosenberg and Abelson, "An Analysis of Cognitive Balancing" (see footnote 19), p. 22. Hovland and Rosenberg very appropriately ask whether experimental subjects, especially in a university setting, may not place a high value on rational consistency, whereas "in real life, people do not particularly value consistency . . . and . . . do not really strive to achieve or conserve it." "Summary and Further Theoretical Issues," in Rosenberg et al., *Attitude Organization and Change* (see footnote 7), p. 221. For an important review and summary of the research on ego involvement and social involvement in attitude change, especially as they relate to threshold for dissonance, see Carolyn W. Sherif, Muzafer Sherif, and Roger E. Nebergall, *Attitude and Attitude Change: The Social Judgment-Involvement Approach* (Philadelphia: W. B. Saunders Co., 1965).

23 Katz, "The Functional Approach" (see footnote 9), p. 199.

gories. [And therefore much of the generalization that exists escapes our analytical schemes and techniques.]

3. Generalization of attitude change is limited by the lack of systematic forces in the social environment to implement that change. Even when people are prepared to modify their behavior [and other attitudes] to a considerable extent they find themselves in situations which exert pressures to maintain old attitudes and habits.[24]

Herbert Kelman's distinction between compliance, identification, and internalization as three processes (or levels) of attitude change are related to the first of Katz's reasons why attitude change is not more generalized. Kelman's distinctions may provide a framework for speculation and research into the generalization of attitude change. *Compliance,* Kelman says, occurs "when an individual accepts influence because he hopes to achieve a favorable reaction from another person or group." *Identification* takes place when the individual "accepts influence because he wants to establish or maintain a satisfying self-defining relationship to another person or a group." *Internalization* involves the acceptance of influence "because the content of the induced behavior—the ideas and actions of which it is composed—is intrinsically rewarding . . . [and] congruent with his value system."[25] Implied in this differentiation, and in its theoretical elaboration—though not explicitly stated in the essay—is the notion that attitude generalization is least apt to accompany a response of compliance and most apt to accompany the internalization of attitude change. If, as Katz and others maintain, a person's belief structure shows high consistency and articulation, and if, as Kelman says, internalization of an attitude change involves the integration of the change into the whole belief system, then we would expect that the internalization of the change would have significant and perhaps far-reaching consequences for other attitudes anchored in the belief system. Such a widespread and interlocking change may take place, for example, in the cataclysmic reordering of attitudes and belief structures under conditions of religious or political conversion.

It might also be hypothesized that one's belief structure, and the attitudes closely associated with it, are of necessity so stable in the normal person that only minor attitude changes involving minimal repercussions will be internalized; if so, the consistency defenses of the belief system must be regarded as so strong that no change will be admitted if significant generalization would be necessary. This hypothesis, if true, may be a fourth explanation (added to the three given by Katz above) for the apparent lack of the generalization of attitude change.

[24] *Ibid.,* pp. 200–201.

[25] Herbert C. Kelman, "Compliance, Identification and Internalization: Three Processes of Attitude Change," *Journal of Conflict Resolution,* II (1958), 53.

Until such variables are more clearly understood, we can say only that, for whatever reasons, individuals show a remarkable ability to hold their attitudes and opinions discretely, tolerating a great deal of inconsistency and lack of integration. One cannot predict, on grounds of consistency, what may be the secondary effects of attitude change.

OPINION AND BEHAVIOR: CONSISTENCY AND CHANGE

20

People do not always say what they think. People do not always act as they believe. Difficult as it is to discover attitudes and opinions, it is even more difficult to know when behavior reflects attitudes and opinions. We are not concerned with the problems of sources, development, or measurement of attitudes, or even whether opinions are consistent with attitudes. Here we are raising questions concerning the possibility that attitudes and opinions, under some circumstances, may be quite inconsistent with behavior.

Opinion-behavior inconsistencies are a common fact of life. I may dislike getting out of bed in the morning to go to work; yet I do it. I may loathe one of my colleagues; yet I act decently and perhaps even pleasantly toward him. I may be bored completely at a party; yet I laugh and talk and appear to the hostess to be enjoying myself immensely. As Shakespeare says, "one may smile, and smile, and be a villain."

A single principle seems to govern opinion-behavior inconsistencies: Behavior will be inconsistent with opinions when, in the judgment of the behaver, the larger context of the situation requires inconsistency. For example, I would prefer not having to get out of bed to go to work in the morning; but, even more, I prefer keeping my job. My second and stronger attitude prevails over my first and weaker attitude, although the behavior remains inconsistent with my first attitude. Likewise, my opinion of my colleague is that he is disagreeable, weak, and dull; but I am also of the opinion that the work relationship requires me frequently to act as though I believed him to be pleasant, strong, and interesting. My behavior is inconsistent with one opinion, completely consistent with the other.

But the matter of opinion-behavior discrepancies is hardly ended by the simple statement that inconsistencies exist when the individual believes that the context requires inconsistency (or, in other words, that larger consistencies require smaller inconsistencies). For then the relevant questions only become: What kinds of "larger contexts" require inconsistency and what kinds allow consistency? What devices (avoidance, lies, rationalization) are used, and under what circumstances, when inconsistency seems to be necessary? What kinds of changes (if any) occur in attitudes and opinions when behavior is inconsistent with them?

20.1   Opinion and Behavior: Convergences and Divergences

There are several reasons why people may say what they do not believe:

(a) they do not know what they believe and feel required to say something (we have already considered this matter, in part, under the "don't know" problem in Chapter 4);
(b) they are unable to express what they believe (that is, their ability with language is too limited to express their opinions accurately); or
(c) they are unwilling to say what they believe.

To the extent that persons say what they do not believe, verbal behavior is inconsistent with opinion. Nonverbal behavior may be inconsistent in the same way, because the individual may be unable or unwilling to act consonantly with his opinions.

The survey-research question is one that imposes a second step of consistency or inconsistency in the opinion-behavior dilemma. From the point of view of the opinion researcher, the problem is usually more complex even than the relation of thought to action. The researcher is hardly ever in a position to hear the unprompted expression of opinion at the same time (or in close proximity to) the behavior that is related to the opinion. The measurement task is not ordinarily a matter of observing spontaneous opinion expression and its manifestation in behavior (which may be then judged to be consistent or inconsistent). Rather, the usual case is for the measurement to be in terms of what persons say, in response to a question that is not their own and at a time of someone else's choosing, about what they think and do.

There is, no doubt, a tendency to consistency in the three elements of the complex involving (a) private opinions, (b) verbal expressions, (c) overt behavior. John Dollard believes that opinions, when voiced either spontaneously or in answer to queries, are expressions of "anticipatory" or "forecasting responses"—that is, they give clues to what the respondent believes he would do when faced with choices involving the substance of the question. The clearest political illustration is the answer to the question "Which candidate do you favor?" for the question implies the behavior component; namely, in whose behalf do you intend to act (vote)? Though the opinion poll of candidate preference is the most obvious example of the argument that voiced opinions are anticipatory responses, most survey answers can be thought of as forecasts of behavior; questions about political ideology, policy issues, or political actors may be considered questions about what the respondent would *do* if choices were necessary. If one thinks about the problem in this way, as Dollard suggests, the question of consistency between opinion and behavior becomes one of how well the individual can predict his future behavior at the time that he has to make a statement about it (that is, at the time he expresses his opinion). Dollard makes some useful and unsophisticated generalizations about the psychological and sociological conditions under which opinions and behavior will be consistent:

1. Neurotics will find it difficult to predict their behavior when their own serious conflicts are involved.
2. Persons with poor verbal skills may find it difficult to forecast their own behavior.
3. People who habitually go into effective action after thinking things over can best predict their own actions.
4. The test situation should not be corrupted by extraneous threats or rewards.
5. A man can best predict what he will do in a future situation if he has been in about the same situation before and thus knows what it's all about.
6. A man can predict what he will do in a future situation provided he doesn't have an experience which changes his mind before this situation occurs.
7. A man can better predict what he will do in a future dilemma if he is told exactly what this dilemma will be.[1]

20.2   Opinion Stability and Resistance to Change

Aside from traumatic conversions of the religious variety—and perhaps not even so dramatically as is alleged in these cases—sudden changes in attitude and opinion probably do not often occur. It is probable, too, that the more intensely an opinion is held, the less likely it is to change

---

[1] John Dollard, "Under What Conditions Do Opinions Predict Behavior?" *Public Opinion Quarterly*, XII (1948–1949), 628–632. These are what Dollard calls "common-sense statements"; he rephrases them into social science jargon, but without any increase in clarity or specificity—a nice example of the vernacular's superiority over the affected language of the "expert."

quickly; and the more solidly an opinion is based on knowledge, facts, reason, and common sense, the less likely it is to change quickly or profoundly. It is also true that, regardless of their factual or rational bases, opinions that are important to the personality of the holder are more resistant to change. Opinions are harder to change if they have been expressed publicly and are known by other persons who are important to the opinion holder. Finally, when change is required, there is a strong tendency to make the least change possible.[2]

It should not be thought that behavior changes follow chronologically, any more than logically, after opinion change. In many instances, opinions change, if at all, only *after* related behavior changes. As Berelson and Steiner point out:

Behavior, being visible, is more responsive to extreme pressures and accommodations. OABs [opinions, attitudes, and beliefs], being private until expressed, can be maintained without even being subject to question or argument. And there is no necessary reason for OABs and behavior to be in harmony.[3]

Opinion change is apt to follow behavior change if the behavior is repeated, if it is approved by one's reference groups, and if it is sanctioned by the social environment generally. Under extreme conditions of deprivation, psychological, physical, or both, when support for pre-existing opinion is removed and contrary behavior is forced or strongly urged, very large shifts in attitudes and opinions may occur. The identification of Jewish concentration-camp victims with their captors, and the defection

[2] Experimental evidence may be found for the above statements. For a useful summary of studies before 1954, see Carl I. Hovland, "Effects of the Mass Media of Communication," in G. Lindzey, ed., *Handbook of Social Psychology* (Reading, Mass.: Addison-Wesley Publishing Co., Inc., 1954), pp. 1062–1103, especially pp. 1086–1088. More recent studies include: D. Katz, C. McClintock, and I. Sarnoff, "The Measurement of Ego-Defense as Related to Attitude Change," *Journal of Personality*, XXV (1957), 465–474; M. Deutsch and H. B. Gerard, "A Study of the Normative and Informational Social Influences upon Individual Judgment," *Journal of Abnormal and Social Psychology*, LI (1955), 629–636; S. Fisher, I. Rubinstein, and R. W. Freeman, "Intertrial Effects of Immediate Self-Committal in a Continuous Social Influence Situation," *Journal of Abnormal and Social Psychology*, LII (1956), 200–207; Milton J. Rosenberg and Robert P. Abelson, "An Analysis of Cognitive Balancing," in M. J. Rosenberg et al., eds., *Attitude Organization and Change* (New Haven, Conn.: Yale University Press, 1960), pp. 112–145. Survey evidence is also abundant; see, for example, E. Jackson Baur, "Opinion Change in a Public Controversy," *Public Opinion Quarterly*, XXVI (1962), 212–226; Angus Campbell et al., *The American Voter* (New York: John Wiley & Sons, Inc., 1960), pp. 256–265; and Philip E. Converse, "Information Flow and the Stability of Partisan Attitudes," *Public Opinion Quarterly*, XXVI (1962), 578–599.

[3] Bernard Berelson and Gary A. Steiner, *Human Behavior: An Inventory of Scientific Findings* (New York: Harcourt, Brace and World, Inc., 1964), p. 576, the same page on which the authors quote from Raymond A. Bauer and Alice H. Bauer, "America, Mass Society and Mass Media," *Journal of Social Issues*, XVI (1960), 30–31.

of American soldiers to Chinese Communist "brainwashing" are celebrated examples of such extreme opinion shift following, or concurrent
with, behavior changes.[4]

20.21   Opinion Change among Political Elites

On all these criteria, opinion leaders, more than opinion followers or
"ordinary citizens," are apt to have atttitudes and opinions which are
stable and resistant to change. Political leaders are shown to care more
intensely about the ends and means of public policy and to hold their
opinions more firmly, with greater articulateness and self-consciousness,
and with greater persistence.[5] Given these anchorages to reality, and to
their own personality and social needs, it is not surprising that the opinions of political leaders are least susceptible to whim and to the chance
effects of random information or propaganda stimulation.

On the other hand, precisely because the views of opinion leaders
are tied to reality and are more self-consciously held than those of the
followers, significant changes in the environment of such leaders are apt
to be evaluated more accurately and quickly by them, and are thus more
apt to lead to appropriate changes. Rationality is more apt to characterize
the opinion-change processes of opinion leaders. The collection and
evaluation of relevant information, along with increased use of discussion
and consultative devices, are likely to accompany opinion changes among
social and political elites. Theoretical models that emphasize cognitive
dissonance will be more useful in the explanation of elite opinion change
than they will be in the explanation of nonelite change. In sum, among
political leaders (by contrast with nonleaders), opinion change is apt to
be less volatile, more deliberate, more informed by social fact and trends,
and more predictable; and at the same time (in a free society), more
gradual and incremental in its pace and scope.

[4] The Jews who identified with their Nazi guards and the soldiers who "confessed" and
defected to the Chinese Communists were few and were extremely deviant cases; see
Bruno Bettelheim, "Individual and Mass Behavior in Extreme Situations," in Eleanor
E. Maccoby et al., *Readings in Social Psychology* (New York: Holt, Rinehart and
Winston, Inc., 1958), pp. 300–310; and, for a balanced assessment of the practices of
Communist brainwashers, see Albert D. Biderman, "The Image of 'Brainwashing,'"
Public Opinion Quarterly, XXVI (1962), 547–563.

[5] Herbert McClosky, Paul J. Hoffman, and Rosemary O'Hara, "Issue Conflict and
Consensus among Party Leaders and Followers," *American Political Science Review*,
LIV (1960), 406–427; Robert S. Hirschfield, Bert E. Swanson, and Blanche D. Blank,
"A Profile of Political Activists in Manhattan," *The Western Political Quarterly*, XV
(1962), 489–506; and Herbert McClosky, "Consensus and Ideology in American Politics,"
American Political Science Review, LVIII (1964), 361–382.

Even in the most celebrated cases of elite opinion change, there is reason to believe that the change processes are longer in germination and less dramatic in scope than the publicity of announcement would suggest. In January of 1945, Michigan's Senator Arthur H. Vandenberg, who was the most influential Republican foreign-policy leader in the U.S. Senate, made a famous speech in which he declared his support for the United Nations and, in general, for active participation by the United States in world affairs. The speech was widely thought to mark a sudden break with Vandenberg's past views, which had been strongly noninterventionist, even isolationist. Yet Vandenberg himself did not regard this speech as being an about-face; his son and biographer said that the speech

was generally (although mistakenly) regarded as a great turning point in the Senator's attitude. . . .

He fully realized that he was going to make an important proposal, but he had little idea, as he admitted later, that he was "taking off" into a new era, or perhaps more correctly that this speech would be regarded as the point at which he definitely abandoned forever the last vestige of the isolationism with which the public still associated him.[6]

The Senator's son (and then administrative aide) described his father's condition for many months before the January 10, 1945, speech as one of "soul searching," and as that of a man who had come to an "acceptance of certain realities regarding foreign policy," and who gradually, between 1941 and 1944, "had fully accepted in his own mind the extensive future role of the United States in international affairs."[7]

Vandenberg's acceptance of internationalism, besides being less dramatic and sudden than it was said to be, illustrates the importance of rationality and reality for opinion leaders. The historic posture of nineteenth-century America, that of aloofness from the affairs of Europe, Asia, and Africa, was finally seen as inconsistent with the actual condition of the United States in 1944 and 1945. The dissonance between Vandenberg's perception of international reality and Vandenberg's former isolationist views was too great; change had to occur in his opinions.

The Vandenberg case illustrates another difference between elites and nonelites in opinion change. The very fact of leadership positions is both cause and consequence of the leaders' greater ability to sense the needs of self and others, and the social ramifications of their own behavior. The Senator was very conscious of his role as a Republican leader and, as he remarked in a letter written while he was working on his famous speech,

---

6 Arthur H. Vandenberg, Jr., ed., *The Private Papers of Senator Vandenberg* (Boston: Houghton Mifflin Co., 1952), p. 131.

7 *Ibid.*, p. 125. "The whole world changed . . . with World War II, and I changed with them," Vandenberg later wrote (p. 139).

he was worried that the Republican Party would not change its policies consistently with the changing political world. His party, he said, had "to be far more realistic about the 'social revolution' which has swept the entire world (and to which we cannot expect to be immune) than we were when last we were in power."[8] The forces which impelled him to opinion change were thus not only his reality testing as an individual, and the cognitive dissonance he found between his old image of the world and his new one, but also his notion of what was expected of him as a leader of his party. Afterward, he wrote: "It seemed to me that it had to be a Republican voice from the then minority benches which had to undertake this assignment. This, in turn, narrowed the responsibility to a point where I felt it was a personal challenge to me."[9]

Finally, the Vandenberg example illustrates the point that minimum rather than maximum change occurs even in the most dramatic cases. His son points out that the Senator "did not record much about the January 10th speech at the time, except to express his surprise at the reaction to it. 'I still don't understand what clicked so terrifically,' he wrote his wife late in January."[10] The public response may be thought of not so much as a reaction to Vandenberg's change, perhaps, as an indication that he had properly assessed his leadership role in articulating the latent or incompletely expressed attitude and opinion changes of many prewar isolationists during the war years. In any event, Vandenberg's opinion change was no more extensive than it needed to be; he remained a conservative, an American nationalist and patriot, and a staunch leader of the opposition party in all ways that were consistent with his new belief in a bipartisan foreign policy.[11]

20.22   Nonelite Opinion Change

We have repeatedly pointed out that for most people political questions are not important. Politics and public issues play only small and episodic parts in the lives and thoughts of most individuals. This low

8 *Ibid.*, p. 129.

9 *Ibid.*, p. 130.

10 *Ibid.*, p. 144.

11 Another, if less dramatic, illustration of elite opinion and behavior change may be found in Senator Everett McKinley Dirksen's (R., Ill.) championship of the civil-rights bill of 1964. Before that year, Senator Dirksen's record was one of opposition to extensive Federal intervention in civil-rights matters. When questioned on his change of mind, he argued that social and political events (his reality testing) and his leadership responsibilities (his self-image) were responsible for his behavior change; quoting Victor Hugo, he declared that "nothing is more powerful than an idea whose time has come." *New York Times*, May 18, 1964.

salience has great significance for opinion-behavior consistency and inconsistency. If people have little motivation, little knowledge, and few occasions to experience relevant stimuli, they will display a great range of attitudes, opinions, and verbal behavior, often logically and politically inconsistent.

McPhee, Anderson, and Milholland have described the way political opinions are held by nonelites, and the way these opinions change under varying social conditions.[12] When ordinary people are asked for political opinions, what emerges is a hodge-podge (almost) of independent and often inconsistent statements of opinion:

> The person has an observable opinion only when he is prompted to react, for example, by a dinner party, interview, or whatever. Thereafter, "out of sight, out of mind," that is, he soon forgets these casual responses. . . . [W]hen some months later he is again prompted to respond on this topic, it is a *new* response independent of the first . . . If another opinion on a related topic was also elicited at the first time, it is not only independent of the first opinion . . . but independent "of itself" when a new version of it is given at some second time a month or two later. No "dynamic interactions" could have gone on between the two topical opinions meanwhile, for neither really existed in the interim as a continuous entity. No more than, if we observe a man tipping his hat to a lady on two occasions a month apart, we assume he held his hat that way all month as one continuous response.[13]

The authors of this essay persuasively argue that two or more expressed opinions, given casually and in an off-hand manner by a person who has little interest in the subject, probably will be independent of each other, and may be logically inconsistent. Such opinions may be related in some loose way to larger, more general, attitudes; but unless these relationships become recognized by the individual, no inconsistencies will be felt and there will be no tendencies to bring the disparate opinions together for comparison or change to greater consistency. If, later, the same question is answered a different way, this does not mean that change has occurred, but merely that the earlier question and answer, being unimportant, were not remembered. In such cases, analytical theories like Festinger's notions of cognitive dissonance are inappropriate; only when attitudes and opinions are important to him will the individual care whether they are consistent with one another.

When giving their opinions, people have both internal and external

---

12 William N. McPhee, Bo Anderson, and Harry Milholland, "Attitude Consistency," in William N. McPhee and William A. Glaser, *Public Opinion and Congressional Elections* (New York: The Free Press of Glencoe, 1962), pp. 78–120. Unfortunately, this article is very poorly written and cannot be recommended to any except advanced students who have a high capacity for puzzle solving and a high toleration for jargon, bad English prose, and superfluous mathematics.

13 *Ibid.,* p. 91. Copyright 1962. Reprinted by permission of The Macmillan Company.

reasons for consistency or inconsistency. Such reasons, as McPhee, Anderson, and Milholland point out, have to do with underlying dispositions and with the momentary importance attached to the matter at the time the opinion is given. The underlying, or "motivational," variables that were assumed by these authors to be significant for their study were (a) *partisanship* (the tendency to adopt or hold beliefs consistent with the general policy of the respondent's party), and (b) *environment* (community support for or against the party's general policy). The importance attached to the issue at the moment of response was measured by internal and external "attention" variables: (a) *interest* (the person's own ranking of interest from "a great deal" to "none"); and (b) *salience* (the person's evaluation of how much the community cared about the issue). When a person has high internal motivation and high interest, opinions are most apt to be consistent and change is least apt to occur. This is the general case of the opinion elites. If, in addition to high internal motivation and interest, there is strong environmental support for consistent opinions, and if the community is seen to regard the issue as a matter of importance, then there will be the highest consistency and least change of opinion over time.

Conversely, when persons have little internal motivation and interest, and when the environment is seen as being both unsupportive and uninterested, then there will be greatest inconsistency and most apparent change over time. This is the general case of the apathetic person who, instead of giving the more honest answer of "don't know" or "don't care," gives casual answers to questions about public issues.

The probability of a person's having opinions consistent with one another and, at the same time, behavior consistent with the opinion sets that are relevant will then be a function of the person's interest and knowledge as well as his estimation of how important the matter is to others with whom he identifies. Consequently, change toward greater internal consistency of opinion sets and opinion-behavior pairings will depend upon increase in internal motivations (interest and knowledge) or increase in environmental motivations (perceptions of importance to others). Internal and environmental motivations are obviously tied together; those most informed and interested are better able to judge the modal opinions of groups important to them (although even the best informed often seriously misjudge the opinions of others).[14]

Among the several practical applications of this way of conceptualizing opinion and behavior consistency is the meaning it gives to political campaigns. As McPhee, Anderson, and Milholland point out, campaigns

---

[14] Warren Breed and Thomas Ktsanes, "Pluralistic Ignorance in the Process of Opinion Formation," *Public Opinion Quarterly*, XXV (1961), 382–392.

increase the environmental motivations, making issues and political opinions temporarily more salient and allowing persons whose opinions and behavior are idiosyncratically inconsistent to learn what the "party line" and what majority or peer-group sentiment may be, or to ponder the issues more carefully, and thus to increase consistency, rationality, and predictable behavior. Their summary statement[15] of the relations between consistency and motivation (internal and external)—a statement which has meaning for mass media and political leadership generally, as well as for campaigns—may be paraphrased as follows:

> In the longer run, the learning and holding of inconsistent opinions and inconsistent behavior patterns is less likely if the individual has stronger, rather than weaker, internal motivations and is surrounded by others similarly motivated. In the shorter run, changes of opinion and behavior in the direction of greater consistency seem to be a result of increasing the individual's attention to the topic.
>
> In the absence of *public* attention to a matter, *private* opinions show a great range of scope and contradiction. When a matter commands greater public attention, private opinions narrow in range and become less inconsistent. Inattentive people, when asked to give opinions, show large dispersions or much idiosyncratic response; attentive people show narrow dispersions and response which is more environmentally oriented and more clearly based on the logical consistencies of social reality.

20.3 The Functional Uses of Opinion and the Processes of Opinion-Behavior Change

In the previous chapter, we considered the various functions which attitudes and opinions serve for individuals. These may be categorized as the knowledge, utilitarian, value-expressive, and ego-defensive functions (listed roughly in order from the most superficial to the deepest levels of meaning for the personality). Consistency or inconsistency of opinions and behavior will depend in part on the functions which opinions serve. If an opinion serves only a knowledge or utilitarian purpose, it will be more susceptible to the "drive to consistency" and will be more consistent with related or socially "appropriate" behavior than if it serves value-expressive or ego-defensive functions.

Katz suggests a number of conditions under which change could be expected in attitudes and opinions serving one or more of these four functions. His categories of change conditions may be integrated with a

---

[15] McPhee, Anderson, and Milholland, "Attitude Consistency" (see footnote 12), pp. 102–111.

conceptualization of opinion change developed by Herbert C. Kelman. As we have seen (p. 336), Kelman distinguishes three processes of opinion change: *compliance, identification,* and *internalization:*

> *Compliance* can be said to occur when an individual accepts influence from another person or from a group because he hopes to achieve a favorable reaction from the other.
> *Identification* can be said to occur when an individual adopts behavior derived from another person or group, because this behavior is associated with a satisfying self-defining relationship to this person or group.
> *Internalization* can be said to occur when an individual accepts influence, because the induced behavior is congruent with his value system.[16]

What happens, in terms of functions and processes, when individuals are under pressure to change opinions or behavior—that is, when change-provoking stimuli are perceived? Whether such persons change opinions or behavior will depend on why they hold the opinions they do, how important these existing opinons are to them, and what techniques are available to hold or change them. Opinions held for knowledge or utilitarian reasons are apt to be changed easily when the stimulations for change include increased or more accurate knowledge, or if adjustment (the utilitarian function) is facilitated by discarding the old and adopting the new opinions or behavior. Opinions held for value-expressive or ego-defensive reasons will not be changed so easily, despite whatever components of reason, knowledge, or utility may accompany the arguments for change; in such situations, the familiar psychological processes of denial, conversion, and rationalization may occur.[17]

Let me suggest how these elements might appear in political life, using a recent example of elite behavior. In the civil-rights debate of 1964, Democratic senators were asked by the Johnson administration to support a bill to guarantee greater political and social equality for Negroes. Those who opposed the bill did so for a variety of reasons: some out of racial prejudice, some for reasons of constitutional interpretation, some because they did not believe that, on balance, the legislation would achieve the goals sought. Some might be inclined to change their

---

[16] Herbert C. Kelman, "Processes of Opinion Change," *Public Opinion Quarterly,* XXV (1961), 62–65.

[17] Denial is a form of psychological evasion, which, as the name implies, allows the individual to refuse to believe in the existence of the change-promoting stimulus. Conversion is the process by which a threatening stimulus is made into an unthreatening stimulus by distortion or complete change of character. Rationalization is the finding of acceptable explanations for opinions or behavior the individual believes he must justify. See Robert P. Abelson, "Modes of Resolution of Belief Dilemmas," *Conflict Resolution,* III (1959), 343–352.

Table 20–1. *Hypothesized Change Probabilities for Senators Opposed to Bill Sponsored by Own Administration When under Pressure from Administration to Vote for the Bill*

FUNCTIONS SERVED BY EXISTING OPINION	PROCESSES OF CHANGE		
	COMPLIANCE	IDENTIFICATION	INTERNALIZATION*
KNOWLEDGE	High probability of change, if administration arguments are informative and logical	High probability of change, if administration's arguments show why senators should accept its interpretation of the "facts of the case"	
UTILITARIAN	High probability of change, if administration arguments show advantages to senators (i.e., logrolling, etc.)	High probability of change, if administration arguments show why a pro-administration vote will be beneficial to mutual interests (such as party)	
VALUE-EXPRESSIVE	Moderate probability of change, if rationalizations made easier for senators	Moderate to low probability of change, depending on administration's demonstration that common values are best served by change of opinion or behavior of senators	Low probability of change, depending on a fundamental reordering of belief structure (not likely to occur quickly or through political argumentation)
EGO-DEFENSIVE	Moderate to low probability of change, if rationalizations are made easier for senators	Moderate to low probability of change, depending on senators' obtaining greater ego satisfaction out of alliance with administration than from retaining existing opinions	Low probability of change, depending on its becoming more satisfying of ego needs than retention of existing opinion

* If I understand Katz and Kelman correctly, value-expressive and ego-defensive functions, which depend on deep-lying personality needs, are internalized; but opinions held for knowledge and adjustment, being relatively superficial and unimportant to the personality, are not internalized. The concepts of value-expressive and ego-defensive functions, and of internalization, are heavily indebted to psychoanalytic theory; see for example, Irving Sarnoff, "Psychoanalytic Theory and Social Attitudes," *Public Opinion Quarterly*, XXIV (1960), 251–279.

opinions (or at least deliver their votes) by what Kelman describes as the process of *compliance;* such a course might be expected from senators who oppose the bill on utilitarian grounds, but be less likely if their opposition were based on value-expressive or ego-defensive needs. Some senators might be inclined to change their opinion on the bill through the process Kelman calls *identification.* Thus, they might believe that loyalty to the Johnson administration, or to Democratic Party leadership, required them to overcome their opposition to the bill. Here again, change through the identification process would occur more easily in cases where the opposition opinions served knowledge or utilitarian functions rather than value-expressive or ego-defensive functions. Senators who were prosegregationist in principle, for reasons having to do with their self-image or ego needs, would not easily have their opinions or behavior changed by appeals to secondary-group ties such as those of party loyalty or leadership. The administration and party strategy, of course, was one of strengthening their identification with reluctant senators, but their chances of success were small with senators whose personality needs were met in part by segregationist views. Finally, opinion or behavior change through the process of *internalization* was not to be expected from senators who opposed the bill. In short, opponents of the bill might come to support the bill through the processes of compliance or identification, but probably only if their opposition was originally based on reasons that did not involve their self-images or their egos.

Functional uses of opinions and change processes are summed up, in an admittedly impressionistic way, in Table 20–1, which is generalized to situations of administrative attempts to change opinions or behavior of senators of the President's party.

OPINION CHANGE AND POLICY CHANGE

Opinions matter for policy. The reason is simple: Opinions are usually reflected in votes; and, in a democracy, votes—if ever so indirectly—make policy.

Whatever science there is in government is the science of probabilities—of the probabilities that those who participate in government, however much or little, from the President to the once-in-a-lifetime voter, will behave in predictable ways. All analyses of political relationships rest on such probabilities. For policies and administrative ways which are long settled, and to which the power network of the society is well adjusted, the probabilities of predictable behavior are very high. In the 1960s, support for the U.S. social-security system is very high, and policy makers in Washington can rely on the routine compliance of 99 per cent or more of those involved. In the middle 1930s, that was not the case, however; the opinions of those involved were then so sharply polarized that the probability of obtaining the agreement was perhaps no greater than 60 per cent.

Now, it may be objected that when a policy is at the legislative stage, as the social-security system was in 1935, the probabilities of agreement will be smaller than later, when the policy has been adopted and has proven successful. Precisely. This is the difference between a policy when it is a proposal and a policy when it is a program. At one time in the history of the U.S. it was literally unthinkable that the federal government should establish a nation-wide system of pensions for workers in private industry. At least until the beginning of the twentieth century, this was an idea that could not have been seriously put forward in the political arena—and I do not think that it was even dreamed of in American political philosophy. The probability of agreement to such an idea was nil, or close to it. From 1900 to 1935, the notion of a national old-age pension system grew from an idea to a proposal, and, at length, to a proposal that commanded enough attention both in governmental and non-governmental circles that it became a bill in Congress. Given such notice, the elite and mass opinions on the subject rapidly increased in number, intensity, and polarization. Then, in the time of decision, the legislators, with ears to the ground and to the White House and to their fellow legislators' words, testing probabilities and consciences as they deliberated to a vote, passed the measure. No one knows whether a majority of the people—or a majority of the *important* people (whoever they are)— favored the Social Security Act of 1935. In the nature of representative government, such knowledge is unattainable. We know that a majority— indeed a large majority—of the U.S. Congress favored the bill and must have believed that it was not only sound policy, but one that the American people, on the whole, would support. As it turned out, they were right—if that is what they thought. Considerable opposition remained for several years after the passage of the act, but noncompliant behavior was quickly tested and discouraged, and American business found that it could live and prosper. Support for the policy has grown and, though some political extremists would abolish the social-security system, it seems likely that 90 per cent or more of the American people favor the policy. In other words, the probability of support is extremely high.[1]

21.1   Ideas, Opinions, and Policies

Perhaps one can generalize the interdependence of opinions and the political process, as public policies evolve from private thoughts. In Chapter 6, we described the opinion-policy process; that was a description of political sociology based on the group theory of politics, and it was somewhat static in that no account was taken of changes in numbers, intensities, or salience of individual or group opinions. The scheme we offer here has different components, although it interlocks with the earlier presentation in many ways, most of which are obvious.

Public policies evolve from governmental responses to human needs and desires. All public policies were once merely *private ideas*. Private ideas, when shared by large numbers of individuals, become *proposals*. Proposals, when they are adopted by governmental authorities, become

[1] Key uses the popular support in the 1960s for the social-security system as an example of what he calls a "supportive consensus." My distinctions between the nature of opinion distributions during the proposal and program stages of policy making are similar in part to Key's differentiations between "permissive," "supportive," and "decisive" consensus. See V. O. Key, Jr., *Public Opinion and American Democracy* (New York: Alfred A. Knopf, Inc., 1961), pp. 29–37. See also, on the notion that popular support for an idea increases after it is enacted into law, Paul F. Lazarsfeld, "Public Opinion and the Classical Tradition," *Public Opinion Quarterly*, XXI (1957), 46–47; Lazarsfeld cites A. C. Dicey, *The Relations between Law and Public Opinion in England During the Nineteenth Century* (London: Macmillan Co., 1920).

public policies. So simplified, these three stages are clear, although it must be at once obvious that, while the distinction between a proposal and a public policy is marked by an official act (by an executive signature or a legislative engrossment) and by a point of time (the "effective date"), no such sharp distinction can be made between an idea and a proposal. Clues might be offered in an attempt to make the distinction more operational— percentage of people who know about or support the idea, or numbers and estimated political strength of groups that favor the idea—but the marginal cases, as in all such matters, must be left to individual judgment. The simplified trichotomy is thus:

Idea (private) —————————→ Proposal —————————→ Policy (public)

Immediately we elaborate. More extreme than ideas are unthinkable thoughts—which may be called *latent ideas,* but which are proscribed by the culture and will be given the name of *sacrilege* (though I mean, of course, to free the word from its narrow religious connotations). Beyond policy is *tradition,* which may be called *assimilated policies,* and which is required by culture (just as sacrilege is forbidden by culture). As we noted in Chapter 10 (on opinions and cultural patterns), in modern societies, very little is forbidden to ideas; sacrilege is almost an extinct commodity in the Western world, and it is rapidly disappearing in non-Western lands. On the other hand, considerable tradition, in its post- or ultrapolicy form, exists. The English common law is perhaps the best example of the dynamic relationship between tradition and policy. The body of practices from which the common law is drawn (or which *is* the common law—a distinction, mainly semantic, which I mention only to ignore hereafter) is precisely a tradition about which there is so much agreement that conflict seldom arises. When conflict does arise over this tradition, a policy statement—that is, a judicial application of the common law—has to be made to settle it; but it can hardly be denied, if one accepts the common-law system at all, that such a tradition is ordinarily beyond contention. With sacrilege and tradition added, the schema becomes:

[Sacrilege]◄————► Idea (private) ————→ Proposal ————→ Policy (public) ◄————► [Tradition]

Let us add a simple representation of opinion, not to take account of the rich variety of views which flower in the attentive public at the proposal stage, but simply to represent the probability of agreement. Thus:

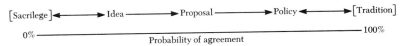

[Sacrilege]◄————► Idea ————→ Proposal ————→ Policy ◄————► [Tradition]

0% ——— 100%
Probability of agreement

Greater precision would require me, since I use the language of probabilities, to label the left end of the continuum "Approaching 0 Per Cent" and the right end "Approaching 100 Per Cent"; but perhaps the readers who care will bear in mind that I understand the subtlety involved, and they will accept this as the rough creation which all such schema are in the social sciences.

Greater detail and concern for realism will move us to represent some of the characteristics of the proposal stage. Between idea and proposal comes agitation, education, and diffusion of the idea. Organization and politicization follow or come about concurrently as the numbers of supporters (and, very likely, opponents, too) grow and as the intensity of opinions increases. At some point, public notice is taken of the *idea-become-proposal,* and governmental officials move for its transformation into policy. In this way, the proposal takes the form of a motion, a resolution, a bill, or an executive order. Intensification of opinions and non-governmental-organization efforts proceed rapidly at this stage, and at some time a decision is made to stop the proposal (temporarily or permanently, as time will reveal) or to move it to the policy stage:

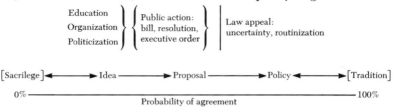

One other element needs to be added to our schema: a representation of numbers and intensities of opinions. As the proposal stage moves to a climax, the general case will exhibit a maximization of involvement, both mass and elite, in terms of intensity and notoriety. In short, more people will care more about the proposal (keeping in mind that even *more* people may not be a large percentage of the population). After the decision is made to end it at the proposal stage or to move it on to the policy stage, both intensity and notoriety fall off. If the proposal fails to become policy, its supporters lose some interest, out of discouragement and rationalization, and its opponents withdraw somewhat from the battle. If the proposal becomes policy, its supporters tend to rest on their laurels and its opponents suffer what has become known as the *fait accompli* effect—namely, the withdrawal of emotional attachment and a rationalization of the changed state of affairs on the part of the losers.[2] Size of the interested public, and the intensities of opinions, may be represented by the crosshatch area in the completed schema on page 355.

The political salience of an issue is the amount of political heat generated by the issue, a measure of its importance, and a composite of numbers and intensities of opinions.

[2] See Robert E. Lane, *Political Life* (New York: The Free Press of Glencoe, 1959), pp. 178–179.

Two points should be made about the schema—although both are quite obvious. The first is that in any given case history of policy development great distortion from the model may appear. The idea-to-proposal-to-policy stages may be completed before there is sufficient politicization and political salience to ensure a high enough probability of

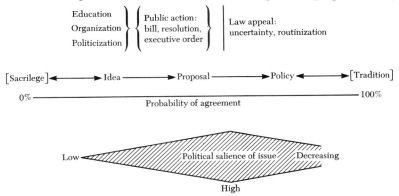

agreement—this is what happened in the case of the hurried, unpopular, and unenforceable Eighteenth Amendment. Conversely, the probability of agreement on an issue may be very high, but because of a volatile and episodic political salience or because of institutional advantages enjoyed by minorities, the proposal may never become policy: compulsory military training is a case in point (see Chapter 6); perhaps even a better example is the proposal for a conflict-of-interest law which would apply to Congress, which would command widespread popular support, but which has been avoided by a Congress understandably reluctant to limit its own freedom. The second point is that the schema has no necessary time schedule built into it. The whole process may be very quickly experienced, as was the case with the creation of a federal policy toward the making and the use of nuclear energy.[3] On the other hand, decades, even centuries may elapse in the evolution of a proposal from an idea.

The schema illustrates why existing policy (the status quo) has the advantage over proposals. Once acceptance for policy has become widespread and salience has decreased, the probability of agreement rises while the level of importance goes down. Real or imagined advantages may be found in the policy, and, as lives are adjusted to the demands and benefits of the policy, support for it increases. Or, at the very least, attention is reduced by the adoption of a better-the-known-evil perspective. At an even higher level of generalization there is a presumption in favor of existing policy, a presumption compounded of the ease of the

[3] See Harold P. Green and Alan Rosenthal, *Government of the Atom* (New York: Atherton Press, 1963), pp. 1–5.

habit principle, the majesty of the law, and desire for social stability which can only be achieved when there is much agreement on many governmental policies.

21.2   Opinion Change and the Opinion-Policy Process

The conceptualization above is, quite obviously, still incomplete as an explanation of the way an idea becomes public policy through a "natural history" involving the spread of the idea, the mobilization of support, the debate about alternatives, and the legislation of the idea as policy into governmental routines. Still missing is a generalization about the political process by which the proposal becomes law in the context of the official and unofficial machinery of a representative democracy. We have not shown how the dynamics of increased political salience and increased probability of agreement are related to the institutional dynamics of policy change. We have not accounted for the role of governmental agencies (legislatures, executives, and courts, in that order of importance), or for the roles of parties and pressure groups. To do so, even in a preliminary and inadequate way, we may recall our conceptualization of the opinion-policy process, first set forth in Chapter 6.

The original model of this opinion-policy process was limited to the interactions of expressed opinions, through group memberships and alignments, on legislative action. Majority, minority, and effective opinions were differentiated and some consideration was given to the way group memberships mediate the opinions of individuals so that the language of politics speaks of "carrying the farm vote," "alienating labor," or "losing favor in the business community." The initial model of the opinion-policy process, as given in Chapter 6, frankly adopted the point of view which has become known as the *group theory of politics*—a point of view which, however inadequate it may be for the nuances of political explanation and prediction, represents what I regard to be the most useful basic orientation to the study of American politics. Using this model, let's see if we can show, figuratively, how changes in opinion distribution and levels of politicization operate through political groups and governmental institutions to effect policy change.

Let us suppose that at any given time (Time A) the patterns of individual and group support for a policy are as represented in Figure 21–1. In this figure, the numbers represent individuals, the lettered boxes represent groups, and the length of the lines connecting individuals with groups represents the importance of the group's policy stand for the individual. Finally, a solid vertical line to a lettered box indicates that the group is a member of the *coalition of effective opinion*—that is, the group favors the policy—while a broken horizontal line indicates group opposition to the policy.

Pressure to change policy may come from any source. But policy will not change unless individuals change opinions and change behavior. Among the many reasons for change of opinions at the individual level is the effect of the policy itself. Once established, a policy will enjoy the

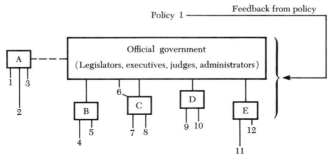

Figure 21–1. Representation of Individual and Group Opinions on Policy before Change (at Time A)

generalized tendency of the *fait accompli* effect (as indicated above), but it will also, to some degree, bring about specific changes in individual opinions. Some persons will feel benefited by the policy and its application; some will feel injured. If the political influence generated by the benefited is greater than that generated by the injured, there will be increased specific support for the policy in addition to the generalized support stemming from the *fait accompli* effect.

As individual opinions change, the balance of opinion within and among groups changes also. These changes combine in various ways—with many changes offsetting one another, of course—which will be reflected in the policy-making processes and in amended or new policies. Figure 21–2 is a representation of how individual and group changes in net opinion distribution results in policy change. Over time, policy *1* becomes policy *2*.

A summary description of what happened to change policy *1* to policy *2* is as follows: Individual *1* is as supportive of policy *2* as he was opposed to policy *1*; his measure of attachment (length of line) to his group in its support for policy *2* is the same as was his group attachment on its opposition to policy *1*. Individual *2* was only weakly agreed to his group's position on policy *1* and has shifted his attachment on this issue to group *B*, which now opposes policy *2*. Individual *3*, who more strongly supported group *A* on policy *1*, has also associated himself with group *B*'s opposition to policy *2*. Individual *4* changed, without alteration in his group support, from a favorable view toward policy *1* to an opposing opinion on policy *2*. Individual *5*, however, shows less agreement with group *B*'s opposition to policy *2* than he showed with the group's support of policy

1; but note that, as must often be the case in fact, he still regards the group as a reference and identity object. Individual *6,* before the policy change, enjoyed direct as well as group access to governmental actors; after policy change, he regards group *B* as a reference object for his opposition to policy *2.* Individuals *7* and *8* have lost some interest in the

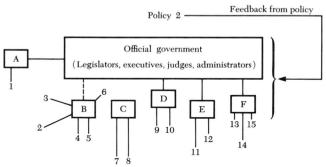

Figure 21–2. Representation of Individual and Group Opinions on Policy after Change (at Time A¹)

issue, concurrently with the change to policy 2, and as a consequence of this, and of individual *6*'s shift of reference group from *C* to *B*, group *C* now takes no stand on policy 2. Individuals *9* and *10,* and group *D,* with which they both identify, now support policy 2 as strongly (or as weakly) as they supported policy *1;* the same situation obtains for group *E* and individuals *11* and *12;* and the generalization is that neither policies 1 nor 2 are very important to groups D and E, but that they are part of the coalition supporting the policies, both before and after change, because their other policy interests make such a course seem effective to them. Group *F* is a new group, or a group newly politicized in the interests of policy *2,* and the individuals (*13, 14,* and *15*) who identify with it are generally close to it on this policy issue. One might suppose that it was in part the activation of this new group, and the expansion of the interested public by individuals *13, 14,* and *15,* that resulted in the change from policy *1* to policy *2.*

In response to changes in the opinion environment, the individuals and agencies labeled *Official Government* will make adjustments in their own thinking and behavior. Some of these adjustments will be of a regularized and bureaucratic nature—change-promoting forces may have to follow prescribed forms of petition, bill drafting, and orderly progression from district to central officials; and change-resisting forces will have the same or other channels of institutionalized access or influence.

Beyond the general constraints of bureaucracy, there are other sets of variables that have significance for the processes by which opinions are translated into public policy. First, the influence of opinion in policy making will vary with the specific organizational context within which the decision makers operate. If the governmental agencies have elaborate and specialized services for collecting and processing information about public opinion, they are likely to pay more attention to the distribution of popular and group views on the issues at stake. Governmental agencies obviously vary in the extent to which they are able and willing to provide such facilities for collecting and analyzing opinion distributions. Historically, among U.S. federal agencies, the State Department and the Agriculture Department have provided more of such services for policy makers than have such departments as Interior and Defense. Most governmental agencies at state and local levels make little or no effort to provide decision makers with systematic intelligence on the distribution of opinions.

Second, the time demands of the decision situation will have important consequences for the opinion-policy process. If the situation is regarded as one of crisis, there will be little time to measure and weigh the opinion distributions on the matter at hand. A crisis situation is one in which there is a short period of time in which to respond to a basic threat that was not anticipated by the decision makers. Under such circumstances, public opinion will be less important in the decision. The development of U.S. atomic-energy policy in 1945–1946 is a case in point. The 1961 decision to block Soviet expansion in Cuba was another case in which public opinion was less influential than it was in, say, the 1948 decision to provide massive aid to European countries through the Marshall Plan.

Finally, the impact of opinions will vary with the personality characteristics of the decision makers. Some political leaders are inclined to attach less importance to public opinion—or, if they grant its importance in the policy-making processes, to show great confidence in their abilities to judge it for themselves. Thus, Woodrow Wilson was not disposed to accept advice on either the importance or the status of popular or group opinions on the issues with which he was confronted as President. Presidents Kennedy and Johnson, on the other hand, have seemed much more inclined to pay attention to polls, newspaper reports, and professionals who were reputed to have their "ears to the ground." Thus, these factors, internal to the official government—generalized bureaucratic routinization, specialized services for reporting and assessing public opinion, crisis level of the decision situation, and personality differences of decision makers—must all be considered in the elaborated model of the opinion-policy process.

Political parties enter the opinion-policy process in two ways: first, in their efforts to determine who the office holders will be in the official government; and second, in their efforts to mediate and compromise the conflicts among interest groups. American political parties are primarily interested in winning public office. To win public office under two-party conditions, a candidate must normally receive a clear majority of the vote. To win a clear majority of the votes, a candidate must attract from individuals and groups greater support than his opponent attracts. The art of politics consists, then, in gaining and keeping a coalition of support greater than an opponent's coalition of support. Politicians and political parties are thus the policy brokers of the American democracy—softening, mediating, and reconciling the intergroup conflict, and, at the same time, "peopling" the government with legislators, executives, judges, and administrators, whose function it is to make and carry out policies that are tolerable for most groups, if perfect for none.

The above description of the function of parties is familiar to all. To represent this in Figure 21–1 is a difficult matter, however, because the political party embraces all the elements shown in that figure. The parties bind individuals and groups together with the official government; the party apparatuses within the governments provide organization and procedures for the processes by which proposals become transformed into policy; and the parties, through their mass organizations and the communications media, provide a vital element in the feedback channels that are so important for opinion stability and opinion change. The parties—to use an organic analogy, dangerous as they can be—are like the lymphatic system of the human body, not separable and discrete like the lungs or heart but generally infused throughout the whole organism. Like the lymphatic system, the parties inform and sustain the body politic, sometimes highlighting differences but more often compromising conflict, searching out and supporting leaders and spokesmen who are also representative men, and providing channels for all who care about the continuation of the democratic dialogue.

In the end, however, even this more elaborate representation of the opinion-policy process, including the overlay of the party system, like all such schema, is much too simple and anemic to catch the richness of complex human and governmental processes. For any adequate understanding of the dynamics of opinion and policy change, one must envision the varied involvement of thousands of groups and potential groups, and of tens or hundreds of thousands of individuals, some caring a lot and others not much, some with skills and resources at their command and others with little—all initiating, responding, evaluating, calculating, and projecting their strategies toward the reduction of their grievances and the enhancement of their happinesses. Such is the process of government where individuals are free to form, hold, and revise their opinions, where their opinions may be openly expressed and related to behavior, and where social institutions encourage such opinion-holding individuals to participate—as their inclinations and abilities permit—in the public enterprise.

INDEX

HM
261
H 4

6526

CAMROSE LUTHERAN COLLEGE
LIBRARY

Date Due		
FEB 18 1971		
FEB 8 1971		
FEB 7 1972		
FEB 2 3 1972		
APR 4 1974		
April 6 10 A.M.		
FE 12 '77		